# The Counseling Practicum
## and Internship Manual

**Shannon Hodges, PhD, LMHC, ACS,** is professor and coordinator of the Clinical Mental Health Counseling program at Niagara University. He has 20 years of counseling experience in community agencies, university counseling centers, and overseas. He is a former director of a university counseling center and clinical director of a county mental health clinic, and has another 10 years of experience in supervising collegiate living groups. He has 25 years of experience in teaching school counselors, mental health counselors, and undergraduate psychology students. He has authored numerous professional publications, including books, book chapters, journal articles, and essays. He has also served on the editorial review boards of several journals including the *Journal of Counseling and Development, Journal of Counseling and Values, Journal of Mental Health Counseling,* and *Journal of College Counseling.* He has received awards both for his teaching and for his writing. Dr. Hodges is a longtime member of the American Counseling Association (ACA), the American Mental Health Counselors Association (AMHCA), and several ACA affiliate divisions. His book *101 Careers in Counseling* is a popular text for counselors and those considering the counseling profession. His most recent mystery novel with a counselor as protagonist is *The Lonely Void: A Bob Gifford Counselor Mystery.* Shannon has taught and counseled overseas and made professional presentations on four continents and in numerous countries. When he is not teaching or writing, he enjoys reading, jogging, and traveling to remote areas of the globe. He and his wife, Shoshanna, live in historic Lewiston, New York.

# The Counseling Practicum and Internship Manual

## A RESOURCE FOR GRADUATE COUNSELING STUDENTS

### Second Edition

**Shannon Hodges, PhD, LMHC, ACS**

**SPRINGER PUBLISHING COMPANY**

NEW YORK

Springer Publishing Company, LLC
11 West 42nd Street
New York, NY 10036
www.springerpub.com

*Acquisitions Editor*: Nancy S. Hale
*Composition*: MPS Ltd, India

*ISBN*: 978-0-8261-2843-0
*e-book ISBN*: 978-0-8261-2844-7

*Student Resources ISBN*: 978-0-8261-3259-8
*Student Resources are available from www.springerpub.com/hodges*

17 18 19 20 / 7 6 5 4

The author and the publisher of this Work have made every effort to use sources believed to be reliable to provide information that is accurate and compatible with the standards generally accepted at the time of publication. The author and publisher shall not be liable for any special, consequential, or exemplary damages resulting, in whole or in part, from the readers' use of, or reliance on, the information contained in this book. The publisher has no responsibility for the persistence or accuracy of URLs for external or third-party Internet websites referred to in this publication and does not guarantee that any content on such websites is, or will remain, accurate or appropriate.

**Library of Congress Cataloging-in-Publication Data**

Hodges, Shannon, author.
    The counseling practicum and internship manual : a resource for graduate counseling students / Shannon Hodges. — Second edition.
        p. ; cm.
    Includes bibliographical references and index.
    ISBN 978-0-8261-2843-0 — ISBN 978-0-8261-2844-7
    I. Title.
    [DNLM:  1. Counseling.   2. Internship, Nonmedical.   3. Vocational Guidance.  W 55]
    BF636.65
    361'.060711—dc23

                                                                                2015028644

Printed in the United States of America by McNaughton & Gunn.

*In memory of Michael T. "Maz" Mazurchuk, alumnus of the Niagara University CMHC program, and Dr. Morgan Brooks, Associate Professor of Clinical Mental Health Counseling, Niagara University*

# CONTENTS

# PREFACE

This text originated from my interest in and commitment to promoting the counseling profession as separate and distinct from related fields, such as social work and psychology. Many practicum and internship texts combine discussions of these noble professions in an amalgamation that blurs the numerous boundaries that exist between them. My intention is to offer a counselor's practicum and internship manual targeted at and to be used specifically in graduate counselor education programs.

As a professional counselor and counselor educator who has supervised numerous professional counselors in the field as well as graduate counseling students, I believe it is essential that our profession maintain a distinction from the related fields of psychology and social work. Having made this statement regarding distinctiveness, I wish to emphasize that I have nothing but respect for professional psychologists and social workers and the excellent work they do in the mental health field. At the same time, the counseling profession must take the lead in educating, promoting, and advocating for itself. Of the three professions, counseling is the only one that trains students primarily in the practice of counseling. Although psychology and social work programs certainly do an excellent job in educating and training future psychologists and social workers, counseling is an ancillary, as opposed to a primary, function for professionals in those fields. This text is written by a counselor and counselor educators for students in graduate counseling programs.

I struggled to develop this book for several years, toying with various outlines and then promptly consigning them to the recycle bin. Finally, in the winter of 2009, I became more serious and developed a prospectus for publication, and the people at Springer Publishing Company were interested enough to take me up on my desire to publish this book. As a child, I recall Reverend Stanley Cooper, our minister, preaching on the topic of "Be careful what you wish for." Brother Stanley was more accurate than I could ever have imagined, as writing a book was very hard work indeed (at least it was for me!). Recently, I have updated the text for this second edition and hope counselor educators and counseling students will find the text worthwhile. **In addition, accompanying Student Resources are available for download from Springer Publishing Company's website: www.springerpub.com/hodges.**

**The Student Resources are available for download from Springer Publishing Company's website: www.springerpub.com/hodges.**

Naturally, your practicum and internship experience will vary greatly depending on your specialization (e.g., school counseling, mental health counseling, rehabilitation counseling), the type of placement (e.g., inpatient, outpatient, public versus private school), your particular supervisor, and the beliefs, attitudes, and experiences you bring to practicum and internship. Because the practicum/internship is the backbone of any counseling program, I encourage you to make the most of your experience by being proactive. Ask questions of your supervisor, take advantage of any training your practicum/internship site offers, and be willing to ask for assistance when you feel you need it. I also encourage my students to "make mistakes" because that suggests you are trying to stretch your skills and learn. It is crucial that you reflect on and learn from your mistakes so that you will be less likely to repeat them.

I would like to share my own practicum/internship experience in the hope that it proves illustrative. From the winter of 1986 through late spring of 1987, I had a very challenging and rewarding practicum and internship at a small college counseling center at what was then known as Western Oregon State College (now Western Oregon University). The college, then with an enrollment of some 3,000 students, was a close-knit college community, where relationships were strong and virtually everyone knew everyone else. The practicum/internship provided a complete therapeutic experience involving providing individual, group, and the occasional couples counseling, career advising, psychoeducational workshops, resident advisor training, crisis intervention, guest speaking in undergraduate classes, and teaching a two credit-hour course for "reentry" students. (Reentry students were those returning to college after an extended absence.) The experience was often intense and required considerable reading, viewing of videos, attending meetings, and providing advocacy for students.

Each week, the director, Dr. Merlin Darby, who was a very skilled and encouraging supervisor, would lead a staff meeting wherein the five interns would take turns presenting difficult cases. Everyone would critique the intern who presented the case. The director was popular, very experienced, and had a knack for coming up with key phrases that assisted my fellow interns and me in seeing angles previously hidden from view. Although we were not always comfortable in presenting cases, the director was very considerate and temperate in his critique. Each week it seemed that I learned something constructive that I had previously lacked. The meeting would occasionally include a representative from the medical staff providing medical consultation.

In addition to operations within the counseling center, I was frequently called on to consult with faculty, student affairs staff, and parents. Our offices, although decidedly not fancy, were spacious, with ample bookshelves, comfortable furniture, and tasteful throw rugs to accent the décor. The support staff was generally very supportive and seemed to value our work. For me, the internship placement was almost ideal. I felt myself a key component of the campus and a valued member of the counseling staff. Then one day in late spring, I completed my internship and later graduated with my master's degree from the Oregon State University Counselor Education program.

My entry into full-time community counseling work was an abrupt wake-up call into the baser realities of the profession. Suddenly, I was working in a residential psychiatric center, on what was a swing shift during the week with a double shift on Saturdays. I had no real office, as we operated on milieu treatment, with an entirely group focus. As the newest member of the treatment team, I felt like an outsider and although the staff was courteous, the center was not the homey, close-knit pleasant environment that the college counseling center was. Our clients, who were called *patients*, were typically of three types: adolescents placed in the center by their families for psychiatric care, those adjudicated by the juvenile court system, or children or adolescents discharged from the state psychiatric hospital. Unlike the college population, they were oppositional, often defiant—hardened by serious physical, sexual, and emotional abuse and parental neglect—unhappy to be there, and definitely uninterested in what treatment we could provide. To top it off, the psychiatric center forced me to work with a behavioral-type program when I considered myself a humanistic, person-centered counselor.

I was overwhelmed, frustrated, and unhappy with my job, and wondering if I had made a mistake in entering the field. I longed for the comfy confines of a college campus, where I could be part of a learning environment dedicated to supporting students well on their way to fulfilling their dreams, not a residential center where much of my efforts involved confronting sex offenders and violent adolescents. Needing advice, I sought out my former supervisor Dr. Darby at the college counseling center. He listened patiently, then explained that most counselors do not begin by working in college centers, but in treatment facilities like the one in which I currently worked. He encouraged me to stick the job out until I found something else and challenged me to see the potential in the tough kids I counseled. He also encouraged me to stretch my therapeutic skills by learning what I could from the psychiatric center's behavioral approach.

In a short time, I found my former supervisor's counsel very wise. Soon, I began to get along better with the staff and my relationships with many of the patients improved. I also came to feel that the job was far more demanding of me emotionally and psychologically, and required far more therapeutic skills than my internship. In time, even the behavioral system began to make real sense to me, as it provided needed structure in the adolescents' lives. I still preferred working with college students (who can be quite challenging themselves!), but I had learned the value of broader clinical experience. The entire experience forced me to grow and adapt in ways I could not have previously imagined. In fact, the seeds of my transition to cognitive behavioral therapy were planted during this time. While I have not jettisoned my humanistic side, I find clients often need specific skills, thought stoppage, reframing, scaling questions, and so forth, to accompany genuineness, empathy, and unconditional positive regard.

I mention my personal story to illustrate a broader point. Namely, many graduate counseling students complete their practicum/internship in an environment where they feel secure, challenged, respected, and safe. Then the experience abruptly ends and they are released into a broader, sometimes less certain, and perhaps "scarier" environment. In my nearly 25 years of experience in the field, I have discovered my own rocky beginnings are very common for many recent graduates of counseling programs.

A more salient point to my story is that I have come to see my former job at the psychiatric center as a critical link in my beginnings as a professional counselor. Had it not been for the intense struggles the job required, I wonder if I would have developed the resilience needed for more in-depth psychotherapeutic work. The demands of a residential psychiatric center counseling a population resistant to therapeutic intervention were likely the best thing that could have happened to my career. But at the time, because I was in the midst of such intense experiences and numerous struggles, I could not have known that and I struggled with the opportunity and growth it offered. Looking back on my experience nearly 30 years since, everything looks so much different. What formerly was an unpleasant and unsatisfying experience, I now view as one of my most fulfilling professional experiences. My only advice, and I offer it with some trepidation knowing how unwelcome unsolicited advice can be, is even if you do not enjoy your practicum or internship, *do* learn from it, as such knowledge may be an unexpected asset later on.

Regardless of your own professional experiences, I hope you will find this text to be helpful and illuminating regarding your path toward becoming a professional counselor. Although we have many specialties and divisions in our field, we are indeed one counseling profession. So, welcome to the profession of counseling! I wish all of you a long, meaningful journey full of both challenge and fulfillment. Counseling is a career full of real challenges but also intrinsic rewards.

# ACKNOWLEDGMENTS

A lot of work goes into writing a book. In my undergraduate days, I imagined writing books, articles, and so forth, to be exciting, exotic work (yes, I was *very* naïve!). The past 25 years, however, have taught me that writing involves far more perspiration than inspiration. Still, for those of us who write—regardless of *what* we write—there is something very alluring in this process. Speaking for myself, the topics for books occur to me at odd moments—driving long hours through very remote deserts in the Australian Outback, in South Africa's Drakensberg Mountains, trekking through a Central American jungle, or simply sitting in my office—then take long periods of dormancy before the concepts emerge into full creations. While writing is very hard work, it brings me much satisfaction and the intrinsic rewards are priceless.

Writing a book also takes a lot of people behind the scenes, providing opportunity, encouragement, and critique. I wish to thank my wife Shoshanna for continuing to encourage me in my writing endeavors. She believed in me when there was little evidence to support her faith. Also, I send a hearty thanks to Nancy S. Hale and her colleagues at Springer Publishing Company for providing me the opportunity to write and publish this book. I hope you will find your faith in me well founded.

**Author's Note:** A percentage of the sales of this text will be donated to the Rev. Michael T. Mazurchuk and Dr. Morgan C. Brooks Memorial Scholarship fund at Niagara University. The scholarship will assist graduate students in the CMHC program in continuing their studies. *Maz and Morgan, you are always close in our hearts.*

# ONE

# INTRODUCTION TO THE COUNSELING PROFESSION AND THE PRACTICUM/ INTERNSHIP

Congratulations! You've completed a portion of your graduate program in counseling and are preparing for practicum and/or internship! The practicum and internship experience is the backbone of any counseling program. You have reached an exciting time in your academic career and now you will begin working with people as opposed to simply reading case studies from a textbook. If you are like most students I have taught and supervised, it's likely you are experiencing a variety of emotions: enthusiasm, anxiety, anticipation, uncertainty, and a myriad of others. Regardless of the amount of classroom preparation you already have, starting your initial practicum will be unlike any other academic experience.

Beginning a practicum/internship represents a major step in your development. Although previously you may have practiced in-class techniques with peers and made recordings of mock counseling sessions with friends, you will now begin counseling actual clients. In my experience, the initial practicum or internship tends to be the most challenging experience in the curriculum. Although students may have mastered the individual techniques and performed well in mock counseling sessions, establishing a therapeutic relationship with real clients presenting serious issues requires a different skill set. The initial experience at the onset of practicum can leave the most resilient of students feeling overwhelmed by the demands of the counseling relationship. Fortunately, if you have reached this point, survival rates are high.

The practicum and internship are important in counselor development because instead of reading about, for example, depression, acting out behavior, alcoholism, and bipolar disorder, you will actually be assisting people struggling with these and other developmental and/or mental health issues. You will also receive an education in the inner workings of your field setting—whether a school, mental health, addictions, or residential psychiatric setting. You will encounter numerous counseling professionals who will demonstrate various approaches to their work (e.g., cognitive behavioral therapy [CBT], person-centered therapy, dialectical behavioral therapy [DBT], integrated therapy). Ethical and legal issues will be paramount and it is hoped that you will receive training in crisis intervention, the chain of command in the event of a trauma, and how to deal with potentially litigious situations, among other issues.

You may be wondering, "How can I survive my practicum and internship?" The goal of this book is to provide orientation and guidance to help you successfully navigate your field placements. First, this chapter will discuss various general issues regarding the counseling profession itself; then it will offer a brief overview of the practicum/internship process. Future chapters will discuss many of these issues in more detail. But, as first things should come first, let us review some basics of the counseling profession.

## IDENTITY

Since the origins of the counseling profession in 1952, the American Counseling Association (ACA; originally named the American Personnel and Guidance Association) has been the flagship counseling organization. As an organization, the composition of ACA has been mixed, "like a ball of multicolored yarn," and sometimes within ACA there has been an emphasis within the specialties of counseling as opposed to the overall profession (Bradley & Cox, 2001, p. 39). "Other professions such as medicine have overcome the divisiveness that comes within a profession where there is more than one professional track that practitioners can follow. ACA has not been as fortunate" (Gladding, 2009, pp. 26–27). Essentially, counseling specialty area organizations often came and went in different directions than the flagship organization, sometimes to the detriment of ACA.

Fortunately, as the counseling profession has grown stronger, achieved licensure in all states and major territories, and been more accepted by the public, ACA has begun to benefit from this progression. The recent 20/20 initiative, *Principles for Unifying and Strengthening the Profession* (2010), involving 29 counseling organizations, represents a key step toward professional unity. The 20/20 initiative includes long-range planning and solidified leadership working toward common goals across all 29 counseling organizations. Though this major step toward unification has taken far longer than some would like, it provides a blueprint for future growth and continued unity. As a graduate student reading this text, you will be called on to play a major role in the development of a unified counseling profession. Although there are numerous choices and options beginning counselors can make to enhance the profession, this author recommends the following:

1. As the ACA is *the* flagship organization, all counselors, regardless of counseling specialty (e.g., school counseling, mental health counseling, rehabilitation counseling), should hold membership their entire professional lifetime.
2. All counselors should also hold a membership in their specialty area. For example, school counselors should maintain membership in the American School Counselor Association (ASCA), mental health counselors should

join the American Mental Health Counselors Association (AMHCA), and so forth.

3. All counselors should join their respective state counseling organization. State organizations assist ACA and other national affiliate organizations with lobbying on the state and local levels. This ensures a stronger counseling presence at the state level and helps strengthen ACA, ASCA, AMHCA, and other national organizations.

If beginning counselors reading this text simply follow these three suggestions, they will help the counseling profession achieve increased parity across the board with their mental health colleagues in psychology and social work.

Because the counseling profession is broad—encompassing ACA, 20 affiliate organizations, and other professional counseling organizations such as the National Board for Certified Counselors (NBCC) and the Council for Accreditation of Counseling and Related Educational Programs (CACREP) and others—unity remains a work in progress. Still, as readers are the counseling profession's future, I am optimistic that the profession will be far more unified in the future. As an illustration of unity's success, ACA's membership now exceeds 56,000 members, representing a continued membership increase the last several years (David Kaplan, personal communication).

## Definition of Professional Counseling

Though it is likely that most readers of this text have studied counseling in depth, some may not have come across a precise definition of "counseling." Until recently, there was no consensus on how counseling was to be defined. Although most definitions of counseling likely were more similar than different, strength tends to come in precision, especially in defining the term forming the cornerstone of our profession (i.e., counseling). Fortunately, delegates of the groundbreaking 20/20: A Vision for the Future of Counseling arrived at the following succinct definition of counseling at the 2010 national conference of the ACA: "Counseling is a professional relationship that empowers diverse individuals, families, and groups to accomplish mental health, wellness, education and career goals" (Linde, 2010; May, 1981, p. 5). Granted, any definition of a vocation as broad as the counseling profession is likely only scratching the surface with regard to professional functions and responsibilities.

Who we are as a profession is clearly crucial to our identity as professional counselors, and having a common definition represents a very important step for the counseling profession.

## Maturation of a Profession

The counseling profession has come a long way since its creation in 1952 as the American Personnel and Guidance Association (interestingly enough, the term "counseling" was not selected as part of the title). The first state to pass a counselor licensure law was the state of Virginia in 1976. Currently, with the passage of California's counselor licensure in 2009, all 50 states, Washington

DC, and Puerto Rico have enacted counselor licensure. This achievement especially in the face of opposing mental health professions represents a major accomplishment. Regardless of the feat, there are still a few goals the counseling profession is working toward. The major initiative still to be accomplished is Medicare reimbursement for licensed counselors (see the following paragraph on Medicare). Counselors having graduated from CACREP-accredited counseling programs have also been approved to work in the Department of Veterans Affairs (VA) hospitals. Unfortunately the VA has been tediously slow at hiring professional counselors; however, this is likely to change over time, albeit slowly.

Consensus on how counseling is defined represents a critical point for the profession; otherwise, what type of an organized profession cannot agree on how its namesake is defined? Cashwell (2010) refers to the 20/20: A Vision for the Future of Counseling initiative as "maturation of a profession" (p. 58) from adolescence into early adulthood. Cashwell (2010, p. 58) also breaks down this growth process into several recognizable benchmarks that have recently been met:

> The passage of California Senate Bill 788, resulting in California becoming the 50th U.S. state with counselor licensure.
>
> Regulations implementing the Mental Health Parity Act and Addiction Equity Act of 2008, essentially mandating that insurance companies use the same limits and cost-sharing requirements for mental health and addiction services as used for other services.
>
> Results of the Institute of Medicine's (IOM) TRICARE study, which recommended removing physician referral and supervision requirements for counselors' services, ultimately paving the way for independent practice for professional counselors under the Department of Defense's TRICARE program:
>
> There is *one* organization, ACA, that serves as our professional membership organization.
>
> There is *one* accrediting body, CACREP, that serves to promote professional counselor preparation.
>
> There is *one* organization, the American Association of State Counseling Boards, involved in the organization of state licensure boards, which regulate the practice of counseling.
>
> There is *one* national credentialing body, NBCC, that monitors voluntary national certification of counselors.
>
> Today, the number of CACREP-accredited programs is rapidly approaching 600 (as of 2015 nearly 700), with CACREP now integrated into the language of many state licensure laws.

Cashwell (2010, p. 59) goes on further to express there are still several marking points before the counseling profession reaches full adulthood. These are:

> Far too few professional counselors are members of ACA. Counselor educators should encourage ACA membership among students as a commitment to lifelong learning and professional growth, not as a short-term requirement or a way to get liability insurance.

Licensure regulations, often initially written in ways necessary to glean passage of laws in the face of oppositional lobbying, should be reviewed by state boards with a focus on strengthening professional identity. In many states, it is far too easy for people with professional identities other than that of counselor to become licensed. Licensure regulations that ensure that licensees are trained and identify as professional counselors will greatly strengthen the Counseling profession.

## Medicare: The Counseling Profession's Next Frontier

Probably the biggest remaining hurdle for the counseling profession is the privilege of billing Medicare. Licensed counselors, unlike licensed psychologists and social workers, currently are not approved to bill Medicare for services provided to their clients. For this to change, both Houses of the U.S. Congress must pass federal legislation to be sent to the president to sign into law. The counseling profession has come very close, seeing passage of a bill in both the U.S. House of Representatives and the Senate at separate times. Though efforts to gain Medicare billing privileges have yet to succeed, the counseling profession is consistently getting its message before the House and Senate and counselor vendorship for Medicare is a matter of time. Also, the ACA website has made lobbying senators and congressional representatives very easy and convenient. Simply go to the ACA's website (www.counseling.org), click on the "Public Policy" link, and then the link titled "Legislative Update," which will offer several options including one for lobbying Congress on Medicare reimbursement for counselors. I would encourage every graduate student reading this text to use ACA's website to contact and lobby their senators and congressional representatives to support counselors in gaining Medicare billing privileges.

It must also be mentioned that some counseling students may be placed in a practicum or internship where they are being supervised by a related mental health professional such as a social worker, psychologist, marriage and family therapist, and so forth. Your supervisor may even oppose counseling's effort to gain Medicare privileges. If they do oppose this effort, treat them with respect even though you will disagree with their position on this issue. Remember, you are in a vulnerable position with regard to your relationship with your field supervisor and will likely need a letter of reference when you are applying for a job. In addition, developing the ability to dialogue, or at the very least to disagree respectfully, is one of the most useful skills anyone can develop. So, support your national organizations' efforts to achieve Medicare reimbursement (ACA, ASCA, AMHCA, etc.), but respect your supervisors' and colleagues' rights to disagree.

## PROFESSIONAL COUNSELING ORGANIZATIONS

As a graduate student in a counseling program, it is important for you to understand that you are becoming a part of a larger profession. In addition to your graduate counseling department, there are local, state, national, and international counseling organizations that you may join and become active. Professional activity is essential for the health and well-being of the counseling profession and graduate students represent the lifeblood of these organizations and the profession. Many of these organizations also play an important role in the practicum and internship process.

Throughout this book, I will mention organizations such as ACA, ASCA, AMHCA, the American Rehabilitation Counseling Association (ARCA), and others that represent the counseling profession. These professional organizations advocate and lobby for the profession, offer professional standards and guidance, and publish helpful journals, books, DVDs, and more. For this reason, it is my strong opinion that all professional counselors and graduate students should purchase a membership in ACA (and/or ASCA, AMHCA, ARCA, etc.). I will primarily advocate for ACA membership because ACA is the national umbrella organization and it's my belief that professions are as strong as their national organization (consider the American Psychological Association [APA] as an example). In addition, I would encourage counselors (and graduate counseling students) to maintain membership in their specialty area, whether that area is in school counseling, mental health counseling, rehabilitation counseling, and so forth. Keeping an active membership with these organizations is an investment in the profession's future. Failure to maintain professional membership is akin to divesting in the professional stock of the very profession you—and thousands before you—have worked so hard to enter. So, keep your membership current; it will provide both you and the field important dividends.

In the following sections, I briefly describe some of the key organizations that you will likely encounter as a student or over the course of your professional career.

## American Counseling Association

The flagship organization for counseling is the ACA. ACA was founded in 1952 as the American Personnel and Guidance Association (APGA) and much later was renamed to more accurately reflect the organization (Gladding, 2009). ACA has some 56,000 members, making it the world's largest counseling organization. ACA has 19 divisional affiliates including the aforementioned ASCA, ARCA, AMHCA, and many more. For a complete list of ACA divisions, as well as other relevant counseling associations, see Appendix A. For students in a graduate counseling program, the *ACA Code of Ethics* (ACA, 2014a) is the primary ethical code; however, ASCA has a separate ethical code, as do AMHCA, ARCA, and all ACA affiliate organizations.

Although you may have studied ethical and legal issues in an ethics course, it has been my experience as a director of two clinics and longtime counselor educator that graduate students cannot read enough about ethical issues. Therefore, throughout this book, I will refer to the ACA's code of ethics (and occasionally those of the ASCA, AMHCA, etc.). Furthermore, although other books may discuss the ethical codes of other professions (such as APA or the National Association of Social Workers), it is my intent to keep the discussion specific to the counseling profession's codes of ethics. The recently revised *ACA Code of Ethics* can be accessed and downloaded from ACA's website at www.counseling.org. Graduate counseling students are encouraged to read and regularly refer to their profession's code of ethics, as they will be held legally responsible for understanding and practicing within ethical parameters. ACA divisions such as ASCA, AMHCA, and so on also have separate codes of ethics that can be accessed through their respective websites. Again, as the flagship organization, my counsel is that *ACA Code of Ethics* represents the flagship of the profession and all students should read and refer to it.

Professional ethical codes are not meant to be exact road maps, but rather exist as a guide to assist counseling professionals in making decisions in the best interests of their clients (Wheeler & Bertram, 2015). For example, let's say you have been counseling Yvonne, a fourth-grade girl struggling with her parents' divorce. Her teacher asks you how Yvonne is doing in counseling, expressing that she wants to help. You feel caught between your desire to protect confidentiality and at the same time be helpful. Based on your understanding of the *ACA Code of Ethics* and/or *ASCA Code of Ethics*, how would you proceed?

This is the type of situation students will face while on practicum and internship. Students frequently are dismayed to learn that ethical codes are not written in stone—rather, they are living documents, shaped by court decisions, legislative initiatives, and professional changes. A more thorough exploration of legal and ethical issues is covered in Chapter 3.

## Council for Accreditation of Counseling and Related Educational Programs

CACREP sets standards for many professional counseling education programs. CACREP guidelines include the required parameters for practicum and internships for counseling students in Addiction Counseling; Career Counseling; Clinical Mental Health Counseling; Marriage, Couple, and Family Counseling; School Counseling; Student Affairs and College Counseling; and Counselor Education and Supervision (CACREP website, 2014; for a complete list of CACREP-accredited counseling programs, go to www.cacrep.org/directory/directory.cfm). As of this writing, CACREP reports 684 accredited counseling programs with 40 more in process of accreditation. Graduates of CACREP-accredited counseling programs have been approved to work in VA hospitals and are able to bill TRICARE without physician referral, among other advantages. CACREP-accredited counseling programs have increased substantially in the last decade and the trend looks likely to continue.

Some related programs are not accredited by CACREP. The Commission on Accreditation for Marriage and Family Therapy Education (COAMFTE), established by the American Association for Marriage and Family Therapy, is the accrediting agency for clinical programs in Marriage and Family Therapy, which are separate from Marriage and Family Counseling program accredited by CACREP (for a complete list of COAMFTE-accredited programs, go to www.aamft.org/cgi-shl/twserver.exe?run:COALIST).

There has recently been an issue with master's-level psychology programs not being eligible either for accreditation by the APA (APA accredits only doctoral programs in psychology) or CACREP. The recent Master's in Psychology and Counseling Accreditation Council (MPCAC; www.mpcacaccreditation.org) lists 27 accredited programs (and counting) as of this writing. It's likely that MPCAC-accredited programs will grow as master's in psychology programs desiring accreditation have no other option, at least currently. Counseling programs that do not meet CACREP accreditation—typically those housed in psychology departments—may also choose to become MPCAC accredited. The limitation is MPCAC graduates are not yet eligible to work in VA hospitals and may have trouble billing TRICARE absent physician referral. Still, MPCAC offers an option for many master's-level counseling and psychology programs.

The Council on Rehabilitation Education (CORE) is the accreditation organization for rehabilitation counseling programs (for a complete list of CORE-accredited programs, go to www.core-rehab.org/progrec.html). Recently, CORE and CACREP have affiliated and time will reveal whether these two organizations will in fact merge. My own belief is a merger would make operational sense and is in the best interests of both organizations.

CACREP has set forth practicum and internship criteria for graduate counseling programs, which are discussed later in this chapter.

## National Board for Certified Counselors, Inc.

NBCC is a voluntary organization that credentials counselors (NBCC, 2015). Most counselors who earn a credential from NBCC are National Certified Counselors (NCC) or Certified Clinical Mental Health Counselors (CCMHC; for a complete list of all NBCC certifications, go to www.nbcc.org).

National certification came during a period when counselors were not licensed so as to provide the profession with a national credential (Remley & Herlihy, 2014). Certification, unlike licensure, is an optional credential. However, students should be aware that most state licensure boards have adopted one of the NBCC's examinations as the state licensure examination. Some states use the National Counselor Examination (NCE), whereas others use the National Clinical Mental Health Counselor Examination (NCMHCE). The Certified Rehabilitation Counselor Examination (CRCE) is administered by the Commission on Rehabilitation Counselor Certification (CRCC), a separate organization from NBCC.

The NBCC awards the designation of NCC to counseling professionals who successfully pass the examination. (Applicants from a CACREP-accredited program may take the NCE or CCMHC in their final semester of their counseling program.) The NCC credential was launched by NBCC in 1983 by the ACA and since that time over 80,000 counselors have become NCCs. An NCC is the prerequisite for all specialty certifications with NBCC (see the following). NBCC has become an independent entity from ACA, though both organizations remain committed to promotion of the counseling profession.

NBCC also awards counseling credentials in specialty areas of mental health (Certified Clinical Mental Health Counselor), addictions (Master Addictions Counselor), and school counseling (National Certified School Counselor). These specialty area certifications require additional coursework and professional experience as well as the passing of an examination. Counselors seeking certification in a counseling specialty area must first obtain the NCC certificate.

## Center for Credentialing and Education

CCE is an affiliate of NBCC and provides services to organizations, professionals, and the public (CCE, 2015). CCE provides specialty credentialing for counselors and related professionals in nine areas. The specialty certifications are:

**Approved Clinical Supervisor (ACS):** For counselors or related mental health professionals having obtained licensure or certification. ACS represents a recent standard in supervision.

**Distance Credentialed Counselor (DCC):** DCC represents to employers and the public that credentialed holders have met established requirements to provide distance counseling. Given the increased popularity and ubiquity of distance counseling, DCC is a credential soon to become popular.

**Educational and Vocational Guidance Practitioner (EVGP):** EVGPs have international competencies for career professionals.

**Human Services-Board Certified Practitioner (HS-BCP):** The HS-BCP credential was designed for human service professionals seeking to advance their careers by acquiring an independent credential.

**Virginia Substance Abuse Counselors:** CCE administers the examination for Certified Substance Abuse Counselors (CSAC) in the Commonwealth of Virginia.

**Board Certified Coach:** The BCC credential likely is the most rapidly expanding certification the CCE offers, given numerous professionals advertise as "coaches." BCC sets a standard for counselors and other professionals interested in professional coaching.

**Distance Credentialed Facilitator:** Previously the DCF credential targeted professionals in career development. DCFs offer their services via Skype, e-mail, the Internet, telephone, and so on. The DCF credential has recently been discontinued.

**Global Career Development Facilitator:** GCDF is a relatively recent credential focusing on international work in the career and facilitation field.

**Thinking for a Change-Certified Facilitator:** T4C was developed for corrections professionals, although it is open to counselors and other professionals.

Naturally, counselors likely will be interested in several of these certificates. Interested counselors or students will find more information on the CCE website at www.cce-global.org.

## Council on Rehabilitation Education

CORE sets the standards and qualifications for becoming a Certified Rehabilitation Counselor (CRC). Applicants who have completed a CORE-accredited master's degree program are eligible to take the CRC examination upon graduation. Applicants from non–CORE-accredited programs must complete a 600-hour internship supervised by a CRC and additional employment under the supervision of a CRC. The CORE requirements for practicum and internship are covered later in this chapter.

Because I have mentioned various national counseling organizations, I have provided a list of the 20 ACA affiliate organizations, plus an additional organization: Divisions and affiliates of the ACA:

American College Counseling Association (ACCA)
Association for Child and Adolescent Counseling (ACAC)
American Mental Health Counselors Association (AMHCA)
American Rehabilitation Counseling Association (ARCA)
American School Counselor Association (ASCA)
Association for Adult Development and Aging (AADA)
Association for Assessment in Counseling and Education (AACE)
Association for Counselor Education and Supervision (ACES)
Association for Creativity in Counseling (ACC)
Association for Lesbian, Gay, Bisexual, and Transgender Issues in
    Counseling (ALGBTIC)
Association for Multicultural Counseling and Development (AMCD)
Association for Specialists in Group Work (ASGW)
Association for Spiritual, Ethical, and Religious Values in Counseling
    (ASERVIC)
Counseling Association for Humanistic Education and Development
    (C-AHEAD)
Counselors for Social Justice (CSJ)
International Association of Addictions and Offender Counselors (IAAOC)
International Association of Marriage and Family Counselors (IAMFC)
Military and Government Counseling Association (MGCA)
National Career Development Association (NCDA)
National Employment Counseling Association (NCEA)

Appendix A has this list of ACA divisions with some basic information and each organization's current website.

Be aware of your own ACA divisional affiliate and changes it may make for the future. For example, all school counselors should be aware of ASCA's National Model titled *The Role of a Professional School Counselor* (2003), which states that appropriate activities for school counselors include "working with one student at a time in a therapeutic, clinical mode" (Kraus, Kleist, & Cashwell, 2009, p. 60). ASCA's National Model also defines a school counselor as "a certified licensed educator trained in school counseling with unique qualifications and skills to address all students' academic, personal/social and career development needs" (Kraus et al., 2009, p. 60). I mention the ASCA National Model because, along with the 20/20 initiative mentioned earlier, it represents one of the more significant changes in the counseling profession. All students enrolled in school counseling programs should be aware of the ASCA National Model and how it affects their future roles as professional school counselors. It is likely that other national affiliate organizations of ACA will, like ASCA, undertake major efforts to define their professional scope of practice. This is another reason counselors should hold professional memberships as they are then more likely to maintain an awareness of changes within their profession.

## COUNSELOR LICENSURE

To protect public safety, states and major territories have established licensure for various mental health professionals, including social workers, marriage and family therapists, and, of course, counselors. Professional counselors are now licensed in all 50 states, the District of Columbia, and Puerto Rico. Licensure laws establish minimum standards for counseling and related mental health professions. Each state and territory has a licensure board responsible for reviewing applications and issuing licenses, handling ethical complaints regarding potential counselor malpractice, and enforcing state/territory regulations regarding the practice of counseling. In some states, one board is responsible for overseeing the practice of counseling as well as social work, marriage and family therapy, and so forth.

Unlike certification, licensure is the primary credential counselors seek as it is required for professional practice, billing insurance, diagnosing and treating mental disorders, and other requirements of professional practice. The basic state licensure requirements are listed in Appendix B. For a complete list of state-by-state requirements, check the *Licensure Requirements for Professional Counselors*, published and updated annually by the ACA (2014b).

Within the United States, a number of different titles are used to identify licensed professional counselors. The following are among the most common:

- Licensed Professional Counselor (LPC; LPC is by far the most common licensure name and has been recommended by the American Association of State Counseling Boards as the preferred title)
- Licensed Mental Health Counselor (LMHC)
- Licensed Clinical Professional Counselor (LCPC)
- Licensed Clinical Mental Health Counselor (LCMHC)

Obtaining licensure is usually a three-step process. The first step involves completion of a master's degree in counseling. The second requires the accumulation of the state required number of post-master's clock hours while supervised by a licensed mental health professional (e.g., licensed counselor, social worker, psychologist, psychiatrist). Most states require individuals to accumulate between 2,000 and 3,000 supervised clock hours (ACA, 2014b). Finally, the individual must pass the required counselor examination. Some of the examinations are the following:

- NCE—administered by the NBCC, this is the most common examination used by states for licensure
- NCMHCE—also administered by the NBCC, this examination focuses more specifically on mental health practice and is used by a smaller number of states as the licensure examination

- Counselor Preparatory Comprehensive Examination (CPCE)—administered by the CCE, an affiliate of NBCC; this is not a credentialing exam. The CPCE is used in some 300 graduate counseling programs as a formal evaluation for students and the academic program.
- CRCE—administered by the CRCC, passage of this examination is also accepted in some states for licensure of rehabilitation counselors.
- Examination for Clinical Counselor Practice (ECCP)—also administered by NBCC, passage of the ECCP is required to obtain the CCMHC credential issued by NBCC (passage of the NCMHCE is also accepted). Currently, two states accept passage of the ECCP as their state licensure examination: Illinois and North Carolina.

Because of the many variations in counselor licensure among states, I recommend *Licensure Requirements for Professional Counselors* (ACA, 2014b). This text provides licensure requirements for all 50 states and territories, including required counseling program, credit hours, licensure examination, post-master's supervision hours, whether a temporary permit is required prior to licensure, and so forth.

## OCCUPATIONAL OUTLOOK FOR COUNSELORS

The counseling profession has expanded considerably in the past 60-plus years. Originally, counselors worked primarily in schools, college career centers, and in public and private agencies devoted to career or vocational guidance. Today, counselors work in a broad variety of settings, including schools, addiction treatment centers, residential psychiatric centers and hospitals, college and university counseling centers, rehabilitation clinics, and many more. The U.S. Bureau of Labor Statistics (BLS) estimates that in 2012, there were 637,800 professional counselors in the areas tracked, and BLS estimates this number will expand to some 769,700 by 2022 (BLS, 2014–2015). Although all specialties of counseling are expected to grow, some will increase more dramatically than others (Table 1.1).

As you can see from Table 1.1, the future of employment in the counseling profession is very promising, although stronger in some specialty areas than others. My recommendation is that you stay current of the always shifting employment landscape by regularly reviewing the employment outlook in your area, state, and region. BLS updates occupational projections every 2 years (you can review their findings online at www.bls.gov and search on "counselors"). For creative arts counselors (e.g., art therapists, dance therapists, music therapists), check with your professional organization for employment information. While BLS does not yet track employment numbers and future projections for creative arts counseling fields, such occupations and jobs do indeed exist. Furthermore, the recommendation here is for the various creative arts organizations to unite and lobby BLS to track their profession as well. Likely, it would be wise for ACA, NBCC, and other counseling organizations to assist the creative arts professions and lobby BLS as well.

**TABLE 1.1   Projections Data From the National Employment Matrix**

| Occupational Title | Employed in 2012 | Projected Employed in 2022 | % Change |
|---|---|---|---|
| Counselors (all) | 637,800 | 769,700 | + |
| **Breakdown by specialty area:** | | | |
| Substance abuse and behavioral disorder counselors | 89,600 | 117,800 | +31 |
| School and career counselors | 262,300 | 293,500 | +12 |
| Mental health counselors and marriage and family therapists | 166,300 | 214,500 | +29 |
| Rehabilitation counselors | 117,500 | 140,900 | +20 |
| Genetic counselors | 2,100 | 900 | +41 |

*Note:* Genetic counselors are included due to BLS tracking and because it is a related field. BLS does not currently track creative arts counselors (e.g., art therapists, dance therapists).
*Source:* Data from Bureau of Labor Statistics (2014–2015). (Be aware that BLS projections are updated periodically.)

Genetic counseling was also included in Table 1.1. despite the fact that most, if not all, genetic counseling graduate training program are separate from traditional counseling departments. Genetic counseling, while different from, say, mental health counseling, arguably is a related counseling profession and as much so as, say, rehabilitation counseling and addictions counseling. As counseling occupations and roles can vary significantly, genetic counseling would appear to fit as well as any other counseling specialty area. Perhaps in the future, the National Society of Genetic Counselors (a leading professional organization) and the American Board of Genetic Counselors (genetic counseling's credentialing board) will develop ties with ACA and other counseling organizations. Regardless, genetic counseling will become a rapidly growing profession in the next decade.

## PRACTICUM VERSUS INTERNSHIP

Faculty, counseling literature, field supervisors, and counseling students will often use the terms *practicum* and *internship* interchangeably. There are, however, some important distinctions between these terms. In this text, we consider practicum to be the first field placement for counseling students. Compared to the internship, practicum typically requires fewer *clock hours* (the total number of hours the student is required to complete) and fewer *direct client contact hours* (hours where the student is in direct contact with clients). Because practicum is the initial placement, expectations will be more flexible than internship. Practicum is, in a sense, a "preinternship" to determine whether the student is appropriate to proceed to internship.

Internship, on the other hand, *usually* begins the semester after the practicum has been completed and requires more clock hours and more direct client contact hours. Most counseling programs usually require one semester of practicum and two to three semesters of internship. (For counseling programs on the quarter system, internship may be spread over four to five quarters.) Naturally, this also depends on state licensure and certification laws. Mental health counseling programs, for example, sometimes require 800 to 1,000 hours of internship while school counseling program would seldom require more than 600 (ACA, 2014b). (*Note:* CACREP accreditation standards require 600 hours of internship and 100 hours of practicum though programs may exceed these requirements.)

Most of the guidance and information presented throughout this book will apply equally to the practicum and/or internship; thus, the term *practicum/internship* will typically be used to refer to field placement. When a distinction between the two is necessary, the text specifically delineates which of the two field placements is referred to.

## PRACTICUM/INTERNSHIP REQUIREMENTS

Because practicum and internship are so different from the typical classroom, graduate counseling students may naturally be confused regarding the requirements for successful completion. All CACREP-accredited counseling programs must follow specific guidelines for the practicum and internship experience (CACREP, 2009 Standards[1]).

For practicum, CACREP requirements are:

- A clinical placement in a particular field setting (school, agency, treatment center, etc.)
- A minimum of 100 clock hours over a minimum 15-week academic term
- At least 40 clock hours of direct service with actual clients
- Weekly interaction that averages 1 hour per week of supervision throughout the practicum by a program faculty member, a student supervisor, or a site supervisor who is working in biweekly consultation with a program faculty member
- An average of 1.5 hours per week of group supervision that is provided on a regular schedule throughout the practicum by a program faculty member or a student supervisor. A student must also be supervised by a properly credentialed field site supervisor (e.g., licensed, certified) in the agency, school, hospital, and so on.
- Evaluation of the student's counseling performance throughout the practicum, including a formal evaluation after the student completes the practicum

---

[1] CACREP standards will be upgraded and published in 2016. Be advised regarding changes.

For the practicum experience, a triadic model of supervision, though not CACREP required, is often encouraged. In the triadic model of supervision, three roles are specified: the supervisor, the supervisee, and the role of observer (Boylan & Scott, 2009). The supervisor's role is conducted by the field site supervisor, who directly observes the practicum student's work through co-counseling and reviewing tapes or DVDs. The supervisor then provides ongoing feedback in a 1 hour weekly setting. Many counseling programs also use what is called site-based supervision, where the students are supervised 1 hour per week (individual or group setting) in the practicum or internship, then for at least 90 minutes in a weekly classroom environment. Given the popularity of Skype and other distance technology, these media are becoming more common for supervision. Distance-based supervision is an area that is certain to grow steadily given the economics of time and distance.

For an internship, CACREP requirements are:

- The same type of clinical placement as practicum
- 600 clock hours, begun after successful completion of the practicum
- At least 240 clock hours of direct service, including experience leading groups
- Weekly interaction that averages 1 hour per week of supervision throughout the internship, usually performed by the on-site supervisor
- An average of 1.5 hours per week of group supervision provided on a regular schedule throughout the internship and performed by a program faculty member
- Evaluation of the student's counseling performance throughout the internship, including a formal evaluation after the student completes the internship by a program faculty member in consultation with the site supervisor (CACREP, 2009 Standards)

Again, some counselor education programs will exceed CACREP standards and may require additional clock hours and contact hours. A few states with two-tier licensure mandate more than 600 hours of practicum-internship during the graduate program for the higher-tier license. Students should confer with their faculty advisor to ensure the placements they are considering can meet CACREP standards or any other standards the program is based upon. As mentioned earlier in the chapter, COAMFTE is the accrediting agency for clinical programs in Marriage and Family Therapy (separate from CACREP's accredited Marriage and Family Counseling programs). COAMFTE's standards of accreditation require 500 direct contact hours and numerous other requirements (these can be accessed through www.aamft.org/about/coamfte/AboutCOAMFTE.asp). International counseling credentialing will likely be based on different standards. Such international standards may be organizations (e.g., British Association of Counselling and Psychotherapy, Australian Counselling Association, Korean Counseling Association) or the state, territorial, or national government of the particular country in which the counseling program resides.

Rehabilitation counseling programs are accredited by CORE, which is now affiliated with CACREP. Their practicum and internship requirements are stated in the Accreditation Manual for Rehabilitation Counselor Education Programs (these are available at www.core-rehab.org/accrman.html). Since the publication of the first edition of this manual, however, CORE and CACREP have become affiliated and developed a new credential, Clinical Rehabilitation Standards (CLRC). Many questions remain, however, such as whether CLRC graduates will be eligible to sit for the Certified Rehabilitation Examination (CRE). CLRC graduates will be able to sit for the NCE examination, as the program will hold dual accreditation as a CACREP CMHC program. CLRC program graduates thus may be eligible for employment in VA hospitals. Previously, CORE-accredited rehabilitation graduates were not eligible for employment in VA hospitals.

It will be interesting to observe how the CORE–CACREP relationship develops and what that will mean for the profession of rehabilitation counseling. Given the affiliation between the two accreditation organizations, this author has to believe that a merger is inevitable. What that merger will look like is speculation at this point, though CACREP certainly is the larger of the two organizations. Any change regarding the affiliation between CACREP and CORE will hopefully be in the best interests of the rehabilitation counseling profession and the broader counseling field.

We will now look at some of the practicum/internship requirements in more detail.

## Contact Hours

For practicum, a minimum of 100 clock hours are required, but 40 of these must involve direct services to students or clients (CACREP, 2009). Direct contact hours most typically include counseling (individual, group, couples, and family), intakes, psychoeducational trainings, presentations to classes, and so on. Your graduate program should have forms available for documenting student clock and contact hours. (An example of such a documentation form can be found in Exhibit 1.1.) Naturally, the contract between the counseling program and the sponsoring agency should specify contact hours so that the student and the agency are clear as to program requirements for practicum and internship. Each counseling program should maintain a program manual and either print it for all students or make it available on the counseling program's website. The latter approach of a virtual handbook holds the advantage of accessibility, cost savings, and environmental sustainability and is the direction all publishing is moving toward.

For internship, counseling students need to record a minimum total of 600 clock hours with 240 hours of direct contact. Internship is typically split into two or three semesters, with the student documenting the same types of activities noted in the preceding practicum section. As a student proceeds from practicum to internship I and then internship II, he or she will likely be given more responsibility.

**EXHIBIT 1.1   Hourly Activities Log**

**Weekly Practicum/Internship Hours Log**
**Practicum: 100 Clock Hours (40 direct hours required within this total)**
**Internship: 300 Clock Hours (120 direct hours required within this total)**

| Date | Direct Hours* | Clock Hours** | Supervisor Signature |
|------|---------------|---------------|----------------------|
|      |               |               |                      |
|      |               |               |                      |
|      |               |               |                      |
|      |               |               |                      |
|      |               |               |                      |
|      |               |               |                      |
|      |               |               |                      |
|      |               |               |                      |
|      |               |               |                      |
|      |               |               |                      |
|      |               |               |                      |
|      |               |               |                      |
|      |               |               |                      |

**Total Direct Hours Completed** _____        **Total Clock Hours Completed** _____

_____        _____

**Student Signature**        **Date**

_____        _____

**On-Site Supervisor Signature**        **Date**

_____        _____

**University Supervisor Signature**        **Date**

\* Direct Hours—Individual, group, couples, family counseling, co-counseling, intakes, assessment, phone crisis counseling, psychoeducational or support groups, and any direct contact with clients.

\*\* Total Clock Hours—Any work activity that does not involve direct contact with clients. Practicum requires a minimum of 100 clock hours, of which 40 hours should be direct contact. Internship requires 300 clock hours, of which 120 hours should be direct contact.

Note: Counseling students need to track their practicum/internship hours in a log format to be signed by their on-site clinical supervisor and the university supervisor at the conclusion of each semester. The university supervisor keeps the log in the student's file.

## Practicum/Internship Class

The practicum/internship class time (called *group* in CACREP guidelines) involves a review of counseling responsibilities. Classroom activities include the following:

- Viewing and critiquing recordings of counseling sessions or mock counseling sessions
- Providing and receiving critique from faculty and peers
- Role-playing problematic scenarios encountered during the practicum/internship
- Discussing various therapeutic approaches and interventions
- Sharing by students their practicum/internship experiences and receiving support and suggestions from the instructor and peers
- Discussing ethical and legal issues that emerge during practicum or internship
- Providing support for students during practicum and internship

Practicum/internship class is discussed further in Chapter 6.

## Academic and On-Site Supervision

Counseling students are required to spend an average of 1 hour per week in individual, on-site supervision at their placement throughout the practicum. In addition, practicum students must meet weekly in a small group format run by a program faculty, adjunct faculty, or counselor education doctoral student. During practicum, the practicum–internship coordinator or designee maintains biweekly consultation with field site supervisors. A brief explanation of the triadic supervision model was previously mentioned. Though not all counseling practicum programs in the United States will be run using triadic supervision, it has become a popular model for many counseling programs.

### Site Supervision

The individual supervisor–counselor meetings provide an opportunity for more in-depth exploration of the counselor's skill, effectiveness, and professional ethics. The clinical supervisor or professor will generally be concerned with issues such as the following:

- What strengths does the student possess?
- What struggles does the student appear to be having?
- How is the student adapting to the school/agency?
- Is the student able to write effective, accurate, and concise case notes?
- Does the student display the required counseling knowledge, therapeutic skills, and professional dispositions necessary for a professional counselor-in-training?
- Can the student establish and facilitate the therapeutic encounter?
- Can the student develop adequate treatment plans?

- Does the student understand his or her current professional limits?
- Can the student manage the caseload he or she has been assigned?
- Can the student receive feedback without becoming defensive?
- Does the student understand how to apply the code of ethics?
- Can the student display both empathy and at the same time set appropriate boundaries with clients?
- Should a client suddenly disclose that he or she is in crisis, would the student know how to proceed?
- Does the student understand the seriousness of confidentiality?
- How well does the student understand cultural issues in counseling?
- Does the student get along well with agency/school staff?

The list of potential site supervisor questions and concerns is much longer than those listed here, but this should give you a good idea of the types of issues you may discuss with your supervisor. Supervision is discussed in more detail in Chapter 6.

It is hoped that you now have a brief introduction to counseling and your practicum/internship experience. In the next chapter, we look at how to select and evaluate a potential practicum/internship placement.

## REFERENCES

American Counseling Association. (2014a). *ACA code of ethics*. Alexandria, VA: Author.

American Counseling Association. (2014b). *Licensure requirements for professional counselors*. Alexandria, VA: Author.

Boylan, J. C., & Scott, J. (2009). *Practicum and internship: Textbook and resource guide for counseling and psychotherapy* (4th ed.). New York, NY: Routledge.

Bradley, R. W., & Cox, J. A. (2001). Counseling: Evolution of the profession. In D. C. Locke, J. E. Myers, & E. L. Herr (Eds.), *The handbook of counseling* (pp. 27–41). Thousand Oaks, CA: Sage.

Bureau of Labor Statistics. (2014–2015). *The occupational outlook handbook* (2014–2015 ed.). Washington, DC: U.S. Department of Labor.

Cashwell, C. S. (2010, May). Maturation of a profession. CACREP Perspective. *Counseling Today*, 52(11), 58–59.

Center for Credentialing and Education. (2015). *Credentials/resources/applications*. Alexandria, VA: Author. Retrieved from http://www.cce-global.org/

Council for Accreditation of Counseling and Related Educational Programs (CACREP). (2009). *CACREP accreditation standards*. Retrieved from www.cacrep.org/2009standards.html

Gladding, S. T. (2009). *Counseling: A comprehensive profession* (6th ed.). Upper Saddle River, NJ: Merrill/Prentice Hall.

Kraus, K., Kleist, D., & Cashwell, D. (2009, September). Professional identity: ACES, CACREP, NBCC share concerns. NBCC Perspective. *Counseling Today, 52*, 60.

Linde, L. (2010, May). From the president: Counseling is. . . . *Counseling Today*, 52(11), 5, 37.

May, R. (1981). *Freedom and destiny*. New York, NY: Norton.

National Board for Certified Counselors. (2015). *Certification*. Alexandria, VA: Author. Retrieved from http://www.nbcc.org/Certification

Remley, T. P., & Herlihy, B. (2014). *Ethical, legal and professional issues in counseling* (4th ed.). Upper Saddle River, NJ: Pearson.

Wheeler, A. M., & Bertram, B. (2015). *The counselor and the law: A guide to legal and ethical practice* (7th ed.). Alexandria, VA: American Counseling Association.

# TWO

# SELECTING AND APPLYING FOR A PRACTICUM/INTERNSHIP

The practicum and internship are the backbones of any graduate counseling program (and in related training programs in social work, marriage and family therapy, psychology, etc.). Depending on the type of program and the particular institution you attend, you will spend anywhere from 400 to 1,200 clock hours on your practicum and internship experience (American Counseling Association [ACA], 2014), depending on whether your program is Council for Accreditation of Counseling and Related Educational Programs (CACREP) accredited and also your state's requirements for licensure. For many counseling students, practicum and internship offer the first opportunity to work with clinical populations. Practicum and internship are challenging in a far different manner than standard classes, as counseling students now grapple with real people having genuine struggles. It's common knowledge that good field site supervisors on practicum and internship are very helpful in guiding students through the maze of client issues, while "poor" supervisors may exacerbate a practicum/internship student's learning trajectory. Choosing an appropriate supervisor and practicum/internship site is vitally important. Likely, most counseling programs do their best to place a student in the appropriate school or agency. Still, placement is a very inexact science and poor "fits" occur. It's also accurate to mention poor supervisors do exist in the field. In this chapter, I discuss all aspects of selecting the appropriate practicum/internship site.

## SELECTING A PRACTICUM/INTERNSHIP

Procedures for choosing a practicum and internship setting will vary depending on the counseling program. For example, in some programs, the faculty may actually select all the clinical placements, and then assign the students to particular settings. In some cases, the program has an agreement with a particular agency or agencies, schools, and so forth. Some students will chafe at this approach due to lack of input while others will be relieved the site is chosen for them. Although this method is regressive in nature, it does lessen the burden for the students.

A more common method of selection involves students and faculty working jointly on practicum and internship selection. In many cases, the student meets with his or her faculty advisor and discusses the types of placements that might match up with the student's interests and aptitude. The important considerations are for students and faculty advisors to meet and discuss the student's interests regarding practicum and internship along with what is realistic. Some counseling program placements are limited due to geography (rural usually), local competition (competing area counseling, social work, and psychology programs), theoretical orientation (e.g., pastoral counseling program will target specific placements as will programs in addictions counseling), student transportation (does the student have a vehicle or reliable access to mass transit), and so on.

One of the first tasks for you as a student seeking a practicum is to meet with your faculty advisor or field placement coordinator to discuss your interests. Begin thinking and researching the types of placements (or field settings) that you are interested in well ahead of deadlines. This means if you must have a placement by mid-August, make sure you seek out your faculty advisor or practicum–internship coordinator in late fall or early spring term of that academic year. Be aware of the differences in counseling ages, issues (such as addictions), public versus private school, and sectarian issues (e.g., a strong pro-choice student may be a poor fit for, say, a Catholic agency). If you are in a school counseling program and looking for a placement, be aware that elementary school placement responsibilities are significantly different from those in high schools. Counseling students who are interested in mental health, rehabilitation, or other community-based programs will have several variables to consider: inpatient or outpatient, addictions (outpatient or residential), college counseling center, community college counseling center, correctional setting, and so forth. Your advisor can point you in the direction of possible placements that are within your area of interest. Your advisor should also be able to inform you whether or not your practicum aspirations are realistic. For example, some placements will not accept master's-level students, others may insist on taking only social work interns, and some placements may require the student to intern for 2 full years, which may not be in the student's best interest if he or she wishes to change placements after 1 year. This may be disappointing, but you need to know this information before investing too much time in the search process.

Now, because of the huge increase in graduate counseling programs since I matriculated into a master's counseling program three decades ago, necessity dictates my covering an unpopular though realistic issue regarding practicum and internship placement. Clearly there are counseling programs that place the onus of securing a practicum and internship squarely on the shoulders of the student with minimal or no help from faculty. This unfortunate—perhaps unethical—situation largely is a vestige of underfunded, understaffed programs. There also has been a proliferation of master's-level counseling programs over the past decade, some of which are marginally funded, over enrolled, and may provide little guidance to students regarding practicum and internship placement. Unfortunately, as institutions increasingly target programs as "revenue" streams, overcrowded understaffed programs are likely to increase. In my opinion, this is a serious concern both for the profession and for students interested in graduate counseling programs. Sadly, the students are always the primary victims in such scenarios.

At the very latest, I recommend that after meeting with your advisor, you brainstorm some six to eight possible placements that are within your areas of interest. Then, get busy with a web search. Many local agencies, schools, and other institutions will have websites that you can research for more information. The following sections in this chapter show particular issues to target as you do your research for a placement. Having run community and university counseling programs, I can tell you that students who have done their homework on a given placement are far more likely to be selected. Students who answer, "I don't know why I want to do my practicum/internship here" won't get a placement at said agency as this suggests a lack of maturity and that the student did not do due diligence. So, know who the school or agency serves and be able to answer pertinent questions regarding why you would be a good fit for that particular placement. This will be doubly true when you are applying and interviewing for jobs after you complete your graduate studies.

As you gather information about various placement settings, you would be wise to keep track of the relevant details about each potential placement (e.g., how interested are you on a 1 to 10 scale with 10 as the highest?), along with your impressions about their suitability for you. Suitability has to do with interest, type of placement (e.g., middle or high school, inpatient or outpatient, addictions or mental health). Basically, the school or agency will be asking itself if it trusts you to represent it and you should ask the same regarding that placement. Exhibit 2.1 offers a practicum/internship site information form that you can use to keep track of each site that you evaluate.

Students should also be aware that it takes a great deal of effort on the part of the faculty to establish relationships with schools, hospitals, clinics, and college counseling centers. Because of the work involved, many counseling programs have long-standing agreements with particular schools and agencies. Such agreements ensure that the counseling program will have enough placements and the agencies will have practicum and internship students to help with their workload. Thus, the decision to seek a practicum with a given school or agency should not be taken lightly, because one bad performance by a student could jeopardize an entire placement. It is also worth mentioning that practica and internships provide a school or agency with a trial period and occasionally, provided the student counselor has performed well and that there is an opening, a job offer from said placement is a possibility. Again, possible employment depends on the school's or agency's policies, budget, and guidelines. Furthermore, your relationship with your field site supervisor at the school or agency will be critical to future employment. Faculty recommendations certainly are very important but a practicum or internship supervisor can specifically address a former student's performance in a workplace-type environment (e.g., "Does Sally get along with colleagues? Is she an ethical practitioner? How does she handle difficult clients/students?"). Having written recommendations for more than 20 years and received calls from potential employers, the previous questions come up in virtually every call. No school or agency professional has ever asked, "What grade did Sally make in class X or Y?" Grades are important, but professional dispositions are even more so.

**EXHIBIT 2.1    Practicum/Internship Site Information Form\***

Date of Contract: _____ /_____ /_____

Agency/School/College Site: _____

Address: _____

_____

_____

_____

Phone: (_____ ) - _____ Website: _____

Contact Name: _____

Contact's Job Title: _____

Contact's Phone Number: (    )_____ - _____ ext. _____

Contact's E-Mail: _____

Write a brief description of the site, population it serves, whether inpatient or outpatient, and anything that seems pertinent.

_____

_____

_____

_____

_____

Student's versus site's schedule: How well does your schedule match that of the site (e.g., Do you need weekend and evening hours for practicum/internship)?

*(continued)*

---

EXHIBIT 2.1   **Practicum/Internship Site Information Form\*** (*continued*)

Based on my contact with this site (phone conversation, e-mail, interview, etc.), does the site seem:

A. Very interested in me doing a practicum/internship with them.
B. Moderately interested in me doing a practicum/internship with them.
C. Not interested in me doing a practicum/internship with them.

Based on my understanding of this placement, I would rate my interest in this site as:

Uninterested          Low          Average          Above Average          High

I would rate my fit (e.g., values, type of population served, view of staff and supervisor) for this site as:

Poor                    Average                    Good                    Excellent

Next step: Do you have a formal interview set up with this site? Yes/No

If you have an interview set up, consider the following checklist:

1. Do you have an up-to-date résumé?
2. A cover letter?
3. Directions to the site?
4. Have you visited its website to learn about the agency and the clients it counsels?
5. If you know someone who has interned at the site, have you spoken to him or her regarding his or her experience?
6. Do you have any concerns about this site? If so, how serious are they?
7. Have you spoken with your faculty advisor about this site?
8. Have you done any mock interviewing in order to prepare for a potential interview? (*Note:* Not all practicum/internships will require a formal interview, although many will. Treat a practicum/internship interview as serious as a job interview. It's good practice for the future.)

---

\*This form is to assist you in gathering information regarding potential practicum and internship placements. Copy this form and use it as a worksheet when searching for a placement. Use one sheet per placement.

## Clinical Populations

A key question to consider is what type of clients you are interested in counseling. For students in school counseling programs, the issue is more basic. You will complete your practicum in an elementary, middle, or high school. Granted, there are variations on the theme, such as private schools, schools serving specialized students (e.g., schools for the visually impaired, the deaf), as well as those educating "at-risk" or exceptional learners. Although all these settings involve counseling school-based populations, various responsibilities may vary considerably. Additionally, a school counseling intern's role will also depend on the supervising school counselor and the philosophy of the school principal. For example, some principals restrict counselors to academic counseling while others who believe school counselors should also provide personal counseling. Some schools provide ample group counseling and others will offer very little. Naturally, there is much variation in school counseling placements.

Counseling students in mental health counseling, rehabilitation, marriage and family counseling, and the like will choose between inpatient versus outpatient clinics, addictions versus mental health, or a hospital or residential addictions treatment center, working with children, adolescents, adults, couples, families, and so forth. Like their school counseling colleagues, there may be wide variation regarding duties. Some addiction agencies may provide the intern with only group counseling and other agencies with only individual counseling experience. Inpatient sites generally will be much different than outpatient mental health or addiction placements. My own experience is that outpatient placements *usually* provide more in-depth counseling. This may be due to the fact that most inpatient client stays are brief and thus counseling may be group support and brief check-in sessions, while outpatient treatment is the more traditional 1-hour session for 8 to 12 sessions. Still, both inpatient and outpatient placements serve as valuable training grounds for future professional counselors.

Again, all students should carefully consider the population they are interested in counseling and discuss their interests with their advisor. Now, despite whatever you may have heard, completing a practicum and internship in, say, an addictions clinic does not mean you will be required to work in addictions for the rest of your professional career. A practicum and internship spent counseling in a high school does not mean you will never get a job counseling in a middle school. Fortunately, the skills and interventions required can be tailored to various ages and populations. One exception: If you are enrolled in a marriage and family counseling or therapy program, you will, of necessity, be required to counsel couples and families (Gladding, 2009), so some restrictions will apply.

Naturally, your interests may not be as clearly defined at this point in your counseling career particularly if you are a younger graduate student. Do not overly stress regarding your potential placement because there is plenty of flexibility in the counseling field. It is not uncommon for counselors to begin their careers in one specialty area (e.g., addictions) and move to one totally different area (e.g., mental health counseling). Some lateral moves within the profession will require more education or training (e.g., moving from an agency setting to a school setting, mental health counselor to art therapist), whereas others will effect no change other than a focus on a different population (counseling children to counseling adults).

Here are some questions regarding client population for consideration in selecting a practicum/internship:

- What clinical populations would I like to counsel? I am interested in counseling this populations because _____.
- Do I prefer inpatient or outpatient settings? Why?

- What are the advantages or disadvantages to a practicum/internship in an elementary school? A middle school? A high school?
- Does the philosophy of the site match my personal values? This is particularly an issue with some private schools and agencies. What populations does the clinic's nondiscrimination statement include and exclude? Some agencies are pro-choice and others staunchly antiabortion. Some placements discriminate against gay and lesbian people—in direct violation of many (ACA/ASCA/AMHCA, etc.) codes of ethics. (Speak with your advisor regarding this issue.)
- Would I like the challenge of a special population such as a prison, jail, or state psychiatric hospital? Why would a correctional setting be a good fit as a practicum/internship?
- How diverse are the students and/or clients the school, college, or agency serves?
- What training opportunities are available at this placement? Many placements provide additional training opportunities through workshops or in-service trainings (e.g., dialectical behavioral therapy [DBT] groups, specialized training with sex offenders and other mandated populations).

Some of these questions address *multicultural competencies* as espoused by Sue, Arredondo, and McDavis (1992) and later adopted by the Association for Multicultural Counseling and Development (AMCD; Arredondo et al., 1996). The definition of *multicultural* has recently been more broadly defined to include issues of disability, socioeconomic status, religion, sexual orientation, and culture, as well as race or ethnicity. Some of the beliefs, knowledge, and skills of culturally skilled counselors are the following:

> Culturally skilled counselors understand their own cultural heritage. They recognize the limits of their multicultural competency and expertise. They understand how their own cultural heritage may contribute to their biases and how racism may affect their personality and work. They are constantly seeking to understand themselves as racial and cultural beings and are actively seeking a nonracist identity. They seek consultative help, are familiar with relevant research, and are actively involved with clients outside the counseling setting. They can send and receive verbal and nonverbal communications accurately and appropriately. (Arrendondo et al., 1996)

Many counseling programs, particularly those accredited by CACREP or the Council on Rehabilitation and Education (CORE), address the various multicultural competencies through their curriculum, training, portfolio requirements, and diverse practicum and internship placements (Remley & Herlihy, 2014). An important factor in your development is to begin to consider multicultural issues when you counsel clients. No one needs to be a cultural anthropologist to be culturally competent. Rather, when you do work with the culturally different, read up on the culture of the client and if you are unsure about something, ask your client for clarification. Most clients will appreciate that you were respectful enough to ask about their culture. Furthermore, given the literally thousands of cultures (and subcultures) in the world, no one can be an expert in all. The important consideration is to be respectful and acquire new information. Cultural issues are discussed in more detail in Chapter 7.

## Level of Responsibility

It is also important to remember that as you progress from practicum through internship you will likely be given more responsibility with each successive placement. Your clinical supervisor's first priority is to ensure the emotional well-being and safety of the clients he or she serves. As you increase in skill and confidence levels, your supervisor is likely to give you more autonomy. My own experience is that practicum often is a student's most challenging placement because usually it's the first. Most graduate counseling students have not done anything quite like counseling work and there may be an initial culture shock, particularly in inner-city or specialized schools (those serving special-needs students) and inpatient psychiatric populations. Practicum supervisors are more likely to restrict the student responsibilities until they observe the student successfully managing them. Naturally, supervisors will vary considerably regarding what activities they allow the practicum student to perform. Most practicum supervisors will likely bring the practicum student along slowly, utilizing observation then co-counseling with an experienced clinician. A few, however, may believe in immediate immersion in which case the practicum student begins immediate counseling. Fortunately most supervisors, ever mindful of liability, will be of the former as opposed to the latter school.

Another factor to consider is that, on your placement, you may work alongside doctoral interns from counselor education, counseling psychology, clinical psychology, social work, and other programs. Doctoral students will naturally be given more responsibility and autonomy than master's-level students. This may be frustrating for graduate students in master's degree programs, but master's-level students should bear in mind that this is not a personal criticism, but rather reflects a higher level of training. Master's-level counseling students who matriculate on to doctoral programs in counselor education, counseling psychology, and the like will likely appreciate the greater degree of latitude at that point.

## Your Site Supervisor

Your site supervisor will play a key role in your practicum/internship experience. In addition to clinical issues, site supervisors also serve as mentors and role models. CACREP requires the following for on-site supervisors (CACREP, 2009 Standards):

- A minimum of a master's degree in counseling or a related profession with appropriate certifications and/or licenses
- A minimum of 2 years of pertinent professional experience in the program area in which the student is enrolled

- Knowledge of the program's expectations, requirements, and evaluation procedures for students
- Relevant training in counseling supervision

Ideally, your on-site practicum supervisor will be a professional credentialed in counseling. It is much easier for, say, a licensed counselor to mentor a graduate student in counseling than a graduate student in a social work program. Likewise, a student in a school counseling program is best suited to have a licensed or state-certified school counselor providing supervision than a school psychologist. Because of the proliferation of the various mental health professionals, however, social workers or psychologists often supervise graduate counseling students and professional counselors in the workplace. Although these related mental health professionals may do a very good job of supervising, it's unlikely they will be as informed about issues specific to the counseling profession, or be advocates for counseling organizations (such as the ACA), as they would for their own professional organizations (American Psychological Association [APA], National Association of Social Workers [NASW], etc.). Finally, all the mental health professions have their own codes of ethics. Fortunately, these ethical codes are more similar than different (Remley & Herlihy, 2014). However, if your on-site clinical supervisor is a social worker or psychologist, he or she likely will not be familiar with ACA's ethical code. This means your faculty advisor or practicum/internship classroom instructor becomes even more important to you. You will be held legally responsible for practicing within your profession's code of ethics and thus it is imperative for you to read and understand it (Remley & Herlihy, 2014; Wheeler & Bertram, 2012).

While you are investigating a practicum site, here are some questions to ask regarding your site supervisor:

- In which mental health profession is your practicum supervisor credentialed (e.g., counseling, psychology, social work)?
- What is your practicum supervisor's primary code of ethics?
- What credentials does your practicum supervisor hold (licensed counselor, licensed clinical social worker, state-licensed or state-certified school counselor, licensed psychologist, etc.)?

Although the various organizations may be initially confusing to you, the practicum provides an opportunity to begin to understand the larger scope of the mental health profession. Furthermore, you will spend your professional career working alongside psychologists, social workers, marriage and family counselors/therapists, and other mental health professionals. Establishing a respectful, working relationship across disciplines is a must for counselors and anyone else in the broader mental health profession. On your practicum and internship, as well as during your future professional career, you will work in multidiscipline teams with many different mental health professionals and this provides an opportunity to work collegially across disciplines. Cross-disciplinary collaboration likely provides the best possible opportunity to deconstruct the various silos that have long plagued the mental health profession.

An important consideration for all counseling students to be aware of involves the varying licensure standards regarding supervision during the practicum/ internship. Many states simply specify that the graduate counseling student must be supervised by a mental health professional licensed in a core discipline (e.g., counseling, social work, psychology). Others, such as the state of Massachusetts, require the student to be supervised by a licensed mental health professional with 5 years counseling experience. Because I teach and supervise counseling students in various parts of the United States, our program makes all students aware of such variations. Therefore, ask your faculty advisor about any licensure requirements in your state. Even better yet, check out your state's licensure requirements online (a complete list of state licensure boards and websites is located in Appendix B). The American Counseling Association publishes a manual with licensure requirements from all states and territories, which is a worthwhile resource (ACA, 2014).

If asked about their theoretical orientation, many counseling supervisors would likely state they have an integrated or eclectic approach (Corey, 2013; Ivey & Ivey, 2007). Others may strongly identify with particular therapeutic approaches, such as solution-focused therapy (SFT), narrative therapy, DBT, cognitive behavioral therapy (CBT), Gestalt therapy, and so forth (Corey, 2013; Gladding, 2009). In many cases, the theoretical orientation of your supervisor may not radically change your experience as a supervisee. For example, a supervisor trained in CBT may not be significantly different than one operating from solution-focused therapy or reality therapy. A supervisor whose theoretical orientation is psychodynamic, or one who uses eye movement desensitization and reprocessing (EMDR), likely will use a far different approach. This is not a criticism of any particular approach, but recognition of the reality that some approaches will require a different style of supervision due to the nature of the material involved. Regardless of the supervisor's theoretical orientation, supervision is critical to the practicum or internship student's development as a counselor.

The theoretical orientation of your supervisor notwithstanding, I strongly suggest that you "study up" on your supervisor's approach. For example, if your supervisor informs you that he or she uses CBT in counseling, you will want to read up on it. It would also be advisable to ask your supervisor to recommend books, journal articles, and DVDs on CBT. The supervisor's particular approach to counseling likely will be strongly correlated to his or her supervision approach. It is likely wise to ask a potential supervisor what supervision theoretical approach he or she uses when interviewing for a practicum or internship. You might ask your field site supervisor what are his or her philosophy and approach to supervision. (Theoretical approaches to counseling supervision are discussed in Chapter 6.)

If the field site and university supervisor emphasizes one particular approach, it carries the advantage of narrowing the scope of practice for a practicum/internship student and gives the student the opportunity to develop a clear theoretical orientation. A disadvantage is that you may not learn enough about other viable therapeutic approaches. Furthermore, it is important to be aware of the research, which suggests that using any particular theoretical approach is far less important, in terms of overall effectiveness, than therapeutic attachment (Duncan, Miller, Wampold, & Hubble, 2010; Wampold, 2001). More interesting, some research suggests theoretical orientation may account for only a small portion of therapeutic success (Duncan et al., 2010), though many researchers will dispute this (Corey, 2013).

## Accreditations and Affiliations of the Site

Practicum/internship placements are naturally going to have wide variation depending on the type of placement. A high school setting differs from a community mental health clinic, a psychiatric ward in a hospital, an inpatient addictions treatment center, a correctional setting, or a university counseling center. Part of your continuing education in the broader mental health field lies in understanding the variations among the numerous settings, the professionals that staff them, and the various accreditations such placements hold. Many counseling programs will separate school practicum/internship students from mental health, addictions, or rehabilitation placements for the weekly or biweekly classroom part, although some counseling programs mix practicum and internship classes for convenience and to better assist students in understanding the nuances of the counseling profession (e.g., school vs. mental health counseling vs. rehabilitation counseling). Counseling is carried out in all these types of placements, but naturally student interns' responsibilities in a school counseling office will be distinct from a residential psychiatric center (few school counselors will use the *Diagnostic and Statistical Manual of Mental Disorders*, fifth edition [*DSM-5*], for example.)

In Chapter 1, we have discussed the importance of accreditation for graduate educational programs in counseling. Similarly, many practicum sites will hold national certifications. National agencies that accredit clinical placements include the International Association of Counseling Services (IACS), The Joint Commission (TJC, formerly the Joint Commission of Health Care Organizations), and the Commission on Accreditation of Rehabilitation Facilities (CARF). These national accreditations are separate and distinct from educational, programmatic accreditations such as CACREP, APA, NASW, Commission on Accreditation for Marriage and Family Therapy Education (COAMFTE), American Association of Pastoral Counselors (AAPC), and so on. This text focuses on CACREP accreditation given that the target audience is graduate counseling students (although non-CACREP programs and even undergraduate psychology and social work classes have used this book for field placement).

Field settings that have earned a national certification in their respective fields (e.g., CARF for rehabilitation counseling and AAPC for pastoral counseling centers) will likely have a stronger reputation in the mental health field and may provide a more enriching practicum or internship experience than unaccredited facilities. Having made this statement, placements in unaccredited agencies and college counseling centers should not be viewed with disdain. Accreditation, although a probable indicator of quality, does not guarantee a successful placement though it does signify that the setting has met the standard in the field. Accreditation furthermore does not ensure supervision will be better than in unaccredited treatment facilities, though again, likely it implies higher quality.

If you are looking at a practicum placement and you notice that it is, for example, CARF accredited it would be wise to go to the CARF website and read up on the agency. The same would apply to any other listed accreditation, whether IACS, CORE, or AAPC. When you interview for a practicum or internship, you want to be able to demonstrate your knowledge of an accreditation, its mission, and how accreditation impacts patient or client care. You will also need to understand how the accreditation impacts the services the agency delivers. It is also a good idea to ask the interviewer how accreditation has improved his or her agency. Going on an interview and being unaware of an agency's accreditation or being unaware of the ramifications of the accreditation will hurt your chances for placement. So, know the agency you are interviewing with and be able to address why you would be a good intern there.

Names and websites of common agencies:

- Commission on Accreditation of Rehabilitation Facilities (CARF): www.carf.org
- International Association of Counseling Services (IACS): www.iacsinc.org
- The Joint Commission (TJC): www.jointcommission.org
- American Association of Pastoral Counselors (AAPC): www.aapc.org

These are the most common accreditations counseling practicum and internship students likely will encounter. Again, be aware of how these respective accreditations may impact your practicum and internship responsibilities. Your field site coordinator or faculty advisor is a good resource when you have questions, as is your field site supervisor.

## Professional Practices and Resources

In addition to understanding the type of setting of your practicum (e.g., school, rehabilitation, inpatient/outpatient addictions), you will need to be aware of professional and developmental issues within the setting. For starters, you want to ask about the orientation process your placement offers to new practicum and internship students. Some agencies and schools have formalized training requiring a student to spend several days learning the agency, its operation, and rules and regulations. Others, particularly smaller agencies or schools, will have very brief, informal training that may last but an hour. You would be well advised to ask whether the school or agency has a policies and procedures manual. If so, ask if you can borrow a copy and see your field site supervisor if you have concerns or questions. In all settings, you will want to know the organization's guidelines, which hopefully will be contained in a formal document (printed or online) and made available to you. Your supervisor may ask you about CACREP, your professional code of ethics (ACA, ASCA, CORE, etc.), and related information. A free exchange among the student, counseling program representative, and field site supervisor is a healthy approach as naturally questions are going to come up, particularly if the school or agency has not previously taken interns from the student's program.

## THE INFORMATIONAL INTERVIEW

After you have selected a few placements, contact them to see about arranging informational interviews. I would counsel students seeking a practicum to contact the appropriate person at the desired sites directly using the phone or e-mail. Do not simply send out résumés and cover letters without first contacting the site directly. First of all, the site may not have a placement for you, in which case your résumés and cover letter will be ignored and likely recycled. Second, most clinical supervisors, or their designee (such as the personnel department), prefer to be contacted directly by phone or e-mail, even though they are busy people. Your faculty advisor and/or the practicum/internship site coordinator will likely have many contacts themselves and soliciting their opinion is a prudent practice. Your professor or practicum and internship coordinator may even be able to streamline the application process for you.

Many schools and agencies will have established guidelines that require the student apply first, and then be called for an interview. Others, however, have very informal procedures and will be happy to arrange an immediate informational interview. Be sure to check with your selected site to see if an informational interview is a possibility. Some potential placements have a formalized application process requiring completing an application (often online), attaching résumé and cover letter, along with three letters of recommendation or references to contact. On this latter point, make sure a reference can give you a robust recommendation; otherwise, words of faint praise may torpedo your plans. Do not simply assume a reference will provide you a strong positive recommendation. Remember this when the time comes to apply for jobs postgraduation as well.

Whether the interview is informational or more formal, you need to practice answering questions that your interviewer is likely to ask. I suggest you work with your advisor and/or the campus career center. You may also check texts such as *What Color Is Your Parachute?* (Bolles, 2015), or one I coauthored with Amy Reese Connelly, *A Job Search Manual for Counselors and Counselor Educators: How to Navigate and Promote Your Counseling Career* (Hodges & Connelly, 2010). You will need to be prepared to answer questions related to the setting you are interested in. For example, if you are interviewing with a representative from an inpatient psychiatric center, be aware of what types of issues it treats, patient/client/student ages, number and training of staff, or whether it operates from a particular therapeutic orientation (e.g., CBT, EMDR, rational emotive behavior therapy [REBT]) because these issues likely will come up in the interview. The more informed you appear regarding the agency you are interviewing with, the better your chances of being offered a placement.

You should always have five to eight questions prepared that you can ask the interviewer. Even if you think you are very well informed regarding the school or agency, ask questions anyway. You may discover more in-depth information and questions suggest you have done your homework on the potential placement. Saying "I don't have any questions" suggests a lack of research, arrogance, or, perhaps, disinterest in the school or agency. "The Formal Interview" section later in this chapter offers a sample of questions you can ask or may be asked. As with every opportunity, be as fully prepared as possible.

## APPLYING FOR THE PRACTICUM/INTERNSHIP

Once again, some college counseling centers and agencies will have a formal application process that requires that you fill out an application packet, whereas others have an informal process where you are instructed simply to show up on a certain day and time for an interview. One large university where I have placed students has a very extensive application process, including a résumé or curriculum vitae (CV), cover letter, letters of recommendation, and a formal interview with several members of the counseling staff. Formality tends to be more common with doctoral students, although master's degree students will want to be prepared for all contingencies. Here are some tips to remember:

1. Is there a formal application for the practicum/internship? If so, make sure you are aware of all the application requirements.
2. If there is an application form, photocopy it and draft your answers in ink, then go back and type the answers in if you have access to a typewriter. In some cases, the site may send you an electronic copy, in which case, you can save the document, then type and edit freely on your computer. The e-copy of a job application form is rapidly making typed applications obsolete.
3. Make sure all words are spelled correctly. As the cliché goes, you do not get a second chance to make a first impression. Most egregiously, if you are applying for a practicum or internship in a school setting, misspelled words and poor grammar will weaken your application.
4. Know the due date for the application. You might be a strong candidate, but a late application makes a statement about your lack of organization and follow-through. In many cases, an application arriving after the deadline will simply be recycled.
5. If you do not understand something on the application, contact the site and ask for clarification. This illustrates initiative and provides another contact with the potential placement.
6. Ask your faculty advisor or practicum/internship coordinator to read over your application prior to submitting it. They may have suggestions on how to improve your application.
7. Does the application process require letters of support from faculty members or others? If so, give your reference ample notice before the deadline. Ample notice would be 10 to 14 days. Do not drop the reference request on them 3 days before the deadline.

## Your Résumé or Curriculum Vitae

When planning to apply for a practicum or internship, I suggest you operate as if you are applying for a professional counseling job at a school, agency, or university counseling center. This involves having an updated and effective résumé or CV. A résumé generally is a one- or two-page summary of your skills, experience, and education; a CV is longer and more detailed. For master's-level counselors and counselor education students, a one- to two-page résumé is standard. For doctoral students in counselor education, use the CV model. Having made the previous statements on résumé and CVs, given the virtual world we all live in, the rules for résumés and CVs seem to be evolving. During my master's program in counseling, going beyond a one-page résumé was viewed as the cardinal transgression. Times have changed considerably as the print CV or résumé is giving way to the electronic version. Recently, I have even noticed three-page virtual résumés with employers seemingly unbothered with the length. Still, play it conservatively and stay within two pages for your résumé.

Because this book targets practica and internships, I will not offer detailed information about how to write an effective résumé, CV, or cover letter. However, Exhibit 2.2 shows a sample of a cover letter used in applying for a practicum position and Exhibit 2.3 shows a sample of a résumé typical for the internship-level student. In addition, some basic information and further career resources can be found in Chapter 12 and in Bolles' iconic *What Color Is Your Parachute?* (2015) and Hodges and Connelly's *A Job Search Manual for Counselors and Counselor Educators: How to Navigate and Promote Your Counseling Career* (2010).

## The Formal Interview

As previously mentioned, interviewing for a practicum or internship varies considerably. Some potential placement sites will request an interview with a clinical director and a select staff. In other cases, a single counselor or social worker will conduct the interview. Regardless of the possible variations, you will want to be thoroughly prepared and take a few copies of your résumé or CV to the interview.

The following are some key questions to anticipate and be able to satisfactorily answer during the interview:

- Why are you interested in applying for a practicum/internship at this agency or school?
- How might our school/agency/hospital fit with your long-term professional goals?
- What specific skills and abilities make you suited for this placement?
- What are your personal and professional strengths?
- What key weaknesses would you like to target for improvement?
- What questions do you have for me/us?
- What counseling theory do you primarily work from?
- Why should we accept you as a graduate intern?

See Chapter 12 for more interview questions and suggested answers, as well as certain inappropriate questions that should not be asked on an interview.

Here are some questions for you to ask the interviewer or interviewing committee during the interview:

- Who would be my primary supervisor? What are his or her training and credentials in counseling and supervision?
- Is the agency accredited? If so, by what accrediting organization?
- What types of counseling-related responsibilities would I be carrying out (e.g., individual, group, couples, family counseling, psychoeducational groups, mediation)?
- What theoretical orientation do staff counselors use (e.g., cognitive behavioral, solution-focused)?
- Will there be opportunities for additional training?
- When can I expect to hear a decision regarding a placement?

---

**EXHIBIT 2.2  Sample of Practicum Application Cover Letter**

March 17, 2016

Ms. Alice Ajanja, MS, LMHC, NCC
Director of Pathways Clinic
Ivy, NY 14221

Dear Ms. Ajanja:

Thank you for taking the time to speak with me on the phone regarding a practicum at Pathway Clinic. I look forward to our interview this Thursday at 1:00 p.m. I feel very positive regarding the potential of serving my practicum and internship at your clinic during the following year. I understand your agency serves many immigrant children, adolescents, and adults. As an immigrant myself, I understand the particular challenges that presents.

In addition to completing the first of my 3-year clinical mental health counseling program at Old Main College, for 2 years I also have served as a Big Sister through the YWCA–YMCA's Big Brother–Big Sister program. Since fall 2015, I have volunteered for the evening crisis line through Sunflower House and was given a letter of recommendation by my supervisor (enclosed).

I enjoy challenging opportunities serving high-needs populations, as I believe timely intervention is especially important in clients developing sound mental and emotional health. I would welcome the opportunity to learn from your supervision in the next academic year.

Respectfully,

*Elisa Botha*

Elisa Botha
Graduate Student in Clinical Mental Health Counseling
Old State College
Ivy, NY 14221

Encl.

---

Actors, musicians, athletes, and politicians prepare well in advance of their big event and you should do the same in preparing for an interview. Get with a friend, fellow student, or better yet a career counselor at your institution and practice answering questions such as those mentioned previously. You might also have a friend or the career counselor videotape your mock interview and then provide critique. You do not need to be perfect, but interviewers will be impressed by prompt candidates, thorough answers, well-groomed applicants, good posture, and appropriate eye contact. Interviewers will be unimpressed by poor grooming, showing up late, interviewees who seem uninformed as to the school or agency function, and who answer "No, I have no questions," when asked. So, prepare for the interview so that you will *be prepared* for the interview.

When you have completed the interview process, always follow up with a thank-you letter. Interviewers will appreciate this simple gesture. Thank-you letters also illustrate that you know how to lay the foundation for future positive

---

**EXHIBIT 2.3   Sample of Internship Résumé**

**Leslie Hawkins**
3333 Cataract Avenue
Niagara Falls, NY 14305
(716) 861-4441
Lhawkins@gmail.com

## SUMMARY OF QUALIFICATIONS

- Compassionate, conscientious helping professional with 3 years of classroom experience (serving what type of students? Mainstream? Special education?)
- Candidate for a Master's Degree in School Counseling
  - Completed three semesters of supervised field experience working with teachers and at-risk students
  - Currently working on fourth semester of experience with school counselors and at-risk students
- Familiar with the needs of emotionally disturbed and learning-disabled students

## EDUCATION

**Niagara University** Lewiston, New York
Master of Science in School Counseling, expected May 2017

**State University of New York at Oswego,** Oswego, NY
Bachelor of Arts in Special Education, August 2012
Minor: Psychology (leave GPA off—focus on the Dean's List note)
- Completed 25 semester hours in Adolescent Education
- Made the Dean's List for three semesters

## RELATED EXPERIENCE

1/14–2/11   **Mill Middle School,** Williamsville, NY
            **School Counseling Intern**
- Observed individual and group counseling sessions with sixth-grade students
- Observed an IEP meeting with the Committee on Special Education
- Gained an understanding of the placement protocol for students with IEP's and other accommodation needs

2/20–present   **89th Street Elementary School,** Niagara Falls, NY
               **School Counseling Intern**
- Observed individual and group counseling sessions with students in grades pre-kindergarten through sixth

Fall 2011–Spring 2012   **SUNY Oswego Pride Alliance Executive Board,** Fredonia, NY
                        **Public Relations Director**
- Assisted in organization and promotion of events for the Pride Alliance, a student group geared towards the LGBT students and their allies on campus
- Participated in weekly meetings with other members of the Executive Board to discuss and plan topics for general body meetings and events throughout the semester
- Helped facilitate and lead weekly general body meetings that consisted of, on average, about 50 people

*(continued)*

**EXHIBIT 2.3   Sample of Internship Résumé (*continued*)**

- Created posters, online event announcements, and programs for every event that was sponsored or co-sponsored by the Pride Alliance
- Mentored various LGBT students on campus, both during and outside weekly office hours
- Was co-captain of the Pride Alliance "Relay For Life" team during the on-campus fundraiser in the spring of 2012
- Collaborated with other multicultural groups on campus when facilitating and creating co-sponsored events

Spring 2011      **Dunkirk Middle School,** Dunkirk, NY
                        **Volunteer Tutor**
- Worked two-on-one with a sixth-grade, at-risk student twice a week
- Prepared a weekly lesson plan
- Kept track of student's progress with pre- and post-test assessments

January 2011    **Gaskill Middle School,** Niagara Falls, NY
                        **Student Observer**
- Observed seventh- and eighth-grade classrooms, including some inclusive classes
- Assisted seventh-grade students in writing and illustrating children's books
- Assisted eighth-grade students with group reading and discussion of selected novels
- Worked one-on-one with eighth-grade student at a first-grade reading level on reading a selected book

January 2010    **Niagara Falls High School,** Niagara Falls, NY
                        **Student Observer**
- Observed 11th-grade Regents and Advanced Placement classes
- Graded practice Regents Exams and vocabulary quizzes

January 2009    **Niagara Falls City School District,** Niagara Falls, NY
                        **Student Observer**
- Helped teachers hand out and collect assignments
- Aided students in their in-class reading and writing tasks

Summer 2007    **Niagara Falls City Recreational Department,** Niagara Falls, NY
                        **Daytime Recreational Aide**
- Supervised children at a local playground for 5 hours a day, Monday–Friday
- Served lunches that were provided by the city

9/06–5/07       **St. Teresa's Parish,** Niagara Falls, NY
                        **Volunteer Sunday School Teacher**
- Taught a lesson once a week to a class of about 10 to 15 elementary-aged students

**OTHER EMPLOYMENT**

5/10–present    **Supermarket Liquors & Wines,** Niagara Falls, NY
                        **Cashier/Customer Service/Stock**

Spring 2010      **SUNY Oswego,** Oswego, NY
                        **Night Desk Attendant** (For what office?)

4/08–9/09       **Niagara Falls State Park,** Niagara Falls, NY
                        **Cashier and Tour Guide**

*(continued)*

---

**EXHIBIT 2.3   Sample of Internship Résumé (*continued*)**

**ACTIVITIES**

- Take Back the Night Walk, Fall 2008
- SUNY Oswego Pride Alliance, Fall 2008–Spring 2012
- Intramural Broomball, Fall 2009–Spring 2012
- Oswego Gospel Choir, Spring 2010–Fall 2011
- *The Vagina Monologues,* Fall 2011–Spring 2012
- Relay For Life, Spring 2011 and Spring 2012

(*Note:* I always include a short list of hobbies as it provides a more complete picture of you and may help create a connection through shared interests or highlight something interesting.)

---

relations. Should you be accepted by this practicum/internship site, such follow-through will be important in interagency relations. Given we live in the 21st century, thank-you e-mail messages will work just fine and are more immediate.

## THE PRACTICUM/INTERNSHIP CONTRACT

Prior to beginning the practicum or internship, the student, the practicum/internship coordinator, and the on-site supervisor should sign a contract agreeing to the basic counseling and related responsibilities the student will be performing. Such contracts may be called a learning contract, a practicum and internship contract, and so forth. Regardless, the agreement should explicitly delineate responsibilities of the student, faculty, on-site supervisor, counseling program, and clinical setting. Contracts are critical for the student, agency/school, and counseling program to understand specific realms of responsibility. The contract also specifies who faculty should contact in the event issues arise during the placement. All parties—student, field site supervisor, and faculty or practicum/internship coordinator—should keep a copy of the contract.

At institutions where I have worked, the practicum/internship contract is developed by the faculty, and then critiqued by the college or university's legal counsel to ensure legal issues are covered. Some agencies will also have their own contract and require the student, faculty, and on-site supervisor to sign. It is critical that supervisors and students develop a mutual understanding regarding the knowledge, skills, and dispositions that the placement and graduate counseling require. For example, CACREP-accredited counseling programs have specific responsibilities for practicum and internship regarding clock hours, direct contact hours, and supervision. The duties, obligations, organizational guidelines, and so forth should be made clear prior to the beginning of the placement.

Naturally, no contract can cover all eventualities, but the contractual language should be clear and easily understood by all parties. The contract should address the following:

- Weekly supervision by the on-site supervisor and the faculty advisor. CACREP and CORE standards require 1 hour of supervision per week carried out in an individual or group format

- The clock hours and direct contact hours the student is required to complete each semester
- The type of clinical duties the student will be assigned. Examples may include individual, group, couples, family counseling, addictions assessments, academic advising, whether the student will conduct testing and assessment and what types, intakes, and so forth
- The name of the on-site supervisor, faculty representative, and student intern
- How conflicts are to be addressed
- The right to terminate on behalf of both the counselor education program and the organization if either party feels the relationship is not working. This termination agreement protects the student, program, and placement
- Duration of the internship. Some contracts specify that the placement will last for the duration of the student's practicum/internship (anywhere from 600 to 1,000 clock hours depending on the program), although others spell out an expectation of one academic year

Documents for practicum and internship are offered in Appendix C.

## FINAL ISSUES TO CONSIDER

Exhibit 2.4 offers a checklist of issues to consider and tasks to complete as you begin your search for a practicum/internship placement. In addition, here are a few final points to bear in mind:

- Have you purchased student liability insurance? ACA and the American Mental Health Counselors Association (AMHCA) now include student liability insurance in the cost of student membership, so purchasing a student membership in ACA or AMHCA is recommended as opposed to simply purchasing student liability coverage. Some counseling programs will, of course, require students to maintain membership in ACA, AMHCA, ASCA, or another professional affiliate. In my own opinion, requiring a student membership is a worthwhile requirement that includes professional development as well as ethical and legal issues. (ACA has an ethics e-mail and phone number students can use: 1-800-347-6647 [×314] or ethics@counseling.org.)
- Have all parties agreed that the student is a good fit for the placement and the placement a good fit for the student?
- Have all parties agreed to and signed the practicum and internship contract? Can all parties live up to the specifications in the contract? Is the supervisor appropriately credentialed (e.g., licensed or certified); can the field site supervisor give the required 1 hour of weekly supervision? (This can be an issue!) Be specific!
- Have all parties met to finalize the agreed-upon supervision, beginning and ending dates of the practicum/internship, and how to work out potential student counselor–supervisor conflicts?
- It would be wise for you to read up on the school's or agency's policies and procedures manual. (If it lacks a manual, this is a red flag!) Then give yourself adequate time to adjust to the real-life setting.

---

**EXHIBIT 2.4   Practicum and Internship Checklist***

- **Get a working résumé** (if you lack one): Examine your work background for skills, experiences, and interests related to the type of placement you desire. Make sure your résumé is accurate, up to date, and targets the particular area (e.g., school, agency, college counseling center, correctional facility).

- **Examining your résumé, what types of experiences do you have that would assist you in doing counseling work?** (e.g., have you been a BA/BS chemical-dependency counselor, case manager, special education teacher or aide, staffed a collegiate living group as either a resident director [RD] or a resident advisor [RA], worked as a camp counselor?) Related experience usually helps when looking for a practicum as it implies you understand the demands of human services work.

- **Coursework:** Be prepared to explain specific courses and additional training you have had that could bolster the case for the school or agency to select you. Have you been trained in diagnosis, treatment planning, assessment, or couples and family counseling? Have you had additional training in creative arts therapy (e.g., dance therapy, art therapy, music therapy), trauma counseling, mediation, and so forth?

- **Interests and orientation:** What type of setting do you prefer? Inpatient? Outpatient? Elementary, middle, or high school? Would you want a setting that provides familiar work or one that offers something new? (For example, if you have been a middle school teacher, would you want to be placed in a middle school counseling office, or would you prefer a different setting?)

- **Scheduling:** Because most graduate students in counseling programs also work, perhaps have families and numerous other demands, what type of placement would best fit your schedule? For example, if you work day shifts during the week, you may need a placement that offers evening and weekend work. Be realistic regarding time commitments, travel to your placement, academic requirements, and such.

- **Types of clients:** What types of clients are you interested in working with? Examples include age, cultural background, special populations, and so forth. If you are unsure about what types of clients you would like to counsel, you may wish to speak with your academic advisor to clarify your interests.

- **Ongoing training opportunities:** When examining potential placements, does the school, agency, or university counseling center offer in-service training? If so, what types (some placements will provide training on various topics such as dialectical behavioral therapy [DBT], mediation, play therapy, etc.)? Some placements will offer training free of charge or at a discount to practicum and internship students.

- **Theoretical orientation:** Do any of the placements you are considering operate on one theoretical approach (e.g., cognitive behavioral therapy [CBT], eye movement desensitization and reprocessing [EMDR], psychodynamic, a particular spiritual approach)? Consider this issue carefully, as some agencies may not fit well with your values. Is there a potential conflict regarding theoretical approach, spirituality, or something else?

- **The supervisor:** Have you met with or are you familiar with the supervisor? Checking with your faculty advisor and students who have been supervised at a particular school, agency, or college counseling center is a good idea. Also, what type of qualities would you want a supervisor to possess? What type of supervisor would you work best with?

- **Do you have concerns regarding the placement (or placements) you are considering?** Any issues of safety, supervision style, professional fit, and so forth (e.g., does counseling in a prison, psychiatric hospital, or other residential setting with higher risk clients intimidate you?).

- **Career issues:** What are your career goals (e.g., I want to run an addictions treatment clinic)? How well does the placement you are considering fit with your career goal(s)?

*(continued)*

---

**EXHIBIT 2.4 Practicum and Internship Checklist\* (continued)**

What types of placements would be most beneficial to your future career plans? (Be aware that your plans may change.)

- **Additional considerations:** What other issues or concerns do you have regarding practicum and internship?
- Make sure you have thoroughly examined your résumé and cover letter for typos regarding spelling, correct dates, educational and work history, and so forth. DO NOT LIE ON YOUR RÉSUMÉ OR CV! Present yourself in an appealing, professional, and accurate manner.

---

\*This checklist is designed to assist you in planning for the types of field placements that will best fit your background, interests, and orientation.

It is hoped that what you have read so far has helped you choose and achieve your desired practicum/internship placement. In Chapter 3, I give a brief overview of common legal and ethical issues you may encounter.

## REFERENCES

American Counseling Association. (2014). *ACA code of ethics*. Alexandria, VA: Author.

American Psychiatric Association. (2013). *Diagnostic and statistical manual of mental disorders* (5th ed.). Arlington, VA: Author.

Arredondo, P., Toporek, M. S., Brown, S., Jones, J., Locke, D. C., Sanchez, J., & Stadler, H. (1996). *Operationalization of the multicultural counseling competencies*. Alexandria, VA: Association of Multicultural Counseling and Development.

Bolles, R. N. (2015). *What color is your parachute? A practical manual for job-hunters and career-changers*. Berkeley, CA: Ten Speed Press.

Corey, G. (2013). *Theory and practice of counseling and psychotherapy* (9th ed.). Belmont, CA: Thomson Brooks/Cole.

Council for Accreditation of Counseling and Related Educational Programs (CACREP). (2009). *CACREP accreditation standards*. Retrieved from www.cacrep.org/2009standards.html

Duncan, B., Miller, S. D., Wamplod, B., & Hubble, M. (2010). *The heart and soul of change: Delivering what works in therapy* (2nd ed.). Washington, DC: American Psychological Association.

Gladding, S. T. (2009). *Counseling: A comprehensive profession* (6th ed.). Upper Saddle River, NJ: Merrill/Prentice Hall.

Hodges, S., & Connelly, A. R. (2010). *A job search manual for counselors and counselor educators: How to navigate and promote your counseling career*. Alexandria, VA: American Counseling Association.

Ivey, A. I., & Ivey, M. B. (2007). *Intentional interviewing and counseling* (7th ed.). Belmont, CA: Thomson Brooks/Cole.

Remley, T. P., & Herlihy, B. (2014). *Ethical, legal and professional issues in counseling* (4th ed.). Upper Saddle River, NJ: Pearson.

Sue, D. W., Arredondo, P., & McDavis, R. J. (1992). Multicultural counseling competencies and standards: A call to the profession. *Journal of Multicultural Counseling & Development, 20*, 64–88.

Wampold, B. E. (2001). *The great psychotherapy debate: Models, methods, and findings*. Mahwah, NJ: Lawrence Erlbaum.

Wheeler, A. M., & Bertram, B. (2012). *The counselor and the law: A guide to legal and ethical practice* (6th ed.). Alexandria, VA: American Counseling Association.

# THREE

# ETHICAL AND LEGAL ISSUES

Ethical codes have been a part of the medical and health care professions for some 3,000 years. The first professional ethical code was established by Hippocrates, a Greek physician. His *Hippocratic Oath* is still taken by medical school graduates in the 21st century (Remley & Herlihy, 2014). To protect the public, ethical codes have been established in many other professions, such as law, psychiatry, social work, and certainly counseling.

For counseling students, reading and understanding the recently updated 2014 edition of the *American Counseling Association (ACA) Code of Ethics* is a vital requirement as student and professional counselors are ethically and legally bound to follow their ethical code (Remley & Herlihy, 2014; Wheeler & Bertram, 2015). The basic core of the *ACA Code of Ethics* involves a concept known as *beneficence*, or doing what is in the best interest of the client (Wheeler & Bertram, 2015). Functioning in the client's best interests includes protecting confidentiality, practicing within your scope of competence, avoiding harm, avoiding conflicts of interests regarding your clients, and refraining from sexual and business relationships with clients, to mention a few. These types of ethical issues and many others are discussed in this chapter. Counselors practicing in various specialty areas must also be familiar with the ethics of their particular specialty (e.g., American School Counselor Association, American Rehabilitation Counseling Association, American Mental Health Counselors Association [AMHCA]). This text focuses primarily on the *ACA Code of Ethics* as it represents the counseling profession's flagship organization.

Beyond the ethical code, counselors must also comply with existing federal and state laws. In fact, an important component of ethical practice is an awareness of state and federal laws with regard to professional practice (Wheeler & Bertram, 2015). Like ethical codes, state and federal laws are in a constant state of flux, influenced by legislative action, court decisions, politics, and societal changes. The landmark *Tarasoff v. The Regents of the University of California Berkeley* case and the Health Insurance Portability and Accountability Act (HIPAA) federal legislative action, both of which are discussed in this chapter, illustrate important examples of how legal and legislative decisions impact the counseling profession. Counselors who do not follow state and federal laws may be prosecuted in criminal courts. Furthermore, civil litigation against a counselor may result when said counselor has breached ethical guidelines such as fraudulent advertising, sexual intimacy with clients, and counselor incompetence.

## COMPETENT ETHICAL PRACTICE FOR COUNSELORS

The mere reading of ethical standards is not the last word in ethical practice, but rather, a commencement. Students in counselor education programs, as well as professional counselors, need ongoing training and consultation regarding competent ethical practice. The most basic ethical requirement is that counselors "practice only within the boundaries of their competence" (ACA, 2014, Section C.2.a). But, how can a counselor exactly determine his or her parameter of competence? It is difficult to answer this question because counseling is a very broad profession involving inpatient, outpatient, addictions, college and university counseling, rehabilitation counseling, school counseling, and so on, and many of these specialty areas are vastly different in scope of responsibility. However, just as an attorney could never be competent in every area of law (no matter what those large billboard ads might suggest!), counselors could never be competent to offer services in all therapeutic areas and counseling disciplines (Barnett & Johnson, 2015). A counselor who is skilled in treating individuals may not be adequately trained and competent in counseling families. Counselors who are very skilled in counseling adult clients with severe mental disorders may not be competent in counseling elementary school children. The critical issue for all counselors regardless of area is to have adequate education, training, experience, supervision, proper licensure and/or certification, ongoing continuing education, and so forth. Naturally, no license, certification, or degree can guarantee competence, but all are specifics suggesting competence. It must also be understood by all counselors that striving for competence is a lifelong endeavor (Corey, Corey, Corey, & Callanan, 2011).

Competence is a serious legal and ethical issue because society expects professionals to be competent and asserts this standard through state licensing boards, professional codes, and the legal system (Wheeler & Bertram, 2015). Counselor competence is the second most frequently reported area of ethical complaint after sexual misconduct (Corey et al., 2011; Neukrug, Milliken, & Walden, 2001). Therefore, students reading this text must begin carefully considering this critical issue of counselor competence as it will be the primary consideration in the remainder of your counseling career. The *ACA Code of Ethics* (2014) recommends consultation (Standard C.2.e.) and peer supervision (Standard C.2.d.) as a means to evaluate one's ongoing effectiveness as a counselor. Continuous self-monitoring, self-assessment, and self-reflection also assist with developing maintaining competence (Johnson, Barnett, Elman, Forrest, & Kaslow, 2012).

## HEALTH INSURANCE PORTABILITY AND ACCOUNTABILITY ACT (HIPAA)

One of the most far-reaching and influential congressional legislative actions with regard to the health and mental health field is HIPAA. Congress passed this sweeping legislation in 1996 to ensure people would be able to maintain insurance coverage when changing jobs and in response to concerns of privacy regarding the electronic transfer of records (Remley & Herlihy, 2014; Wheeler & Bertram, 2015). Counselors' and other mental health professionals' billing insurance must comply with HIPAA standards.

Given that inpatient and outpatient agency practicum and internship sites will be subject to HIPAA regulations, it is very important that counseling students understand it. Even field placements such as university counseling centers, most of which technically are not required to follow HIPAA (i.e., do not bill insurance) generally comply with HIPAA. Naturally, your supervisors will likely provide both training and oversight regarding HIPAA and other federal policies impacting professional practice. Still, it is a good professional practice to be proactive and read the HIPAA requirements. You may visit the HIPAA website (www.hhs.gov/ocr/hipaa). In addition, professional counseling organizations, such as ACA, AMHCA, and others, periodically offer training in HIPAA compliance. The periodical *Counseling Today* frequently offers information on HIPAA compliance.

## INFORMED CONSENT

*Informed consent* means that clients must know and understand basic issues about the process of counseling: their rights, counselor responsibilities, fees charged, counselor training, access to records, and limits to confidentiality, and how to register formal complaints among others. The counseling relationship is built on the foundation of trust, which provides a context for ongoing therapy (Pope & Vasquez, 2011). With rare exception clients are not experts in the mental health arena and must, of necessity, rely on their counselors to provide them with the information necessary to become active participants in therapy and make informed choices (Handelsman, 2001; Herlihy & Corey, 2015).

During informed consent, counselors must provide the client with information pertinent to the counseling relationship. As stated earlier, this includes fees, counselor training, and such, but also outlines the client's rights and responsibilities, including provisions for mandated clients, the client's right to terminate counseling, expectations (e.g., client and counselor are both punctual, fees are paid on time), emergency plans for counselor vacation and after-hours coverage, and so forth. Written documentation of these issues is a must, given possible liability issues (Wheeler & Bertram, 2015). In fact, HIPAA requires written documentation of informed consent (Madden, 1998). Counselors in the field should provide clients with a document outlining informed consent with a place for clients to sign and date indicating they have read and understood the document. Client's understanding of informed consent is also impacted by numerous factors such as age, education, mandated versus voluntary status, intellectual impairment, and cultural differences. It also is important to remain open to an alternate means of dispensing informed consent such as an interpreter or translator (Wheeler & Bertram, 2015). The critical issue is for counselors to do everything within reason to ensure clients have understood informed consent.

It is worth noting that informed consent in couples, family, and group counseling is more complex than in individual therapy. Most important for the client to understand is that confidentiality cannot be guaranteed when there is more than one client in the session (Remley & Herlihy, 2014). Counselors involved in group, family, or couples counseling must carefully explain the nature of counseling and how and why confidentiality is critical to the therapeutic process. Counselors must also work with groups, couples, and families to determine how a breach of confidentiality might be dealt with.

The *ACA Code of Ethics* (ACA, 2014, Section A.2.b) outlines the information that should be discussed with the client when obtaining informed consent:

- The purpose, goals, techniques, procedures, limitations, potential risks, and benefits of counseling services
- The counselor's qualifications, including relevant degrees held, licenses and certifications, areas of specialization, and relevant experience
- Arrangements for continuation of services should the counselor become unable to continue counseling
- The implications of the *Diagnostic and Statistical Manual of Mental Disorders*, fifth edition (*DSM-5;* American Psychiatric Association, 2013), diagnosis, use of assessments, and reports
- Fees and billing information (generally not applicable in schools and most college or university counseling centers)
- Confidentiality and its limits
- The client's right to inspect his or her record and to participate in counseling treatment
- The client's right to refuse any recommended services or modality change and be advised of the consequences of refusal especially with regard to legally mandated clients

In addition to those issues suggested by the *ACA Code of Ethics*, numerous counseling professionals have recommended that additional information be included:

- A description of the counselor's theoretical orientation (written in clear language the client can understand) or a brief statement regarding the counselor's philosophical approach to counseling (Corey et al., 2011)
- Information regarding the logistics of counseling, such as length and frequency of sessions, procedures for making and canceling appointments, policies regarding phone contact between sessions, and how to contact the counselor in the event of an emergency
- Information regarding insurance reimbursement, including the fact that any diagnosis assigned will likely become part of the client's permanent health record and the risks inherent with this (Welfel, 2012)
- Information alternatives to counseling, such as 12-step groups, support groups, self-help books, medication information, and other supportive services

- When applicable, a statement regarding video or audio taping, along with a statement that the client's case may be discussed with the clinical supervisor or a consultant (Corey et al., 2011)
- The client's recourse if dissatisfied with counseling services, including names and contact information for supervisors and addresses and phone numbers of licensing boards and professional organizations (Remley & Herlihy, 2014; Welfel, 2012)

Exhibit 3.1 offers a sample informed consent form that a client might sign.

---

**EXHIBIT 3.1    Informed Consent for Clients**

**Jane Doe, MS, LMHC, NCC**
**1719 Freud Lane**
**Therapy, NY 10017**
**jane.doe@aol.com**
**Phone: (123) 456-7890**

**My Qualifications**
My practice includes counseling with children, adolescents, and couples. I am also a New York State Certified Mediator. I hold a master's degree in Mental Health Counseling, am a Licensed Mental Health Counselor (LMHC), and a Nationally Certified Counselor (NCC). I have postgraduate training in cognitive behavioral therapy from the Beck Institute in Philadelphia. My postgraduate experience includes 15 years as a community mental health counselor and I hold memberships in the American Counseling Association and the American Mental Health Counselors Association.

The clinic's fees are set by your insurance carrier, so you want to consult your carrier for any questions. For uninsured clients, we offer a sliding fee scale with minimum fees set equal to the lowest billable insurance carrier ($60.00 per session). Most insurance carriers will allow 8–10 sessions.

**The General Course of Counseling**
I appreciate that you have come to our clinic and I want to be thorough and specific in helping you achieve the goals you have set. My job is to provide assessment and counseling and work conjointly with you to set treatment goals. It is true that in counseling success depends on the client actively wanting to change. Counseling is not an exact science, and at times the counselor, in consultation with you, may need to revise the goals of treatment. Some assessment will be carried out at the intake time and other assessments may be added later for further clarification. Unless otherwise stated, all counseling sessions are 50 minutes long.

If you have been mandated for treatment to this agency, you will be required to sign a Release of Information Form so this counselor and the agency can provide necessary information to the agency, parole officer, court, or other official that mandated your treatment.

Anytime you have questions regarding your treatment, please feel free to ask.

---

*(continued)*

---

**EXHIBIT 3.1  Informed Consent for Clients (*continued*)**

**Record Keeping and Confidentiality**
Ethically and legally, I am required to keep records of all our contacts. Legally, you have the right to see all information generated between us. You must provide explicit permission for information to be revealed, unless the law specifies otherwise (see exceptions to confidentiality). Thus, with your written consent, I will provide information to anyone with a legitimate need. You are also entitled to a copy of any records generated in this office. This clinic keeps records for 10 years past the last date of contact. Then, because of space and privacy concerns, records are destroyed in compliance with state law and professional ethics.

**Exceptions to Confidentiality**
The following are general legal/ethical exceptions to confidentiality (check with your state or province as there is variation):

- When child abuse/neglect is suspected.
- When elder abuse is suspected.
- In the case of imminent danger of suicide.
- In the event of a clear and specified threat to a third party.
- If a life-threatening contagious disease threatens a third party (e.g., AIDS, HIV).
- When a client provides written permission (i.e., Release of Information Form).
- If a judge mandates a release of information.
- If a client sues a counselor or makes false charges against a counselor.

**Client as Consumer**
As a client in counseling, you are encouraged to participate actively and fully in your own treatment. Many counselors will assign homework activities, reading, and so forth. You are encouraged to follow through with as many homework assignments as possible. In addition, keep your counselor apprised when you cannot complete out-of-session assignments so that the two of you can make a new plan. Also, if you feel you do not fully understand something, ask your counselor for clarification. Clients who take an active approach to their treatment are likely to make more therapeutic progress than those who are passive.

**Your Rights as a Client**
Although you are encouraged to discuss the issues with your counselor first, if for any reason you believe your rights have been violated, you have a right to file a grievance.

**For Ethical Issues**
American Counseling Association (ACA)
5999 Stevenson Ave.
Alexandria, VA 22304
1-800-347-6647 (×314)

New York State Board for Mental Health Counselors
State Education Department
Office of the Professions
89 Washington Ave.
Albany, NY 12234-1000
www.op.nysed.gov

I have read and understand all information presented here in the informed consent document.

_____          _____

Name                                                              Date

## CONFIDENTIALITY AND PRIVILEGED COMMUNICATION

The effectiveness of the counselor–client relationship is constructed upon trust. Confidentiality is the cornerstone of counseling and arguably the most important ethical concept in the delivery of counseling services. Without confidentiality, clients would be far less likely to disclose personal or sensitive information, and many would refrain from seeking counseling services entirely (Herlihy & Corey, 2015; Miller & Thelan, 1986; Remley & Herlihy, 2014). Within the mental health profession, confidentiality is viewed as essential to the counseling relationship. Clients need to know that their counselors will respect their privacy, whereas counselors know that an effective counseling relationship is built on a foundation of trust. Clients involved in a deeply personal relationship like counseling have the right to expect that what they divulge in sessions will be kept private (Corey et al., 2011; Herlihy & Corey, 2015; Wheeler & Bertram, 2015). Naturally, concerns regarding a counselor's ability to protect the right of confidentiality frequently emerge. However, complaints against counselors for breach of confidentiality are actually quite rare. Various studies have shown that less than 5% of complaints to ethics boards involve a breach of confidentiality (Garcia, Salo, & Hamilton, 1995; Pope & Vasquez, 1998, 2011).

On the other hand, in one study, 62% of psychologists surveyed reported that they had unintentionally violated their clients' confidentiality (Pope, Tabachnick, & Keith-Spiegel, 1987). Some of the unintentional violations of confidentiality are listed here:

- Sending confidential information through the Internet: Web-based counseling presents serious challenges to privacy due to hacking concerns.
- Violations through e-mail exchanges: Counselors and clients should always assume e-mail is not a confidential method of information delivery and should refrain from disclosing names, personal information, and other data, in e-mail.
- Violations over the telephone: Telephone transmission of information may not be secure, particularly those using mobile phones.
- Violations via fax: Client information is frequently faxed from one organization to another; given how busy most offices are, confidential information can easily be passed on.
- Confidential information left on answering machines: Counselors in private practice should use an answering service and refrain from leaving any details on an answering machine.
- Discussing cases in insecure locations: Remley and Herlihy (2014) relate a story of two counselors discussing a client in a crowded elevator, only to discover that the client was standing behind them!
- Completing confidential documentation in public places: Once while sitting in a coffee shop, I noticed the woman at the table next to me was writing her case notes and seemed untroubled by the look of astonishment on my face. Make sure you take the same precautions in documentation as you take when counseling and do it behind closed doors.

Clearly, there are many ways counselors can unintentionally violate a client's confidentiality. Graduate students in counseling programs must be very diligent in maintaining client privacy. Although it is natural for students to want to debrief with one another, bear in mind your ethical obligations are the same as those of professional counselors (ACA, 2014, Section F.8.a). Your communications must not reveal any sensitive information that would allow third parties to readily identify a client. Case notes, assessments, and recordings of sessions must be stored in secure locations with access limited to faculty and on-site clinical supervisors.

## Privileged Communication

The legal concept of *privileged communication* refers to any conversation that takes places within a protected relationship, such as that between an attorney and client (Wheeler & Bertram, 2015). The law often protects against forced disclosure of such conversations, although there are exceptions. In most states, counselor–client communications are protected from disclosure similar to that of physician–patient or attorney–client communications. More importantly, the privilege applies when the counselor is called as a witness in an administrative hearing or courtroom (Wheeler & Bertram, 2015). Counselors should understand however, that the privilege usually belongs to the client (the holder of the privilege), though the counselor may be charged with the responsibility of protecting the privilege (Wheeler & Bertram, 2015).

The application of privileged communication to the mental health field arose in the groundbreaking legal case, *Jaffee v. Redmond et al.* (1996), which was the first U.S. Supreme Court case to uphold the concept of a psychotherapist–patient privilege in federal court. In the *Jaffee* case, a policewoman sought counseling from a licensed social worker after she fatally shot a suspect during a stabbing incident. The family of the decedent sued the police officer, police department, and the city, alleging use of deadly force in violation of the suspect's civil rights. In legal proceedings, the plaintiffs learned that the police officer had been in counseling and sought to compel the social worker to testify at the trial and turn over case notes and records on her counseling sessions with the officer. The case made its appeals eventually winding up at the U.S. Supreme Court. The Supreme Court ruled the social worker could not be compelled to reveal the private records of her sessions with the policewoman. The case was the first to uphold the concept of psychotherapist–patient privilege that applied to psychiatrists, psychologists, social workers, counselors, and so forth.

Counselors should be aware, however, that not all states expressively grant counselor–client privilege in state court proceedings. Counselors who get subpoenaed should always seek the advice of their supervisor and/or that of their legal counsel. Counselors should never simply comply with a subpoena as doing so may constitute a violation of confidentiality and privacy (Remley & Herlihy, 2014; Wheeler & Bertram, 2015). Rather, let legal counsel work with the judge to address the subpoena.

## Exceptions to Confidentiality

Confidentiality is not an absolute or static concept, as courts and legislative actions are constantly reshaping its parameters (Wheeler & Bertram, 2015).

Federal guidelines such as HIPAA also proscribe permissible exceptions to confidentiality. As was stated previously, clients should be made aware at the beginning of the counseling relationship the legal limits of confidentiality (Wheeler & Bertram, 2015). It is important to discuss the occasions in which confidentiality may be breached, because clients may not be aware that confidentiality is not absolute. Counseling students may fear that enumerating the limits of confidentiality could inhibit a client's disclosure, although this does not appear to be a realistic concern (Baird & Rupert, 1987).

There are several general and common exceptions to confidentiality (Remley & Herlihy, 2014; Wheeler & Bertram, 2015):

- In cases of suspected abuse or neglect (child abuse, elder abuse, vulnerable populations)
- When the client is a danger to self
- When the client is a danger to others
- Clients planning future crimes
- Legal proceedings when counseling records may be subpoenaed (this would include a former client suing a former counselor in which case the client could not assert privilege communication)
- When a client has signed a release of information
- When the client is a minor, confidentiality would go to the parent or guardian
- Clients with serious communicable diseases (e.g., HIV, AIDS)

### Suspected Abuse

In most states, laws have been enacted for the teachers, health care workers, and mental health professionals regarding *mandated reporting* of suspected abuse (Remley & Herlihy, 2014). This law generally applies in cases of suspected child abuse or neglect, although in some states it is also applied to other vulnerable populations such as older persons or the disabled (Wheeler & Bertram, 2015). Under mandated reporting statutes, if a child tells a counselor he or she is being physically or sexually abused, if the child has bruises or other injuries indicative of abuse, or if the counselor has other reasons to believe the child is being physically, sexually, or emotionally abused, the counselor is required to notify the appropriate authorities (typically a department for child welfare or children's services). Under the law, counselors cannot be sued for good faith reporting of suspected child abuse (Wheeler & Bertram, 2015).

After the report is made, a caseworker will be assigned to investigate. If the caseworker determines probable cause for abuse or neglect, he or she will refer the case to local law enforcement authorities. If, after an investigation, the authorities determine that abuse is occurring, the next step may be legal action for criminal prosecution of the abuser(s) or civil action to determine the best placement for the child's welfare. In many cases, the child will be removed from the home for a period (and in some cases, permanently). Child abuse and neglect are discussed further in Chapter 9.

### Suspected Child Abuse: A Reality Check

Students in counseling programs should be aware of the delicate issues involving child abuse and neglect. Even when children are removed from the home, they may be going to a foster care placement that can be abusive or neglectful. Furthermore, in most cases, my experience is the child often is returned to the abusive or neglectful home. Basically, there are not enough foster care placements (and many are not viable ones), and residential care options (e.g. orphanages, residential treatment facilities) are expensive in the long term. Basically, reporting suspected child abuse, while required, is no panacea.

### Danger to Self and Others

Probably the most common situation in which a counselor will be required to breach confidentiality arises when a client makes direct and specific threats of suicide or of harm to a third party. The legal and ethical issues that arise in these situations are discussed in the *Tarasoff* case (*Tarasoff v. The Regents of the University of California Berkeley*, 1976). The case began when a psychologist at the university counseling center received a viable threat from a student, Prosenjit Podder; he intended to kill his former girlfriend (Tatiana Tarasoff) when she returned from overseas. The psychologist reported the student to the university police, who briefly detained him for questioning but then released him when he promised to have no contact with Tarasoff when she returned to the United States. Tragically, when Ms. Tarasoff returned to campus, Mr. Podder murdered her. The Tarasoff family sued the psychologist, psychiatrist, university counseling center, campus police, and the university's Board of Regents claiming no one from Berkeley notified them of the danger. The Supreme Court decided that specific responsibilities and obligations arise on the therapist's part from the special counselor–client relationship and that this relationship may create additional responsibility on the part of the counselor. Specifically, the Supreme Court ruled:

> One a therapist does in fact determine, or under applicable professional standards reasonably should have determined, that a patient poses a serious danger of violence to others, he bears a duty to exercise reasonable care to protect the foreseeable victim of that danger. (p. 345)

Not all threats of violence may be serious ones; however, if a client makes an explicit threat regarding violence and has a plan to achieve it, then the *Tarasoff* case would definitely apply. If a client discloses thoughts, feelings, or intentions that place the client or an identifiable third party at risk, you must document the threat, the appropriate action taken, as well as notify the proper authorities. Competent documentation is essential in crisis situations, as they may ultimately involve the legal system. Should a case proceed to court for an involuntary commitment to a psychiatric center, for example, or even a correctional facility, the case record will be carefully scrutinized by lawyers, the judge, and other professionals. You want to demonstrate in writing that you were thorough in your counseling, assessment, and decision making, and that you did every-thing possible to ensure the client's safety. (Working with potentially violent or suicidal clients is discussed in more detail in Chapter 9.) A good maxim to remember is "If it ain't written down, it didn't happen the way you say."

Some state courts have issued decisions that limit or contradict the *Tarasoff* ruling. In Florida's *Boynton v. Burglass* (1991), counselors may breach confi-dentiality to prevent imminent harm, but they are not mandated by law to do so (Wheeler & Bertram, 2015). The case originally pertained to a psychiatrist but the *Boynton* judge clarified the ruling also applied to all psychotherapists. Therefore, in Florida, counselors may breach confidentiality to prevent clear and imminent harm to someone, but there is no mandatory duty as exists under the landmark *Tarasoff* decision. Counselors in Florida should be mindful of new case law that may further define the scope of duty to warn and protect (Wheeler & Bertram, 2015).

Texas also declined to adopt the *Tarasoff* ruling. In 1999, the Texas Supreme Court held in *Thapar v. Zezulka* that counselors have no common law duty to warn readily identifiable third parties of a threat against them. By statute, Texas counselors are permitted to make disclosures to law enforcement or medical personnel in situations where there is an identifiable risk of imminent injury. However, there is no specific grant of immunity built into the Texas statute, which could create a decision-making challenge for the counselor (Wheeler & Bertram, 2015). The bottom line, of course, is for counselors to know and oper-ate within the laws of their respective state or territory and seek clarification from supervisors or legal counsel when they are unsure of legal issues.

### Clients Planning Future Crimes

Most legal cases impose liability on a counselor for failure to warn and protect a third party only when there is resulting personal injury (Wheeler & Bertram, 2015). However, the Vermont Supreme Court ruled the *Tarasoff* duty could also apply in a property damage case. In *Peck v. Counseling Services of Addison County, Inc.* (1985), a client informed his counselor he planned to burn down his father's barn. But, under exploration of the issue, he then promised the counselor he would not commit the arson. However, the client did in fact burn down the barn whereupon the client's father sued for damages. The Vermont Supreme Court ruled arson could pose a grave risk to human life and ruled for the plaintiff and against the counselor and her agency. Thus, in some states *Tarasoff* carries an expanded duty for counselors.

If a client discloses that he or she is planning to commit future crimes, the counselor is required to disclose this information in 17 states when the client is under investigation by law enforcement officials (Glosoff, Herlihy, & Spence, 2000). These states are Alaska, Arizona, Idaho, Illinois, Indiana, Kansas, Louisiana, Massachusetts, Montana, New Mexico, Oklahoma, Oregon, South Carolina, South Dakota, Tennessee, and Washington; and the District of Columbia. Types of criminal activity included in this exception are the distribution of con-trolled substances, selling stolen goods, and fraudulent schemes (Welfel, 2012).

Counselors confronted by such circumstances should confer with their supervisor and legal representative to ensure they are in compliance with the law and their professional ethics.

### Legal Proceedings

Typical legal proceedings in which counselors may encounter forced disclosure involve cases of suspected child abuse, child custody, and civil litigation against counselors (Remley & Herlihy, 2014). In such cases, the counselor may be subpoenaed by an attorney to provide information from counseling sessions with a client. In the event you receive a subpoena to appear at a legal proceeding, but no mention is made of records, do not take records with you unless instructed to do so by your attorney (Remley & Herlihy, 2014). When a subpoena is issued to you by a lawyer, your first step is to consult your supervisor. Your supervisor (or you if you are the supervisor) should consult the attorney to determine whether the subpoena is valid and whether you should respond (Remley & Herliny, 2014; Wheeler & Bertram, 2015). An attorney will review the subpoena and advise you what steps need to be taken. For example, the attorney could ask the lawyer who issued the subpoena to withdraw it, file a motion with court to quash the subpoena, or advise you to comply with the subpoena. The critical point here is *do not try to deal with a subpoena without legal advice from an attorney.*

When a former client brings a case against a former counselor, the client's records no longer fall under the protection of "privileged" as discussed previously (Wheeler & Bertram, 2015). In such cases, the counseling records are considered to be evidence that is necessary to establish the legal facts. If a client decides to file an ethical complaint against a counselor or sue a counselor for any reason, the client must waive the right to confidentiality. This provides the counselor the opportunity to defend himself or herself against the client's claims.

In any case of forced disclosure, counselors must seek legal advice from competent counsel. Schools, agencies, hospitals, and other institutions all have attorneys who will be able to deal with the subpoena. If you receive a subpoena (which is unlikely, but could happen), report it immediately to your supervisor. Given the possibility that counseling records could be subpoenaed, however, it behooves counselors to be judicious in what they write in the records. Should any counselor or graduate counseling student be subpoenaed, his or her written records (e.g., case notes) are likely what will be called into question. Chapter 5 discusses ways to take effective and comprehensive case notes.

### Client Release of Information

This exception is based on the client's right to release information. The *ACA Code of Ethics* states, "Unless exceptions to confidentiality exist, counselors obtain written information from clients to disclose or transfer records to legitimate third parties. Steps are taken to ensure that receivers of counseling records are sensitive to their confidential nature" (ACA, 2014, Section B.6.g). Many clients in counseling will waive this right, especially when insurance reimbursement is concerned. Still, counselors must be certain to educate clients regarding written release of records and document such actions. (*Note:* Documentation, particularly in counseling services, clearly is the "devil in the details.")

A release from confidentiality does not give a counselor approval to release client information to anyone but to specified third parties who would have a legitimate need to know. Additionally, the counselor must establish whether that third party will be able to respect the client's sensitive information. If the counselor has any hesitation about the wisdom of releasing the client's information to a particular person, the counselor should discuss his or her concerns with the client so that the client can make an informed decision.

### Minor Clients or Legally Incompetent Clients

Issues of confidentiality and privileged communication become much more complicated when minor clients or incompetent adults are involved. Minors and legally incompetent adults cannot enter into legal contracts. Thus, their parents or guardians essentially make legal decisions for them (*in loco parentis*). Counselors must balance the rights of minor clients and incompetent adults with their parents' or guardians' need to know regarding specifics of counseling sessions (Remley & Herlihy, 2014). At the same time, however, counselors have ethical obligations to such clients themselves (ACA, 2014, Section B.5.a). These issues can be particularly problematic in school settings, where the counselor also has the added responsibility of working within the framework of school district policies and his or her own school's principal.

There are also significant legal variations across states and territories. For example, the definition of *minor* varies; in many states, adulthood begins at 18 years of age, but in some it is 19 or 21 years (Wheeler & Bertram, 2015). Furthermore, some states provide that 16-year-olds can withhold certain information from their parents, such as the use of birth control. The variations among state laws certainly make for challenging and confusing situations for counselors. Because of the complexities involved, Gustafson and McNamara (1987) recommended that therapists should create a written protocol that explicitly states the conditions of and limits to confidentiality in counseling minor clients. This protocol would be reviewed with each minor client involved, signed, and kept in the record. Providing a written record reduces the potential for confusion and protects the counselor, school, agency, or other party that may be involved should legal issues arise.

It is also worth mentioning that legal issues involving minors usually also involve their parents or legal guardians. Parents and guardians should also be aware of the parameters of confidentiality with regard to their children's therapy. Interestingly, while minor children cannot enter into contracts, school counselors evidently do not need parental or guardian permission to counsel school children (Remley & Herlihy, 2014). For example, parents may inform the school counselor or principal that they do not want their daughter seeing the counselor. But if the principal and counselor have good reason to believe the child needs counseling, they could proceed with counseling. Though counseling against parental wishes might seem insensitive, there may be compelling reasons for doing so. For example, I can recall one case where a father did not want his daughter in counseling. The school principal and counselor went against the father's wishes citing the minor daughter's depressed and withdrawn behavior. During a session with the school counselor, the daughter disclosed her father had been sexually abusing her.

### Clients With Serious Communicable Diseases

Counseling clients with serious communicable illnesses raises several ethical and legal issues. Significant concerns for counselors involve confidentiality of client disclosures, the risk of discrimination against clients if their health status is not protected, and the welfare of third parties at risk for infection because of contact with the client (Welfel, 2012).

Mandated disclosure regarding communicable diseases is one of the more recent ethical and legal issues the mental health profession has faced and perhaps the most controversial, because legal scholars continue to debate the merits of disclosure in this arena (Anderson & Barret, 2001; Harding, Gray, & Neal, 1993; Wheeler & Bertram, 2015). The *ACA Code of Ethics* outlines guidelines for counselors regarding disclosure in cases of communicable diseases:

> When clients disclose they have disease commonly known to be both communicable and life threatening, counselors may be justified in disclosing to identifiable third parties, if the parties are known to be at serious and foreseeable risk of contracting the disease. Prior to making a disclosure, counselors assess the intent of clients to inform the third parties about their disease or to engage in any behaviors that may be harmful to an identifiable third party. Counselors adhere to relevant state laws concerning disclosure about disease status.
>
> (ACA, 2014, Section B.2.c)

A gray area in most state laws covering communicable diseases refers to mandated disclosure by physicians and other health care providers and is often vague on the responsibilities of mental health professionals (Welfel, 2012). Furthermore, state laws on mandated disclosure of serious communicable illnesses vary widely. Most states allow or demand disclosure in cases of serious communicable illnesses, although some states mandate privacy for the client. In states that mandate privacy, a counselor could potentially be sued for disclosure to third parties (Welfel, 2012). Given such complexities and varying laws regarding disclosure in this arena, counselors must seek legal advice about the regulations that govern mandated disclosure and privacy.

An added note regarding potentially contagious, life-threatening diseases is that *ACA Code of Ethics* has made a significant change from the 2005 edition. Previously, the ethical code read: "prior to making a disclosure, counselors confirm that there is such a diagnosis ..." (ACA, 2005, Section B.2.b). When my colleagues and I on the 2014 Ethics Revision Task Force reviewed and revised the Code, we realized the impossibility of confirming such a diagnosis. For example, it's unlikely a physician would disclose such to a third party absent a legal mandate to do so given HIPAA regulations. Second, the client may refuse to disclose the name of his or her physician. The language in the 2014 revision seems to me (naturally) a more functional one.

### Counseling Terminally Ill Clients

Counselors working with terminally ill clients, whether in hospice or other agencies, may face several ethical, legal, moral, and spiritual issues. Terminally ill clients whose pain and suffering are intense may wish to examine the option of euthanasia during counseling sessions. The topic of "rational" (sic) suicide (Humphrey, 1996) raises many complex issues: Are counselors under the same obligation to prevent terminally ill clients from committing suicide as they would other suicides? Does a terminal diagnosis actually change the counselor's duty to warn and protect? Does a client have a right to die? Are clients who wish to hasten their own death considered rational, or should they be considered mentally ill? The 2005 edition of the *ACA Code of Ethics* discussed the matter at length:

> *Counselor Competence, Choice and Referral.* Recognizing the personal, moral, and competence issues related to end-of-life decisions, counselors may choose to work or not work with terminally ill clients who wish to explore their end-of-life options. Counselors provide appropriate referral information to ensure that clients receive the necessary help.
>
> *Confidentiality.* Counselors who provide services to terminally ill individuals who are considering their own deaths have the option of breaking or not breaking confidentiality depending on the specific circumstances of the situation and after seeking consultation or supervision (ACA, 2005, Section A.9).

The most recent revision of the *ACA Code of Ethics* (2014), however, removed the previous section on end-of-life counseling due to the fact the language could put the counselor in violation of state laws (i.e., "option of breaking or not breaking confidentiality"). The changes from the 2005 ethical standards to the 2014 ones illustrate the need for counselors to stay current in their profession and be aware of revisions to the code of ethics as such codes are living and not static documents. The next revision of the *ACA Code of Ethics* likely would occur roughly 10 years after the 2014 version, though court decisions could also impact the code before that time.

Counselors who work with terminally ill clients should now be familiar with these ethical statements, but also must be aware of state laws. Naturally, when working with end-of-life issues and decisions, counselors may find it necessary to consult a legal professional for guidance.

---

*The Case of Harriet*

Harriet is a 70-year-old former advertising executive who has lived a full and active life. An all-conference cross-country runner in college, she completed numerous marathons, half-marathons, and other athletic events. She was married and raised three children, and has eight grandchildren. Harriet, a widow, was diagnosed with inoperable liver cancer and given 6 months to live. She seeks counseling services from Malcolm to help her address end-of-life issues. After a couple of sessions, Harriet states that she will discontinue debilitating radiation and chemotherapy treatments; she goes on to say that if the pain becomes too unbearable, she will take her life. Malcolm wishes to continue counseling Harriet but decides he must break confidentiality should Harriet discloses a suicide plan.

1. What do you think about Malcolm's decision? Do you agree? Disagree? Why?
2. Are Malcolm's actions defendable on ethical, legal, and/or moral grounds?
3. What do you see being in Harriet's best interests?
4. If Malcolm approached you for consultation regarding Harriet, how would you advise him?

---

## Recommendations for Practicum/Internship

Here are some recommendations to consider if you are faced with an issue of confidentiality during your practicum/internship:

- Know your school's or agency's policies on breaching confidentiality. Keep a copy of the written policy at your disposal.
- Anytime you see the need to break confidentiality, consult with your site supervisor as soon as possible.
- Keep your practicum/internship advisor apprised regarding crisis situations.
- Make sure that you have properly documented a clear rationale for breaching confidentiality in the case notes. You never know when a file may be subpoenaed or a judge mandates court disclosure. A general guideline is "If it's not written in a file, it didn't happen."
- In the event you are subpoenaed, do not immediately comply with the order; this could mean you have violated confidentiality. Go immediately to your supervisor, who will notify the school or agency attorney. Let the legal professionals fight the legal battles.

## TECHNOLOGY AND CLIENT RECORDS

Many counseling agencies, schools, treatment centers, and private practitioners now maintain client records, schedules, and financial information on computer software. New technology, however, brings about new risks. Hackers may compromise the system and have access to sensitive client information; thus, security is paramount. Records must also be backed up in the event that data are lost. There are numerous software programs on the market specifically designed for counseling professionals' use. These programs can assist counselors in the creation and management of client records, including scheduling, billing, treatment planning, progress notes, reports to outside professionals (e.g., judges, child welfare, parole and probation), and client termination summaries, to cite a few. Three such programs are TheraScribe (www.therascribe.com), Therapist Helper (www.helper.com), and Notes 444 (www.notes444.com), among many others. With the advent of the super technology era, it's likely all records will be kept by virtual means, which requires no warehousing. Keeping virtual documents, however, does leave the door open to hackers.

Counselors must also maintain records for the minimum period set forth by federal or state law. Some states mandate 7 years, others 10 years (Wheeler & Bertram, 2015). Counselors may also wish to keep client records for years after treatment has ended because former clients have been known to request copies of case notes or counselors may need client records to protect themselves against litigation (Wheeler & Bertram, 2015). If there is no set minimum period for retention of records, a general practice is to keep records for a minimum of 7 years (Remley & Herlihy, 2014; Wheeler & Bertram, 2015). As a professional counselor, should your school or agency have a particularly sensitive record that you believe wise to retain for a period longer than required, it would be prudent to have legal counsel advise you on the matter.

Counseling agencies, schools, and other mental health treatment or rehabilitation centers would be wise to adopt an official record retention policy. Records should be kept and transmitted in accordance with HIPAA requirements, professional ethics, and federal and state laws. The record retention policy should specify how records will be stored, where they will be stored (the location must be secure), and how and when they will be destroyed (Wheeler & Bertram, 2015).

## BOUNDARY ISSUES: DUAL RELATIONSHIPS IN COUNSELING

*Boundary issues* in counseling typically involve *dual* or *multiple relationships*. According to Herlihy and Corey (2015), dual or multiple relationships occur when counselors take on roles outside the therapeutic encounter. Dual relationships can involve combining the role of counselor with that of minister, teacher, colleague, committee member, friend, relative, and so forth. In certain settings, multiple relationships are not only expected but they may be required. For example, school counselors will interact with students beyond the school counseling office. Pastoral counselors will be expected to have multiple relationships if they counsel as part of their ecclesiastical duties. Counselors working on small college/university campuses likely will encounter clients and former clients outside the counseling center. Counselors in residential treatment settings (e.g., correctional, addictions, psychiatric) are required to treat patients in counseling sessions (individual or group), but also interact with them at lunch, on the grounds, and so forth. Certainly counselors practicing in rural or remote areas will have no option but to have multiple relationships with clients. As a counselor who has practiced in rural and occasionally in very remote areas (Outback Australia), such settings require strong though flexible boundaries. The critical factor in multiple relationships is to ensure client privacy in areas where privacy is difficult to achieve. The 2014 ACA Code of Ethics has explicitly outlined guidance for managing counselor–client boundaries in Section A.6. Counseling students should carefully review this section of the ethical code as it appears boundary violations (or *perceived* boundary violations) are the primary reason for ethics complaints against counselors (Herlihy & Corey, 2015; Remley & Herlihy, 2014). Most multiple relationships likely are not ethical violations, but counselors must take care to ensure client's rights are not compromised when relationships extend beyond the session. Naturally, some multiple relationships are ethical violations as noted in the following paragraph.

A sexual relationship between a counselor and a client represents a dual relationship whereby the counselor has committed an egregious ethical (and in some cases and certain states a legal) violation. Sexual relations between counselors and clients are explicitly forbidden under the ACA Code of Ethics. For other dual relationships, however, the issue is less clear. The most recent revision of the ACA Code of Ethics recognizes that dual relationships are not necessarily unethical. Under Section A.5 ("Roles and Relationships with Clients"), the standard states:

> Sexual and/or romantic counselor-client interactions or relationships with current clients, their romantic partners, or their family members are prohibited. This prohibition applies to both in-person and electronic interactions or relationships. (ACA, 2014, Section A.5.a)

Sexual relationships with former clients, their romantic partners, or their family members also are prohibited for a period of 5 years following the last professional contact (Section A.5.c). This prohibition applies to both in-person and electronic means. In fact, the code specifies there would need to be 5 years of no personal or professional contact with the former client and counselor. Should the counselor pursue a romantic/sexual relationship with a former client after the required 5-year no-contact period, said counselor must do in-depth work to ensure such a relationship would not be harmful to the former client. Given the intense focus on prohibiting sexual intimacies between counselors and clients, it might surprise many to learn one of the most common malpractice allegations and litigation against mental health professionals is sexual misconduct (Pope & Vasquez, 2011). From my viewpoint of nearly 30 years in the counseling field, it seems such relationships would be fraught with numerous potential hazards to the former client. Thus, my suggestion is counselors should never enter into romantic/sexual relationships with former clients. As a point of comparison, the National Association of Social Workers ethical code prohibits sexual relationships with former clients (Remley & Herlihy, 2014).

The 2014 code also prohibits other multiple relationships with clients. Prohibitions include not soliciting client testimonials (Section C.3.b), promoting counselor products (Section C.3.f), and engaging in bartering with clients unless the counselor can document such is not harmful to the client (Section A.10.e). Anytime a counselor has a concern regarding whether the dual or multiple relationship is an ethical one, the counselor should take steps to clarify the relationship. The clarification process could involve reviewing relevant sections of the ethical code, consulting with a colleague, and doing intense self-reflection involving exploring motivations for a dual/multiple relationship. Basically, should you be prosecuted or investigated by the licensing board, ACA, or another relevant body, you will be asked to defend your actions. So, make sure your actions are in the best interests of the client, document that, and be able to articulate a clear and succinct defense should the need arise.

While the code of ethics no longer prohibits all nonprofessional relationships per se, ethical codes are about the best interests of the client. Determining what is in the client's best interests, however, is not always easy or straightforward. The critical factor in dual/multiple relationships is for the counselor to refrain from involvement in counselor–client relationships that could compromise the therapeutic encounter or be potentially harmful to the client. Herlihy and Corey (2015) identified four characteristics of dual relationships that make them problematic:

First, potential dual relationships can be *difficult to recognize*. They can evolve in subtle ways. For example, a counselor may accept an invitation from a client to go out for coffee. This may lead to more social encounters until the relationship has progressed into a sexual one.

A second characteristic of dual relationships is that their *potential for harm ranges along a wide continuum*—from extremely harmful to benign or even beneficial.

But because the onus of responsibility is on the counselor and not on the client, counselors must discern through consultation whether the potential benefit of crossing boundaries with a client outweighs the risks and harm.

---

### The Case of Alice

Alice, age 28, seeks counseling from Steve, a licensed mental health counselor in an employee assistance program her employer contracts with. Alice's goal is to resolve issues of sexual abuse from her father that she endured when she was a teenager. After 3 months of counseling, Steve initiates a sexual relationship with Alice. He rationalizes his behavior by convincing himself that she is benefiting from a healthy sexual relationship with a positive adult concerned about her sexual well-being. Alice, on the other hand, feels somewhat confused. She feels in love with Steve but wonders about the nature of their relationship and whether Steve has done this before. She is also aware that Steve is in violation of his professional ethics, if not of the state law. She wants to discuss her concerns with Steve, but also does not want to lose him either as a romantic partner or a counselor. Needing advice, Alice comes to your counseling office. She states that above all, she does not want you to breach confidentiality by reporting on Steve. How would you advise Alice?

*The Case of Hector*

Hector has been coming to see Tomasina, his counselor, for nearly 6 months. Through counseling, Hector has gained the self-confidence to complete his college degree. Hector requests Tomasina attend his graduation and graduation party because he credits counseling with Tomasina for making it possible for him to achieve his goal. After reviewing the code of ethics, giving the matter some thought and consulting with a colleague, Tomasina agrees to attend Hector's graduation.

1. What are the differences between Steve's and Tomasina's motivations regarding entering a dual relationship with their respective clients?
2. What potential for harm could result from Tomasina's attending Hector's graduation and graduation party?
3. What potential harm could come from Steve's affair with Alice?
4. What potential harm—if any—could come to you, the counselor Alice seeks out for advice?
5. If you were a counseling supervisor, how would you have advised Tomasina?
6. What are the ethical issues a counselor must consider regarding dual/multiple relationships with clients and former clients?

The examples illustrate the extremes of dual relationships and counseling. Steve's motivations are suspect and a clear violation of ethics regardless of whether or not the relationship is mutually desired. Even if the client pursues the sexual relationship and wants it to continue, the counselor has committed a serious ethical violation. Tomasina's decision to attend graduation and the graduation party has a low probability of harming the client. The *2014 ACA Code of Ethics* specifically states that an example of a potentially beneficial interaction is "attending a client's formal ceremony" (e.g., wedding or commitment ceremony, graduation; ACA, 2014, Section A.6.b).

A third characteristic is, with the exception of sexual dual relationships, that there is very little consensus among mental health professionals regarding the propriety of dual relationships (Herlihy & Corey, 2015). Some, such as Lazarus and Zur (2002), have taken the position that it can be very beneficial for a counselor to engage in dual relationships with some clients. Others have taken an opposing stance. St. Germaine (1993) suggests that the power differential between the counselor and the client makes it impossible for them to have a truly healthy relationship. It is also possible that counselors can knowingly or unknowingly exploit a client when dual roles are in play. Tomm (1993) points out that the dual role itself is not necessarily problematic; rather, it is the counselor's tendency to exploit clients or misuse power.

Unfortunately, there is a paucity of research regarding the impact of dual roles and the effectiveness of counseling (Pope & Vasquez, 2011; Remley & Herlihy, 2014). There also is no clear consensus among counseling professionals on this issue and in many cases the surrounding culture may have as much impact as anything else. For example, while working in remote Australia I encountered an addictions counselor who treated indigenous Australians. He stated while practicing in an urban setting in Melbourne he saw clients exclusively at the office. But, when he relocated to remote, indigenous central Australia, the local tribe expected him to participate in kangaroo hunts and certain cultural ceremonies. He explained nonparticipation would risk his relationships with the indigenous community and thus he often participated though admittedly such made his practice complicated. The recommendation here is that at this point in your student counseling career, limit dual/multiple relationships as much as possible.

The fourth characteristic that makes boundary issues so complex is that *some dual relationships are unavoidable* (as in the preceding Australian Outback case). For example, counselors practicing in rural, isolated communities may find it impossible to avoid dual roles with clients. Having spent almost 20 years practicing in rural communities, I would frequently discover a current or former client working on my car at the dealership, ringing up my grocery bill at the supermarket, or serving with me on a community agency. In some rural communities, there may be only one counselor for a 100-mile area making referrals nearly impossible. As previously mentioned for school counselors, dual relationships are simply a fact of the school environment. Counselors in the military also face many of the same challenges (Johnson, Ralph, & Johnson, 2005) as do members of particular subcultures (Lazarus & Zur, 2002). People's political affiliations, ethnic identities, religious values, and so forth, can often lead to dual relationships as clients often seek counselors with similar values (Johnson et al., 2005).

---

### The Case of Ginger and Kimber

Kimber has been a client of Ginger for several weeks. They both live in a small and remote community of 2,000 people in the western United States, nearly 70 miles from the nearest town. Kimber's husband and Ginger's partner serve on the advisory board for a local charitable organization. The husband and partner develop a friendship and want to begin a social relationship that includes all four parties.

1. How should Ginger respond when her partner suggests this social contact?
2. Do you think Kimber should inform her husband that Ginger is her counselor and that she would not be comfortable in such a social relationship?
3. What potential risks are posed for Ginger and Kimber should a social relationship develop?
4. Does the fact that they live in such an isolated community change the issue? If yes, how so?
5. If you were Ginger's supervisor, how would you advise her? (Remember, the onus in multiple relationships is on the counselor, not on the client.)

## SEXUAL INTIMACY WITH CLIENTS

The most destructive and egregious form of dual relationships with clients is that involving sexual intimacy. The prohibition regarding sexual relationships is designed to protect clients from sexual and emotional exploitation. The ethical codes of all major helping professions specifically prohibit sexual relationships with clients (Wheeler & Bertram, 2015). Ignoring this ethical standard has led to client abuse and has been the downfall of otherwise capable counselors (Herlihy & Corey, 2015; Remley & Herlihy, 2014). Lamb and Catanzaro (1998) found that 8% of clinicians surveyed admitted to sexual violations with clients. It is likely that this statistic is low because of underreporting among various therapists surveyed. This statistic seems even more egregious when considering all the educational efforts, numerous ethical codes (ACA, APA, NASW, AAPC, AAMFT, etc.), lawsuits, press coverage, and so on, for mental health professionals caught breaching this inviolable ethical standard. Likely, mental health professionals who violate the standard believe they won't be caught.

In addition to ethical standards, many states have laws against counselor–client sexual relationships (Wheeler & Bertram, 2015). This makes a counselor–client sexual relationship not only an ethical matter but also a criminal one. Moreover, it is important to note that sexual relationships are considered a crime even if the client is a willing participant and of legal age (Wheeler & Bertram, 2015). Should you have a sexual relationship with a client the least you will lose if discovered is your job. You could lose your license, certification, spouse/partner, livelihood, be sued, and in some states even go to prison. Be aware!

Along with criminal laws, all states have laws that carry civil suits and damages for sexual intimacies with clients (Wheeler & Bertram, 2015). The *2014 ACA Code of Ethics* expands this prohibition to include "sexual or romantic client interactions or relationships with former clients, their romantic partners, or family members ... for a period of 5 years following the last professional contact" (ACA, 2014, Section A.5.c). The language also expands on the ethical responsibilities of a counselor who might wish to become involved in a romantic relationship after 5 years by cautioning that the counselor must demonstrate forethought and document (in written form) whether the interactions or relationship can be viewed as exploitative in some way and whether there is still potential for harm to the former client. Again, the onus is always on the counselor to demonstrate they have *done no harm* to the client.

### Maintaining Professional Boundaries

Clearly, counselors involved in sexual impropriety with the clients they serve risk doing long-term and severe emotional damage to the clients. This is to say nothing of the professional damage to the counselor, his or her colleagues, employer, family, and the profession in general. Simply put, counselors should not have sex with their clients, period.

Corey et al. (2011) emphasize several points that are especially relevant for students in graduate programs. It is common, and human, to experience an attraction to clients. Therefore, the matter of counselor–client attraction must be recognized, processed, and dealt with. A fundamental aspect of such training recognizes the distinction between attraction and acting on that attraction. Students must feel it is safe to discuss feelings of attraction with their professors and clinical supervisors without the fear of being judged or criticized. If need be, graduate students should seek out professional counseling to help them clarify and separate personal and professional issues related to attraction.

Unfortunately, some research suggests that despite ethical training and education, students who disclosed client attraction to their supervisor did not develop an appropriate understanding of the ethical boundaries regarding that attraction (Housman & Stake, 1999). A small percentage (7%) even thought that sex with a client might be ethical and therapeutic. On the other hand, 47% thought that any sexual feelings for clients were unacceptable. The former group could run into serious ethical and legal problems, whereas the latter may have difficulty because they may be unable to address feelings of attraction due to believing such feelings are morally or ethically wrong.

Recognizing that attraction is natural is the most realistic approach to take. There are some warning signs for counselors to pay attention to when they feel an attraction for a client:

- Giving the client extra time beyond the session
- Dressing up on the days you see that particular client
- Revealing inappropriate personal information to the client, such as your relationship status, type of person you are attracted to, and so forth
- Daydreaming about romantic escapades with the client
- Agreeing to meet with the client outside the treatment center, school, and so forth
- Encouraging the client to call you after hours even if it is not an emergency
- Initiating physical contact with the client
- Offering or accepting gifts from the client
- Considering how to manage the 5-year no-contact clause in the code of ethics

## Other Boundary Issues of Concern

Besides sexual relationships with clients, counselors should be cautious and judicious about entering into other dual relationships. Bartering with a client for goods and services is not prohibited by the *ACA Code of Ethics*, although a counselor should be very cautious about the practice. A common form of bartering involves the exchange of services. For example, a client might be a self-employed contractor having difficulty paying for counseling. He may offer renovation work in return for counseling services. This agreement raises many questions: Is it a fair exchange of services? Also, what if the counselor is unhappy with the renovation work? Conversely, what if the client is unhappy with the counseling? What happens if the client decides to leave counseling but has not finished the renovation work? What happened if the client sues the counselor (or vice versa?). Clearly such counselor–client relationships are fraught with concerns. Advice: Refrain from such dual/multiple relationships when the potential risks seem to outweigh the client rewards.

The *ACA Code of Ethics* offers guidelines for counselors to help them determine whether a potential bartering arrangement might be acceptable. The code states that counselors may participate in bartering only if three criteria are met: the relationship is not exploitive or harmful and does not place the counselor in an unfair advantage, if the client requests it, and if such arrangements are an accepted practice among professionals in the community (ACA, 2014, Section A.10.e). Still the counselor must tread very lightly regarding bartering and avoid it in most circumstances.

Social relationships have been discussed previously. Essentially, counselors should limit social relationships to special occasions (e.g., funerals, weddings) as much as possible. When counselors blend the roles of counselor and friend, they create a conflict of interest that compromises the objectivity needed for good professional judgment (Pope & Vasquez, 2011). Counselors will meet clients in outside social contexts without prior planning on either's part. Therefore, counselors should discuss with their clients how they might be affected by encountering the counselor outside the office and how such chance encounters should best be handled.

At times, clients will offer gifts to their counselors. As a counselor who has had his or her fair share of gifts offered (though nothing fancy or expensive), I can attest to the discomfort a counselor feels in choosing to maintain clear boundaries and a desire to not hurt the client's feelings (which could jeopardize therapy). One agency I worked in had a written policy prohibiting staff from accepting any gifts from clients. This policy was written into the informed consent form clients signed at the onset of counseling. Naturally, even if advised of such prohibitions, some clients will forget or will try to present a gift anyway. Whether to accept or not to accept a gift may also depend on its monetary value. Few counselors would accept a costly work of art from a client, though most would likely accept a crayon drawing from a child. Evidently, many mental health professionals would express the monetary value of the gift was the critical aspect. Borys (1988) discovered that 84% thought that it is ethically permissible to accept a gift worth less than $10, but only 18% thought that it is ethical to accept a gift worth $50 or more. The code of ethics makes this statement:

> Counselors understand the challenges of accepting gifts from clients and recognize that in some cultures, small gifts are a token of respect and gratitude. When determining whether or not to accept a gift from clients, counselors take into account the therapeutic relationship, the monetary value of the gift, the client's motivation for giving the gift, and the counselor's motivation for wanting to accept or decline the gift. (ACA, 2014, Section A.10.f)

As per Section A.10.f. of the *2014 ACA Code of Ethics*, it may also be prudent to consider the client's motivation. A client may be offering a gift as a small token of sincere gratitude. This would be considerably different from a client offering a gift as a means of manipulation. Remley and Herlihy (2014) recount an example of the client who was an excellent baker; the counselor accepted the first two baked offerings. When the client came with the third treat, the counselor used the situation as a means of exploring the client's motivation. Counselor–client exploration regarding motives behind gifts, while delicate, could also be the pathway to a deeper and more honest therapeutic relationship.

Counselors should also be aware of cultural considerations. Giving and accepting gifts is a common practice in many cultures as a means of showing gratitude and respect (ACA, 2014, Section A.10.f; Sue & Sue, 2012). Counselors need to ensure as much as possible that their own discomfort at being presented with a gift does not overshadow their sensitivity to what the gift means to the client (Remley & Herlihy, 2014; Sue & Sue, 2012). When counselors do choose to accept a gift, they should notify their supervisor. It might also be a good idea to document the gift in the case notes, its relative monetary value, and why the counselor accepted it.

---

*The Case of Jim*

Jim is an addictions counselor working on a tribal reservation in the American Southwest. As a member of the tribe, Jim is acutely aware of the delicate boundary between cultural expectations and professional ethics. Because he works in a traditional healing community, he is occasionally expected to visit clients in their homes, have meals with the client's family, and participate in spiritual purification ceremonies with them.

1. What types of ethical and boundary difficulties would you expect Jim to face in this scenario?
2. How does Jim's culture change his professional situation?
3. How might Jim manage both ethical responsibilities and cultural expectations? Or, what would be realistic regarding the balance between maintaining ethical boundaries and cultural norms?

There are many counselors in a similar situation to Jim. An interesting aside to note is that I have noticed that legal discussions regarding situations such as Jim's tend to be quite different from those regarding mainstream, dominant, White culture. It would be interesting to hear from Jim's tribal legal counsel regarding any ethical and legal risks of Jim's situation.

---

## LIABILITY INSURANCE

For counselors practicing in the United States, professional liability insurance is an absolute necessity. Although graduate counseling students on practicums and internships are far less likely to be sued than professional counselors, they are not immune to litigation (Wheeler & Bertram, 2015). Counseling students in Council for Accreditation of Counseling and Related Educational Programs (CACREP)–accredited programs are required to carry student liability insurance, and many non-CACREP programs now require coverage as well. Fortunately, students who purchase a membership with the ACA or the AMHCA receive student liability insurance as part of their membership. Students may also purchase student liability insurance through many independent carriers.

For a client plaintiff to prevail in a malpractice lawsuit against a counselor, the plaintiff must prove the following elements (Prosser, Wade, & Schwartz, 1988):

1. The counselor had a duty to warn the client to use reasonable care regarding providing counseling services.
2. The counselor failed to conform to the required duty of care.
3. The client was injured.
4. There was a reasonably close casual connection between the conduct of the counselor and the resulting injury (known as *proximate cause*).
5. The client suffered an actual loss or was damaged.

Malpractice is the legal term pertaining to civil litigation against counselors and related mental health professionals. As in the preceding list, malpractice is based on negligence, or failure to foresee an injury the professional should otherwise foresee. Malpractice is state regulated and typically applies only when the professional is state-licensed or certified (Wheeler & Bertram, 2015). Malpractice is commonly found in the following types of cases:

1. The procedure used by the counselor was not within the realm of accepted practice.
2. The technique used was one the counselor was not properly trained to use (lack of professional competence).
3. The counselor failed to follow a procedure that would have been more helpful.
4. The counselor failed to warn and/or protect others from a violent client.
5. Informed consent to treatment was not obtained.
6. The counselor failed to explain the possible consequences of the treatment.

(Wheeler & Bertram, 2015, p. 46)

Thus, significant factors in protecting yourself against malpractice is to read and understand your professional ethics, practice within them, seek supervision and consultation when necessary, continually upgrade your professional skills, and consult with an attorney should the need arise.

The good news regarding litigation against counselors and other mental health professionals is that proving all of these elements of malpractice is difficult (Remley & Herlihy, 2014). Roughly 20% of cases filed against mental health professionals result in a judgment against the therapist (Conte & Karasu, 1990). Still, even an unsuccessful lawsuit could potentially end a counselor's practice (Remley & Herlihy, 2014), and being sued is stressful, expensive, and time consuming (Remley & Herlihy, 2014). Once again, the best way to deal with lawsuits is to lessen the risk of litigation by practicing within the boundaries laid out in the *ACA Code of Ethics*, be meticulous in writing case notes, limit dual relationships as much as possible, refrain from romantic relationships with clients, receive ongoing supervision, and continue upgrading your education through your professional life. These simple recommendations are no guarantee against being sued, but they lower a counselor's window of vulnerability to lawsuits.

# REFERENCES

American Counseling Association. (2005). *ACA code of ethics*. Alexandria, VA: Author.

American Counseling Association. (2014). *ACA code of ethics*. Alexandria, VA: Author.

American Psychiatric Association. (2013). *Diagnostic and statistical manual of mental disorders* (5th ed.). Arlington, VA: Author.

Anderson, J. R., & Barret, R. L. (Eds.). (2001). *Ethics in HIV-related psychotherapy: Clinical decision making in complex cases*. Washington, DC: American Psychological Association.

Baird, K. A., & Rupert, P. A. (1987). Clinical management of confidentiality: A survey of psychologists in seven states. *Professional Psychology: Research and Practice, 18*, 347–352.

Barnett, J. E., & Johnson, W. B. (2015). *Ethics desk reference for counselors* (2nd ed.). Alexandria, VA: American Counseling Association.

Borys, D. S. (1988). *Dual relationships between therapist and client: A national survey of clinicians' attitudes and practices* (Unpublished doctoral dissertation). University of California, Los Angeles.

Boynton v. Burglass, 590 So. 2d 446 (Fla. Dist. Ct. App. 1991).

Conte, H. R., & Karasu, T. B. (1990). Malpractice in psychotherapy: An overview. *American Journal of Psychotherapy, 44*, 232–246.

Corey, G., Corey, M. S., Corey, C., & Callanan, P. (2011). *Issues and ethics in the helping professions* (9th ed.). Belmont, CA: Brooks/Cole-Cengage.

Garcia, J., Salo, M., & Hamilton, W. M. (1995). Report of the ACA Ethics Committee: 1994–1995. *Journal of Counseling & Development, 72*, 221–224.

Glosoff, H. L., Herlihy, B., & Spence, E. B. (2000). Privileged communication in the counselor–client relationship. *Journal of Counseling & Development, 78*(4), 454–462.

Gustafson, K. E., & McNamara, J. R. (1987). Confidentiality with minor clients: Issues and guidelines for therapists. *Professional Psychology: Research and Practice, 18*, 503–508.

Handelsman, M. M. (2001). Accurate and effective informed consent. In E. R. Welfel & R. E. Ingersoll (Eds.), *The mental health desk reference* (pp. 453–458). New York, NY: Wiley.

Harding, A., Gray, L., & Neal, M. (1993). Confidentiality limits with clients who have HIV: A review of ethical and legal guidelines and professional policies. *Journal of Counseling & Development, 71*(1), 297–305.

Herlihy, B., & Corey, G. (2015). *ACA ethical standards casebook* (7th ed.). Alexandria, VA: American Counseling Association.

Housman, L. M., & Stake, J. E. (1999). The current state of sexual ethics training in clinical psychology: Issues of quantity, quality, and effectiveness. *Professional Psychology: Research and Practice, 30*(3), 302–311.

Humphrey, D. (1996). *Final exit: The practicalities of self-deliverance and assisted suicide for the dying*. New York, NY: Dell Trade Paperback.

Jaffee v. Redmond et al. 1996 WL 314841 (U.S. June 13, 1996).

Johnson, W. B., Barnett, J. E., Elman, N. S., Forrest, L., & Kaslow, N. J. (2012). The competent community: Toward a vital reformulation of professional ethics. *American Psychologist, 67*(7), 557–569.

Johnson, W. B., Ralph, J., & Johnson, S. J. (2005). Managing multiple roles in embedded environments: The case of aircraft carrier psychology. *Professional Psychology: Research and Practice, 36*, 73–81.

Lamb, D., & Catanzaro, S. (1998). Sexual and nonsexual boundary violations involving psychologists, clients, supervisees, and students: Implications for professional practice. *Professional Psychology: Research and Practice, 29*(5), 498–503.

Lazarus, A. A., & Zur, O. (Eds.). (2002). *Dual relationships and psychotherapy.* New York, NY: Springer Publishing Company.

Madden, R. G. (1998). *Legal issues in social work, counseling, and mental health.* Thousand Oaks, CA: Sage.

Miller, D. J., & Thelan, M. H. (1986). Knowledge and beliefs about confidentiality in psychotherapy. *Professional Psychology: Research and Practice, 17,* 15–19.

Neukrug, E., Milliken, T., & Walden, S. (2001). Ethical complaints made against credentialed counselors: An updated survey of state licensing boards. *Counselor Education and Supervision, 41,* 57–70.

Peck v. Counseling Services of Addison County, Inc. 499 A.2d 422 (Vt. 1985).

Pope, K. S., Tabachnick, B. G., & Keith-Spiegel, P. (1987). Good and poor practices in psychotherapy: National survey of beliefs of psychologists. *Professional Psychology: Research and Practice, 19,* 547–552.

Pope, K. S., & Vasquez, M. J. T. (1998). *Ethics in psychotherapy and counseling: A practical guide for psychologists* (2nd ed.). San Francisco, CA: Jossey-Bass.

Pope, K. S., & Vasquez, M. J. T. (2011). *Ethics in psychotherapy and counseling: A practical guide for psychologists* (4th ed.). Hoboken, NJ: Wiley.

Prosser, W. L., Wade, J. W., & Schwartz, V. E. (1988). *Cases and materials on torts* (8th ed.). Westbury, NY: The Foundation Press.

Remley, T. P., & Herlihy, B. (2014). *Ethical, legal and professional issues in counseling* (4th ed.). Upper Saddle River, NJ: Pearson.

St. Germaine, J. (1993). Dual relationships: What's wrong with them? *American Counselor, 2,* 25–30.

Sue, D. W., & Sue, D. (2012). *Counseling the culturally different: Theory and practice* (6th ed.). New York, NY: Wiley.

Tarasoff v. The Regents of the University of California Berkeley, 13 Cal. 3d 177, 529 P.2d. 533 (1976).

Tomm, K. (1993, January/February). The ethics of dual relationships. *The California Therapist,* 7–19.

Welfel, E. R. (2012). *Ethics in counseling and psychotherapy: Standards, research, and emerging issues* (5th ed.). Belmont, CA: Brooks/Cole-Cengage.

Wheeler, A. M., & Bertram, B. (2015). *The counselor and the law: A guide to legal and ethical practice* (7th ed.). Alexandria, VA: American Counseling Association.

# FOUR

# CLINICAL ISSUES IN PRACTICUM/INTERNSHIP

In this chapter, I'll offer a brief overview of common clinical issues you may encounter at the practicum/internship site, along with suggestions and examples to assist you in counseling and assessment. Students beginning the practicum may find the experience difficult at first, because they are actually encountering real people with real issues instead of theoretical scenarios in a textbook or on a DVD or other recording. Compounding the issue is the amount of information and data that accompanies counseling. The type of method, the information gathered, and how records are managed and stored vary from setting to setting. Perhaps the most important concept for graduate counseling students to keep in mind when they are providing counseling is that the quality of the therapeutic relationship is likely more important than the particular technique or theoretical approach. Empirical research has validated this concept (Duncan, Miller, Wampold, & Hubble, 2010; Wampold, 2001). So, practicum and internship students, if you remember nothing else, it's about the relationship.

Although no one chapter or text could possibly cover all the clinical issues and skills you need, this chapter will outline some of the basic skills that you should be aware of: building the therapeutic alliance, handling intake and basic assessments, understanding counseling techniques, and other basics. The next chapter discusses clinical writing skills that you will need to document your sessions.

## BUILDING THE THERAPEUTIC ALLIANCE

The most critical factor in establishing the counseling relationship is creating an attachment with the client or clients (Beck & Weishaar, 2008; Duncan et al., 2010; Rogers, 1951). Creating this alliance involves a process of establishing trust, respect, openness, and the willingness to take emotional risks (Beck, 2011; Ellis, 2001). Once an alliance is established, the client can begin to disclose to the counselor the reasons he or she has sought out counseling. The initial interview is your first and best opportunity to begin establishing such an alliance. Ivey, Ivey, and Zalaquett (2012) suggest a structured model for the initial interview:

- Building rapport and structuring a process that has as its purpose the building of a working relationship with the client
- Gathering information, defining the problem, and identifying client assets to determine why the client has sought out counseling and how he or she views the issue
- Determining outcomes, which enables the counselor to plan therapy based on what the client is seeking, the client's viewpoint, and what life would be like without the existing problems
- Exploring alternatives and confronting incongruities, which is a critical task for the counselor to assist the client in resolving his or her problems
- Generalization and transfer of learning, which are the processes whereby changes in the client's thoughts, feelings, and behaviors are carried out in his or her everyday life

Weinrach (1989) advocated that counselors address issues most frequently raised by clients when beginning therapy. This may include some of the following questions:

- How often can I expect to have an appointment?
- How might I reach you in an emergency?
- What happens if I forget an appointment?
- How confidential are counseling sessions?
- What do I do in an emergency?
- When is it time to end treatment?
- What are my financial responsibilities?
- How often do I obtain reimbursement from insurance?

Beginning counselors should be aware that the counseling process may be new as well as intimidating to clients beginning therapy. Because clients come to counseling feeling burdened, overwhelmed, depressed, anxious, frustrated, even hostile, and so forth, they may not be well attuned to the therapeutic process. So, you must of necessity be thorough in the intake and informed consent process and solicit from your clients whether or not they understand their rights and responsibilities. Furthermore, encourage them to ask for clarification whenever they have questions or are confused about a therapeutic matter. Questions like those just mentioned can help clarify the counseling relationship and address the client's basic concerns.

It is also worth noting that not all clients enter the counseling relationship voluntarily. *Mandated clients* (those who are required to enter counseling by a spouse, boss, correctional facility, probation officer, judge, principal, dean of students, or another person) are a reality in all clinical settings, and mandated clients are likely to show less investment in the counseling process (Cox & Klinger, 2011; Hodges, 2011). Regardless of whether the client has come voluntarily or is mandated, the process of initiating therapy begins with acknowledging the issues listed previously.

## INITIAL INTAKE FORM

The intake form is a common information gathering form. Many counseling settings will use some variation of this form to gather basic information about a new client. Intake sheets typically include name, address, family history, previous counseling and psychiatric treatment, medications, and other information. The intake is usually common in mental health settings, although many schools use a similar form (sometimes called a developmental history form; Sommers-Flanagan & Sommers-Flanagan, 1999).

Exhibit 4.1 offers an example of an intake form.

---

**EXHIBIT 4.1 Initial Intake Form**

NAME: _____ DATE: _____/_____/_____

Address: _____ City: _____ State: _____

Zip Code: _____ Phone: _____ (H) _____ (W/C)

**Identifying Information**

Age: _____ Date of Birth:_____ / _____ /_____ Place: _____

Sex: Female _____ Male _____ Height: _____ Ft. _____ In. Weight: _____ Lbs.

Occupation: _____

Marital Status: M _____ S _____ D _____ Sep. _____ Other: _____

Spouse's/Partner's Name: _____ Age: _____

Occupation: _____ Employer: _____

Name(s)/Ages of Children (If applicable):

_____

_____

_____

_____

Referral Source: _____

Address of Referral Source: _____

---

(continued)

**EXHIBIT 4.1    Initial Intake Form (*continued*)**

**Treatment History**

Are you currently taking medication?        Yes: _____    No: _____

If yes, name of medication(s): _____

Provider of medication(s): _____

Have you received previous psychiatric/psychological treatment?

Yes: _____    No: _____

If yes, name the provider: _____

Dates of Counseling/Psychiatric Treatment: _____

_____

Has any close relative ever had psychiatric treatment or been committed to a psychiatric hospital?    Yes: _____    No: _____

If yes, please explain:

_____

_____

_____

What factor(s) led you to seek counseling services? _____

_____

_____

Symptoms: _____

_____

Treatment Outlook: If you were to feel better, what would be different?

_____

_____

What personal strengths do you possess that can help with your treatment?

_____

_____

(continued)

**EXHIBIT 4.1   Initial Intake Form (*continued*)**

## Family History

Mother's Name: _____   Living: _____   Deceased: _____

Father's Name: _____   Living: _____   Deceased: _____

Brother(s)/Sister(s):

Name: _____   Age: _____   Living: _____   Deceased: _____

Name: _____   Age: _____   Living: _____   Deceased: _____

Name: _____   Age: _____   Living: _____   Deceased: _____

## Educational History

High School: _____

  Location: _____

  Dates Attended: _____ Degree: _____

College/University: _____

  Location: _____

  Dates Attended: _____ Degree: _____

Technical School: _____

  Location: _____

  Dates Attended: _____ Degree: _____

Graduate/Professional: _____

  Location: _____

  Dates Attended: _____ Degree: _____

## INITIAL ASSESSMENT

The types of assessment you conduct with clients will vary greatly depending on your setting and client population. An educational placement, such as a middle school, will require considerably different data than a residential psychiatric center. Proper assessment is influenced by the following considerations (Hayes, 2013):

- Who is making the assessment? Is a counselor making the assessment? A psychologist?
- Where is the assessment taking place? In a high school counseling office? In a correctional setting?
- When is the assessment occurring? Junior year in anticipation of preparing for college or technical school? Or prior to beginning graduate school?
- Why is the assessment being undertaken? Has the client been referred for counseling and assessment because of concerns about his or her mood? Is the client mandated?
- How is the assessment conducted? By computer? By pen and paper?

In mental health settings, some variation of the Mental Status Examination (MSE) is likely to be conducted as part of the intake process (Seligman, 2004). School counselors, however, are unlikely to use the MSE, although they may use some type of developmental questionnaire. The MSE is designed to provide the counselor with baseline information regarding the client's appearance, affect, cognitive functioning, orientation, judgment, short- and long-term memory, insight, and more (Polanski & Hinkle, 2000).

Although not a standardized psychological instrument, the MSE is frequently used in mental health settings for the purposes of assessment, diagnoses, and treatment of mental disorders. Typically conducted during the initial intake interview, the MSE can provide counselors with helpful categorized information for formalizing objective and subjective client data. Although numerous formats of the MSE exist, the two versions provided here offer examples of the MSE. Exhibit 4.2 shows a brief version of the MSE, and Exhibit 4.3 offers an MSE for older children, adolescents, and adults.

## COUNSELING TECHNIQUES

Most counseling programs offer graduate training from various theoretical approaches (Gladding, 2009). In your program, you may study theoretical approaches such as psychodynamic, client-centered, rational emotive behavior therapy, cognitive behavioral therapy, solution-focused, narrative and existential, just to name a few. Because they explore so many counseling theories, students often put together an integrative approach, meshing techniques from this list of various theories. The proliferation of approaches and techniques can definitely be confusing for students regarding what particular theoretical set of techniques to use with which particular client.

---

**EXHIBIT 4.2   Mental Status Examination (Brief Version)\***

**Now, I am going to ask you a series of questions to test your concentration and memory. Answer to the best of your ability. Okay, any questions before we begin?**

**Orientation to Time:**

What year is this? (1 point)
What season is this? (1 point)
What is the month and date? (1 point)
What day of the week is it? (1 point)
(Maximum of 4 points)

**Orientation to Place:**

What is the name of this institution/school/agency? (1 point)
What floor are we on? (1 point)
What city and state are we in? (1 point)
What county is this? (1 point)
(Maximum of 4 points)

**Immediate Recall:**

I am going to say three objects. After I say them I want you to repeat them. They are "ball," "flag," and "tree." Now say them. Remember them because I will ask you to repeat them later. (Interviewer: 1 point for each; maximum of 3 points)

**Attention:**

(Choose from either of the following items but not both)

Serial 7s. Subtract 7 from 100 and continue until I tell you to stop. (Interviewer: Continue until subject makes an error. 1 point for each correct answer up to a maximum score of 5 points)

Spell the word "world" backwards. (1 point for each correct letter; maximum of 5 points)

**Delayed Recall:**

What are the three words I asked you to remember? (1 point for each; maximum of 3 points)

**Naming:**

Show subject a pen and wristwatch and ask to name them. (1 point for each; maximum of 2 points)

**Repetition:**

Repeat the following sentence exactly as I say it. "No ifs, ands, or buts." (1 point for each word; maximum of 3 points)

**Stage Command:**

"Now I want to see how well you can follow instructions. I'm going to give you a piece of paper. Take it in your right hand, use both hands to fold it in half, and then put it on the floor." (1 point for each command; maximum of 3 points)

(continued)

---

**EXHIBIT 4.2   Mental Status Examination (Brief Version)\* (*continued*)**

**Reading:**

Show the subject a headline written on the following page and ask him or her to read what it says silently and then to do what it says. (1 point; *Note:* You may write anything. The point is to see if the client understands it.)

**Copying:**

Give subject a clean sheet of paper and ask him or her to copy the geometric design printed on the next page. (1 point)

**Writing:**

On the same sheet of paper, ask the subject to write a complete sentence. (1 point)

**Scoring Procedures:**

Total (Maximum Score) = 30

***Note:***

Scores of 23–30 indicate expected or *normal functioning*. Scores lower than 23 suggest the presence of *cognitive impairment*.
23–30 = *no cognitive impairment*
18–23 = *mild cognitive impairment*
0–17 = *significant cognitive impairment*

*MSE scores may be invalid if the subject has less than a ninth-grade education, is intoxicated, or is under the influence of other drugs.*

Adapted from Folstein, Folstein, & McHugh, 1975; Polanski & Hinkle, 2000.

\*A Mental Status Examination (MSE) is a common subjective form of assessment that typically accompanies a clinical intake. This MSE is a common example of a brief or short version. Short versions are often used in clinical settings to regularly assess change in a client.

---

**EXHIBIT 4.3   Mental Status Examination for Older Children, Adolescents, and Adults\***

The areas to be covered for the written Mental Status Examination report:

**Prior to beginning, explain:**

1. Who you are? (Certified School Counselor, Licensed Professional Counselor, etc.)
2. What setting are you in? (school, hospital, clinic, prison, etc.)
3. Why is the MSE taking place? (teacher request, standard procedure, client mandated by court or parole and probation, etc.)
4. Informed consent. (Confidentiality and its limits, training or education, fees—if applicable, rights and responsibilities of person being assessed, etc.)
5. Always ask the person being assessed, "Do you have any questions?"

*When interviewing a client, always remain calm and in control. Exaggerated verbal and nonverbal responses may invalidate the interview.*

(continued)

---

**EXHIBIT 4.3    Mental Status Examination for Older Children, Adolescents, and Adults\* (*continued*)**

---

**A. Heading**

Name:

Age:

Date of Birth:

Gender:

Interview Site:

Date of Interview and Report:

Person Making the Referral:

Reason for Referral:

**B. Appearance and Behavior**

1. How did the client present himself or herself?
2. How did the interviewee look? (Note grooming, height, weight, facial appearance, special adornments, jewelry.)
3. How did the interviewee act during the interview? (Note any bizarre gestures, postures, repetitive movements, poor eye contact, slow movements, excessive movements, etc.)
4. Was the interviewee's behavior appropriate for his or her age, education, and vocational status?
5. How did the interviewee relate to the interviewer (e.g., was he or she wary, friendly, manipulative, approval seeking, hostile, superficial)?

**C. Speech and Communication**

1. How was the general flow of the interviewee's speech? (e.g., Was it rapid, controlled, hesitant, slow, pressured?)
2. Does the interviewee have speech impediments?
3. How was the general tone and content of the interviewee's speech? (Note, for example, over- or underproductivity of speech, flight of ideas, paucity of ideas, loose associations, rambling, tangentially, neologisms, bizarre use of words, incoherence, etc.)
4. What was the relationship between verbal and nonverbal communication?
5. Was there a relationship between tone and content of the communications?
6. How interested was the interviewee in communicating?

**D. Thought Content**

1. What did the interviewee discuss? (Note, for example, content that he or she brought up spontaneously.)
2. What were the problem areas?
3. Were there any recurring themes?
4. Were there any signs of psychopathology, such as obsessions, delusions, hallucinations, phobias, or compulsions?

*(continued)*

**EXHIBIT 4.3 Mental Status Examination for Older Children, Adolescents, and Adults\* (continued)**

### E. Sensory and Motor Functioning

1. How intact were the interviewee's senses—hearing, sight, touch, and smell?
2. How adequate was the interviewee's gross motor coordination?
3. How adequate was the interviewee's fine motor coordination?
4. Were there signs of motor difficulties such as exaggerated movements, repetitive movements (tics, twitches, tremors, bizarre postures, slow movements, or rituals)?

### F. Cognitive Functioning

1. What was the general mood of the interviewee (e.g., was he or she sad, elated, anxious, tense, suspicious, or irritable)?
2. Did the interviewee's mood fluctuate or change during the interview?
3. How did the interviewee react to the interview (e.g., was he or she cold, friendly, cooperative, suspicious, or cautious)?
4. Was the interviewee's affect appropriate for the speech and content of the communications?
5. What did the interviewee say about his or her mood and feelings?
6. Was the self-report congruent with the interviewee's behavior during the interview?

### G. Insight and Judgment

1. What is the interviewee's belief about why he or she was coming to the interview?
2. Is the belief appropriate and realistic?
3. Is the interviewee aware of his or her problem and the concerns of others?
4. Does the interviewee have ideas about what caused the problem?
5. Does the interviewee have any idea about how the problem could be alleviated?
6. How good is the interviewee's judgment in carrying out everyday activities?
7. How does the interviewee solve problems of living (e.g., impulsively, independently, responsibly, trial and error)?
8. Does the interviewee make appropriate use of advice or assistance?
9. How much does the interviewee desire help for his or her problems?

### H. Questions to Ask the Interviewee

(*Note:* This section is geared to older children, adolescents, and adults. For preschool and K–2, many of these questions may be inappropriate.)

**Key:** Questions 1–4 and 8–10 test general orientation to time, place, and person, respectively; 11–16 test recent memory; 17–20 test remote memory; 21–23 test immediate memory; 24–25 test insight and judgment; and 26–28 test oral reading and spelling skills.

1. What is today's date?
2. What day is it?
3. What month is it?
4. What year is it?
5. Where are you?
6. What is the name of this city?
7. What is the name of this clinic? (or school, university counseling center, etc.)
8. What is your name?

*(continued)*

---

**EXHIBIT 4.3    Mental Status Examination for Older Children, Adolescents, and Adults\* (*continued*)**

9. How old are you?
10. What do you do?
11. Who is the president of the United States?
12. Who was the president before him?
13. Who is the governor of this state?
14. How did you get to this clinic (or school counseling center)?
15. What is your father's name?
16. What is your mother's name?
17. When is your birthday?
18. Where were you born?
19. Did you finish elementary school? (if appropriate)
20. When did you finish high school? (if appropriate)
21. Repeat these numbers back after me: 6-9-5, 4-3-8-1, 2-9-8-5-7.
22. Say these numbers backwards: 8-3-7, 9-4-6-1, 7-3-2-5-8.
23. Say these words after me: ball, flag, tree.
24. What does this saying mean: "A stitch in time saves nine"?
25. What does this saying mean: "Too many cooks spoil the broth"?
26. Read back the three words I gave to you earlier. (ball, flag, tree)
27. Write the words given previously. (ball, flag, tree)
28. Spell these words: spoon, cover, attitude, procedure.

**I. Conclusion**

At the conclusion of the Mental Status Examination report, write your name and credentials:

Adapted from Hodges (2014).

---

\*Longer versions of the MSE are more typically used when a client is beginning counseling. The format presented in this exhibit represents one example of an MSE. The Mini Mental Status Examination is much briefer (usually half the questions) and likely as valid and reliable as the longer MSE. Some agencies will use the MMSE in place of the MSE as a time-saver.

The reality is that counseling is a trial-and-error and retrial process between the counselor and client. There is no-one-size-fits-all approach that faculty and clinical supervisors can give to students. Student counselors in a practicum/internship may simply need to try different theoretical approach techniques. The more you use various techniques, the more you can learn and build on your existing skill set. Here are some basic counseling techniques and interventions you will likely use in practicum and internship:

- Open-ended questioning: "What brought you in for counseling today?"
- Reflection of feeling: "How did you feel when …?"
- Paraphrasing: "So, it sounds like you were upset at …."
- Summarizing: "It sounds like you believe that you are beginning to feel a sense of confidence regarding recovering from your divorce. You are reaching out to friends, attending a weekly support group, even contemplating dating again. That sound about right?"

- Scaling question: "On a scale of 1 to 10, with 1 meaning you feel *very depressed* and 10 meaning you feel *great*, where would you put yourself?"
- Gestalt empty chair technique: "Ok, let's say your father was sitting in that empty chair beside you. What would you want to say to him regarding his verbal abuse?" Also, the empty chair technique can be conducted using a psychodrama approach, where the client will sit in the empty chair and play the role of the absent person (e.g., father, mother, spouse). The client will also play themselves.
- Reframing: "You mentioned 'I always fail.' But earlier I heard you say you just completed a college degree. It seems to me it might be more accurate to say, 'I have my failures, but I'm also successful.'"
- Homework: "Ok, here is what I'd like you to do between now and next week's session. You have talked about a desire to make friends. So, I'd like you to speak with three new people in the next week. Then, we'll discuss how that goes in next week's session."
- Artwork (with younger clients): "Ok, Ellen, I have some paper and crayons. I'd like you to draw your family on this large sheet."
- Role play: This is similar to the empty chair technique discussed previously. Clients, especially couples and families, are primed for role plays. Individual counseling also should involve role plays from time to time. Role plays are often used for issues involving confrontation, asking for a date, assertiveness with a roommate, setting limits with a parent, and so forth.
- Miracle question: "Alright, say when you woke the next day the issue(s) that brought you to counseling were resolved. What would then be different about your life? What would others notice was different about you? How would this miracle change your life?"
- Self-reflection: "Now, you have mentioned continuing to have very angry thoughts about your former spouse that upset you. Now, in the future when those thoughts recur, here is what I'd like you to do. The technique is called reframing, where you will replace negative thoughts with healthier, more realistic ones. So, you'll replace those thoughts with: 'It's unfortunate our marriage did not work out. But now I have the chance to have a healthy relationship.'"
- Self-talk: "Instead of saying 'I'm a loser' whenever you have a disappointment, I'd like your self-talk to be: 'Okay, that was disappointing, but I'll improve and eventually be successful.'"

The preceding is only a brief list of several techniques that students likely will use on their practicum and internship. Do not let yourself get too overwhelmed by techniques, because they take time to learn. Also, keep in mind that theoretical approach and technique may not be the most important aspect of counseling success and likely will be secondary to the theoretical alliance. As per the preceding list, you will get to practice what you preach to clients. Most people preach better than they practice, but be patient with yourself. As a cognitive counselor I'd encourage you to carefully monitor and revise your self-talk from defeatist to realistic and proactive.

When you use techniques and interventions, give the client time to answer before moving on to the next intervention. Remember, pause time is cultural and while some cultures may take but one second to respond, non-Western cultures (and indigenous U.S. cultures) may take 3 to 4 seconds (Sue & Sue, 2012). Present yourself as calm and engaged, suggesting to the client(s) that he/she/they is/are your only point(s) of focus. Clients will likely be encouraged that you are attending to them so intently. In fact, it is unlikely that anyone else will attend to clients the way that their counselors do. After all, counseling, unlike friendship, is a one-sided relationship and all about the client(s). It is also very important to be genuine when you are counseling clients. Although there is no exact formula on authenticity, it starts with understanding your own beliefs, attitudes, and values and remaining nonjudgmental when the client's beliefs, attitudes, and values are different from yours. This sounds easy when read in a text, but clients with radically different political, spiritual, educational, sexual, social, and/or cultural backgrounds may challenge you in ways you have not considered. It also is important to remind you that a referral based on value conflict is not considered ethical. In fact, the only ethical reason for referral is incompetence (Standard A.11.b).

One of the most critical aspects of the practicum experience is learning to trust your own instincts (Gladding, 2009). Some counselor educators might call this process learning to listen to your "inner voice." A supervisor of mine was once fond of saying, "When you have spent time counseling, you develop an inner counselor as your guide. This guide is honed through education, experience, self-reflection, and intuition. Learn to heed this voice." To become a successful counselor, each student in training must learn to recognize his or her own voice and to put the suggestions of that inner voice into action. Listening to our inner voice is likely another path to becoming the genuine practitioner, which Carl Rogers (1942, 1951) wrote about decades ago. In addition, understand that the inner voice will not be perfect regarding what technique or intervention to use with a client, because counseling is an inexact science and will require you to use many different skills. Still, awareness of your own inner counselor voice is likely the most reliable path to take in the counseling experience, particularly when nothing else seems to be working.

## THE CLINICAL RECORD

Keeping accurate client records is vital to effective counseling and ethical practice. Remley and Herlihy (2014) suggest client records contain the following information:

- Intake information: This category includes personal demographic data about the client, such as name, address and phone number, date of birth, gender, ethnicity, education, marital status, and previous psychiatric and counseling history.
- Assessment/testing information: Assessment provides specific information the counselor might otherwise not have on areas such as current drug use, depression, suicidal ideation, hopefulness, and so forth.

- Psychological and/or educational or career assessment: The Beck Depression Inventory-II, Minnesota Multiphasic Inventory-2/A (MMPI-2/MMPI-A), Strong Interest Inventory, Myers-Briggs Type Indicator, SAT/ACT, and so on.
- Psychosocial family assessment: Assesses the client's current level of functioning in his or her family and/or his or her community. In the past, the *Diagnostic and Statistical Manual of Mental Disorders (DSM)* system asked for a Global Assessment of Functioning or a Children's Global Assessment Scale (GAF/CGAS). While the *DSM-5* (American Psychiatric Association, 2013) eliminated—unfortunately—the multiaxial system and GAF/CGAS, counselors should consider scaling-type questions based on client functioning. Higher scores on a 1 to 10 or 1 to 100 scale suggest greater autonomy and higher functioning.
- Vocational and educational situation: How stable is the client's employment status? What is his or her level of education or desired education?
- Drug and alcohol assessment: Assesses past and current use of chemical substances through interviewing and testing with the Alcohol Use Disorders Identification Test (AUDIT), Michigan Alcohol Screening Test (MAST), Substance Abuse Subtle Screening Inventory-3 (SASSI-3), and other tests related to drug and alcohol addiction and abuse.
- Health assessment: Assessment of recent health issues, surgeries, procedures, and current use of medications.
- Treatment plan: The treatment plan identifies and sets the parameters for how counseling is to be carried out, including statement of the problem, treatment goals, and steps to reach the goals.
- Case notes: Documentation of progress, clinical impressions, evaluation of each session, and homework assigned to the client (see Chapter 5 for more on how to write effective case notes).
- Termination record: A summarization of treatment, success, lack of success, and so forth (see Chapter 11 for more on client termination).

## CLOSING THE SESSION

Standard counseling sessions are typically 50 minutes (there may be some variation for group, couples, and family counseling). Counselors, especially new ones, should try to begin and end sessions on time, because this illustrates to clients the importance of set beginnings and endings. Counselors who allow sessions to begin late and extend beyond the parameters are modeling poor boundaries to the client. Such "loose" behavior on the part of the counselor may ultimately be unhealthy for the client in jobs, relationships, and in other social encounters. Of course, this statement is culture specific. Western cultures tend to value more rigid timelines, whereas some Eastern and indigenous cultures have more flexibility regarding time (Lee, 2003, 2006; Sue & Sue, 2012). Still, counselors must be cognizant of timely schedules, because clients and colleagues will likely expect you to be prompt and lack of timeliness may create a backlog. (*Note:* In my own experience, physician appointments seldom have been on time. Counseling appointments have very different expectations.)

Many beginning counselors do have difficulty closing sessions with clients who insist on pushing the session beyond its limits. There is the old adage of the client who says nothing of note for 49 minutes, then drops a bombshell ("I'm pregnant," "My home is being foreclosed," "I've just flunked out of college," etc.). I have experienced many such incidents myself. If a client truly is in crisis—that is, a danger to himself or herself or others—then do not let the client leave (see Chapter 9 for more information on clients in crisis). In the absence of such a risk, it is important that you stay as close to the set parameters as possible.

Benjamin (1987) emphasizes two important concerns in closing a counseling session. First, both the counselor and the client should be aware that the session is ending. This means the counselor has covered time limits in the intake session. Counselors would also be wise to make some statement during closing time like, "Ok, it looks like our time is about up ...." Second, no new material should be presented during the closing. If the client "drops" something on you at the very end of the session, you might say, "That's an excellent starting point for next time" (if it is not a crisis).

When it comes to ending sessions, be brief and simple. Remind the client of time limits by saying, "We have just 5 minutes left." This can help the client refocus and also serves to keep the session on track. You might also say something like, "Time is almost up. Could you summarize what you learned today?" Gladding (2009) emphasizes that it is helpful to have the client summarize what happened in the session. This emphasizes the client's responsibility by forcing the client to reflect back on the salient points and recap them. This is also a tacit way of illustrating that the counselor values what the client sees as the important points of the session. The counselor certainly can provide the summarization, but it prevents the client from achieving momentum. Some counselors use nonverbal gestures such as standing up or pointing to their watch. There are many ways to end the session. The best guideline is to be clear, low key (so as not to hurt the client's feelings), and firm. Then, the final aspect of session termination is setting an appointment for the next session.

## FINAL SUGGESTIONS

Here are some suggestions for your transition to the practicum/internship experience:

- Remember, in the beginning, everyone was a rookie. Give yourself time to make the transition. When you feel stressed and overwhelmed, check in with your supervisor. Also, get to know your fellow practicum students. You can be good supports for one another. In fact, some graduate students have even begun practicum support groups.
- As you begin practicum, be aware that you will be critiqued. The important aspect here is to be open to critical feedback. Even with the most benign and constructive type of feedback, it is natural to experience some degree of defensiveness. Be open to the feedback from your on-site clinical supervisor and your faculty practicum supervisor. But do not be afraid

to ask clarifying questions (see Chapter 6 for more information on critique and feedback).

- Take initiative. Clinical supervisors are generally impressed with practicum and internship students who read and ask questions regarding agency, school, or university counseling center policies. If there are written policies and procedures manuals at your site (and there should be!), read the manual and ask your supervisor any question you might have about school/agency policies.
- Make a point of showing up on time for all your shifts. Interestingly, in all my years as a counselor educator, one of the most common complaints is tardy practicum/internship students.
- Complete all responsibilities in a timely manner. Make sure all case notes are written and filed after each session (or certainly before you leave the practicum site).
- Make sure you take care of yourself. Counselors cannot begin to help people in need unless they are emotionally healthy themselves. Make time for stress-reducing activities that you enjoy, such as physical fitness (jogging, cycling, swimming, power walking, yoga, aerobics, etc.), and centering activities such as meditation, prayer (for those so inclined), reading, and so forth. Incidentally, self-care is part of your ethical code (American Counseling Association, 2014) and possibly one of the ethical tenets given least attention.
- Understand that counseling actual people can be a complex endeavor. Give yourself time to adjust as counseling is unlike any experience you have previously had.

## CONCLUSION

Finally, I tell all my students not to be afraid of making mistakes. In fact, I instruct them they *should* make mistakes, because making mistakes indicates they are stretching their skill set. One of the worst mistakes student counselors can make is being inert because of "fear of saying something wrong." "Good" clinical supervisors are not going to chastise a student counselor for a basic semantic mistake and if they do this would be good information for your program faculty and practicum and internship coordinator. Fortunately it's unlikely you will tell the client something that will be permanently damaging. You will commit occasional errors of commission and omission, because every counselor, no matter how talented and experienced, does. If you believe you have offended the client, honesty is the best policy ("I apologize. I may have offended you by that question/comment. Let me try and rephrase ...."). Very few clients will expect perfection from their counselor (and should a client expect perfection that would be an issue for the two of you to explore!). The critical factor is that you are able to learn from your mistakes. Be proactive and solicit advice from your on-site supervisor and university supervisor.

Finally, one of the best skills you can begin to hone is the power of self-talk and self-reflection (Beck & Butler, 2005; Ellis, 1999). As you proceed through your practicum and internship experience notice how your self-talk evolves. Ideally, your self-talk should become more proactive ("I'm making real improvement as a counselor" type) and less negative or uncertain ("I can't possibly help anyone"). Granted, some graduate students will not be appropriate for counseling work but that's different than having negative, or as Ellis (1999) would say, irrational self-talk. Even if you honestly believe you are not a good fit for the counseling profession I would encourage you to adopt proactive self-talk such as: "It's unfortunate that I am not a good fit for counseling work but I will find another career and can still be helpful to others in my own way." Essentially, while everyone *cannot* be a counselor, everyone *can* be a helper in some fashion. Monitor your self-talk through self-reflection and revise it to be more optimistic and realistic. You will feel better, function better as a counselor, and your personal life likely will be more rewarding.

## REFERENCES

American Counseling Association. (2014). *ACA code of ethics*. Arlington, VA: Author.

American Psychiatric Association. (2013). *Diagnostic and statistical manual of mental disorders* (5th ed.). Alexandria, VA: Author.

Beck, A. T., & Weishaar, M. (2008). Cognitive therapy. In R. J. Corsini & D. Wedding (Eds.), *Current psychotherapies* (8th ed., pp. 263–294). Belmont, CA: Thomson Brooks/Cole.

Beck, J. S. (2011). *Cognitive behavior therapy: Basics and beyond* (2nd ed.). New York, NY: Guilford Press.

Beck, J. S., & Butler, A. C. (2005). Treating psychotherapists with cognitive therapy. In J.D. Geller, J.C. Norcross, & D.E. Orlinsky (Eds.), *The psychotherapist's own psychotherapy: Patient and clinician perspectives* (pp. 254–264). New York, NY: Oxford University Press.

Benjamin, A. (1987). *The helping interview*. Boston, MA: Houghton Mifflin.

Cox, W. M., & Klinger, E. (Eds.). (2011). *The handbook of motivational counseling: Concepts, approaches, & assessment* (2nd ed.). West Sussex, England: Wiley.

Duncan, B., Miller, S. D., Wamplod, B., & Hubble, M. (2010). *The heart and soul of change: Delivering what works in therapy* (2nd ed.). Washington, DC: American Psychological Association.

Ellis, A. (1999). *How to make yourself happy and remarkably less disturbable*. Atascadero, CA: Impact.

Ellis, A. (2001). *Overcoming destructive beliefs, feelings, and behaviors*. Amherst, NY: Prometheus Books.

Folstein, M. F., Folstein, S. E., & McHugh, P. R. (1975). "Mini-mental state": A practical method for grading the cognitive state of patients for the clinician. *Journal of Psychiatric Research, 12*(3), 189–198.

Gladding, S. T. (2009). *Counseling: A comprehensive profession* (6th ed.). Upper Saddle River, NJ: Merrill/Prentice Hall.

Hayes, D. G. (2013). *Assessment in counseling: A guide to the use of psychological assessments procedures* (5th ed.). Alexandria, VA: American Counseling Association.

Hodges, S. (2011). *The counseling practicum and internship manual: A resource for graduate counseling students*. New York, NY: Springer Publishing Company.

Hodges, S. (2014). *Clinical mental health counseling manual*. New York, NY: Niagara University College of Education.

Ivey, A. E., Ivey, M. B., & Zalaquett, C. P. (2012). *Intentional interviewing and counseling: Facilitating development in a multicultural society* (7th ed.). Belmont, CA: Cengage Learning.

Lee, C. C. (Ed.). (2003). *Multicultural issues in counseling: New approaches to diversity* (3rd ed.). Alexandria, VA: American Counseling Association.

Lee, C. C. (Ed.). (2006). *Counseling for social justice*. Alexandria, VA: American Counseling Association.

Polanski, P. J., & Hinkle, J. S. (2000). The mental status examination: Its use by professional counselors. *Journal of Counseling & Development, 78*, 357–364.

Remley, T. P., & Herlihy, B. (2014). *Ethical, legal and professional issues in counseling* (4th ed.). Upper Saddle River, NJ: Pearson.

Rogers, C. R. (1942). *Counseling and psychotherapy*. Boston, MA: Houghton Mifflin.

Rogers, C. R. (1951). *Client centered therapy*. New York, NY: Houghton Mifflin.

Seligman, L. A. (2004). *Diagnosis and treatment planning in counseling* (3rd ed.). New York, NY: Kluwer.

Sommers-Flanagan, R. S., & Sommers-Flanagan, J. S. (1999). *Clinical interviewing* (2nd ed.). New York, NY: Wiley.

Wampold, B. E. (2001). *The great psychotherapy debate: Models, methods, and findings*. Mahwah, NJ: Lawrence Erlbaum.

Weinrach, S. G. (1989). Guidelines for clients of private practitioners: Committing the structure to print. *Journal of Counseling & Development, 67*, 299–300.

# FIVE

# CLINICAL WRITING AND DOCUMENTATION IN COUNSELING RECORDS

Writing clear and descriptive clinical case notes is very different from most other types of writing. By now, you have likely had lots of experience writing American Psychological Association (APA)-style research papers in your counseling classes. You may also have written poetry, short stories, journal articles, and maybe even website blogs. In these cases, the objective is to entertain, persuade, or inform. Unlike these aforementioned types of writing, your objective in writing case notes is merely to create an accurate and informative record of treatment and client progress (or lack thereof). Although it is likely that training in counseling skills receives the most attention in graduate programs, clarity in clinical writing may be even more important (Mitchell, 2007; Seligman, 2004; Wheeler & Bertram, 2015), especially should a client's file be subpoenaed and the counselor required to testify and defend his or her case notes in a courtroom. This chapter is designed to provide an overview on writing clear, concise, and effective case notes. "Counselors have an explicitly stated legal and ethical duty to create and maintain client records on every client" (Wheeler & Bertram, 2015, p. 203). Failure to maintain adequate records could also form the basis of malpractice as it breaches the standard of care expected from a mental health professional (Wheeler & Bertram, 2015). Counseling students should remember that like all other counseling training, developing good, clear, and concise clinical writing skills takes time and comes through experience. Your practicum and internship placements likely are good beginning points for developing good clinical writing skills. Having made such a statement, it is also noteworthy to admit that many counselors and supervisors are not good clinical writers.

Remember, when writing case notes, you are not writing for a wide audience—in fact, in most cases, you actually hope your case notes never see the light of day! You must be aware, however, that your notes are not simply for yourself but serve as treatment history for future clinicians, human service professionals, law enforcement personnel, the client, and, shudder, even the courts. An ineffective clinical writer who makes numerous grammatical errors or leaves out pertinent information will lose his or her professional credibility at minimum, and, at maximum, could be on the short end of a lawsuit. Should the unlikely and unfortunate event of a lawsuit against you come to pass, you want the written case record to support your therapy. Without adequate documentation of adherence to the *American Counseling Association (ACA) Code of Ethics* as well as failure to document competent treatment, a counselor's legal and ethical vulnerability is increased (Mitchell, 2007; Remley & Herlihy, 2014; Wheeler & Bertram, 2015).

Unfortunately, many graduate counseling programs seem to put little emphasis on training students in writing clinical case notes (Cottone & Tarvydas, 2003; Hodges, 2011). This is of great concern when one considers that what is (and is not) recorded in case notes can be the difference between legal culpability and sound legal standing (Wheeler & Bertram, 2015). Many professions, such as medicine, train students with the expectation that their notes will be read by various professionals and that they must always be ready to defend whatever is in the record (Remley & Herlihy, 2014). The *2014 ACA Code of Ethics* requires counselors to maintain counseling records and furthermore to provide adequate documentation (ACA, 2014). Adequate documentation is not explicitly defined though often includes case notes, a treatment plan, *Diagnostic and Statistical Manual of Mental Disorders* (DSM; American Psychiatric Association [APA], 2013) diagnoses, any testing, and documentation from previous clinical and other providers (e.g., psychiatric records, previous counseling, law enforcement).

Case notes are one of the most important records for counselors as they are records counselors generate themselves. Most writers are made, not born (and my experience is that this includes all types of writing—clinical, fiction, poetry, magazine, etc.). As a college professor and a writer myself, I can verify that writing does not come easy to most people. (It certainly has not come easy to me!) Most of us struggle to transform our thoughts into coherent sentences and paragraphs that address what needs addressing. The best teacher for writing case notes is some combination of instruction, reading an experienced clinician's case notes, perusing appropriate reference texts on writing case notes, suggestions from clinical supervisors and/or colleagues, and practice, practice, practice writing your own. During your practicum or internship, ask for tips from veteran counselors regarding effective case notes. Notice how they have learned to write, what they put in their notes, and, just as important, what they leave out. The specific style and content will vary from one counselor to another, and in differences regarding the types of clients being counseled or evaluated. However, the professionalism of skilled colleagues will likely be consistent. This is also an area where your onsite field supervisor should be your coach. Your field supervisor may critique your case notes and, if not, feel free to ask him or her to do so. Students in school counseling placements likely will have far less documentation than those in agencies, hospitals, and correctional facilities. Nevertheless, because good professional writing is essential across many areas of the counseling field, school counseling students would be wise to develop their case note writing as well, as they have also been compelled to testify in courts of law.

## CLIENT RECORDS AND THE STANDARD OF CARE

In the distant past, it was common for counselors and other mental health professionals to intentionally refrain from keeping client records (Wheeler & Bertram, 2015). This unfortunate (and now unethical) practice is, necessarily, and thankfully, passé. Over the past two decades, the standards regarding information, storage, and transmission of client records have all been raised. Failure to maintain adequate client records could form the basis of a claim of professional malpractice because it breaches the standard of care expected of a practicing mental health professional (Wheeler & Bertram, 2015). As previously mentioned, the *2014 ACA Code of Ethics* is explicit regarding a counselor's duty to record adequate records: "Counselors create, safeguard, and maintain documentation necessary for rendering professional services" (ACA, 2014, Standard A.1.b). Well-documented client counseling records are possibly the most effective tool counselors have for establishing client treatment protocols, ensuring an ongoing standard of care, and supporting competent care.

Ethical and legal standards impact all counselors. Regardless of the setting you ultimately work in, whether school, hospital, correctional facility, or university counseling center, you will need to become competent and skilled in writing clear case notes and not merely because you may be compelled to testify in a court of law, an ethics hearing, or defend your case notes to your workplace supervisor. Aspirational ethics require a counselor to strive to exceed basic ethical parameters. Thus, should you find yourself in these unfortunate and sometimes traumatic experiences and your case notes become the focus of examination, you will be in a stronger position. On this matter I can speak from experience. As a director of a county clinic early in my career, I was compelled to go to court regularly. In every case, the attorneys focused most of their attention on the written records, either my own or that of one of the clinicians I supervised. Essentially I learned the hard way that I (and others) had to be prepared to defend anything we recorded in case notes. After all, although a client's or counselor's memory will fade with time, written records remain.

### Standard of Care: Clinical Management

Clear, concise case notes and well-maintained clinical records clearly assist in the clinical case history and provide a rationale for past and current treatment. Because the nature of counseling implies continuous growth and change, case notes should reflect how the client is progressing in his or her treatment. Case records provide documentation of quality care, including what has worked, what has not worked, and why. Case records also ensure some degree of protection from legal liability by demonstrating and documenting the strategic planning on the part of the counselor and treatment team. Case notes also establish that the counselor conducted himself or herself as a competent professional (e.g., was ethical, within legal parameters). After all, written records are the only concrete proof the counselor has regarding client treatment and therapeutic progress. As it is often said in the mental health field, "If it ain't written down, it don't exist." So, make sure the critical areas of treatment are adequately recorded. As a counselor you will deal with three conflicting principles (Mitchell, 2007, p. 17):

1. The client's right of confidentiality versus the counselor's obligation to protect society
2. The client's right to receive service in the least restrictive setting versus the counselor's obligation to provide close supervision, continuous monitoring, and a safe environment
3. The client's right to die versus the counselor's obligation to save lives

One of the more distressing issues that can arise in counseling is when a client discloses the intent to harm himself or herself or other parties. When clients disclose thoughts, feelings, or intentions that place themselves or an identifiable third party at risk, the counselor must document the threat, and the appropriate action taken, as well as notify the proper authorities. Competent documentation is essential in crisis situations, as such are likely to involve the legal system. Should a case proceed to a court for an involuntary commitment to a psychiatric center, correctional facility, referral to child protection caseworkers, or to court officials, the case record will be carefully scrutinized.

## DOCUMENTING COMPLICATED END-OF-LIFE ISSUES

Having written the previous paragraph emphasizing the very real need to protect clients (and others), the finer nuances of self-harm call out for additional elaboration. Clearly, all competent counselors would quickly intervene in cases of foreseeable harm regarding a child, an adolescent, or an adult. But for seniors in counseling, particularly those with terminal illnesses the issue of protecting the client versus client autonomy likely is murkier for many counselors. The ethical dilemma of a client's right to die has long been debated in Western society and as of this edition (2015) only three states—Oregon, Washington, and Vermont—have enacted physician-assisted suicide. While right-to-die issues and situations are far more common in the medical profession, counselors and other mental health professionals may also grapple with this thorny issue.

The issue confronting counselors is how to respond when a terminally ill client discloses the intention to end his or her life. Under typical circumstances the counselor would have an ethical (and legal) duty to take action to prevent the client from carrying out a suicidal intent. Said action likely would involve breaching confidentiality to prevent the client from attempting suicide. But with elderly, terminally ill clients many counselors may have conflicting emotions. A critical factor beyond the counselor's feelings include (a) who is the client (the terminally ill patient or the family members); (b) who has legal competence to determine what course of action is in the best interest of the patient (the terminally ill patient or a health care guardian); (c) the strongly held views by everyone involved concerning the proper (moral, ethical, and legal) course of action; (d) state laws that may be more or less prescriptive in terms of the duties and responsibilities of health and mental health professionals; and (e) the values of the counselor who is providing services (Wheeler & Bertram, 2015, pp. 182, 183). The *2014 ACA Code of Ethics* (ACA, 2014, Standard B.2.b) provides some guidance at least with regard to professional ethics:

> Counselors who provide services to terminally ill individuals who are considering their own deaths have the option to maintain confidentially, depending on applicable laws and the specific circumstances of the situation and after seeking consultation or supervision from appropriate professional and legal parties.

As a member of the ACA Ethics Revision Task Force that revised and developed the 2014 edition of the *ACA Code of Ethics*, we struggled to revise the end-of-life section of the 2005 edition as members of the task force had various ethical and moral positions—such is natural on sensitive issues. Any counselor counseling a terminally ill client who professes an intention to hasten his or her death likely will tread a legal and ethical precipice. Beyond professional ethics and legal issues, moral and religious issues and the right to self-determination may weight as heavily as any other considerations. The classic ethical question of "What is in the client's best interest?" may be challenging to satisfactorily answer in assisted suicide. The more pragmatic issue for readers of this text is how and what to document in such a situation. My advice—which may not be very helpful—is to seek good consultation from a seasoned, trusted colleague and to obtain legal advice. While few counselors have faced end-of-life euthanasia, *some* have and in the future more are certain to be forced to confront this issue.

Quality documentation also facilitates continuity of care from one counselor to another counselor or related professional (Wheeler & Bertram, 2015). Whether the transfer is temporary (e.g., the counselor is on vacation or out of the office) or permanent, the case record provides continuity of care. In such cases, well-written, up-to-date case notes are a means of communicating important information to a new clinician or court official. It could also be argued that clear, concise, and effective case notes are "in the client's best interest."

## Standard of Care: Legal Implications

Clearly this text has been quite emphatic regarding the legal implications of counseling as litigation casts a very long shadow over the mental health profession. Counseling records sometimes become legal documents in court cases—such as when clients are involved in custody battles, malpractice litigation, workers' compensation, probation hearings, charges of abuse, involuntary commitments to psychiatric hospitals, and so forth. The standard of practice regarding records and the documentation of counseling services continues to evolve, often through legal changes. The full impact of congressional acts such as the Health Insurance Portability and Accountability Act (HIPAA) have yet to be tested in court (Wheeler & Bertram, 2015), but counselors should assume the highest standard. The *Tarasoff v. The Regents of* the *University of California* case (1976), *Jaffee v. Redmond et al.* (1996), and *Thapar v. Zezulka* (1999) have all impacted the counseling profession in significant ways (e.g., established the duty to warn in *Tarasoff*, psychotherapist [including counselor] privilege in federal court in *Jaffee*, and in *Thapar* a judge ruled Texas counselors have no duty to warn nor immunity should they do so). Case notes should reflect that the counselor made the client aware of his or her rights through informed consent (see Chapter 3). Clients must clearly understand the limits of confidentiality, and that a counselor will need to break confidentiality under certain required circumstances (e.g., danger to self or others, legally mandated court testimony, child abuse). Fortunately, few cases will not evolve into a judicial hearing, but the counselor must prepare each case record with the understanding that the case could proceed to court. Also, always remember that with a legally mandated client, a court official (or parole or probation officer/committee) likely will be reviewing the file, and your case notes, reports, and assessment findings could make a significant difference in a client's life.

So, assume that the client record you are creating will wind up being scrutinized in a courtroom or another formal and serious forum. This foundation will assist you in carefully creating a well-documented file that will accurately reflect the client's progress. Because client records can become public records (as in court proceedings), counselors should not include identifying information about third parties (such as family members, extramarital lovers, etc.) unless that information has a direct bearing on the client's treatment.

Clearly, client records do not always reflect a favorable impression on the client and may be detrimental in a legal hearing. For example, if counseling a convicted sex offender who has been noncompliant with treatment, for ethical and legal purposes your written record must reflect that. In some cases, you may actually find a client likable and want to inflate said client's compliance and progress in counseling. Clearly, however, such inaccuracy could be construed either as malpractice, falsifying a legal document, or both, which could jeopardize a counselor's career (Mitchell, 2007; Remley & Herlihy, 2014; Wheeler & Bertram, 2015). Essentially, your ethical integrity and potential legal standing to practice are a professional lie as much in your writing acumen as with your clinical skills. The wrong lesson to learn from this chapter is that documentation and case notes are an impossible chore. Frankly, the simpler you make your case notes, likely the better off you will be. Be thorough, but be concise as possible. Furthermore, work to ensure that the case file is complete and that additional documentation (e.g., treatment plan, assessment, records from other providers) is present.

## Standard of Care: HIPAA Compliance

As discussed in Chapter 3, counselors who practice in public and private settings, where insurance is billed, fall under HIPAA of 1996. The major intent of HIPAA was to address electronic transmission of client care information through media such as the Internet. State laws have been crafted to ensure further HIPAA compliance, especially with regard to client privacy (Wheeler & Bertram, 2015).

Some counselors, such as school counselors and counselors working in college and university counseling centers, may be exempt from HIPAA, although many of the latter may attempt to operate in compliance with HIPAA regardless of a given desire to meet a higher standard of care.

HIPAA will primarily impact the counselor with regard to electronic transmission of mental health record (e.g., progress notes, treatment plan, assessment). Privacy refers to the basic right of a person to be left alone and to control his or her personal information (Wheeler & Bertram, 2015). The term *privacy* is often used interchangeably with the term *confidentiality*, though confidentiality typically refers to a professional's (i.e., counselor) ethical duty and privacy is what the client reserves to protect his or her personal information from third parties. The HIPAA Privacy Rule (2013) was established by federal action to provide a greater sense of patient privacy previously lacking due to variations in state laws. This amendment to HIPAA arose as a result of concerns that transmission of health care information through the Internet and other electronic means could lead to gaps in protection of patient confidentiality. The HIPAA Privacy Rule applies to both paper and electronic transmissions of protected health information (PHI) by covered entities. Covered entities are health and mental health professionals who transmit any PHI such as health care claims, health plan enrollment, and coordination of benefits (Wheeler & Bertram, 2015). These would include counselors, billing insurance and sending such information through electronic or paper means. Incidentally, counselors must also be aware of state law if their state of residence *exceeds* HIPAA standards of client/patient protection of privacy.

Counselors are strongly advised to keep abreast of HIPAA changes that may impact their obligations to clients. The HIPAA Privacy Rule of 2013 also specifically permits clients to receive copies of their records in electronic form and/or have the records sent in electronic form to third parties, provided health records are transmitted through electronic means (Wheeler & Bertram, 2015). While it is difficult to predict specific changes to currently existing federal privacy law, given the global virtual world we inhabit, future regulation regarding privacy is certain to occur.

## CASE NOTES

Given the time, effort, and referencing in this text regarding legal issues, it should be clear legalities, as well as professional ethics, are paramount for counselors. While the prose in this text is heavy on legal rulings, court cases, and congressional acts, there is much uncertainty in select areas of mental health care. Counseling records include two broad sections of information identified by HIPAA as PHI. PHI examples include (a) client demographic information (e.g., name, date of birth, address, telephone number, e-mail address) and (b) diagnosis, prognosis, treatment plan, progress to date, dates of service (beginning and end of client sessions), participants in session, and financial data (charges, payments, balance) (Wheeler & Bertram, 2015). This type of PHI is confidential but under appropriate circumstances may be accessed by third-party providers such as insurance companies.

Case notes are given an added level of protection if they are maintained in a separate physical or electronic location. This means that disclosure of case notes requires a separately executed client authorization if the case notes are maintained in a separate file (Remley & Herlihy, 2014). Naturally, counselors can easily integrate case notes within a single file and such is common practice. In such practices, case notes would fall under the general guidelines governing disclosure (see Chapter 3). While many counselors would argue the need to maintain "psychotherapy" case notes separately given what appears to be added protection against subpoenas, one may wish to proceed with caution. Two files require an extra location—either electronic or physical—to file confidential case records. This means an added complication and one extra step with every record. My own experience through decades in mental health and higher education is things get misplaced. Thus, many counselors prefer to have just one case record.

Although HIPAA provides a definition of psychotherapy notes, important questions remain unanswered. For example, would standard SOAP notes (to be discussed later in this chapter) be considered *psychotherapy notes*? In my experience, many agencies assume they are. What about the couples, family, or group counselor who considers the couple, family, or group as the client? How would this approach be affected by HIPAA? Or what about the counselor who has ethical concerns regarding the legitimacy of *DSM* diagnoses, based on past and present cultural and gender discrimination (Schwartz & Feisthamel, 2009) and refuses to use the system? These and other relevant questions regarding HIPAA remain unanswered (Bertram & Wheeler, 2015). Given past history (e.g., *Tarasoff, Jaffee*), the courts may eventually be called upon to decide such issues.

## Standard of Care: Risk Management Strategy

The final reason for keeping records is very simple. Well-documented case files provide effective defense for counselors responding to lawsuits or ethical complaints (Remley & Herlihy, 2014; Wheeler & Bertram, 2015). Should questions arise about what the counselor did, or, as in legal and ethical hearings, failed to do, well-documented records provide protection. If you are accused of incompetence, malfeasance, and violating legal or ethical parameters, and your treatment actions were not adequately noted in the record, you have little defense. Clear case notes, assessments, treatment plan, and so forth are essential documents that provide a rationale for treatment. Case files are also typically read by colleagues and supervisors in the same agency, school, and hospital, and this collateral oversight and support strengthens the counselor's case. A question counseling students likely have at this point is, "What constitutes adequate documentation?" This is an excellent question; unfortunately, "adequate documentation" is not explicitly defined. Nevertheless there are some clearly understood parameters of "adequate" documentation:

- Client identification information (e.g., name, age, gender)
- Previous treatment (e.g., medical, mental health, educational—whatever is pertinent and available)

- Informed consent document: states client's rights and responsibilities including parameters of confidentiality, and so on
- Financial arrangements (e.g., insurance, private pay, employee assistance program)
- Clinical assessment and/or *DSM-5* diagnosis
- Release of information (if pertinent)
- Collateral information (test results, letters regarding client educational, psychological and/or vocational history, reports, information regarding the client obtained from other sources, past clinical records, communications from third parties)
- Treatment plan
- Case notes
- Academic standing, grades, and so on (P–12 school settings)
- Anything else pertaining to the treatment of the client
  (Adapted from Wheeler & Bertram, 2015)

Wheeler and Bertram (2015) refer to high-risk cases, such as those involving potentially suicidal clients, clients who express homicidal intent, HIV-positive clients with multiple sexual partners, and cases of suspected abuse. From a risk management standpoint, they recommend such cases to be fully *documented* through the following steps:

- *At-risk situation*: Document what the client did or said that suggested she or he was considering engaging in or was actively engaging in a high-risk activity. Be clear and specific. Example: "Client stated she had a plan for suicide by swallowing pills after session today." Or, if more subtle: "Client said he was really getting 'tired of his ex-wife's obnoxious new boyfriend and planned to take him out.'" Then explain that you clarified with the client what "take him out" meant.
- *Assessment*: Based on your clinical experience and knowledge of the client, document the severity level of this threat. Clearly explain how you determined the severity level. Did you use a standard assessment such as the Beck Depression Inventory-II (BDI-II), Adapted SAD PERSONS Scale, Danger Assessment Instrument, specific intake questions, review of past client history, scaling questions (1 to 10 with 1 being low and 10 high), and so on? Standard assessments with a research base behind them always are an advantage (e.g., BDI-II, Minnesota Multiphasic Inventory-2 [MMPI-2], Drug Attitude Inventory [DAI]). There is nothing necessarily wrong with using subjective assessments in counseling, as they are common. But, as they lack a strong research base and are subject to wide reliability and validity concerns, a prudent counselor would pair them with an objective test. Subjective tests lacking research support may also be more open to question in a courtroom.
- *Options*: List the options you consider as appropriate responses based on your assessment. Listing options demonstrates that you were thinking broadly and that you considered a range of alternatives before reaching a decision.
- *Rule out*: Briefly describe what options you ruled out and why each was determined to be inappropriate. These descriptions clarify your clinical decision making and make the case that you acted appropriately.

- *Consultation and/or supervision*: If there is time, obtain and document any colleague's consultation or supervision you received to evaluate and clarify a course of action.
- *Actions taken*: Describe the options you chose, including what you said and did. This helps clarify how you implemented the options you determined to be appropriate.
- *Follow-up*: Document what happened, what you did, and how things progressed until there was resolution.

(Adapted from Wheeler & Bertram, 2015)

My experience has taught me the wisdom of one additional step: *Consult your supervisor*. Anytime that you encounter a high-risk case, consult with your supervisor as soon as possible, document that you consulted her or him, and note any suggestions. From past experience as a supervisor, I can tell you that a supervisor's worst nightmare is to be caught unaware because a counselor did not apprise them of a high-risk situation. Because supervisors ultimately are held to a higher standard than line counselors and other therapists, they inherit greater liability. So, consult your supervisor immediately in potential high-risk situations. Needless to say, failure to apprise your boss regarding a high-risk, potentially litigious situation is very poor job security!

As a counselor-in-training, you must understand that no amount of protection is absolute. However, should you maintain an up-to-date case file, document clear case notes, treatment plans, and so forth, and follow the suggestions in the previous discussion of high-risk cases, you will have the odds on your side. But regardless of how thorough you are regarding case notes, adequate documentation, and consultation with your supervisor, the risk remains, albeit very small. Furthermore, while as a student you "likely" fall under your university's liability, this issue seems unclear as graduate students generally are not considered university employees. Thus, carrying student liability insurance is a must. As previously noted, most counseling programs likely require students to purchase liability insurance. Student membership in ACA, American Mental Health Counselors Association (AMHCA), American School Counselor Association (ASCA), and other professional counseling organizations carries student liability along with the membership.

## RECOMMENDATIONS FOR RECORD KEEPING

As discussed in Chapter 3, agencies and settings differ in terms of how they take, maintain, and store records. Many are moving to electronic-based notes systems. Whether your school or agency uses paper or electronic records, Mitchell (2007) offers the following advice regarding record keeping:

- Service providers need timely, accurate, and comprehensive information. Lack of information can impede quality of care because the decision-making process is placed at risk.
- An organization must comply with its own written policy related to record keeping and confidentiality. In the event of litigation or allegations

of unethical conduct, "failure to comply" can be used against the service provider.

■ One way to avoid misuse of information is to have trained employees who are committed to protecting the privacy of each client. (p. 45)

Mitchell (2007) also offers eight assumptions counselors should make regarding electronic records:

1. The counseling record will be subpoenaed and the court must understand what went on in counseling.
2. The counselor may or may not be with the agency when it happens. Someone else will have to read and understand what the counselor wrote.
3. Legislation that opens a record to the client exists now or will be passed. In fact, the *Code* [*ACA Code of Ethics*] already provides the client with reasonable access to records.
4. The counselor's notes will not be accurate if he or she takes days or weeks to write a note, so they should be written as soon as possible. [Practicum and internship students will not be retained if such delays occur!]
5. The note will be the best possible reflection of the counselor's professional abilities.
6. Client contact is not considered a professional service until the counselor's entry is in the record.
7. The notes may be used by an official board of inquiry [e.g., licensure board, ethics panel, etc.].
8. The service documentation and personnel file may be requested by a board of inquiry [essentially, a board of professional counselors charged with reviewing ethics complaints] in the event of allegations of unethical conduct. The *ACA Ethical Code* also requires that counselors cooperate with investigations. (p. 46)

Counselors never know who might be called on to inspect a client's file. Therefore, always write case notes and organize the client's file with the assumption that what is written will be read and evaluated at some point in the future. Keeping this possibility in mind should not overly inhibit you, but should help you keep close to the facts. It is important to remember the following:

■ Your clients have a legal right to review their record.
■ Your clients have a right to demand that you provide copies of case notes to their physician, other mental health professionals, and attorneys.
■ Your clients have a right to subpoena your case notes. If they sue you, they lose their right to privacy as the counselor has a right to protect himself or herself in a lawsuit.
■ Third parties can also subpoena case notes when involved in legal cases involving the client, even over the client's or counselor's objections. You will need your attorney to address subpoenas. Do not simply send documents the subpoena requests as you may then be guilty of violating the client's privacy.

- The legal representatives of deceased clients, in most states, have a right to inspect the deceased client's case notes. But deceased clients maintain confidentiality and a right to privacy absent legal rulings. Should a family member who is not the deceased client's legal representative request to view his or her loved one's file, you likely will need to refuse. (Check with your attorney as state laws may vary.)
- In cases of litigation, case notes and other confidential documents may become public. Thus, prepare your clients for the possibility. When counseling mandated clients, apprise them that a third party may request copies of pertinent documents or information regarding treatment.
- Make sure you have been very thorough regarding the client's rights during informed consent.
- Once again, you may be compelled to testify regarding why you wrote what you wrote in the case notes. Essentially, once you write something in a case file, you are responsible for defending what you wrote.

## GENERAL RECOMMENDATIONS FOR WRITING CASE NOTES

There are three key points to keep in mind with regard to case notes. One, case notes provide a tracking record of the client's treatment, progress, or lack of progress. Two, case notes provide clear documentation of decisions and actions the counselor has made during treatment. Three, case notes provide a rationale and defense for the counselor should an ethical or legal issue arises. Case notes also provide evidence that the counselor is following best practices—in other words, what any clinically sound, ethical counselor would do in similar circumstances.

### Objective Versus Subjective Information

One important element is the ability to distinguish objective information (who said what, or what you directly witnessed during a session) from subjective impressions (conclusions you developed as a result of counseling the client). Quite often, because of the large volume of clients you will see and because of the passage of time, you may confuse the objective with the subjective. It is very important that you are able to separate what was actually observed or documented from what you believe to be the case. (I know from experience lawyers will hammer away on this issue!) Objective documentation is what you will be held accountable for in a court case should you be unfortunate enough to be the object of such. For example, do not write "The client seems to be a drug addict" especially if you have no direct evidence of addiction. The client may not be an addict and recording of such libelous information could significantly harm the client and be grounds for a lawsuit against you (Wheeler & Bertram, 2015). On the other hand, if the client is being treated for chemical dependency, noting that fact that "… the client appears to have be abusing substances based upon own admission, drug screenings, and his answers on the SASSI-3" would be accurate record keeping. Just remember, objective information is what the client has said, done, and is verifiable. For example: "The client has been court mandated for addictions evaluation and counseling after being cited for Driving Under the Influence (DUI)" or whatever is accurate.

## Keep Comments Concise

Because a client may be verbose, client quotations should be kept to a minimum and only the most significant should be included, otherwise counselor accuracy may be called into question (Cameron & turtle-song, 2002). Hart, Berndt, and Caramazza (1985) suggest that an individual is able to accurately recall only vestigial bits of verbatim information. (*Note:* My experience is many counselors overstate their memory of counseling sessions.) This suggests that after a 50-minute counseling session, a counselor's ability to recall specific information with any accuracy is questionable (unless of course the session has been recorded). So, keep quotations to a minimum; note only key words or a brief phrase. Key words or phrases might include plans for suicide, homicide, comments suggesting a dramatic change in life circumstances, a major change in the client's well-being, employment, marital status, and so forth. Quotations may be cited to document inappropriate or abusive language toward the counselor or others. Comments suggesting significant denial should be documented. For example, a father accused of abusing his son with a whip might say, "I only use a whip when necessary!" Because the child's physical and emotional health may be at stake, his comments and likely tone of voice should be recorded. The counselor might note, "When confronted regarding belt marks on his son's legs, the father stated in a loud, defensive tone, 'I only use a whip when necessary!'"

## Note Behavioral Changes

It is also important to document statements that suggest the client may be confused regarding time, place, and person or is experiencing an abrupt change in his or her mental status. For example, if the client becomes disoriented and is confused as to who he or she is, or the circumstances regarding being in counseling, the counselor should record this. To assess the client's mental status, a mental status examination or a mini-mental status examination should be administered (see Chapter 4).

A client's change in attitude, either positive or negative, should be recorded because it serves as evidence for counseling effectiveness or ineffectiveness. A statement such as "Counseling has helped me get sober and put my life back together" might be written as "Client reports 'counseling has been very effective regarding sobriety.'" This information is especially important if the client was mandated to counseling and presented to the first session as oppositional. The goal is not to provide a verbatim account of what the client said, but to reflect current areas of client concern and to support or validate the counselor's interpretations and interventions. Essentially, "successful" counseling is where treatment goals are being realized. This particular area also suggests for mandated clients that the counselor needs a concrete understanding of what the mandating party considers successful. For example, what specific behavioral changes are desired? Naturally, if addiction is the primary issue, sobriety is key. Counselors will further need to assist mandating parties in what is realistic in therapy. A school principal or probation officer saying "She needs to change her behavior" is too vague. Specifically, *what* behavior needs to change? *How* much change is required? *What* would successful therapy look like? These are the types of specifics that referring administrators, magistrates, and parents often seem vague on. As a counselor-in-training you need to gather such specifics in order to more accurately measure client success or nonsuccess.

## Be Judicious and Supportive

Because case notes may be read by insurance officials, court officials, other mental health professionals, and so forth, the counselor should be judicious about the type of information included in the case record. Political, religious, and racial views should not be included in the case notes unless they directly relate to the focus of treatment (Eggland, 1988). The counselor also should not repeat inflammatory statements that are critical of other mental health providers, because such comments could antagonize clinicians and compromise care. Instead of using the actual names of client's object of animus, the counselor might substitute with terms such as "other staff" or "another mental health professional," and so on. It is of further importance to remember that the names a client mentions during counseling sessions should not be included in the record unless those persons have a direct relationship to the client's treatment. So, before including a name, ask yourself, "How is this person's name related to the client's treatment?" Always remember, you are not necessarily getting the *truth* from a client, but rather their perception of the truth. Beyond legalities, fairness to named persons not present to defend themselves would seem sound ethical practice.

Another guideline to follow is to be constructive in how you word case notes (Baird, 2005). Remember again, your clients have a right to inspect the file and you do not want to record anything that might incite additional animus, assign blame, or be personally demeaning. You do want to record an accurate synopsis of the client's treatment, including successes, issues still in progress, relapses, and so forth, but you must be professional and ethical in the manner in which you record these important clinical details. Professional case notes will lessen the probability the client (or another official) will be offended. So, to borrow from Shakespeare, record the truth but do so in a manner that does not appear inflammatory or personally demeaning.

## Keep It Brief

Brevity is the operative word when writing case notes. Counselors should express essential ideas, but keep notations brief because of space and time constraints. Instead of writing, "the client states," use shorthand terms such as "reports," "states," "describes," "indicates," "complains of," and so forth (Cameron & turtle-song, 2002). Instead of writing, "Today the client says, 'I'm having lots of conflicts with coworkers since the last counseling session where we met and talked about jackasses I work with!'" the counselor might write, "Client reports increased conflict at work since last session." Furthermore, because it is obvious that the counselor is the scribe, it is not necessary for the counselor to refer to himself or herself.

Students often ask me, "How long should it take me to write case notes?" My suggestion is a 10-minute time frame, because this is about the maximum time you can expect between sessions (often you may have less, of course). Naturally there are times when you are unable to record case notes until the end of the day. As was previously noted regarding difficulty recalling specific events in particular counseling session, my recommendation is for counselors to keep notes during the session. These brief summaries of critical points can be a real asset in reminding the counselor of the particulars of the session. During days when I had back-to-back sessions for 6 to 7 hours a day, taking brief in-session notes was invaluable to writing accurate case notes as I could not possibly remember all pertinent points and without in-session notes likely would have confused particular issues with clients. Then, when I had written the case note, I shredded handwritten in-session notes. I would also inform clients the purpose behind in-session notes so as to demystify the process. I always informed my clients they could view my in-session notes anytime. Very few clients ever took me up on my offer. Again, do not write anything inflammatory, use actual names, and shred the in-session notes when the official record is recorded.

Further along on the topic of writing in-session notes, I have met a few therapists of the opinion that writing in-session notes was detrimental to therapy. I have found no research to support this opinion and, furthermore, as most counselors cannot recall much of the session, such notes have been essential to me. Naturally, some counselors feel different regarding writing in-session notes and their practice may vary. Your own field site supervisor may have a different practice and that may work for him or her, though it would not function well for me. School counselors may write far fewer case notes, and the structure, expectation, and approach to therapy are typically different in a school versus an agency or hospital. Still, school counseling offices will need to document academic and behavioral information.

## SOAP FORMAT

There are several different formats used for writing case notes (SOAP, DAP [data, assessment, plan], narrative recording, etc.). All are developed to provide a continuity and consistency to a generally subjective exercise on the part of the counselor. Because of its popularity among mental health professionals, I recommend the SOAP (subjective, objective, assessment, plan) format. Exhibit 5.1 shows a sample SOAP write-up form, which uses *DSM* categories.

### Subjective

This section should provide a narrative of the client's feelings, concerns, problems expressed, goals, thoughts expressed, the intensity of problems expressed, and the problems' impact on significant relationships. Relevant comments

**EXHIBIT 5.1** *DSM-5* and SOAP Client Case Note Format

Page 1 of 2

Name(s) and age(s) of client(s): _____

_____

_____

Date:_____ / _____ / _____     Code(s): _____     Session #: _____

Presenting Problem: _____

_____

_____

_____

Medications: _____

Cite Criteria for Primary Diagnosis:

_____

_____

_____

_____

_____

*DSM-5* Preliminary Diagnostic Impressions (For educational and training purposes only. Not intended as a final diagnosis):

*Prescriptive. Not intended as a final diagnosis.*

**Subjective (S):** _____

_____

_____

_____

_____

_____

_____

_____

(continued)

---

**EXHIBIT 5.1**  *DSM-5 and SOAP Client Case Note Format (continued)*

---

**Objective (O):** _____

_____

_____

_____

_____

_____

_____

_____


**Assessment (A):** _____

_____

_____

_____

_____

_____

_____

_____


**Plan (P):** _____

_____

_____

_____

_____

_____

_____

_____


Code:   psy. = psychiatric referral; ac = acute; cr = chronic; R/x = meds; Tx = treatment;
        pr = parental access restricted; wc = ward of court; npr = no previous records

**Counselor's Signature** _____

provided by close family members, court officers, and other officials should also be noted in this section. The client's perception of the issues should be clear to an outside reader of the record. Counselors should be thorough although brief in their summarizations.

*Example of a Subjective (S) Entry:* "I feel very guilty about how my alcoholism has impacted my relationship with my kids." This would be a subjective statement as you may not believe the client or have a realistic way to verify the statement. Using third-person writing style also is acceptable. For example: "Client states 'feeling guilty' regarding inability to manage addiction."

## Objective

The objective section is made up of what can be "seen, heard, smelled, counted, or measured" (Cameron & turtle-song, 2002, p. 288). Generally, there are two types of objective information: outside documented reports and the counselor's own observations of the client's behavior during the session. The latter, the counselor's observations, are composed of any psychological, interpersonal, or physical findings relevant to treatment. Objective information could consist of the client's appearance, verbal and nonverbal behavior, affect, voice tone, body posture, compliance with treatment, oppositional nature, and client's strengths. This section may also refer to the client's mental status and competence to continue treatment. Supportive outside written reports such as psychological or psychiatric reports, assessments, medical records, prison records, school records, and so forth would be included in the objective section. Remember to note any client changes or discrepancies and when they occur (e.g., client becomes irritated in discussing a topic or blushes when a name is mentioned).

The counselor's choice of language in this section should reflect accuracy in content. Terms that seem less precise such as "appeared," "seemed," "possibly," and so forth should be avoided. Naturally, because counseling is not an exact science, some degree of latitude is expected. Terms such as "evidenced by" is a descriptive term that implies direct observation. For example, let us say the client arrived 15 minutes late for session, was unkempt, and had difficulty maintaining his or her focus in session. This behavior is inconsistent with previous sessions where the client was on time and engaged with the process. When writing this in the case notes, the counselor might say, "Appeared depressed as evidenced by tardiness, less involvement in the counseling process, and poorly groomed."

When writing the objective section of the report, the counselor should refrain from using pejorative language ("slob"), stating opinion not supported by facts ("lazy"), and personal judgments ("He is a loser"). Terms that have a negative connotation and are subject to speculation such as "dysfunctional," "rude," "obnoxious," "normal," "abnormal," and the like should be avoided. For example, a counselor should not write, "Client arrived stoned to the session and proceeded to be uncooperative and unprofessional." The counselor might instead record, "Client presented smelling of pot, struggled to maintain focus throughout session, and had difficulty sitting upright in the chair."

*Example of an Objective (O) Entry:* "The client's clothes were wrinkled, soiled, and he was giving off a malodorous smell."

## Assessment

The assessment section is a summarization of the counselor's clinical impressions regarding the client's problem or problems (Cameron & turtle-song, 2002). The assessment section serves to synthesize and analyze the information expressed in the subjective and objective sections. The assessment section includes a psychiatric diagnoses based on the *DSM-5* (APA, 2013). Although there is much controversy regarding use of the *DSM*, and certain diagnoses in particular, *DSM* diagnoses are considered a standard part of treatment (Remley & Herlihy, 2014; Wheeler & Bertram, 2015) and required for financial reimbursement. Diagnoses are simply a reality of professional practice. Ginter and Glauser's (2001) opinion is that the assessment section of the SOAP format includes clinical impressions. Sometimes clinical impressions will be recorded in the form of "rule out" or "rule in" when the counselor is not entirely confident in assigning a diagnosis. Clinical impressions can assist other clinicians in reaching a final diagnosis because they provide guidance on previous assessment. When reporting clinical impressions in the SOAP notes, counselors should clearly identify them as such. Counselors should also identify the evidence for the prospective diagnosis because this documents the clinical process the counselor followed and that the counselor operated within standard procedures.

---

*Clinical Impressions*

Appropriate use of clinical impressions is vital both for writing good case notes and for effective counseling practice. Consider the following example: A counselor working in an outpatient mental health clinic is conducting an intake and assessment for a 6-year-old boy referred by his school counselor for possible attention deficit/hyperactivity disorder (ADHD). The school counselor's report describes the child as having difficulty maintaining his focus for even brief time periods (i.e., 5 minutes), is constantly out of his seat, frequently interrupts his teacher and peers, and has a tendency to self-injury caused by constantly hurrying (e.g., running into chairs, tables, tripping). When the child's history is being taken, the mother discloses that she often consumed alcohol throughout her pregnancy. Although there is not enough evidence for a diagnosis of fetal alcohol syndrome, the counselor's clinical impression is to "rule out fetal alcohol syndrome" and to refer the child for a neurological evaluation. The neurologist can examine the counselor's report and take the information into account as he or she makes a diagnosis.

The assessment portion of the SOAP format is the most likely portion to be read by outside reviewers such as counselors, psychologists, social workers, court officers, child welfare caseworkers, and such (Cameron & turtle-song, 2002). Consequently, counselors should take pains to ensure that the assessment section is supported by the subjective and objective sections, as these portions lay the foundation for a diagnosis or diagnostic impressions. When considering a diagnosis, the counselor should ask the following questions: "Are there sufficient data to support a particular client diagnosis?" (Cameron & turtle-song, 2002), and "Am I prepared to defend my diagnosis?"

The counselor must be prepared to defend any diagnosis he or she renders to parents, colleagues, supervisors, probation officers, and child welfare officials, and if necessary in a courtroom. Naturally considering the full ramifications of a diagnosis can be intimidating, although declining to provide a diagnosis based on the fear of the consequences is also unappealing and possibly unethical. The best advice for counselors is to make the most informed decision possible, and to be able to demonstrate the steps you took to arrive at your diagnosis. Consulting with your supervisor or a trusted colleague is a good idea when you are unsure of selecting a particular diagnosis. It may well be that diagnosis is the "tar baby" of mental health care given the volume of debate and disagreement regarding the *DSM* system and that some researchers have questioned the utility and validity of the *DSM* (Duncan, Miller, Wampold, & Hubble, 2010; Wampold, 2001). Regardless, using the *DSM* classification is typically required for third-party reimbursement and many mental health professionals as well as medical, educational, correctional, and judicial professionals expect a diagnosis. Unless the counselor works in a P–12 school, most university counseling centers, or in a private practice that does not bill insurance, you likely will have to render a diagnosis.

*Example of an Assessment (A) Entry*: "Client's addiction was assessed using the SASST-3 and with a urine analysis (UA) test. SASSI-3 results client was defensive regarding drug use and UA was positive for methamphetamines."

## Plan

The final section of the SOAP format is the treatment plan. The plan is built on the information within the subjective, objective, and assessment sections and should include short-term and long-term goals. This section generally consists of two parts: the action plan and the treatment prognosis. The information to be noted in this section includes the date of the next appointment (or, if it is the final session, to note that this is the final session and include aftercare), interventions used during the session, treatment progress, and homework assigned (if any).

The counselor should note client progress, or lack thereof, in the plan section, because this will have a direct bearing on further treatment. Typically, progress assessments are described in terms such as "good," "fair," "excellent," "guarded," or "poor," accompanied by an explanation supporting the progress assessment. The plan section of the SOAP format completes the case notes section.

---

**TABLE 5.1   SOAP Case Notes Examples**

| Section | Definition | Example |
|---|---|---|
| Subjective (S) | What the client tells you, what pertinent others tell you about the client, how the client experiences the world | Client's feelings, concerns, and problems; comments by clinicians and pertinent others; client's orientation to time, place, and person; client's verbalized attitudes toward helping |
| Objective (O) | Factual information, what the counselor personally witnessed, what was measured through testing or assessment, documentation from other parties | The client's appearance, affect, behavior, test results, and so forth; materials from other agencies to be noted and be attached |
| Assessment (A) | Summarizes the counselor's clinical thinking regarding the patient's diagnosis | Include clinical diagnosis and impressions; may include *DSM* diagnosis (or possible diagnoses) |
| Plan (P) | Describes the parameters of treatment, consists of an action plan and prognosis | Action plan: include interventions used, treatment progress, and direction; include date of next appointment. Prognosis: include the anticipated gains from the intervention |

Adapted from Cameron & turtle-song, 2002, p. 290.

*Example of a Plan (P) Entry:* "Client has been mandated for 12 sessions of addiction counseling. Client will have random UAs to test for treatment compliance, with weekly individual and group counseling sessions to reduce anxiety. The goal is to reduce anxiety scores on the Beck Anxiety Inventory by 50% in 12 weeks. Client was offered weekly secular or Narcotics Anonymous (NA) meetings and chose NA. Will monitor with NA facilitator."

Table 5.1 summarizes each SOAP section and the type of information that should be recorded.

---

*The Case of Pierre*

Pierre is a 28-year-old, Caucasian male, court-mandated client. He was arrested following a domestic dispute involving his female partner. Pierre presents for the first session agitated and oppositional to treatment. He discloses to his counselor, Steve, "I didn't do anything wrong … everybody uses a little force … I was just manning up!" Throughout most of the initial session, Pierre remains defiant. He outlines his struggles in the relationship, explaining how he works 60 hours per week to support

*(continued)*

(continued)

his partner and two kids, and never misses work. He says with much animus, "My damn girlfriend can do anything she wants, but I'm the one that gets arrested!" He demands that the counselor write the judge a letter explaining that he has no problems. Later in the session, Pierre says that he grew up in a physically and verbally abusive home. At age 17, he ran away to live with his maternal grandparents, who seemed to provide the only stability in his life. At age 20, he was arrested twice for driving while intoxicated, and once for a fight at a party. He reports that he feels more aggressive when he has been drinking. Pierre admits to consuming "a couple of drinks a night ... no big deal, you know." He also reports that when he gets angry, he feels like exploding and sometimes becomes violent, punching walls, kicking the trash can, throwing chairs, and occasionally hitting his partner. He also admits that he has "been physical" with his kids on at least two occasions, but maintains that he gets physical only "when they need to be controlled." Before the session ends, he opines, "This counseling is sissy stuff. How the hell are you going to help me with the judge, huh?" Then, he angrily slams the door and storms from the office.

**SOAP Write-Up for Pierre**

S: Client admitted previous use of violence "when they [family] need to be controlled." He reports experience of domestic violence in family of origin. He reports running away from home at age 17 to live with grandparents to escape family violence.

O: Recent history is he was arrested for domestic assault on his female partner and court mandated to counseling. Today was client's initial session and he was guarded throughout most of the session. At session's conclusion, he became agitated when informed he would need to attend treatment for 16 weeks, angrily stating, "Counseling is sissy stuff!" and "How are you going to help me with the judge?" before slamming the door and storming from the office.

A: *DSM-5* Diagnosis: Physical Abuse of Adult [V61.1]. Clinical impressions: Rule out Abuse of Children [V.61.21].

P: Rescheduled for following week (6/12/09) at 3 p.m. Prognosis is guarded because of lack of insight into behavior and mandated client apparently because of a lack of motivation for behavioral change. Will assess potential for future violence using the Domestic Violence Screening Assessment (DMSI). Will refer to 16-week batterers' intervention group in addition to continuing individual cognitive behavioral counseling. Next session plan is to introduce recognizing and stopping anger before it explodes.

6-5-20XX
Steve Washington, LMHC, NCC
Counselor, Jackson County Mental Health

*The Case of Latisha*

Latisha is a 32-year-old, single, admittedly isolated African American who seeks counseling services at Rainbow Counseling Services. She is assigned Maria Jose, a Latina counselor who recently completed her master's in counseling. Latisha appears very shy and reticent, making infrequent eye contact. Her clothes are wrinkled and hair uncombed, and evidences a slight body odor. Maria Jose administers the Beck Depression Inventory-II (BDI-II) and Latisha scores 33 (very high) though indicates she is not suicidal and is hopeful. Maria Jose explains her BDI-II score, inquiring regarding her hopefulness and lack of suicidality. Latisha answers "I get depressed sometimes but wouldn't take my life. I give everything over to God as he is my rock and my support and keeps me afloat … he isn't finished with me yet." Latisha further asks Maria Jose, "Are you a Christian? I would like a Christian counselor." Maria Jose briefly explains her ethical responsibility to be open and fair to clients regardless of spiritual orientation and adds, "You may pray in session if you need and I will be silent and respectful." Latisha seems pleased with this answer and becomes more animated. At the session's end, she makes a follow-up appointment. "You really helped me today!" she says before leaving.

S: Client reports feeling depressed and concurrently that her religious faith in God assists her in coping. Client maintains she has much to live for and that "God isn't finished with me yet."

O: Client appeared lethargic though compliant in session. She was poorly groomed with a slight malodorous smell, and made eye contact infrequently. She did maintain her focus on the session and answered each question on the intake and BDI-II.

A: Client's score of 33 on the BDI-II is very high though she denies suicidality and states she feels hopeful about the future expressing much confidence in her religious faith. Client appears motivated for treatment and seemed to become energized after my agreement she can pray in session while I am silent.

P: Scheduled the next session for 6/12/20XX at 3 p.m. Will readminister the BDI-II at session's end to check progress. Plan to reduce her depression by 50% in eight sessions. Plan to assist client in making two friends for social support and encouraging her to attend regular religious services in her faith as she has identified this as a support.

Regarding the case of Latisha, some students reading the text may have questions regarding Maria Jose's handling of Latisha's religious concerns. In previous eras, counselors often were reluctant to address spiritual issues given that counseling typically was a secular service. More recently, the profession has realized spirituality/religion may be a viable means of emotional support for clients (Cashwell & Watts, 2010; Cashwell & Young, 2011). The critical issue regarding spirituality in session likely involved boundaries and roles. Maria Jose demonstrates her respect for Latisha's values by agreeing to her request to pray in session but maintains her boundary by stating she will be the silent observer. If this session were taking place in a pastoral counseling center, church, synagogue, mosque, and so on, the role and boundary likely would be different. It is worth pointing out, however, that religious leaders who also are professional counselors and members of ACA must also follow *ACA Code of Ethics*. As a former pastoral counselor, professionals in such settings must be very clear during informed consent as to professional roles and boundaries.

## Final Thoughts on SOAP Format

Case notes and client files are legal documents and must be legible (preferably typed), accurate, and concise (Mitchell, 2007; Sommers-Flanagan & Sommers-Flanagan, 1999). A good general guideline to follow is to write your notes immediately after the session, because your memory is freshest at that point. Also, good case notes should be reviewed prior to the next session to facilitate continuity from the previous session to the current one. Furthermore, you may have to transfer the client to another counselor or official; in that case, readable, legible, and coherent case notes will enhance treatment effectiveness and reduce liability. Refrain from technical jargon because it is not descriptive and can be misunderstood should another professional read the file.

For consistency purposes, all client contacts, including phone messages, e-mails (although use of e-mails should be discouraged because of security concerns), letters, and so forth should be recorded using the SOAP format. If an error is made in the record, never erase or use correction fluid. Note the error by either crossing out the error in pen or writing "error" and then record your initials. Should your agency utilize electronic records, use that system to add to the record noting you are making an addition and cite reasons for the addendum. Some agencies even have correction sheet reports for such contingencies, with the counselor explaining the error and signing the document. The mistake and correction should be clearly identified by the counselor.

Document all professional client-related contacts. For example, any pertinent client information provided from a case manager, parole officer, physician, school counselor, and so forth should be noted in the record. At the conclusion of the SOAP format, the counselor should date and sign his or her legal name and include job title and credentials. The counselor should also sign his or her name immediately below the last line of the *plan* section of the SOAP notes.

## REFERENCES

American Counseling Association. (2014). *ACA code of ethics*. Alexandria, VA: Author.

American Psychiatric Association. (2013). *Diagnostic and statistical manual of mental disorders* (5th ed.). Arlington, VA: Author.

Baird, B. N. (2005). *The internship, practicum, and field placement handbook: A guide for the helping professions* (4th ed.). Upper Saddle River, NJ: Pearson/Prentice Hall.

Cameron, S., & turtle-song, i. (2002). Learning to write case notes using the SOAP format. *Journal of Counseling & Development, 80*, 286–292.

Cashwell, C. S. (2010, May). Maturation of a profession. CACREP Perspective. *Counseling Today, 52*(11), 58–59.

Cashwell, C. S., & Watts, J. S. (2010). The new ASERVIC competencies for addressing spiritual and religious issues in counseling. *Journal of Counseling & Development, 55*(1), 2–5.

Cashwell, C. S., & Young, J. S. (2011). *Integrating spirituality and religion into counseling: A guide to competent practice.* Alexandria, VA: American Counseling Association.

Cottone, R. R., & Tarvydas, V. M. (2003). *Ethical and professional issues in counseling* (2nd ed.). Upper Saddle River, NJ: Merrill/Prentice Hall.

Duncan, B., Miller, S. D., Wamplod, B., & Hubble, M. (2010). *The heart and soul of change: Delivering what works in therapy* (2nd ed.). Washington, DC: American Psychological Association.

Eggland, E. T. (1988). Charting: How and why to document your care daily and fully. *Nursing, 18*(11), 76–84.

Ginter, E. J., & Glauser, A. (2001). Effective use of the *DSM* from a developmental wellness perspective. In E. R. Welfal & R. E. Ingersoll (Eds.), *The mental health desk reference* (pp. 69–77). New York, NY: Wiley.

Hart, J., Jr., Berndt, R. S., & Caramazza, A. (1985). Category-specific naming deficit following cerebral infarction. *Nature, 316,* 439–440.

Health Insurance Portability and Accountability Act of 1996 (HIPAA), Pub. L No. 104-191, 110 Stat. 1936 (1996). See also HIPAA Privacy Rule, 45, C.F.R. 160.101-312, 164.106, 164.500-534 (2013).

Hodges, S. (2011). *The counseling practicum and internship manual: A resource for graduate counseling students.* New York, NY: Springer Publishing Company.

Jaffee v. Redmond et al. 1996 WL 314841 (U.S. June 13, 1996).

Mitchell, R. W. (2007). *Documentation in counseling records: An overview of ethical, legal, and clinical issues* (3rd ed.). Alexandria, VA: American Counseling Association.

Remley, T. P., & Herlihy, B. (2014). *Ethical, legal and professional issues in counseling* (4th ed.). Upper Saddle River, NJ: Pearson.

Schwartz, R. C., & Feisthamel, K. P. (2009). Disproportionate diagnosis of mental disorders among African American versus European American clients: Implications for counseling, theory, research, and practice. *Journal of Counseling & Development, 87,* 295–301.

Seligman, L. A. (2004). *Diagnosis and treatment planning in counseling* (3rd ed.). New York, NY: Kluwer.

Sommers-Flanagan, R. S., & Sommers-Flanagan, J. S. (1999). *Clinical interviewing* (2nd ed.). New York, NY: Wiley.

Tarasoff v. The Regents of the University of California, 13 Cal. 3d 177, 529 P.2d. 533 (1976).

Thapar v. Zezulka, 994 S. W. 2nd 635 (Tex. 1999).

Wampold, B. E. (2001). *The great psychotherapy debate: Models, methods, and findings.* Mahwah, NJ: Lawrence Erlbaum.

Wheeler, A. M., & Bertram, B. (2015). *The counselor and the law: A guide to legal and ethical practice* (7th ed.). Alexander, VA: American Counseling Association.

# RECOMMENDED READING

Jongsma, A. E., & Berghius, D. J. (2006). *The adult psychotherapy progress notes planner.* New York, NY: Wiley.

Jongsma, A. E., Peterson, L. M., McInnis, W. P., & Berghius, D. J. (2006). *The adolescent psychotherapy progress notes planner.* New York, NY: Wiley.

McInnis, W. P., & Bughius, D. J. (2006). *The child psychotherapy progress notes planner.* New York, NY: Wiley.

Patterson, T., & McClanahan, T. M. (1999). *The couple and family clinical documentation sourcebook: A comprehensive collection of mental health practice, forms, and records.* New York, NY: Wiley.

Wheeler, A., & Bertram, B. (2015).*The counselor and the law: A guide to legal and ethical practice* (4th ed.). Alexandria, VA: American Counseling Association.

Wiger, D. E. (2005). *The clinical documentation sourcebook: The complete paperwork resource for your mental health practice*. New York, NY: Wiley.

Zuckerman, E. L. (2000). *The clinician's thesaurus: The guide for writing psychological reports* (5th ed.). New York, NY: Guilford Press.

As spiritual issues were noted in the case of Latisha, the following text is a recommended resource:

Cashwell, C. S., & Young, J. S. (2011). *Integrating spirituality and religion into counseling: A guide to competent practice*. Alexandria, VA: American Counseling Association.

# SIX

# MODELS OF SUPERVISION: CLASSROOM AND SITE SUPERVISION

The practicum/internship experience involves not only the on-site clinical experience but also the intense supervision, both in an individual and in a classroom setting. As mentioned in Chapter 1, graduate counseling students in Council for Accreditation of Counseling and Related Educational Programs (CACREP)–accredited programs (practicum and internship) are expected to spend an average of 1 hour per week of supervision with a faculty and on-site supervisor, and for practicum an additional average of 1.5 hours per week of group supervision. In this chapter, I will provide guidance to help you and your fellow students make the most of your supervision experience, both in the classroom and with your on-site supervisor.

## PRACTICUM/INTERNSHIP CLASS

This class is very different from other courses you will take, such as Counseling Theories, Assessment, and Research Methods. Generally, practicum and internship classes are more experientially based and seldom involve examinations, memorizing material, American Psychological Association-style term papers, and so on. Typically, students discuss pertinent aspects of their placement, site supervisor, challenges, aspects they enjoy, what they are learning, issues on the site, and so forth. The practicum class will discuss (and perhaps view recordings of) confidential counseling sessions. Thus, as a graduate student, you must treat the experience as if it were a supervision meeting. Like a supervision meeting in an agency or school, a large part of the practicum or internship classroom experience will involve presenting clinical cases and then receiving critiques from your peers and the professor. Although the practicum class can initially be anxiety provoking, it may eventually develop into a very rewarding and enriching experience. A sample syllabus of the course is provided in Exhibit 6.1.

When possible, practicum and internship students are expected to make recordings of actual counseling sessions. Video recordings are preferable because they allow students to observe nonverbal components of the session, as well as

---

**EXHIBIT 6.1   Sample Syllabus**

---

**Public State University Spring 20XX**
**Graduate Mental Health Counseling Program**
**Department of Educational Leadership and Counseling**

**Professor:** John Doe, PhD, LMHC, ACS

**Office:** 328 D Academic Complex

**E-mail:** professor@counseling.edu

**Phone:** (123) 456-7890 (office)

(123) 456-7890 (home)

**Office Hours:** M 1:00–3:00 p.m.
W 2:00–4:00 p.m.
Th. 1:00–3:00 p.m.
*Or by appointment*

**Course Number and Title**
EDU 679: Mental Health Practicum
Wednesday 4:20–7:05 p.m.
Office # 112

**Catalog Description**
This course is designed to provide graduate counseling students with an introduction to professional issues in mental health practice (counseling, critiquing peers, consultation, professional issues, ethics, etc.) and in preparation for the subsequent counseling internships (EDU 685, EDU 686, and EDU 678). Students will be placed in a counseling setting for a minimum of 100 clock hours and will have weekly group seminars. This course also incorporates the ethical standards of the American Counseling Association ([ACA] www.counseling.org) and those of the American Mental Health Counselors Association ([AMHCA] www.amhca.org). Canadian students may wish to consult the Canadian Counseling Association ([CCA] www.cca.org). Students are also expected to gain relative skills, especially in the realm of consultation with other mental health professionals. Practicum and Internship classes are based upon CACREP standards (www.cacrep.org).

**Textbook**
Hodges, S. (2016). *The counseling practicum and internship manual: A resource for graduate counseling students* (2nd ed.). New York, NY: Springer Publishing Company.

**Educational Philosophy**
The constructivist framework of the graduate Mental Health Counseling program forms the basis for all courses. EDU 679 (Mental Health Counseling Practicum) serves as a foundational class for mental health counselors, including professional roles and identity, a focus on the American Counseling Association's (ACA's) *Code of Ethics and Standards of Practice*. The University Mental Health Counseling program also follows the requirements of the Council for Accreditation of Counseling and Related Educational Programs (CACREP). The eight CACREP core areas are listed as follows:

Professional Identity: *Addressed in EDU 679.*
Social and Cultural Diversity: *Addressed in EDU 679.*

*(continued)*

---

**EXHIBIT 6.1    Sample Syllabus (*continued*)**

---

Human Growth and Development: *Addressed in EDU 679.*
Career Development: *Not addressed in EDU 679.*
Helping Relationships: *Addressed in EDU 679.*
Group Work: May be addressed for the individual student depending on the
    practicum site.
Assessment: *Addressed in EDU 679.*
Research and Program Evaluation: *Not addressed in EDU 679.*

**Course Objectives and Requirements**

- Demonstrate skills in individual/group/relationship counseling using appropriate theoretical and practical perspectives.
- Demonstrate knowledge of professional ethical standards as defined by the ACA and the American Mental Health Counselors Association (AMHCA). Apply knowledge of ethical and legal perspectives to relevant counseling situations.
- Recognize and respond appropriately to professional limitations.
- Become familiar with community resources and know when and where to refer clients.
- Learn the value of providing and receiving professional consultation regarding counseling individuals, couples, families, and groups.
- Learn to give and receive feedback in the seminar format.
- Follow established professional and ethical guidelines regarding counseling multicultural and diverse client populations.
- Weekly attendance in seminar. *More than two absences will result in an unsatisfactory (U) grade. An unsatisfactory grade requires the student to wait until the following year to repeat EDU 679.*
- Read assigned chapters in text and be ready to discuss in the seminar format.
- *A score of 70% or higher on the final ethics examination is also required before a student may progress to EDU 685. The final is based on ethical and legal issues through readings in the text and in-class discussion.*
- *Students must also receive a satisfactory evaluation in their practicum placement to move to Internship I (EDU 685).*
- *Video of a taped 30-minute session with a classroom partner or a client in a professional setting.* Students may counsel from a person-centered, cognitive behavioral, solution-focused, integrative, and so on, framework. In addition, each video will be preceded using the SOAP/*DSM-5* and intake form in your *Mental Health Counseling (MHC) Handbook.* In practicum, the mock video sessions will not be graded. Next semester in Internship I (EDU 685), mock sessions will be graded.
- Learn the nuances of consultation with counselors, other mental health professionals, human services agencies, and law enforcement.
- *All students must provide proof of student liability insurance prior to beginning practicum.* Additionally, students must maintain student liability insurance throughout internship.

**Methods of Instruction**
Weekly sessions will be organized using a seminar approach. It is expected that students will have read and are prepared to discuss previously assigned material (i.e., text). Students will be expected to communicate their experiences in the practicum setting to other students and faculty. Feedback from others in the practicum will enhance students' perceptions and facilitate learning new approaches to counseling. Students will also present a videotape of a role-played counseling session to others in the practicum for

(*continued*)

---

**EXHIBIT 6.1   Sample Syllabus (*continued*)**

feedback on the use of counseling skills. The professor will use the session rating form on p. 27 of the *MHC Handbook*.

**Outline of Course**

| CLASS MEETING DATE | ACTIVITIES |
|---|---|
| Week 1 | Introduction to practicum. Schedule videotape presentations. Textbook information. |
| Week 2 | Read Chapters 1, 2, and 3. Video: Ethical and Legal Issues. |
| Week 3 | Read Chapter 4: Client welfare. |
| Week 4 | View professional video and critique. |
| Week 5 | Student videotape presentation. Read Chapters 5 and 6: Confidentiality, and Records and Subpoenas. |
| Week 6 | Student videotape presentation. Read Chapter 7: Competence and Malpractice. |
| Week 7 | Student videotape presentation. Read Chapter 8: Boundary Issues. |
| Week 8 | Student videotape presentation. Read Chapters 9 and 10: Families and Groups. |
| Week 9 | Student videotape presentation. Read Chapter 11: Evaluation, Testing, and Diagnosis. |
| Week 10 | Student videotape presentation. Read Chapter 12: Private Practice. |
| Week 11 | Student videotape presentation. Read Chapter 13: Technology and Health Care. |
| Week 12 | Student videotape presentation. Read Chapter 15: Supervision and Consultation. |
| Week 13 | View/critique professional counseling videotape. Read Chapter 17: Resolving Ethical and Legal Issues. |
| Week 14 | Last class. Ethics examination. |

**Grading**
The final grade (*S, U,* or *I*) will be determined by class attendance (no more than two absences); a passing score on the ethics examination (70 and above is passing); satisfactory performance on videotapes; and feedback from the students, on-site supervisor evaluation, and the university professor. Satisfactory performance in all the aforementioned areas will result in a grade of satisfactory (*S*). A deficient mark in any of the previously mentioned areas will result in a grade of unsatisfactory (*U*). A *U* grade would result in the student retaking EDU 679 the following year.

**Checklist**

- Satisfactory evaluation by site supervisor and evaluation of supervisor (turn in by final class, December 3).
- Passing the ethics examination (grade of 70 or higher).
- No more than two classroom absences.

(*continued*)

---

**EXHIBIT 6.1 Sample Syllabus (*continued*)**

- Satisfactory performance on videotape—not graded, but demonstrating a basic ability to create a therapeutic environment.
- Must turn in practicum timesheet (see pp. 35–36 in *MHC Handbook*). Turn in by final class.

**Bibliography**

American Counseling Association. (2014). *The ACA code of ethics*. Alexandria, VA: Author.
Herlihy, B., & Corey, G. (2015). *ACA ethical standards casebook* (7th ed.). Alexandria, VA: American Counseling Association.
Wheeler, A. M., & Bertram, B. (2015). *The counselor and the law: A guide to legal and ethical education* (7th ed.). Alexandria, VA: American Counseling Association.

---

give everyone in the class a concrete picture of how the counselor-in-training conducted the session. Unfortunately, during the past several years, placements (at least in my area) seem to be more restrictive regarding allowing practicum and internship students to record sessions. Many programs have been forced to work around such a restriction by having students' record mock sessions with a supervisor. This restriction regarding prohibiting on-site recordings is very unfortunate given counselors-in-training are an important part of this country's mental health treatment. In fact, judging by the Bureau of Labor Statistics, counselors, particularly mental health counselors, addictions counselors, and others, are among the fastest growing mental health professions (Bureau of Labor Statistics, 2015). Such curtailment likely is due to liability concerns on the part of schools and agencies.

There are several procedures to follow when recording client sessions. The *ACA Code of Ethics* (American Counseling Association [ACA], 2014, Section B.6.c) states that clients must be informed when recordings are being made and must give their consent to the process prior to recording the session. Although no legal or ethical requirement stipulates that permission be given in writing, standard practice generally includes written forms of consent. Programs, students and counselors would be wise to follow such practice (Remley & Herlihy, 2014). Exhibit 6.2 shows a sample permission-to-record form.

Students must also understand that information stored on a DVD, Flash drive, or any other device must be kept in a secure setting and then erased after it has been reviewed by the clinical supervisor and/or the practicum/internship class (Wheeler & Bertram, 2015). *Note*: Be careful not to leave sensitive recorded material in unsecure locations. Unless your agency (and you) have an encrypted site, you may put you and your clients at risk. As more and more clinicians utilize technology for counseling and additional clinical services secure software becomes even more critical. Having made this statement, however, I often am flummoxed at hearing counselor, counselor educators, and counseling supervisors bemoan lack of security in advanced technology when many likely

---

**EXHIBIT 6.2    Client Permission to Record Counseling Session for Supervision Purposes**

I/We, _____ hereby grant permission for our counselor to videotape/ audiotape (circle appropriate recording choice) our counseling session on the following date(s):._____

I/We understand that the purpose of this recording is for the clinical supervision of my/our counselor's work. I/We provide for the following people to view the recording:

_____ (Supervisor)

_____ (Practicum/Internship Group)

The above-named persons will also hold the information on the recording confidential. The recording will be erased after the supervisor has reviewed it.

_____    Date: _____
Client Signature

_____
Client Signature

_____
Client Signature

**Parental/Guardian Permission to Record Session Form**
The graduate counseling program at Northern State University conducts a practicum and internship course for the purpose of training future professional counselors. The practicum/internship class is an advanced course requirement of all degree candidates in Northern State University's graduate counseling program. Graduate students in the counseling program are required to record counseling sessions as part of their professional training and development and to be of more assistance to the clients they counsel. The counseling sessions conducted with your child will be reviewed by the student counselor's faculty supervisor (or, in some cases, the supervisor at this site) and a small group of graduate students in the practicum/internship. The faculty supervisor, on-site supervisor, and graduate counseling students are all held to confidentiality and the contents of this recording will not be revealed beyond the course. Once the recording has been played, it will be erased. By signing this form, you give permission for your child to be recorded. Thank you for your cooperation in this important matter.

Parent's/Guardian's name _____

Student Counselor's Signature _____

Date: _____ / _____ / _____

---

think nothing of disclosing sensitive information to a colleague through the telephone, a medium scarcely secure! Regardless, take reasonable precautions to secure recordings and counseling through the medium of technology.

You should review your recording prior to presenting it in class. For counseling students in agencies, generally programs require students to complete an intake form with a Mental Status Examination or Mini-Mental Status Examination, diagnostic form, and SOAP (subjective, objective, assessment, plan) or DAP (data, assessment, plan) case note form regarding the session (see Chapters 4 and 5 for examples of some of these forms), plus a *Diagnostic and Statistical Manual of Mental Disorders*, fifth edition (*DSM-5*; American Psychiatric Association, 2013) diagnosis (if at an agency), and sample treatment plan. These materials will provide you with a format for tying the case together, and will give the rest of the class an organized context of the client's presenting issues, ongoing struggles, counselor observations, and prognosis for treatment. Counseling students in school settings generally will complete more developmental and less "clinical" forms. School counseling forms might include a school-based intake form, possibly with an orientation-times-five questionnaire (e.g., "Who are you?"; "Where are you?"; Who is your father/mother?"; "Why are we talking?"; What day is it?"), grade point average, career/vocational issues, supports, family, and so forth.

## MODELS OF SUPERVISION AND CRITIQUE

There are numerous models of counselor education and supervision (Benshoff, 1993; Borders, 1991). In counselor education programs, supervision serves the dual purposes of monitoring counselors'-in-training performance as well as monitoring the well-being of clients receiving services from graduate counseling students (*ACA Code of Ethics*, 2014, Standard F.1.a). Professional research in counselor supervision recognizes that there are two types of supervision—administrative and clinical (Borders & Leddick, 1987). Administrative supervision focuses on administrators providing supervision to counselors and other employees in an agency, a school, a hospital, and so forth. Clinical supervision, on the other hand, is the process where mental health professionals review the clinical work of counselors or counselors-in-training with the goal of facilitating counselor effectiveness. In this text as well as in counselor education programs, the focus will be on clinical as opposed to administrative supervision. Naturally, counseling students will receive on-site supervision from a licensed counselor, social worker, psychologist, certified school counselor, and so on. Counseling students also receive weekly supervision and training from a faculty member so that supervision and training can be comprehensive.

Borders (1991) advocated an instructional model involving goal setting, reading, and discussion of journal articles, case presentations, and review and critique of counseling sessions by peers and faculty. In this approach, students specify questions they would like addressed and the types of feedback they are seeking. Then, each student presents a recording, which is critiqued by the professor and students in the class. (In this approach, all members of the class will critique the student presenting the case.) Naturally, different students will have different reactions: one student may focus on the nonverbal behavior of the client, whereas another will attend to the content. Some will focus more on specific techniques used and others will be more concerned with whether the counselor paid enough attention to the affective domain. Students might approach the presentation from various orientations: humanistic, cognitive behavioral, or client centered, for example.

During the critique, the supervisor monitors the discussion to clarify the student's comments and to ensure that the feedback is constructive. The student being critiqued can also ask questions to enhance his or her understanding of the intention of the comments and to seek clarification. The supervisor also sets the stage by explaining the approach, appropriate feedback style, as well as modeling how to receive feedback. Another variation is the Structured Group Supervision Model (SGSM) developed by Wilbur, Roberts-Wilbur, Morris, Betz, and Hart (1991). The SGSM uses five phases:

1. The request for assistance statement: In this phase, students may seek support for personal growth, technical skills, and better understanding of the therapeutic process.
2. The questioning period and identification of focus: Students take turns questioning the student presenter.
3. The feedback statements: In this phase, group members may offer feedback related to the session with the intent of assisting the student counselor's continued development. Wilbur et al. (1991) suggest that during this phase the student remains silent and focuses entirely on receiving the feedback. Wilbur et al. also point out that the "silence" reduces the possibility of a defensive response. Group members are instructed to offer critique in the form of statements such as "If this were my client ..." or "What I might do ...."
4. A pause period: Perhaps the most innovative aspect of the SGSM is the pause phase. Following the feedback, there is period of 10 to 15 minutes (5–10 minutes may be a more realistic time frame in some classes) during which the supervisee is encouraged to reflect on the critique while the class takes a short break.
5. An optional discussion period: After the break, the group reassembles and the supervisee responds to the feedback. These reflections may involve comments on the feedback, insights gained from the critique, how the comments were helpful, and what he or she might do differently the next time he or she sees the client.

Other practicum supervisors may be more informal and use a less structured approach to assessment. Many will use a round-robin format where each peer in the class will critique the student counselor. The student being critiqued is not held to silence as in the SGSM, and may ask clarifying questions. The faculty supervisor is generally the last to provide feedback, so as not to unduly influence the student critique.

With any feedback approach used, the instructor would be prudent to explain the nature of feedback at the onset of the semester, and then models appropriate styles of critique (e.g., commenting on the counseling approach and effectiveness versus making a personal criticism). The instructor should also avoid interrupting the feedback to empower students providing feedback. The goal of feedback is twofold: to provide an opportunity for the student counselor to stretch his or her counseling skills and to enhance students' development in providing critique.

## WRITTEN FEEDBACK

After the class discussion, a session rating scale or critique form may be used by students and/or the faculty supervisor to rate the student counselor's effectiveness.

Naturally, the critique form cannot address all areas of the therapeutic encounter, but provides a brief analysis of the relative effectiveness of the student counselor. Exhibit 6.3 shows a sample session rating form. Many schools and agencies serving as practicum and internship settings will have their own critique form.

---

**EXHIBIT 6.3   Student Counseling Session Rating Form**

Date: _____ / _____ / _____

Student: _____     Evaluator: _____

Audiotape: _____     DVD/Videotape: _____     In-Class Role Play: _____

Brief Summary of Session Content: _____

_____

_____

_____

Specific Criteria:                                                Rating (1 = *Least*; 5 = *Best*)

1. Opening:                                                      1  2  3  4  5
Was informed consent thorough and professional? Was confidentiality covered?

2. Rapport:                                                     1  2  3  4  5
Did the counselor establish a good therapeutic alliance (e.g., voice tone, appropriate eye contact, paraphrasing, summarizing)?

3. Attending Skill:                                            1  2  3  4  5
Did the counselor use minimal encouragers and refrain from unnecessary interruptions? Additionally, was the counselor skilled in using therapeutic silence?

4. Open-Ended Questioning:                                     1  2  3  4  5
Did the counselor make appropriate use of open-ended questions?

5. Affective Domain:                                           1  2  3  4  5
Did the counselor demonstrate appropriate empathy?

6. Challenging/Confrontation:                                  1  2  3  4  5
Did the counselor confront the client (if the situation warranted it)?

---

*(continued)*

---

**EXHIBIT 6.3   Student Counseling Session Rating Form (*continued*)**

7.  Solution Skills:                                            1   2   3   4   5

Did the counselor offer appropriate solution-seeking input (through techniques such as the Empty Chair, Miracle Question, Role Plays, etc.)?

8.  Cultural Issues:                                            1   2   3   4   5

Did the counselor appear to understand and respect cultural issues?

9.  Goal Setting:                                              1   2   3   4   5

Did the counselor set effective goals for a follow-up session?

10. Closing:                                                   1   2   3   4   5

Was closing well-orchestrated? Or, was it too abrupt?

11. On the following 1 to 10 scale, how effective was the student counselor in facilitating the counseling session? (1 = *least effective*, 10 = *most effective*) Circle the appropriate number:

        1     2     3     4     5     6     7     8     9     10

12. What the student did best during this session was:

_____

_____

_____

13. Regarding this session, what the student most needs to improve on is:

_____

_____

_____

14. Constructive comments for the student counselor's continued development:

_____

_____

_____

_____

Signature of Evaluator

## OFFERING FEEDBACK TO PEERS

As part of practicum/internship (and throughout your counseling career) you will be involved in critiquing counselor effectiveness and offering suggestions for improvement. Until now, you may not have had much opportunity to hone your feedback skills and will likely need coaching from your instructor and on-site supervisor. Student critiques often run a continuum from overly critical to too vague to overly positive. Overly negative feedback can impinge on a student counselor's confidence, whereas uncritical positive comments provide little educational value. An instructor must strive to create an environment where honest and critical comments are given and received. This latter point requires a deft touch on the part of the supervisor and an open perspective on the part of the student. Supervisors will need to provide constructive feedback while realizing even positive comments may elicit an undesired reaction from a student. It's worth expressing, therefore, that supervision also is a work-in-progress on the part of the supervisor.

Kadushin (1985) offered guidelines for supervisors to follow when critiquing counseling students' work. These guidelines stress the importance of giving feedback that is specific, timely, focused on concrete behaviors, descriptive rather than judgmental, focused on the behaviors of the student rather than his or her personal characteristics, phrased in the form of tentative statements rather than authoritative conclusions, focused on positive issues, and, finally, selective rather than a laundry list. Consider the following example:

> **Unhelpful feedback:** "Hector, I think you need to engage the client more."
> (Too vague. How could Hector "engage" the client? Be specific.)
> **Helpful feedback:** "Hector, I think a specific way you could engage the client in the session might be to ask more open-ended questions such as, 'How could you begin to create healthy friendships?' Or, 'What could you do right now to establish a functional relationship with your father?'" (The feedback in this example was targeted and specific.)

Students in a practicum or internship also receive weekly clinical supervision at their placement from an experienced, licensed, or properly credentialed supervisor. These supervision meetings are designed to target specific issues related to the student counselor's performance at the agency or school. The supervisor's critique will generally focus on the following questions:

- Is the student counselor able to establish the therapeutic relationship?
- Is the student counselor able to set realistic goals with the client?
- What struggles does the student counselor appear to be having?
- How well does the student counselor facilitate therapeutic change during sessions?
- Does the student counselor understand his or her professional ethics? Can he or she use them effectively in session?
- Is the student counselor able to receive constructive feedback and incorporate it into improving his or her counseling skills?

## Supervisory Style

There are various supervisory methods to use with practicum/internship students. The type of supervision provided will mostly depend on the orientation of the on-site clinical supervisor. Although numerous studies have been conducted on the effectiveness of supervision on counselor development, no evidence supports one methodology as being superior to another (Granello & Granello, 2007). Interestingly, only once in my entire counseling career has anyone ever asked me, "What is your theoretical supervision style?" This question was asked of me at an interview for a faculty position in counselor education, not in a treatment facility. But, when you become a supervisor, be prepared to articulate a supervision style. In fact, my belief is that most supervisors in the field would likely be stumped at such a question. Probably your field supervisor has developed his or her own style after several years of experience in both being supervised and providing supervision. Most supervisors are likely influenced most by the person who supervised them during their graduate school training or an influential supervisor when they were newly minted counselors or other therapists.

### *Examples of Clinical Supervision Styles*
### Bernard's Discrimination Model

One of the most commonly employed and researched supervision models is the Discrimination Model, originally published by Bernard (Bernard & Goodyear, 2009). The discrimination model is composed of three separate foci for supervision (i.e., intervention, conceptualization, and consultant) and three possible supervision roles (i.e., teacher, counselor, and consultant). The supervisor could, in any given moment, respond from one of nine ways (three roles × three foci) (Bernard & Goodyear, 2009). For instance, the supervisor may take on the role of teacher while focusing on a specific intervention used by the supervisee in the client session, or the role of counselor while focusing on the supervisee's conceptualization of the work. Because the response is always specific to the supervisee's needs, it changes within and across sessions.

The supervisor first evaluates the supervisee's ability within the focus area, and then selects the appropriate role from which to respond. Bernard and Goodyear (2009) caution supervisors not to respond from the same focus or role out of personal preference, comfort, or habit, but instead to ensure the focus and role meet the most salient needs of the supervisee in that moment. Supervisors utilizing the discrimination model must be very organized and mindful regarding the supervisory relationship and be clear as to what role they are "playing" out with the supervisee.

### Psychodynamic Approach to Supervision

Psychodynamic supervision is based upon Freud's model of transference and countertransference (Frawley-O'Dea & Sarnat, 2001). Frawley-O'Dea and Sarnat (2001) further classify psychodynamic supervision into three categories: patient-centered, supervisee-centered, and supervisory-matrix-centered.

Patient-centered, based on Freud's model, focuses the supervision session on the patient's issues and behaviors. The supervisor assumes a didactic role with the goal of assisting the supervisee to understand and treat the patient. The supervisor is viewed as a dispassionate expert and thus an authority figure. As long as the supervisee agrees with the supervisor, little conflict is inherent (Smith, 2009). Given that the psychodynamic supervisor is posited as an authority figure, some supervisees may have difficulty voicing disagreement particularly if they are struggling with confidence—something not unusual with beginning counselors. Likely, most counseling students are not under supervision from a psychodynamic supervisor (though some practicum and internship students may well be supervised by such, especially in large urban areas).

Supervisee-centered supervision, which focuses on the content and process of the supervisee's experience, became popular in the 1950s (Bernard & Goodyear, 2009). The supervisor's uninvolved, authority role remains the same, but as attention is transferred to the supervisee's experience as a counselor, the approach becomes more experiential than didactic (Bernard & Goodyear, 2009). Still, as the supervisor remains the distant authority figure, the supervisee remains in the position of the "inferior." Proponents of psychodynamic-based supervision would point out that all supervisors would be the authority figure regardless of the supervision model utilized. While this point is true (or should be), the model may lend itself to scrutiny more than a process-oriented conversation.

The supervisory-matrix-centered approach differs in that in addition to focusing on the client, it also addresses the supervisor–supervisee relationship. No longer is the supervisor an austere, uninvolved expert. The relationship is very relational with the supervisor expected to actively participate in establishing a two-way conversation with the supervisee (Frawley-O'Dea & Sarnat, 2001). The relationship also involves an examination of parallel process, defined as the "supervisee's interaction with the supervisor that parallels the client's behavior with the supervisee as the therapist" (Haynes, Corey, & Moulton, 2003).

## Feminist Model of Supervision

Feminist theory asserts that an individual's experiences are reflective of society's dominant values, attitudes, and opinions (Brown & Brodsky, 1992). Feminist counselors view the client's experience within the context of society. Thus, anxiety, depression, bipolar disorder, and so forth, may be viewed as a consequence of an oppressive society (Brown & Brodsky, 1992). Many feminist counselors are ardently opposed to the DSM as a tool of a patriarchal society (Haynes et al., 2003).

Feminist supervisors then may counsel the supervisee to acknowledge power differentials in the client–counselor relationship and encourage the supervisee to understand the role of privilege. Given that the supervisor holds a position of power over the supervisee, the relationship may form grounds for more collaborative discussions, at least to the extent possible. Feminist supervisors may also focus on empowerment of the supervisee and in turn facilitate the counselor's working to empower clients, many of whom may live along the margins of society as disempowered individuals, couples, and families. Feminist models of supervision have become more popular in recent years (Haynes et al., 2003).

## Integrated Developmental Model

The Integrated Developmental Model (IDM) of supervision developed by Stoltenberg (1981) and Stoltenberg and Delworth (1987), and later by Stoltenberg, McNeill, and Delworth (1998), is a popular and well-researched supervision model (Smith, 2009). The IDM describes three levels of counselor development:

> Level 1: Supervisees are generally entry-level students who are high in motivation, but also high in anxiety and fearful of evaluation.
> Level 2: Supervisees are at mid-level and experience fluctuating confidence and motivation, often linking their own mood to success with clients.
> Level 3: Supervisees are essentially secure, stable in motivation, have accurate empathy tempered by objectivity, and use therapeutic self in intervention. (Falender & Shafranske, 2004)

The IDM emphasizes the need for the supervisor to select skills and interventions appropriate to the level of the supervisee. When supervising a level-1 supervisee, the supervisor would want to balance the supervisee's anxiety and dependence by a display of support and direction. If supervising a level-3 supervisee, the supervisor would emphasize autonomy and engage in a more constructivist discussion. The critical factor in IDM is matching feedback with the supervisee's appropriate level, otherwise the supervisee may feel either overwhelmed or restricted. A supervisor who refuses to engage in more parallel conversation with a level-3 supervisee is likely to encounter a high degree of frustration and resistance. Likewise, a supervisor who expects autonomous behavior from a level-1 supervisee likely will increase the supervisee's anxiety.

The IDM has become a popular supervision model and offers many advantages, especially in breaking down supervisees into working stages of development, as such may make sense to supervisees. IDM, however, does have weaknesses as it focuses predominantly on the development of graduate students in training and pays little attention to postdegree supervision (Smith, 2009). Furthermore, IDM presents few suggestions for specific supervision models that are applicable at each specific supervisee level (Haynes et al., 2003). An alternative development model developed by Ronnestad and Skovholt (1993, 2003) addresses IDM's initial weaknesses by providing a framework to describe counselor development.

## Ronnestad and Skovholt's Supervision Model

The Ronnestad and Skovholt model is based on a longitudinal qualitative study conducted by interviewing 100 counselors/therapists, ranging in experience from graduate students to professional counselors/therapists with a mean of 25 years of counseling experience (Ronnestad & Skovholt, 1993). Ronnestad and Skovholt analyzed data and developed a stage model, a theme model, and a professional model of development and stagnation (Ronnestad & Skovholt, 2003). The first three phases (The Lay Helper, The Beginning Student Phase, and The Advanced Student Phase) essentially correspond with the levels of the IDM (Smith, 2009). The remaining phases (The Novice Professional Phrase, The Experienced Professional Phase, and The Senior Professional Phase) are self-explanatory in terms of the relative occurrence of the phase in relation to the counselor's career.

In addition to the phase model, Ronnestad and Skovholt's (2003) research enumerated 14 themes of counselor development. They are as follows:

1. Professional development involves an increasing higher-order integration of the professional self and the personal self.
2. The focus of functioning shifts dramatically over time from internal to external to internal.
3. Continuous reflection is a prerequisite for optimal learning and development at all levels of experience.
4. An intense commitment to learn propels the developmental process.
5. The cognitive map changes: Beginning practitioners rely on external expertise, seasoned practitioners rely on internal expertise.
6. Professional development is a long, slow, continuous process that can also be erratic.
7. Professional development is a life-long process.
8. Many beginning practitioners experience much anxiety in their professional work. Over time, anxiety is mastered by most.
9. Clients serve as a major source of influence and serve as primary teachers.
10. Personal life influences professional functioning and development throughout the professional life span.
11. Interpersonal sources of influence propel professional development more than "impersonal" sources of influence.
12. New members of the field view professional elders and graduate training with strong affective reactions.
13. Extensive experience with suffering contributes to heightened recognition, acceptance and appreciation of human variability.
14. For the practitioner there is a realignment from self as hero to client as hero.

(Adapted from Ronnestad & Skovholt, 2003)

Ronnestad and Skovholt (2003) conclude that counselor development is a complex process requiring continuous self-reflection. They also conclude that, much like the counselor–client therapeutic alignment's robust influence on treatment outcomes, their results suggest a "close and reciprocal relationship between how counselors/therapists handle challenges and difficulties in the client relationship and experiences of professional growth or stagnation" (p. 40).

### Cognitive Behavioral Supervision

Just as cognitive behavioral therapy (CBT) has become a very popular approach to counseling, cognitive behavioral supervision is likewise common (Haynes et al., 2003; Beck, Wright, Newman, & Liese, 1993). Cognitive behavioral supervision makes use of tangible thoughts and behaviors, particularly that of the supervisee's professional identity and his or her reaction to the client (Haynes et al., 2003). Cognitive behavioral techniques used in supervision include setting an agenda for supervision sessions, bridging from previous sessions, assigning homework to the supervisee, and capsule summaries by the supervisor (Beck et al., 1993). The supervisor–supervisee relationship is akin to that of teacher–student and though it is collaborative, it is directive with the supervisor leading.

### Person-Centered Supervision

Carl Rogers developed person-centered therapy with the belief that the client has the capacity to effectively resolve life problems without interpretation and direction from the counselor (Corey, 2013). Similarly, person-centered supervision assumes that the supervisee has the resources to develop effectively as a counselor. The supervisor then is not viewed as an "expert" in the person-centered model but rather an experienced collaborator. The supervisor's role is to establish an environment whereby the supervisee can be open to the supervision experience in order to develop fully as a clinician (Lambers, 2000).

### Solution-Focused Supervision

Solution-focused brief therapy was developed as a therapeutic approach in the 1980s by de Shazer (1985). As the name suggests, the approach focuses on being brief and focusing on solutions as opposed to a focus on problems. Therapeutic attention is devoted to building on the client's idea of a future goal and discovering the inner resources needed in order to achieve this goal (de Shazer, 1985).

Solution-focused supervision lends itself well to clinical supervision as well as in counseling as its interventions are easily transferrable to clinical supervision encounters. The following constructivist questions might be utilized in supervision:

- "So, how were you able to help the client improve his or her mood?"
- "How were you able to gain confidence this past semester?"
- "What have you learned about yourself during your practicum/internship/job?"
- "What would you cite as your clinical strengths?"

When addressing the supervisee's strengths, resources, and skills, the supervisor adopts the persona of the curious inquirer. For example, asking how the supervisee managed a particular situation despite challenges enables the supervisor to acknowledge his or her ability to identify skills utilized in order to identify the particular solution.

One of the solution-focused staples is the Miracle Question. Regarding a focus on specific goals, the supervisee may be asked, "If you went to sleep tonight and a miracle occurred related to your confidence as a counselor (or any issues of concern) where you were more confident, how would your work as a counselor be different? What would you notice? What would I notice?" The

Miracle Question provides the format for the supervisee to drop anxiety and speculate on future success (Kim Berg & Szabo, 2005).

Subsequent supervision sessions focus on solutions rather than problems. Soliciting, "What has improved?" at the onset of a supervision session, as opposed to "How are things?" encourages the supervisee to focus on their clinical growth. At the conclusion of the supervisory session, the supervisor summarizes the supervisee's strengths, skills, and improvement. The solution-focused supervisor provides feedback based upon the supervisee's choice of language. Thus, the importance of active listening coupled with constructivist-type responses is highly emphasized. The following suggestions are offered regarding solution-focused supervision:

■ Utilization of active listening to what the supervisee is saying. (Example: "I hear you saying you are concerned about this client's ongoing depression.")

■ Using constructivist-type responses to assist the supervisee identify strengths, skills, and inner resources. (Example: "If you could bring that client into the supervision session right now, what might you say to him or her now?")

■ Using encouragement by actively demonstrating interest and encouraging a more collegial supervisory relationship, though not an equal one. (Example: "You are making a good effort with this recovery group. Now, here's something to think of for the next session ....")

■ Citing and naming specific supervisee strengths, skills, and resources. (Example: "You have made a lot of progress in confronting relapse.")

■ Use of scaling questions to assist the supervisee in measuring clinical growth. (Example: "On a scale of 1 to 10, with 10 high, how would you rate your counseling skill at this point?")

The goal of a solution-focused supervisory approach to clinical supervision is to enhance the supervisee's experience and lessen his or her degree of anxiety, thus enhancing the likelihood the supervisee will develop more confidence and competence. As the solution-focused supervision approach is more collegial, supervisees may report feeling less anxiety during supervision sessions. It is also likely, however, that some supervisees may find an "over focus" on strengths limiting and may at times prefer explicit criticism. Research on the solution-focused supervision model is not as extensive as more established models and more research is needed in this area of the clinical supervision literature.

## Systems Approach to Supervision

In the systems approach to supervision, the crux of the supervision relationship targets mutual involvement of both parties (Holloway, 1995). Holloway describes seven dimensions of supervision: (a) central supervisory relationship, (b) functions of supervision, (c) tasks of supervision, (d) the client, (e) trainee, (f) supervisor, and (g) the institution. The functions and tasks of supervision are at the foreground of interaction, while the latter four dimensions represent unique contextual factors that, according to Holloway, are covert influences in the supervisory process. Supervision in any particular instance is viewed as reflective of a unique combination of these seven dimensions (Smith, 2009). Thus, a systems approach to supervision covers multiple levels related to the various intersecting "systems" in which the supervisee and client exist. Examples of systems may be schools, businesses, correctional institutions, religious institutions, cultures, families, and so forth.

### Supervision Styles

You may discover that your field site supervisor may have a radically different style than the one supervising your classmate. Some on-site supervisors are quite formal and require a student to tape an entire session. Others will listen to a brief segment of a tape, or none at all. Some supervisors will ask students to work on a particular skill, such as delivering confrontation or using a particular intervention. Supervisors vary greatly across the continuum of styles, opinions, theoretical approaches to counseling, and in how they deliver feedback (i.e., constructivist versus overtly negative in feedback).

It is clear that in the supervisor–student relationship, the power differential rests with the on-site supervisor. Thus, students must become facile in negotiating a delicate balance of appearing open to critique and at the same time developing appropriate assertiveness. Openness to critique would involve listening to feedback that may be critical. The assertiveness aspect of the student's role would be to ask for clarification if he or she was unclear about the message. Consider this example:

| | |
|---|---|
| **Supervisor:** | I need you to work on the treatment plan more, okay? |
| **Practicum student:** | I would like to do that. What specifically could I do to improve my performance in this area? |

If you do not know what your supervisor is suggesting, or if he or she seems vague (such as in the given situation), seek clarity by asking questions. Good supervisors will appreciate your initiative. Granted, there are poor supervisors out there and some of you will have the misfortune of working under them. Having a poor supervisor, however, also provides you the opportunity to learn to deal effectively with such professionals as you will encounter them in your career. When you do get a supervisor who seems to be a poor communicator, is overly critical, sloppy, or seems burned out, you need to find a "safe" area to debrief this. Safe areas could include other practicum or internship students and fellow graduate students in your counseling program.

If you believe your supervisor is incompetent or unethical (as opposed to merely ineffective), your first step would be to talk with your faculty advisor or the coordinator of practicum/internship placement (ethical issues are discussed in Chapter 3). Your advisor would then need to dialogue with your on-site supervisor or the director of the setting in which you have been placed. In many cases, a healthier relationship can be established, although, in some instances, you will likely be assigned a new supervisor. It is also possible that you may need a new placement, although that should be a last resort. It has also been my experience that in most cases (although not all), addressing conflicts with your supervisor paves the way for a more trusting and respectful relationship.

## Site Supervisor as Mentor

You need to develop a strong rapport with your on-site supervisor, as he or she will not only be writing an evaluation of your performance, but will also serve as the natural contact for clinical advice. The following statement is one you need to remember when faced with ethical, legal, moral, or other dilemmas that occur at your placement site: When in doubt, always contact your supervisor at the soonest possible time. This will save both you and your supervisor much anxiety.

Not all questions or concerns are ethical ones. In fact, it is likely most of your questions will turn out to be operational in nature. Operational concerns relate to the ways the placement site carries out treatment, its rules, chain of command, professional orientation of its staff (psychologist, counselor, social worker, etc.), whether the setting holds one of the various accreditations, and so forth. In my more than 20-year experience with practicum and internship placements, most student concerns and conflicts fell into this latter category. Besides paying careful attention to whatever orientation your site provides, you will want to develop your own checklist of questions to ask your on-site supervisor:

- What types of training and professional development are provided to practicum/internship students (many practicum/internship sites will train or send students to training in various techniques, treatment models, etc.)?
- What types of resources are available to practicum/internship students (computers, access to a library, research opportunities, etc.)?
- How are client or patient records kept (online, written and locked in a secure file, etc.)?
- What are the policies regarding taping client sessions (some organizations tape all client sessions and require clients to sign a waiver as part of consent to treatment)?
- What are the emergency procedures in the event of a crisis (e.g., hostage situation; an assault at the setting; death of a client, patient, or staff member; suicide attempt)?
- Although you are a counselor-in-training, your supervisor (or most staff) may be a psychologist. Which code of ethics will you need to know?
- Has your placement informed you of how to address an allegation of sexual harassment, child abuse or endangerment, communicable disease, or any mandated reporting issue?

These questions represent a beginning point; as you proceed through your practicum and internship, you will likely come up with many more questions. Keep your smartphone or a notebook handy so when you have questions and concerns you can write them down. It is also worth mentioning that no policy manual, no matter how thick and comprehensive, can possibly address all contingencies. So, be smart and proactive by keeping notes and asking pertinent questions. Your supervisor will likely be impressed at your initiative. If he or she is not, you may wish to consider whether the setting is the right one for you.

# REFERENCES

American Counseling Association. (2014). *ACA code of ethics.* Alexandria, VA: Author.

American Psychiatric Association. (2013). *Diagnostic and statistical manual of mental disorders* (5th ed.). Arlington, VA: Author.

Beck, A. T., Wright, F. D., Newman, C. F., & Liese, B. S. (1993). *Cognitive therapy of substance abuse.* New York, NY: Guilford Press.

Benshoff, J. M. (1993). Peer supervision in counselor training. *Clinical Supervisor, 11,* 89–102.

Bernard, J. M., & Goodyear, R. K. (2009). *Fundamentals of clinical supervision* (4th ed.). Needham Heights, MA: Allyn & Bacon.

Borders, L. D. (1991). A systematic approach to peer group supervision. *Journal of Counseling & Development, 69,* 248–252.

Borders, L. D., & Leddick, G. R. (1987). *Handbook of counseling supervision.* Alexandria, VA: American Counseling Association.

Brown, L. S., & Brodsky, A. M. (1992). The future of feminist therapy. *Psychotherapy, 29,* 51–57.

Bureau of Labor Statistics. (2015). *Mental health counselors and marriage and family therapists.* Retrieved from http://www.bls.gov/ooh/community-and-social-service-mental-health-counselors-and-marriage-and-family-therapists.htm

Corey, G. (2013). *Theory and practice of counseling and psychotherapy.* Belmont, CA: Thomson Brooks/Cole.

De Shazer, S. (1985). *The keys to solutions in brief therapy.* New York, NY: Norton.

Falender, C. A., & Shafranske, E. P. (2004). *Clinical supervision: A competency-based approach.* Washington, DC: American Psychological Association.

Frawley-O'Dea, M. G., & Sarnat, J. E. (2001). *The supervisory relationship: A contemporary psychodynamic approach.* New York, NY: Guilford Press.

Granello, D. H., & Granello, P. F. (2007). *Suicide: An essential guide for helping professionals and educators.* New York, NY: Pearson/Allyn & Bacon.

Haynes, R., Corey, G., & Moulton, P. (2003). *Clinical supervision in the helping professions: A practical guide.* Pacific Grove, CA: Brooks/Cole.

Holloway, E. (1995). *Clinical supervision: A systems approach.* Thousand Oaks, CA: Sage.

Kadushin, A. (1985). *Supervision in social work* (2nd ed.). New York, NY: Columbia University Press.

Kim Berg, I., & Szabo, P. (2005). *Brief coaching for lasting solutions.* New York, NY: Norton.

Lambers, E. (2000). Supervision in person-centered therapy: Facilitating congruence. In E. Mearns & B. Thorne (Eds.), *Person-centered therapy today: New frontiers in theory and practice* (pp. 196–211). London, England: Sage.

Remley, T. P., & Herlihy, B. (2014). *Ethical, legal and professional issues in counseling* (4th ed.). Upper Saddle River, NJ: Pearson.

Ronnestad, M. H., & Skovholt, T. M. (1993). Supervision of beginning and advanced graduate students of counseling and psychotherapy. *Journal of Counseling and Development, 71,* 396–405.

Ronnestad, M. H., & Skovholt, T. M. (2003). The journey of the counselor and therapist: Research findings and perspectives on professional development. *Journal of Career Development, 30,* 5–44.

Smith, K. L. (2009). *A brief summary of supervision models.* Milwaukee, WI: Department of Counselor Education, Marquette University.

Stoltenberg, C. D. (1981). Approaching supervision from a developmental perspective: The counselor complexity model. *Journal of Counseling Psychology, 28,* 59–65.

Stoltenberg, C. D., & Delworth, U. (1987). *Supervising counselors and therapists.* San Francisco, CA: Jossey-Bass.

Stoltenberg, C. D., McNeill, B., & Delworth, U. (1998). *IDM supervision: An integrated developmental model for supervising counselors and therapists.* San Francisco, CA: Jossey-Bass.

Wheeler, A. M., & Bertram, B. (2015). *The counselor and the law: A guide to legal and ethical practice* (7th ed.). Alexandria, VA: American Counseling Association.

Wilbur, M. P., Roberts-Wilbur, J., Morris, J. R., Betz, R. L., & Hart, G. M. (1991). Structured group supervision: Theory into practice. *Journal for Specialists in Group Work, 16,* 91–100.

# SEVEN

# MULTICULTURAL ISSUES AND CONSIDERATIONS

In the early years of its existence, the counseling profession mirrored the society that encapsulated it: largely Caucasian, male dominated, and middle class (McIntosh, 1998). In 1962, the pioneering counselor C. Gilbert Wrenn suggested that "culturally encapsulated" counselors define reality according to one's set of cultural standards and fail to take into account other cultural frameworks (Remley & Herlihy, 2014). Culturally encapsulated counselors tend to judge other cultural practices through the lens of their own culture and may tend to ignore evidence at odds with their own cultural framework. Consequently, cultural encapsulation tends to lead to stereotyping and biased thinking against other cultures.

Wrenn's (1962) writings dovetailed with other societal movements that hastened the recognition of multicultural viewpoints, including the Vietnam War and the resulting protests, the Civil Rights Era, the beginning of the Gay Rights Movement, and the Women's Movement. These civil and sociocultural movements changed the political and social landscape of the United States and the counseling profession as well (Wehrly, 1991). Counseling professionals finally, although slowly, began to offer multicultural viewpoints in counseling curricula, journal articles, and textbooks. In 1972, the Association of Non-White Concerns in Personnel and Guidance (now known as the Association for Multicultural Counseling and Development [AMCD]) was chartered by the American Counseling Association (ACA). It was in the mid-1990s that the AMCD and the Association for Counselor Education and Supervision (ACES) created the *Multicultural Counseling Competencies and Standards* (Arredondo et al., 1996) for purposes of inclusion in counselor education programs. AMCD's standards provide a format for counselors and counselor education programs to incorporate multicultural training into professional practice and the curriculum of graduate counseling programs.

The very definition of culture has also expanded; for purposes of this chapter, *culture* is broadly defined and includes race, ethnicity, nationality, gender, sexual orientation, socioeconomic class, age, disability, and other factors that may not be readily apparent (Pedersen, 1994). If administered a

Free Association (FA) technique with the key word as "culture," most people's first response likely would be to say "race." (I have experimented with such a FA technique in my assessment course and roughly 90% of initial answers are "race" or "skin color.") This bias in one direction has historically been reflected in educational, social, governmental, and even in professional organizations. For example, as previously noted, the AMCD was chartered as the Association of Non-White Concerns in Personnel and Guidance. Most counseling students in 21st century graduate programs are more facile in recognizing the broad spectrum of culture though many retain culturally encapsulated opinions (Hayes, Prosek, & McLeod, 2010). Given the dynamic, global nature of the 21st century and the likelihood of interacting with a very multicultural world, cultural competence is a necessity counselors deny or ignore at the peril of their career.

Despite the profession's best efforts, however, discrimination remains very active as even many well-intentioned counselors may have internalized issues of bias and practice discrimination without any awareness on their part (D'Andrea, 2000; Kiselica, 1999; McIntosh, 1998). White, mainstream counselors are often reluctant to admit to harboring biased attitudes regarding race (D'Andrea, 2000; Lee, 2003; Sue & Sue, 2012). Ridley (2005) offered several examples of unintentional racism as manifested by counselors:

- Avoiding the issue of cultural differences by claiming to be "color blind"
- Being too color conscious, thus attributing all problems to a client's cultural background
- Failing to recognize one's own issues of bias
- Facilitating codependent relationships with ethnic clients out of a need to be needed
- Misunderstanding a client's defensive reactions to the counselor's stereotypical thinking
- Misunderstanding a client's culturally learned patterns of communication or behavior

Lee (2006) suggests that culturally responsive counseling should be based on three premises: First, diversity is real and should not be ignored; second, differences are just that—differences—and not necessarily deficiencies or indicators of pathology; and third, counselors working with diverse clients must avoid stereotypes and monolithic thinking. A multicultural perspective asserts that diverse clients may hold values and beliefs that are different from those of the counselor. Multicultural counselor education seeks to establish a foundation for cultural pluralism in counselor training, counseling practice, and also in the manner counselors conceptualize multiculturalism. In this chapter, I provide an overview of some of the issues related to becoming a culturally competent counselor.

Finally, the *2014 ACA Code of Ethics* stresses the commitment of counselors to advocate on behalf of their clients. Effective advocacy involves confronting the social issues that adversely impact clients' mental, physical, sexual, emotional, financial, and cultural health. Standard A.7.a addresses the counselor's obligation to "advocate at the individual, group, institutional, and societal levels to address potential barriers and obstacles that inhibit access and/or the growth and development of clients." Thus, given the broad nature of culture and the fact that professional ethics now require inclusion of cultural considerations in all counseling situations, all counseling students must include cultural considerations with each client they counsel.

## SELF-AWARENESS: THE FIRST STEP

The beginning place for developing cultural competence is to acknowledge how your own cultural identity impacts your beliefs, values, and attitudes regarding people in society. For example, you might ask yourself, "What is my culture?" This question may be more complicated than it appears. It involves not only your race but also your nationality, region, religion, political views, gender, socioeconomic status, sexual identity, and even more. All these variations on culture play a large role in our daily actions and meditations (Sue & Sue, 2012), not to mention our interactions with clients. Counselors would be well advised to understand how their view of culture impacts counseling individuals, groups, couples, or families (Association for Specialists in Group Work, 1998; Sue & Sue, 2012). As counselors must first acknowledge their own biases, the following worksheet provides a list of numerous cultures. Read and fill in each blank line with the first thought that comes to your mind. Then discuss with a partner in dyads or triads.

Jew: _____

Muslim: _____

African American: _____

Latino/Latina: _____

Asian: _____

Undocumented Alien: _____

Person on Welfare: _____

Poor Person: _____

Gay or Lesbian Person: _____

Transgendered Person: _____

Evangelical Christian: _____

Disabled Person: _____

Unmarried Parents: _____

Tea Party Republican: _____

Janitor at Your College: _____

White Person: _____

Now consider the case of Stacy:

---

*The Case of Stacy*

Stacy, a White female counselor in a college counseling center is counseling Jin-Lin, a freshman Chinese American student. Jin-Lin is majoring in computer engineering, although he confesses he would prefer to become a high school math teacher. He maintains, however, that his parents would disapprove of him changing his major as they see engineering as higher paying and could offer the family more financial support. Stacy's approach is to explore with Jin-Lin what he wants as opposed to what his family thinks. She asks Jin-Lin if he could confront his parents and explain his own career aspirations as this way his parents would be forced to accept his aspirations over that of his family's.

1. How effective do you think Stacy's approach will be? Why?
2. What would Stacy need to know about Jin-Lin's family and culture to be helpful?

*Consideration:* In Stacy's case, it might help her to understand that many Asian people are uncomfortable with confrontation, and, culturally, family wishes may often be valued over individual desires. Stacy's apparent approach of *treating the client as she would anyone else* could be a serious cultural error. It could also prove a significant stumbling block to further counseling with Jin-Lin. Stacy would be better off helping Jin-Lin explore his feelings related to his family's expectations with the understanding that collectivist cultures may not value individualism as Western cultures likely would.

---

## MULTICULTURAL COMPETENCIES

Pedersen, Draguns, Lonner, and Trimble (2002) and Arredondo et al. (1996) have outlined multicultural competencies for multicultural self-awareness:

- Ability to recognize direct and indirect communication styles
- Sensitivity to nonverbal cues
- Ability to recognize cultural and linguistic differences
- Interest in cultures other than your own
- Sensitivity to the stereotypes and myths of other cultures

- Ability to describe elements of your own culture
- Ability to recognize relationships between and among cultural groups
- Acknowledgment of your own racist attitudes

The final suggestion on this list is the one likely to cause the most discomfort among students and faculty in counselor education programs. Sue (1996) and Arredondo et al. (1996) have discussed how racist attitudes and practices are deeply embedded in the dominant culture. Some students and faculty are likely to argue that faulty assumptions may not necessarily be a reflection of racist attitudes. In the example of Stacy and Jin-Lin, Stacy was very well intentioned regarding her approach, and likely meant no disrespect. Her assumption that *all* clients do what is best for themselves is well-grounded in Western thinking. However, because she is counseling an Asian client, Stacy would have been wise to have asked Jin-Lin what he saw as his options. A counselor's failure to dialogue with his or her client around culturally sensitive issues is likely to be interpreted as cultural arrogance or cultural ignorance. In the case of Stacy and Jin-Lin, Stacy would be well-advised to reflect on the differences in values between a Western and individualist culture, and an Eastern and collectivist one. There is a note of caution that must be mentioned here: Do not make the assumption that simply because you are counseling, say, an Asian client such as Jin-Lin, that said client holds a traditional, cultural worldview. Many people of Asian, Latino, Middle-Eastern, and so forth, cultures may well have ideas that run counter to traditional cultural values. Counselors would be prudent to keep an open mind regarding culture and solicit the client's input when questions arise. Remember, your cultural values may not be the client's. Furthermore, the client may also have different values than the culture in which he or she was raised. So, go light on assumptions and check your impressions with your client.

Clearly, it is worthwhile to remember that clients are individuals; they may not necessarily share or even agree with the values commonly associated with their culture, religion, ethnicity, and other commonly cited cultural preferences. Clearly, assisting clients to examine their own wishes and goals versus those of society and their own culture is a critical aspect of the counseling process. In such instances, however, counselors must take care to provide the client the courtesy of inquiring how his or her options might be influenced by cultural norms. Counselors must also prepare clients to anticipate and address the consequences of going against cultural, family, and other norms. During this process, mainstream counselors must be mindful to refrain from subtly (or *not* so subtly) trying to coerce the client into adopting Western values.

In addition to developing cultural competence, counselors need to continually educate themselves when counseling culturally different clients. Ways of developing cultural awareness involve reading and studying various cultures. Naturally, it would be impossible for a counselor of any culture to be an expert on all others. What is reasonable is for counselors to be open to learning basic information on cultures they encounter in counseling. Instruments such as the Multicultural Counseling Inventory (MCI; Sodowsky, Taffe, Gutkin, & Wise, 1994) can also be used by counselors to assess their own cultural competence and awareness. Consider the case of Steve that follows.

*The Case of Steve*

Steve, a school counseling intern, is working in a public, inner-city high school. Steve is conducting a group information session on college preparation. The 10-person group is composed mostly of female African American and Latina students. The discussion gravitates to the advantages and disadvantages of attending private versus public colleges. Steve notices Juanita, a very good student, has remained silent. Juanita is wearing a cardinal red St. Anne's Catholic School sweatshirt. Hoping to draw her into the discussion, Steve asks her, "Juanita, wouldn't you feel more comfortable at a Catholic college instead of a public state university?"

1. How appropriate or inappropriate was the question Steve posed to Juanita?
2. What are some other strategies Steve could have used to invite Juanita into the conversation?
3. If you had been in Steve's situation, what approach might you have used to encourage Juanita's participation?

In the case of Steve, we see once again a counselor who might have been motivated by good intentions, yet may be practicing in a culturally inappropriate manner. Despite her sweatshirt we do not know for sure if she would be more comfortable at a Catholic institution, nor can we infer Juanita being of a particular religious tradition as students wear shirts of all types. Now, it could well be that Juanita is Catholic and that she *might* prefer a Catholic college, but Steve does not know this to be the case; moreover, she is attending a public college, and he must be careful in the future to refrain from such assumptions.

The following list outlines cultural competencies that are recommended for counselors (Arredondo et al., 1996; Pedersen et al., 2002):

- Knowledge about the histories of cultures other than your own
- Understanding of the implications and ongoing problems of racism, oppression, and stereotyping, and their impact on diverse clients
- Knowledge of the language and slang of other cultures, and of the effect of your own communication style on diverse clients
- Knowledge of resources available for teaching and learning in other cultures
- Knowledge of aspects of traditional counseling approaches that may be inappropriate for counseling clients from diverse cultures
- Understanding of how your own culture is perceived by members of other cultures
- Knowledge of institutional barriers that impede access to counseling services for many clients from diverse cultures

- Professional expertise that is relevant to people in other cultures
- Repertoire of information that people in other cultures will find useful

There are many ways counselors can increase their multicultural competence. There are numerous texts, journal articles (*Journal of Counseling and Development, Journal of Multicultural Counseling*, etc.), DVDs, courses, and workshops. Lee (2001), Sue and Sue (2012), and others have opined that it is of critical importance for most counselors to experience the isolation that members of minority groups have historically experienced. They suggest working in a diverse setting, attending diverse religious and cultural events, and attending social functions for international students. One of the most important resources for your continued development is your clients. Working with people from diverse backgrounds illustrates the importance of culture, spirituality, and customs.

Regarding mainstream counselors experiencing cultural isolation first-hand, experiences such as study abroad, volunteering in emerging countries, and interning in inner-city settings are worthwhile endeavors. Perhaps in the near future graduate counseling students will complete overseas internships in Asia, the Middle East, Central and South America, and so on. Such experiences could result in paradigm changes for counseling students and open new doors to the global counseling profession.

## DEVELOPING CULTURALLY APPROPRIATE SKILLS

Another goal of multicultural education and practice is developing culturally appropriate skills and intervention strategies for counseling diverse clients (Sue, 1996). Becoming culturally skilled as a counselor requires that you go beyond your basic training in counseling techniques (Sue, 1996). Culturally skilled counselors recognize the need to serve as advocates, consultants, and liaisons to community-based organizations representing culturally different people (Lee, 2001). Furthermore, many of the traditional approaches to counseling focus on the needs of the individual, which may not be appropriate in counseling clients dealing with social oppression and discrimination (Remley & Herlihy, 2014). To be an effective counselor, you must develop an array of helping skills that account for not only the individual client, but also the broader society in which your clients reside.

Advocates for multicultural counseling have challenged the profession to embrace a sense of social activism (Lee, 2006). This involves confronting the discrimination that negatively impacts many segments of society. The *ACA Code of Ethics* (ACA, 2014) addresses this; it states that "counselors advocate at individual, group, institutional, and societal levels to address potential barriers and obstacles that inhibit access and/or the growth and development of clients" (Section A.7.a). Such obstacles to development include racism, sexism, homophobia, discrimination against the mentally ill, religious oppression, and so forth.

*The Case of Harriet*

Harriet, a 35-year-old African American woman, approaches a community mental health center seeking counseling. During her intake with Robin, Harriet reports symptoms of depression including loss of appetite, feeling sad, and a general feeling of hopelessness. Harriet denies any recent personal losses, but states, "I've had lots of losses. My father in prison, my brother was killed in gang warfare, my boyfriend abandoned me, and I'm struggling to feed and house my kids." Harriet also states she is working a minimum-wage job though says she wants to get her General Educational Development (GED) certificate but has not had the energy to study. Robin suggests a psychiatric screening for medication in the belief that medication is the most effective method to help Harriet address her depressed mood by the use of an antidepressant.

What do you think of Robin's approach? How helpful is her suggestion regarding medication?

1. What type of strategy might be most helpful for Harriet?
2. What issues and barriers should Robin anticipate when helping Harriet?

Robin might have been more effective had she taken a wider-angle view of the multiple issues impacting Harriet. Instead of focusing solely on medication, she could have explored the resources and social supports available in Harriet's community. Robin's failure to engage Harriet on these possibilities is an example of a well-intentioned counselor missing the forest for the trees. Furthermore, even should Harriet need medication, counseling to address negative thoughts that tend to accompany depression might also prove helpful in lifting Harriet's depression. For many African Americans, faith-based communities are an important source of emotional, spiritual, and even financial support. This is another area Robin should have explored and there is an issue of isolation.

The following are skills and objectives suggested by Arredondo et al. (1996), Lee (2001), and Pedersen et al. (2002):

- Skill at accessing appropriate service agencies and resources in the client's community
- Repertoire of strategies for helping clients cope with culture shock and acculturative stress that may arise from immigration experiences
- Ability to anticipate consequences of events in other cultures
- Fluency in the languages of other cultures
- Comfort in functioning in other cultures
- Skill at finding common ground with members of other cultures while retaining your own racial or ethnic identity
- Skill in helping clients to effectively intervene with institutional barriers and in using community resources when appropriate
- Active involvement in activities aimed at reducing prejudice and enhancing cross-cultural counseling knowledge in the community

## ETHICS AND MULTICULTURAL COUNSELING

The American Multicultural Counseling Association's Multicultural Counseling Competencies offer guidelines for counselors' consideration in their efforts toward multicultural competent counseling. The critical issue in multicultural competence is for individual counselors to put these guidelines into practice (Sue & Sue, 2012). Standards regarding nondiscrimination and honoring diversity are found throughout the code in numerous sections addressing the counseling relationship, assessment, professional responsibility, counselor education and supervision, and research. Multicultural competence requires counselors to keep in mind that the ethical reasoning of counselors is embedded within the counselor's worldview, which is shaped by sociocultural conditioning of which we are often unaware (Helms & Cook, 1999; Remley & Herlihy, 2014).

The *ACA Code of Ethics* (ACA, 2014, Section C.5) states that counselors do not condone or engage in discrimination against prospective or current clients, students, employees, supervisees, or research participants based on age, culture, disability, ethnicity, race, gender, religion or spirituality, sexual orientation, marital/partnership status, language preference, socioeconomic status, immigration status, or any basis protected by law. Many counseling professionals take the *ACA Code of Ethics* a step further, emphasizing that counseling professionals must take an advocate role to prevent and fight against societal discrimination and prejudice (Saltzman & D'Andrea, 2001). For example, a counselor may advocate for physically disabled clients to have access to school buildings; for a gay woman to have a say in the medical care of her long-term partner; for an older client battling age discrimination; and so on. Counselors are encouraged to lobby elected officials to remove barriers of discrimination against individuals and groups.

For student counselors working in practicum and internship placements, this could also mean confronting racist, sexist, and homophobic jokes and culturally offensive language. A simple method of supporting culturally sensitive counseling involves an intense self-examination regarding one's own language, attitudes, and behavior. Student counselors can also join the Association for Multicultural Counseling and Development, and read materials related to multicultural competence (e.g., *Journal of Multicultural Counseling*, and texts such as *Multicultural Issues in Counseling: New Approaches to Diversity*, *Multicultural Counseling Competencies*).

---

*The Case of Paul*

Paul is a gay African American minister of a Christian congregation that actively maintains that being gay is a sin. Although Paul does not agree with the stance his church takes, he is nevertheless very committed to his religious faith. For the past year, Paul has met and begun dating a man he met at a church conference. They have been very careful to keep their relationship a secret, but as the relationship grows, they wish to make it permanent. However, both partners are struggling with

*(continued)*

(continued)

the knowledge that continuing the relationship would mean having to leave their church. Confused about how to proceed, Paul comes to see James, a counselor at a Pastoral Counseling Center. James, a religious person, believes homosexuality is morally wrong and uses the Bible to justify his belief. However, during counseling he is touched by Paul's honesty and humanness and feels torn between his religious convictions and his ethical obligation as a counselor. Feeling very conflicted, James seeks advice from his clinical supervisor.

1. What are the issues James must address in providing counseling to Paul?
2. What ethical issues are involved in this scenario?
3. If you were James' supervisor and he came to you for advice, how would you counsel him to proceed?
4. How does a counselor balance ethical practice and his or her own moral/religious code?
5. Would James be guilty of unethical practice if he refused to counsel Paul because of his religious beliefs? Why or why not?

*Shades of Oppression*

David is a Jewish counselor educator at a public university in the northeastern United States. During David's presentation on preventing discrimination at an ACA conference, Hussein, a young Palestinian professor, stands and begins calling David a hypocrite because of David's well-known support for the State of Israel. David tries to regain control of the presentation, but the crowd has been engaged and is divided over the issue. David's supporters maintain that Hussein's criticism is based in anti-Semitism; his opponents claim David is supporting an apartheid society. Many in the audience are confused regarding what to do, because they see both David and Hussein as representatives of oppressed cultures.

1. If you were at the session, how would you respond? What would help in this challenging situation?
2. If you were a leader in ACA, how would you proceed in this case? What would be your follow-up response?
3. What are the difficult issues involved in the conflict?
4. How might the *ACA Code of Ethics* inform whatever action is taken?

In this case, we see professionals representing two cultures, both of which have faced severe discrimination. Advocacy, in such cases, may well lie in encouraging and facilitating dialogue among such disparate points of view. Counselor educators and professional counseling organizations are clearly in a position to facilitate difficult dialogues. While a conversation between David and Hussein might or might not facilitate lasting change, failure to dialogue on issues of conflict is simply abdicating

(continued)

*(continued)*

professional responsibility. Clearly, in many cases the issues are complex and clear answers may be difficult to discern. The essential factor here likely lies not in agreement as that may not be realistic in such scenarios, but in establishing difficult dialogues. Clearly, such conversation is very difficult for UN experts to say nothing of counselors and counselor educators. Still, complex issues require an earnest response.

---

*The Case of Ali*

Ali recently completed his doctorate in counselor education in a Council for Accreditation of Counseling and Related Educational Programs (CACREP)–accredited counselor education program on the West coast. He holds a master's in clinical mental health counseling and is a licensed professional counselor. He returns to his home country in the Middle East where cultural norms vary considerably from those in the United States. Ali has accepted a job running a counseling clinic and providing individual, family, and group counseling. He begins counseling Ahmed, an engineer who has recently returned home after 5 years working in Sydney, Australia. Ahmed confesses in an early session that he is gay. During his formative upbringing, he managed to suppress his sexual orientation due to religious and strict legal repression. As being gay is punishable by death in their country, Ali well understands the dilemma Ahmed is in. Ahmed recounts it was only in Sydney where he explored his sexuality, eventually forming a partnership with a man. Now back home, his parents expect him to marry soon and have children.

"I don't know what to do," a distraught Ahmed confides to Ali. "Can you help me?"

1. If you were Ali, how might you counsel Ahmed?
2. What are the conflicts involved in this scenario?
3. What would cultural competence in counseling look like in this scenario?
4. What is in the client's best interest here?
5. What do you think is most realistic in this situation?

## FINAL THOUGHTS

The *ACA Code of Ethics* also prohibits counselors from discriminating against groups that do not fall under the current federal nondiscrimination code. On June 26, 2015, the U.S. Supreme Court ruled that states cannot ban same-sex marriage. Gay and lesbian couples now have the same legal rights and benefits as heterosexual couples (CNN, n.d.). Also, many cities and municipalities have enacted nondiscrimination laws designed to protect such vulnerable groups. Two high-profile nondiscrimination court cases involving counselor education training programs, *Ward v. Wilbanks* (2010, 2012) and *Keeton v. Anderson-Wiley* (2011, 2012), illustrate changing U.S. cultural norms and a backlash against such change. The *ACA Code of Ethics* also opens the door to further in-depth discussions regarding what is and what is not unethical behavior when the topic revolves around diversity.

Another complication regarding multiculturalism and discrimination involves the relatively recent expansion of the counseling profession into non-Western societies. In many societies, current cultural practice would be at odds with ACA's nondiscrimination clause, particularly regarding the role of women and nondiscrimination regardless of sexual orientation and religion, to name a few "hot button" topics. There are some societies that provide no equal rights to women and no legal protection from domestic abuse, and where, most egregiously, being gay or lesbian and practicing a religion other than the official government sanctioned one are each punishable by death (Hodges, 2009).

There are no easy answers to multicultural and societal conflicts such as the ones just mentioned. The counseling profession, at least the *Western* counseling profession, has posited itself as a pluralistic one and advocates for the rights of disadvantaged groups (e.g., women, gays and lesbians, the poor). But it is fair to state that many non-Western societies would not agree with ACA regarding much of ACA's nondiscrimination statement. A critical question is: "How ACA and affiliate organizations will remain consistent with their egalitarian policies without, ironically enough, seeming culturally insensitive to many non-Western cultures?" This disconnect between organizational pluralism and cultural variation will likely become a serious issue in the future as the counseling profession becomes more commonplace in Middle Eastern, African, and Asian societies. ACA and other progressive mental health organizations have been reluctant to address these more complex international, cultural issues (e.g., discrimination versus cultural context). What may appear simple, for example, in the United States, may not be so in Saudi Arabia.

Counseling in a diverse world carries many challenges and rewards. A multicultural counseling perspective encourages counselors to become aware of their own biases, values, and assumptions by increasing their awareness of other cultural groups. A multicultural framework also involves developing culturally appropriate intervention strategies to address the particular needs of clients with regard to ethnicity, culture, spirituality, gender, disability, sexual orientation, and socioeconomic standing to name a few. Because of the wide variation in global cultures, no one can reasonably claim to be an expert. Therefore, it is highly recommended for counselors to continue their education well beyond the classroom through workshops, networking, and reading texts on multicultural counseling.

## REFERENCES

American Counseling Association. (2014). *ACA code of ethics*. Alexandria, VA: Author.

Arredondo, P., Toporek, M. S., Brown, S., Jones, J., Locke, D. C., Sanchez, J., et al. (1996). *Operationalization of the multicultural counseling competencies*. Alexandria, VA: Association of Multicultural Counseling and Development.

Association for Specialists in Group Work. (1998). *Principles for diversity-competent group workers*. Alexandria, VA: Author.

CNN. (n.d.). *Map: Same-sex marriage in the United States.* Retrieved from http://www.cnn.com/interactive/us/map-same-sex-marriage/

D'Andrea, M. (2000). Postmodernism, constructivism, and multiculturalism: Three forces reshaping and expanding our thoughts and counseling. *Journal of Mental Health Counseling, 22,* 1–16.

Hayes, D. G., Prosek, E. A., & McLeod, A. L. (2010). A mixed-methodological analysis of the role of culture in the clinical decision-making process. *Journal of Counseling & Development, 88,* 112–119.

Helms, J. E., & Cook, D. A. (1999). *Using race and culture in counseling and psychotherapy: Theory and process.* Boston, MA: Allyn & Bacon.

Hodges, S. (2009, March). Counseling in the twenty-first century: Challenges and opportunities. *Counseling Today, 51*(9), 44–47.

Keeton v. Anderson-Wiley, 733 F. Supp. 2d 1368 (S.D. Ga. 2010), aff'd, 664 F.3d 865 (11th Cir. 2011), appeal dismissed, No. 110-099 (S.D. Ga. June 22, 2012).

Kiselica, M. S. (1999). Confronting my own ethnocentrism and racism: A process of pain and growth. *Journal of Counseling & Development, 77,* 14–17.

Lee, C. C. (2001). Culturally responsive school counselors and programs: Addressing the needs of all students. *Professional School Counseling, 4,* 257–261.

Lee, C. C. (Ed.). (2003). *Multicultural issues in counseling: New approaches to diversity* (3rd ed.). Alexandria, VA: American Counseling Association.

Lee, C. C. (Ed.). (2006). *Counseling for social justice.* Alexandria, VA: American Counseling Association.

McIntosh, P. (1998). White privilege, color, and crime: A personal account. In C. R. Mann & M. S. Zatz (Eds.), *Images of color, images of crime* (pp. 207–216). Los Angeles, CA: Roxbury.

Pedersen, P. B. (1994). *A handbook for developing multicultural awareness* (2nd ed.). Alexandria, VA: American Counseling Association.

Pedersen, P. B., Draguns, J. G., Lonner, W. J., & Trimble, J. E. (Eds.). (2002). *Counseling across cultures* (5th ed.). Thousand Oaks, CA: Sage.

Remley, T. P., & Herlihy, B. (2014). *Ethical, legal and professional issues in counseling* (4th ed.). Upper Saddle River, NJ: Pearson.

Ridley, C. R. (2005). *Overcoming unintentional racism in counseling and therapy: A practitioner's guide to intentional intervention* (2nd ed.). Thousand Oaks, CA: Sage.

Saltzman, M., & D'Andrea, M. (2001). Assessing the impact of a prejudice prevention project. *Journal of Counseling & Development, 79,* 341–346.

Sodowsky, G. R., Taffe, R. C., Gutkin, T. B., & Wise, S. (1994). Development of the Multicultural Counseling Inventory (MCI): A self-report measure of multicultural competencies. *Journal of Counseling Psychology, 41,* 137–148.

Sue, D. W. (1996). Ethical issues in multicultural counseling. In B. Herlihy & G. Corey (Eds.), *ACA ethical standards casebook* (5th ed., pp. 193–197). Alexandria, VA: American Counseling Association.

Sue, D. W., & Sue, D. (2012). *Counseling the culturally different: Theory and practice.* New York, NY: John Wiley & Sons.

Ward v. Polite, 667 F.3d 727 (6th Cir. 2012).

Ward v. Wilbanks, Case No. 09-CV-11237 (E.D. Mich. July 26, 2010).

Wehrly, B. (1991). Preparing multicultural counselors. *Counseling and Human Development, 24*(3), 1–24.

Wrenn, G. (1962). *The counselor in a changing world.* Washington, DC: American Personnel and Guidance Association.

## RECOMMENDED READING

Barret, B., & Logan, C. (2007). *Counseling gay men and lesbians: A practice primer.* Florence, KY: Wadsworth.

Cashwell, C. S., & Young, J. S. (2005). *Integrating spirituality and religion into counseling: A guide to competent practice.* Alexandria, VA: American Counseling Association.

Fukuyama, M. A., & Sevig, T. D. (1999). *Integrating spirituality into multicultural counseling.* Thousand Oaks, CA: Sage.

Harley, D. A., & Dillard, J. M. (Eds.). (2005). *Contemporary mental health issues among African Americans.* Alexandria, VA: American Counseling Association.

Henriksen, R. C., Jr., & Paladino, D. A. (2009). *Counseling multiple heritage individuals, couples, and families.* Alexandria, VA: American Counseling Association.

Lee, C. C. (2012). *Multicultural issues in counseling: New approaches to diversity* (4th ed.). Alexandria, VA: American Counseling Association.

Pedersen, P. B., Draguns, J. G., Lonner, W. J., & Trimble, J. E. (2008). *Counseling across cultures* (6th ed.). Thousand Oaks, CA: Sage.

Perez, R., Debord, K. A., & Bieschke, K. J. (2009). *A handbook of counseling and psychotherapy with lesbian, gay, and bisexual clients.* Washington, DC: American Psychological Association.

Roysircar, G., Sandhu, D. S., & Bibbins, V. E. (Eds.). (2003). *Multicultural competencies: A guidebook of practices.* Alexandria, VA: American Counseling Association.

Sue, D. W., & Sue, D. (2002). *Counseling the culturally diverse: Theory and practice* (4th ed.). New York, NY: Wiley.

Vernon, A., & Clemente, R. (2005). *Assessment and intervention with children and adolescents: Developing multicultural approaches.* Alexandria, VA: American Counseling Association.

# EIGHT

# MANAGING STRESS DURING YOUR PRACTICUM/INTERNSHIP

Among the various mental health disciplines, the counseling profession is unique in that it was conceived with a strength-oriented wellness approach (Gladding, 2009; Myers, Sweeney, & Witmer, 2000; Witmer & Granello, 2005). Such an approach promotes a healthy and balanced life, not only for clients but also for counselors themselves. The intention of this chapter is to assist you in maintaining a healthier, more balanced life as you proceed through practicum and internship. As a future counselor, it is essential that you maintain a healthy lifestyle during your professional years (and well beyond, of course). Healthier counselors will likely be better counselors, and enjoy more productive years in the profession. Self-care is part of the American Counseling Association (*ACA*) *Code of Ethics* as a buffer against impairment (Standard C.2.g) as is monitoring our effectiveness (Standard C.2.d). From my own anecdotal observation over the years, having witnessed many counselors' poor and marginal self-care, it is likely that substandard self-care is the most violated standard in the code of ethics. So, as counselors assisting others in developing healthier lifestyles, it is essential we practice what we teach.

As graduate students in a counseling program, you will also meet counselors, psychologists, social workers, and other mental health professionals who do not practice what they teach. Unfortunately, there are far too many counselors and other mental health professionals who struggle with addictions, codependence, anger management issues, and dangerously inflated egos, and whose behavior you will not want to emulate. You are not expected to have perfect behavior, never get upset, or have a total lack of conflicts. You are expected to learn to manage the challenges of your practicum and internship (and, more significantly, the demands of your life!). As a young graduate student, I had much difficulty in managing the stress involved in working, meeting academic demands, and managing a challenging practicum and internship setting. I hope this chapter provides some insights in recognizing stressors that accompany counseling a struggling population of clients. Furthermore, it is worth mentioning that for some students, their supervisors and fellow graduate students may provide more stress than the population they counsel!

Workplace conflicts, not lack of professional knowledge, are the primary reason people leave their jobs (Bolles, 2015).

## DEVELOPING AND MAINTAINING A HEALTHY AND MINDFUL LIFESTYLE

There are many different pathways, plans, theories, approaches, books, journal articles, and other resources devoted to living a healthy and fulfilling life. The fact that so many authors, counselors, theologians, personal trainers, coaches, and such attempt to provide counseling, coaching, and information to manage stress and teach mindfulness, a balanced diet, exercise routine, and so forth is indicative of just how stressful daily life has become in this postmodern age. As graduate students on a practicum or internship you are no stranger to the challenges of external demands. The practicum or internship experience placed atop family responsibilities, a job, academic work, and financial demands can create great stress in your life (Remley & Herlihy, 2014). The irony of life as a graduate student in counseling is that while you are working to assist your clients to live healthier, more fulfilling lives, the demands of graduate school and practicum/internship can potentially derail your own sense of harmony and balance. Somehow you must learn to effectively address this contradiction and develop a healthy coping mechanism. While every professional likely preaches better than she or he practices, developing healthy routines is essential for good physical, mental, and emotional health.

In this chapter devoted to managing stress on the practicum and internship, I have created several exercises for the purposes of self-reflection. Self-reflection is a critical task not only for counselors but also for anyone in any occupation or walk of life and is a process of examining oneself during times of difficulty or success. The ability to step back from an experience, however successful or disappointing, can be a key skill for personal success as a counselor. I entitle this first section of the chapter "Developing and Maintaining a Healthy and Mindful Lifestyle." It is important for me to acknowledge that I have likely not created anything new in addressing the issues of healthy lifestyle or "wellness," as it is often referred to in the counseling field (Myers et al., 2000). Regardless of how we decide to refer to managing stress, living a balanced life, and mindful living, we usually address the same common themes of how to live a fulfilling, meaningful, and healthy life. I also offer a list of additional resources at the end of this chapter for counseling students to consider.

One of the first topics to address is that of stress. Stress is simply an everyday fact of life for everyone. Stress is an external change to which we are required to adjust our lives. Generally, we think of stress as being negative, such as death of a loved one, unemployment, divorce, and other such challenges. But positive changes in our lives can also bring about stress as well. For example, getting married or partnered, moving across the country for a new job, buying a home, traveling overseas, making your first conference presentation, and, of course, entering graduate school are all exciting experiences, but they can also bring about new stressors that complicate our lives.

We can experience stress from three different sources: the environment, somatic ways, and our thoughts (Davis, Eshelman, & McKay, 2008). Environmental stressors might be conflicts in the workplace, harsh weather, pollution, overcrowding, impoverishment, and living in unsafe areas. Environmental stressors are the ones we commonly see played up in the media, such as the 2009 catastrophic oil leak off the coast of Louisiana, Hurricane Sandy in 2012, slums in major cities, the trauma brought about by natural disasters such as that of the Katrina hurricane, the tsunami in Sri Lanka, and the earthquake in Haiti a few years ago. Environmental concerns clearly illustrate the connection between harmony with the environment and a less stressful life, or the exact opposite. Other common forms of environmental stress might be difficulties with your spouse/partner, roommates, colleagues at the office, and so forth.

The second source of stress is somatic, or how your body interprets stress. High-paced work settings, poor diet, sleep disturbances, and addiction all stress the body. Our reactions to these external demands are influenced by a genetic "fight-or-flight" response inherited from primitive ancestors who dealt daily with life and death issues. These genetic traits were passed on through the subsequent generations to assist people in their adaptation to environmental demands. Consequently, we all have as part of our physiological system the innate tendency to prepare the body to face the stressor or to flee from it. An adaptive example of "fighting" might be the coworker who requests to speak with the party with whom he or she is having conflicts. Unhealthy fighting is when the same coworker screams obscenities at the other party. Adaptive "fleeing" is when someone takes a temporary break from the stressful event (say an argument with their spouse), then returns and asks to speak with the party with whom he or she is having the conflict. Unhealthy fleeing is when the hurt person says, "They don't bother me," when in fact the other person's nasty comments or disrespectful actions do in fact bother him or her. Denial is a type of "unhealthy" fleeing. The critical factor here is "healthy" fighting and fleeing.

The third source of stress derives from our thoughts. How you interpret or label stressful events will in great measure determine how well you resolve stress (Ellis, 2001). One of the ways our assumptions can add to stress is when we mistakenly interpret messages. For example, interpreting your supervisor's grimace to mean he or she is upset with you will likely create stress. But verifying this assumption might clear up the misunderstanding. In the event your boss is upset with you but has not voiced displeasure, addressing the issue is a pathway of moving through the stress. Remember, your supervisor's facial expressions (for example) may or may not have anything to do with you. So, don't overly interpret messages, but certainly investigate them.

## Effects of Stress

Stress is difficult to define in a precise manner because it is a highly subjective phenomenon that differs for each of us. Experiences that are stressful for some are pleasurable for others. For example, some people actually look forward to swimming with sharks (namely, my spouse—but reef and nurse sharks, not Great Whites!) while others (myself) are terrified at the prospect. We respond to stress in different ways: some people eat less when stressed, other overeat, some turn pale whereas others blush, some use healthy coping skills such as exercise and talking with friends, and others self-medicate with alcohol and other drugs. Here are some common signs of stress:

1. Frequent headaches
2. Disturbed sleep
3. Trembling of limbs
4. Neck ache, back pain, muscle spasms
5. Dizziness
6. Sweating
7. Frequent colds
8. Stomach pain
9. Constipation or diarrhea
10. Hyperventilation
11. Frequent urination
12. Decreased sexual desire
13. Excessive worry or anxiety
14. Increased anger or frustration
15. Decreased or increased appetite
16. Depression or mood swings
17. Difficulty concentrating
18. Feeling overwhelmed
19. Feelings of worthlessness
20. Suicidal thoughts
21. Social withdrawal
22. Excessive defensiveness
23. Reduced work efficiency
24. Constant fatigue
25. Feeling less hopeful
26. Elevated blood pressure and heart rate

(Adapted from the American Institute of Stress, 2010)

## Tips for Managing Stress

Because stress is a reality in daily life, you cannot eliminate it. You can, however, manage the stress that comes into your life. The following are several tips for managing stress.

**Tip #1: Recognize stress and deal with it accordingly.**

- Learn to say "no." This may take some practice. Know your limits and stay within them.
- Limit time with people you find stressful to be around. Conversely, maximize your time with people you find affirming and supportive.
- Take a break from stressors. If traffic causes you unmanageable stress, take a different route or use alternative forms of transportation if possible

(e.g., car pool, mass transit, cycling). If the evening news stresses you, take occasional breaks from reading the paper, online news, or watching TV.

■ Refrain from overly discussing upsetting topics (there is a time and place for such discussions, of course, just not too often). If discussing politics, religion, sex, or even sports causes you too much conflict, perhaps refrain from discussing them, at least with select people. If people try and engage you in arguments over these topics, simply inform them, "I don't discuss these topics."

■ Prioritize your schedule. Make "to do" lists in order of what is most important. If there are unnecessary tasks, move them to the bottom of the list or eliminate them.

**Tip #2: Be proactive.**

■ Find constructive ways to express your feelings instead of suppressing them. Practice expressing your feelings with a trustworthy friend and solicit feedback from that friend. This way you will be more prepared to do so on your practicum/internship.

■ Learn to be assertive. There is more on assertiveness later in the chapter.

■ Manage time effectively. Poor time management skills will lead to additional stress. Prioritize your workload and this will help reduce your stress level.

■ Be willing to compromise in conflicts. Do not make all the compromises, but make the ones you can.

**Tip #3: Reframing problems.**
Reframing is a basic counseling technique. Here are some examples of how you might use reframing:

■ Reframe personal conflicts as "growth opportunities" and seek to resolve them.

■ Be realistic and let go of perfectionism. You are going to make mistakes on your practicum/internship. Make them and learn from them. Ask your supervisor for advice.

■ Step back from a stress situation and ask: "How big an issue will this be in 6 months or a year?"

■ On a regular basis, take time to reflect on the successes and blessings in your life. Challenging periods in life have a way of obliterating personal successes. So, take stock of your successes.

**Tip #4: Accept what you cannot change and change what you can.**

■ You cannot control other people. So, focus on how you react to their behavior and strategize more effective ways to deal with challenging people. A potentially more effective approach is focusing more on your goal as opposed to people's behavior. Remember, you cannot control another person's behavior but you can manage your own.

- Get support. Discussing concerns with close friends can be very helpful. For one thing, you realize you are not alone; also, sharing a concern may provide an outside perspective you might find useful.
- Forgiveness. No one is perfect and, with rare exception, other people are not out to make our lives miserable. Learning to forgive perceived slights can free you from negative energy. If you have trouble with forgiving others, counseling may be a viable option for you. Forgiveness often is more for the forgiver than the perceived transgressor.
- Self-reflection. What do I need to change about myself? You might ask a few trusted friends to help you with this. Do they see areas you could improve on? How could you improve on these areas? What would self-improvement look like?

## A Healthy Assets Ledger

To build on your wellness practice, consider the following reflective questions. These questions are for you to use for purposes of self-exploration regarding personal, professional, and spiritual growth.

**Reflective Questions to Consider**

- How well-developed and balanced are the personal, occupational, social, and spiritual (if appropriate) dimensions of your life?
- Who do you say you are? Also, how does who you say you are compare to how others appear to view you? Or, how great is the distance between who you really are and who you want to be? Be realistic, but be honest about this "divide."
- How does this self-view correlate with how significant people in your life view you (you may wish to discuss this with relevant people in your life)?
- What is your most fulfilling time of the week? Why? If you feel a lack of fulfillment during your week, how could you create more meaning in your life?
- How would you describe this stage of your life?
- What issues and/or challenges are creating difficulty for you?
- How could you begin to lessen or better manage these challenges?
- What are your key strengths?
- What skills, hobbies, interests, and talents do you possess?
- What areas of your life would you like to explore? (*Note:* This could apply to personal relationships, travel, continuing education, career, or anything you deem important.)
- In what ways are you dependent on others?
- In what ways are you self-reliant?
- What conflicts are inhibiting your personal growth and professional effectiveness?
- How could you take steps to resolve these conflicts?

### Regarding Major Successes and Failures in Your Life

- When you consider your major successes, what has worked well and why? What did your major successes teach you?
- Regarding your failures, what seemed to go wrong and why? What did your failures teach you?
- What could you do differently next time either to build on success or to ensure you did not fail in the next opportunity?

Exhibit 8.1 represents a self-monitoring system using scaling questions. This assessment technique provides a sense of where you are in the respective domains. The self-rating questions are intended to help provide a constructive method of self-care. This approach is not intended as a substitute to replace good personal, professional, and spiritual growth, but to serve and support wellness in these areas.

## Additional Considerations for Managing Stress

### Setting Limits With Others

- Do you have difficulty saying "no" to other people? If you do, how could you begin to say "no" when you know doing so is necessary? What makes setting limits difficult for you? Guilt? Fear? Something else? How could you begin to practice setting limits with others? For example, saying "no" when you mean no?
- What healthy risks can you undertake to enhance your personal and professional growth?
- When you think about the type of people who cause you stress, what is it that they do stressful for you? Okay, now that you have identified what is stressful about their behavior, how could you manage your stress level around them?

### Developing Connections

- Would you want to make friends with someone like yourself? Why or why not? If "no," what could you change?
- If you feel isolated, how could you begin to develop meaningful relationships?
- If you are in a marriage or partnership and you are not feeling fulfilled, how could you begin to create a greater sense of fulfillment in that relationship?
- If you are not in a relationship and would like to be, how could you begin to create such a relationship? (Or, what qualities would you like in a partner?)
- Recall a difficult period in your life. How did you navigate your way through this time?

---

**EXHIBIT 8.1  Dimensions of a Healthy Lifestyle**

**Spirituality/Religious Life**
My spiritual/religious life provides a sense of purpose and helps me address major life challenges.
(*Note:* An alternate phrasing for nonspiritual/nonreligious people might be: "My sense of life meaning/purpose provides fulfillment and helps me address the challenges in my life.")

        1    2    3    4    5    6    7    8    9    10

(1 = *no help at all*; 10 = *strongly helps*)
If your score was less than five, how could you improve your situation?

**Personal Vision**
"I have a clear vision in my personal, spiritual, and professional life."

        1    2    3    4    5    6    7    8    9    10

(1 = *No vision*; 10 = *I have a clear vision*)
If you do not have a clear personal, spiritual, or professional vision, how could you develop one? Visioning is a key component to success in all these areas.

**Self Worth**
"I feel worthwhile as a human being and have a strong sense of self-acceptance. Although I am not perfect, I feel generally good about myself."

        1    2    3    4    5    6    7    8    9    10

(1 = *I am worthless*; 10 = *My self-worth is very strong*)
If you are experiencing low self-esteem, how could you begin to feel better about yourself? What actions could you take to begin to feel more self-confident?

**Goal Setting**
"I feel self-confident about setting and meeting goals and demands in my life."

        1    2    3    4    5    6    7    8    9    10

(1 = *I lack confidence in my ability to meet demands and the goals I set*; 10 = *I feel very confident in setting, planning, and meeting goals and demands*)
If you lack clear goals in your life, how could you begin to create some clear goals?

**Rational Thinking**
"I believe I perceive my life and life situations in a rational manner. I seldom engage in overly negative thinking."

        1    2    3    4    5    6    7    8    9    10

(1 = *I frequently engage in irrational thinking*; 10 = *I am very rational in my beliefs*)
If you have rated yourself as frequently engaging in irrational beliefs (e.g., "I am a loser," "I am worthless," "No one could ever love me"), how could you begin to think in a more

*(continued)*

---

**EXHIBIT 8.1   Dimensions of a Healthy Lifestyle (*continued*)**

rational manner? (Or, if you are unsure as to whether your beliefs are rational, you might consider asking someone you trust for feedback.)

**Emotional Understanding and Regulation**
"I am in touch with my emotions and am able to express the full range of emotions appropriate to the situation. I also am not governed by my emotions."

1    2    3    4    5    6    7    8    9    10

(1 = *I am not able to regulate my emotions and often express emotions inappropriate to the situation*; 10 = *I am able to regulate my emotions and experience emotions appropriate to the situation*)

If you find you are not experiencing an appropriate range of emotions, or you find you are too often ruled by your emotions, how could you begin to change this? Remember, you will have "negative" emotions, so the task is to regulate them appropriately.

**Resilience**
"I am a resilient person, and able to analyze, synthesize, and make a plan to deal with challenges and projects that come my way."

1    2    3    4    5    6    7    8    9    10

(1 = *I do not feel resilient*; 10 = *I am very confident in my resiliency*)

If you do not feel resilient (or you are not as resilient as you would like) or do not have the ability to resolve difficulties in your life, what could you do to begin to develop more resilience? (*Note:* If you feel stuck on strategizing with this component, perhaps begin by making a list of ways you feel resilient. Or, ask someone who knows you well to list ways they see you as being resilient.)

**Sense of Humor**
"I possess a healthy, appropriate sense of humor that helps me deal with the stresses of life."

1    2    3    4    5    6    7    8    9    10

(1 = *I have no sense of humor*; 10 = *I have a healthy sense of humor*)

If you do not feel your sense of humor is either strongly developed, appropriate, or provides an effective release of stress, what could you change to improve the situation?

**Fitness or Recreation**
"I have a regular weekly fitness/recreational routine that helps me stay physically and emotionally fit."

1    2    3    4    5    6    7    8    9    10

(1 = *I have no activity routine*; 10 = *I have an active physical/recreational routine*)

If you do not have a regular weekly fitness routine, what could you do to change this? (Remember, you do not need to become a marathoner, competitive cyclist, swimmer, or dancer. It is simply about developing a regular routine of 20 minutes a day, at least 3 days a week.)

*(continued)*

**EXHIBIT 8.1 Dimensions of a Healthy Lifestyle (*continued*)**

**Healthy Diet**

"I regularly eat a balanced diet, including healthy vegetables and fruits."

(*Note:* Healthy is not meant to imply you *never* eat unhealthy foods because that's not realistic. In fact, sometimes it is good for the psyche to eat ice cream, cookies, and so forth. Just don't do it too often. Rather, it is about eating unhealthy food in moderation.)

| 1 | 2 | 3 | 4 | 5 | 6 | 7 | 8 | 9 | 10 |

(1 = *My diet is unbalanced and unhealthy*; 10 = *My diet is balanced and healthy*)

If your diet is unhealthy (eating high-fat food, "junk" food, fast food too often), how could you begin to eat a healthier diet? (For in-depth help, you may wish to consult a dietician.)

**Mindful Living**

"I maintain a mindful lifestyle by not abusing alcohol or other drugs, by wearing a seat belt, having regular medical exams, and by refraining from high-risk activities (e.g., casual sex, binge drinking, binge eating, restricting food)."

| 1 | 2 | 3 | 4 | 5 | 6 | 7 | 8 | 9 | 10 |

(1 = *I do not live a healthy, mindful life*; 10 = *I maintain a healthy, mindful lifestyle*)

If you find you are not living a healthy, mindful life, what steps could you take to change this?

**Managing Stress and Anxiety**

"Through my diet, workout routine, friendships, and so forth, I have the ability to manage stress and anxiety. When I find I am unable to manage the stress and anxiety in my life, I check in with close friends and family or if the need arises, I see a counselor."

| 1 | 2 | 3 | 4 | 5 | 6 | 7 | 8 | 9 | 10 |

(1 = *I am regularly unable to manage the stress and anxiety in my life*; 10 = *I am able to manage the stress and anxiety in my life*)

If you find you regularly have difficulty managing the stress and anxiety in your life, how could you begin to manage that stress and anxiety better?

**Sense of Self**

"I feel that my self-identity is strong and well developed."

| 1 | 2 | 3 | 4 | 5 | 6 | 7 | 8 | 9 | 10 |

(1 = *My sense of self is incongruent with who I am because I try too hard to be who others want me to be*; 10 = *My sense of self is very congruent with who I am*)

Some people struggle with their own identity for various reasons, such as enmeshment with family, codependence with a loved one, low self-esteem, and so forth. If you find you are struggling with an inability to develop your own identity, what are some options for exploration (options that would reduce your struggle or help you resolve your personal identity struggles)?

(continued)

**EXHIBIT 8.1   Dimensions of a Healthy Lifestyle (*continued*)**

**Connection to Family or Culture**
"I feel a strong connection to my family or culture."

1    2    3    4    5    6    7    8    9    10

(1 = *I feel no connection to my family or culture;* 10 = *I feel a strong and healthy connection to my family and culture*)

In the event you feel no connection to your family or culture, what would you say accounts for this? Also, how could you begin to make stronger connections to your family and culture?

**Career/Vocational Development**
"I feel a sense of satisfaction in the career I am pursuing" (e.g., mental health counselor, school counselor, rehabilitation counselor).

1    2    3    4    5    6    7    8    9    10

(1 = *No satisfaction;* 10 = *Maximum satisfaction*)

If your chosen career does not provide personal challenge and satisfaction for you, what steps could you take to create more fulfillment and satisfaction? (Or, if you are unemployed, how could your job search become more fulfilling? Or, how could this period of unemployment be more productive?)

**Hobbies**
"My hobbies help me relax and provide a sense of enjoyment."

1    2    3    4    5    6    7    8    9    10

(1 = *I have no hobbies or they provide no sense of enjoyment or relaxation;* 10 = *My hobbies are a pure joy*)

If you lack hobbies or outside interests from work, how could you create some fulfilling pursuits?

**Social Life**
"I have healthy relationships that provide me a sense of emotional connection and help make life more rewarding."

1    2    3    4    5    6    7    8    9    10

(1 = *I have no significant relationships, they are shallow, or provide little in the way of emotional connection;* 10 = *I have healthy and fulfilling relationships and they are an important part of my life*)

If you lack significant personal connections or your relationships do not provide you a sense of emotional connection, how could you begin to address this? (Or, how could you begin to create fulfilling relationships?)

**Intimacy**
"Intimacy, or love, is a central part of my life and my relationship with my spouse/partner provides the grounding, intimacy, and close connection I need." (*Note:* Intimacy could involve sexual intimacy or even a close, nonsexual relationship.)

(continued)

---

**EXHIBIT 8.1    Dimensions of a Healthy Lifestyle (*continued*)**

|   |   |   |   |   |   |   |   |   |   |
|---|---|---|---|---|---|---|---|---|---|
| 1 | 2 | 3 | 4 | 5 | 6 | 7 | 8 | 9 | 10 |

(1 = *Intimacy is largely absent from my life*; 10 = *Intimacy is a large part of my life and provides me with great satisfaction*)

If intimacy seems absent from your life, or seems unhealthy or unfulfilling, what do you need to do to change this situation?

**Questions Regarding Self-Care**
Regarding these dimensions, which do you appear to be strongest? Weakest? How could you improve your strengths and build upon your weak areas? What action could you take to improve your self-care? What supports do you need to create a healthier lifestyle? If you are unsure how to create a healthy self-care lifestyle, who could you ask for help (your doctor, counselor, a nutritionist, your spiritual leader, family member, friend, etc.)?

---

- How do you go about creating meaning in your life?
- Make a list of at least five skills you already possess that you can use to keep yourself well and fit.

### Work and Career

- Are you pursuing the career you truly belong in? Why or why not?
- Why did you choose to pursue counseling as a career?
- What is your dream job or dream career? (Describe in some detail: title, location, etc.)
- How can you begin to create your dream job? What steps are necessary?
- Setting goals is important for success. What are your major goals for the next 5 years?
- In what ways have you changed since entering your graduate counseling program?

### Mentoring

- Who are some people who have inspired you? *Note:* They need not necessarily be people you have met. For example, many have been inspired by the likes of Martin Luther King, Jr., Mahatma Gandhi, Mother Teresa, Dalai Lama, Stephen Hawking, and so forth, even though they have never met these people.
- Name five people and state how they have inspired you.
- Who are some people who share your hobbies and interests?
- Cite some organizations you are actively involved in.
- List some people who share your spiritual beliefs (or who share your personal convictions).

## CONFLICT MANAGEMENT SKILLS

A big part of health and wellness involves managing conflict (Weinhold & Weinhold, 2009). As a future counselor, you will have many opportunities to help clients and fellow students identify, address, and manage conflict. Conflict between people is actually a very natural occurrence; yet many people find conflict to be traumatic and stressful. Conflict need not necessarily be traumatic, however, and if well managed and addressed, it may provide the foundation for personal growth. The critical factor regarding conflict is that we acknowledge it, and then strategize on how to resolve it.

The first step in managing conflict is to admit that it exists. Because counseling can be demanding and stressful work, it is likely you will have ample opportunities to work on developing competence in dealing with conflict. I have listed common assumptions about conflict, and then, a reframed response to these assumptions.

> **Assumption 1:** "All conflict is bad and should be avoided."
> **Reframed response:** Conflict is not necessarily "bad." Acknowledging and addressing conflict can be liberating and improve self-confidence.
>
> **Assumption 2:** "Conflict is awful and terrible."
> **Reframed response:** Conflict is neither "awful" nor "terrible," although refusing to admit or address it can result in poor health.
>
> **Assumption 3:** "I simply can't deal with conflict."
> **Reframed response:** Dealing with conflict is sometimes unpleasant for me. However, the more experienced I become at addressing conflicts, the more confident and effective I become at resolving them.
>
> **Assumption 4:** "When I have conflicts they always 'blow up' into something unmanageable so it's just better to ignore them."
> **Reframed response:** Sometimes my attempts at conflict resolution go awry and tempers can escalate. However, in many, if not most cases, I am able to navigate conflict without causing further injury.

Now, a critical factor beyond admitting the existence of conflicts is how we go about resolving them. Fortunately, people can improve their conflict resolution skills with practice. As a counselor operating from a cognitive framework, I believe conflict resolution is grounded in childhood experiences of observing and participating in family conflicts. Our parents or guardians consciously or unconsciously modeled styles of conflict resolution, which we internalized and then repeated in our conflicts with siblings and peers. Some families are more functional at addressing conflict; children raised in more functional homes will have an early advantage at conflict resolution. Children raised in less functional, dysfunctional, abusive, or neglectful homes will likely have more struggles in resolving conflict as conflict may have been denied or blown up into destructive aggression.

## Conflict Resolution Styles

- The Denier: "Conflict? What conflict?" "Everything's just perfect."
- The Minimizer: "It's not anything to worry about." "No big deal."
- The Overly Responsible Type: "It's all my fault."
- The Avoider: "It's better to avoid conflict regardless of the cost."
- The Aggressor: "You have to get in people's face! That's how you resolve conflicts."
- The Mindful Type: "Ok, there is a conflict. What steps can I take to resolve it?"

Examine the types and think about which type best fits how you generally behave when faced with conflict. No one will always choose only one type, but decide which of the conflict resolution styles most frequently describes you. Now, think about which of these styles you would prefer.

The following questions are aimed to focus your awareness on your current conflict resolution style and how you would like to modify it.

- Which of the mentioned types would usually describe the manner in which I deal with conflict?
- What do I fear about conflict?
- What types of conflict situations do I find most challenging?
- Who were my role models in learning how to address conflict?
- What are my strengths in resolving conflict?
- How effective is my style of conflict resolution?
- In what situations does my approach to resolving conflict work?
- In what situations does my approach to resolving conflict seem ineffective?
- What would I want to change about my style of conflict resolution?
- How could I begin to change my approach to conflict resolution?
- What is one small change I can make that will help me address conflict more effectively?
- My biggest challenge in improving my conflict resolution skills is …
- Think of someone who seems effective in resolving conflict. What conflict resolution skills do they possess?
- What, in my professional training and background, assists me in resolving conflict?
- What types of conflict resolution work do I see myself performing in the future?
- What types of conflict resolution roles would be inconsistent with my future practice as a counselor?
- How would a skill in conflict resolution assist me in becoming an effective counselor?

*Conflict Scenario One*

You have just commenced your practicum. You get along very well with most of the staff and fellow graduate practicum students. However, after a few weeks, you discover another practicum student seems to be constantly belittling you (e.g., "You haven't learned much about counseling, have you?" "Your approach to counseling is all wrong."). You decide not to address the issue, hoping it will just resolve itself. Then, one of the graduate students informs you the student in question is bad mouthing you to the others.

   How would you resolve this apparent conflict? What actions would be most constructive? What would healthy resolution look like? Now, if possible, role-play the scenario out with a classmate or friend. The more you practice resolving conflicts, the more skilled you will become at resolving them. You cannot force the other person to act professionally and respectfully, but you can behave both ways.

*Conflict Scenario Two*

You have completed practicum and are beginning internship at your placement. Your new supervisor seems very harsh with his criticism and is somewhat sarcastic during supervision sessions, making comments such as "This is subpar work!" and "I can't believe your last supervisor saw your work as worthy of passing practicum." Your supervisor also discloses he really did not want to supervise you, but was forced to do so by the director of clinical services. Intimidated and discouraged, you soon discover yourself avoiding him whenever you can; as weekly supervision arrives, your stomach is upset and you feel very anxious. You realize this is an unhealthy situation and you would like to switch supervisors, but worry the answer will be "no" and that your supervisor may hold your actions against you. What steps might you make to deal with this conflict? Who might be supports for you in the challenging situation?

## THE COUNSELING STUDENT AS CLIENT

Counseling work can certainly be very stressful, as clients bring in difficulties of their own, and there may be job conflicts with coworkers. As a graduate student in a counseling program, you have the added complication of coursework, along with seeing clients, balancing a home life, and numerous additional demands. Many counseling programs now mandate a few counseling sessions for their students. Counselors who have had the experience of being clients themselves have a more complete understanding of the therapeutic process (Norcross, Strausser, & Faltus, 1988). Putting yourself in the vulnerable position as a client also provides you the opportunity of experiencing the "other side" of the therapeutic experience and likely can help you develop more empathy for clients and their struggles.

   I can state from experience that many counselors and other mental health professionals sometimes are reluctant to seek counseling services for themselves, out of their fear or arrogance, or simply being unaware of the extent of their personal issues. Self-care is a critical component of effective function for counselors and an issue addressed in the *ACA Code of Ethics* (Standard C.2.g). As a future professional counselor, graduate school is the optimal time to begin addressing your own mental health to ensure whatever personal concerns you have do not impact your counseling work. This is not to say you must be perfect to be a counselor; every counselor, no matter how successful and well-adjusted, has some personal "baggage." Most important, understand your issues and work to improve on them. After all, such is the nature of counseling work.

If you decide that entering personal counseling would be a good idea, you should be aware that many counselors, psychologists, social workers, and other mental health professionals have already reached similar conclusions. Mahoney (1997) reported that 87% of mental health professionals surveyed admitted they had entered personal counseling at some point in their careers. Personal counseling was rated by mental health professionals as second to practical experience as the most important influence in their professional lives. A study of 500 counselors and psychologists revealed that 93% rated the experience from mildly positive to very positive (Baird, Carey, & Giakovmis, 1992). Other notable counseling professionals such as Sam Gladding (2009) have posited personal counseling as a critical growth experience for counselors. In fact, in the event that it has been a lengthy period of time since a counselor was a client, it's likely a good idea to seek counseling services as a mental health "checkup" and to better empathize with the clients being served.

Pope and Tabachnick (1994) conducted a study of more than 800 psychologists, in which 84% admitted to having been in personal therapy. The most often cited reasons for mental health professionals to seek counseling were (in descending order) depression; divorce or relationship difficulty; struggles with self-esteem; anxiety, or career, work, or study concerns; family of origin issues; loss; and stress (Pope & Tabachnick, 1994). Among those surveyed, 85% described the therapeutic experience as very or exceptionally helpful. What these and other studies suggest is that personal counseling can be very important for our own emotional health and personal growth. Furthermore, personal counseling helps counselors and other therapists remain healthy and in doing so they likely are more effective at providing counseling. Furthermore, many counseling professionals have chosen to become helping professionals because of positive, life-transforming experiences through their own personal counseling (perhaps even readers of this text).

In addition to counseling, support groups can serve an important role for counselors and certainly for graduate students. I am not aware of counseling programs that require student participation in support groups, but it is a worthwhile concept, particularly given the stressful nature of graduate study, practicum and internship demands, and because the Council for Accreditation of Counseling and Related Educational Programs (CACREP; 2009) standards essentially mandate training reflective counseling professionals. In my own graduate counseling program, we were required to participate in an intensive growth experience for 3 days. I was both a participant as a master's degree student and later a group facilitator as a doctoral student. My experience in both groups was educational and very informative regarding the power of the group experience on individuals. However, my belief is that an ongoing support group would be more impactful regarding students' personal growth and development.

## FINAL SUGGESTIONS FOR SELF-CARE

Kenneth Blanchard, famous for the best-selling book *The One Minute Manager*, cowrote a follow-up book titled *The One Minute Manager Gets Fit* in 1986. He was motivated to write this book after realizing that he was so consumed with chasing success that he forgot the most important thing: to keep his life in balance (Blanchard, Edington, & Blanchard, 1986). He ate junk food, failed to workout, his weight ballooned, and his blood pressure rose to dangerously high levels (Blanchard et al., 1986). In the book, he listed the following as a means of assessing fitness level:

- I love my job. (Most of the time)
- I use safety precautions like wearing a seat belt in moving vehicles.
- I am within five pounds of my ideal weight.
- I know three methods to reduce stress that do not include the use of drugs or alcohol.
- I do not smoke.
- I sleep six to eight hours each night and wake up refreshed.
- I engage in regular physical activity at least three times per week. (Including sustained physical exertion for twenty to thirty minutes—for example, walking briskly, running, swimming, biking—plus strength and flexibility activities)
- I have seven or fewer alcoholic drinks a week.
- I know my blood pressure.
- I follow sensible eating habits. (Eat breakfast every day; limit salt, sugar, and fats like butter, eggs, whole milk, breakfast meats, cheese, and red meat; and eat adequate fiber and few snacks.)
- I have a good social support system.
- I maintain a positive mental attitude. (p. 36)

The list contains many common-sense items, yet it is clear that many people, including some graduate students and professional counselors, struggle with many of them. Regular medical checkups on an annual basis are also highly recommended. Graduate students who lack health insurance should check with their student health service as medical care is usually subsidized by student fees and is significantly less expensive than off-campus providers. Furthermore, as previously noted, good self-care is an ethical construct (Standard C.2.g); graduate counseling students would be wise to begin working on self-care development. Professions at college and university counseling centers, student health centers, and clergy are in a good position to assist with this.

## CONCLUSION

The practicum and internship experience can be a very demanding and, occasionally, stressful time for a graduate student. The good news is that survival rates are very high and it is likely you will manage stressful times quite well. You should expect occasional times, however, when you feel overwhelmed or "stressed out." These times, though unpleasant, also provide some of the greatest opportunities. You will get to practice the same stress management techniques and skills you have been teaching your clients. This is where self-reflection, reframing, meditation, exercise, friendships, and so forth are so valuable and rewarding. Be aware of your stress and anxiety levels and monitor them closely so that you remain physically and emotionally healthy. A burned-out counselor—one who tries to be everything to everyone—fails to set limits, lacks assertiveness, eats a poor diet, and has no significant friendships, and is likely to be of limited value to his or her clients. So, understand yourself and your emotional and physical limitations and work to stay within them.

## REFERENCES

American Institute of Stress. (2010). *Effects of stress.* Retrieved June 15, 2010, from www.stress .org/topics-effects.htm

Baird, B. N., Carey, A., & Giakovmis, H. (1992). *Personal experience in psychotherapy: Differences in therapists' cognitions.* Paper presented at the Western Psychological Association, Portland, OR.

Blanchard, K., Edington, D. W., & Blanchard, M. (1986). *The one minute manager gets fit.* New York, NY: Quill.

Bolles, R. N. (2015). *What color is your parachute? A practical manual for job-hunters and career-changers.* Berkeley, CA: Ten Speed Press.

Council for Accreditation of Counseling and Related Educational Programs (CACREP). (2009). *CACREP accreditation standards.* Retrieved from www.cacrep.org/2009standards.html

Davis, M., Eshelman, E. R., & McKay, M. (2008). *The relaxation and stress management workbook* (6th ed.). Oakland, CA: New Harbinger.

Ellis, A. (2001). *Overcoming destructive beliefs, feelings, and behaviors.* Amherst, NY: Prometheus Books.

Gladding, S. T. (2009). *Counseling: A comprehensive profession* (6th ed.). Upper Saddle River, NJ: Merrill/Prentice Hall.

Mahoney, M. J. (1997). Psychotherapists' personal problems and self-care patterns. *Professional Psychology: Research and Practice, 28,* 14–16.

Myers, J. E., Sweeney, T. J., & Witmer, J. M. (2000). The Wheel of Wellness counseling for wellness: A holistic model for treatment planning. *Journal of Counseling & Development, 78*(3), 251–266.

Norcross, J. C., Strausser, D. J., & Faltus, F. J. (1988). The therapist's therapist. *American Journal of Psychotherapy, 42,* 53–66.

Pope, K. S., & Tabachnick, B. G. (1994). Therapists as patients: A national survey of psychologists' experiences, problems, and beliefs. *Professional Psychology: Research and Practice, 25,* 247–258.

Remley, T. P., & Herlihy, B. (2014). *Ethical, legal and professional issues in counseling* (4th ed.). Upper Saddle River, NJ: Pearson.

Weinhold, B. K., & Weinhold, J. B. (2009). *Conflict resolution: The partnership way* (2nd ed.). Denver, CO: Love Publishing.

Witmer, J. M., & Granello, P. F. (2005). Wellness in counselor education and supervision. In J. E. Myers & T. J. Sweeney (Eds.), *Counseling for wellness: Theory, research, and practice.* Alexandria, VA: American Counseling Association.

## RECOMMENDED READING FOR MANAGING STRESS

Brinkman, R., & Kirschner, R. (2002). *Dealing with people you can't stand: How to bring out the best in people at their worst.* New York, NY: McGraw-Hill.

Davis, M., Eshelman, E. R., & McKay, M. (2008). *The relaxation and stress reduction workbook* (6th ed.). Oakland, CA: New Harbinger.

Greenberger, D., & Padesky, C. A. (1995). *Mind over mood: A cognitive therapy treatment manual for clients.* New York, NY: Guilford Press.

Myers, J. E., & Sweeney, T. J. (Eds.) (2005). *Counseling for wellness: Theory, research, and practice.* Alexandria, VA: American Counseling Association.

Williams, M. B., & Poijula, S. (2000). *The PTSD workbook: Simple effective techniques for overcoming traumatic stress symptoms.* Oakland, CA: New Harbinger.

## RECOMMENDED READING FOR CONFLICT RESOLUTION

The following books are good resources for ideas, self-reflection, and skill building regarding conflict resolution:

Barsky, A. E. (2007). *Conflict resolution for the helping professions* (2nd ed.). Belmont, CA: Thomson Brooks/Cole.

Fisher, R., & Ury, W. (1981). *Getting to yes: Negotiating agreement without giving in.* New York, NY: Penguin Books.

Gladding, S. T. (2009). *Counseling: A comprehensive profession* (6th ed.). Upper Saddle River, NJ: Merrill/Prentice Hall.

Myers, J. E., Sweeney, T. J., & Witmer, J. M. (2000). The Wheel of Wellness counseling for wellness: A holistic model for treatment planning. *Journal of Counseling & Development, 78*(3), 251–266.

Weinhold, B. K., & Weinhold, J. B. (2009). *Conflict resolution: The partnership way* (2nd ed.). Denver, CO: Love Publishing.

# NINE

# CRISIS INTERVENTION IN PRACTICUM/INTERNSHIP

No area of professional counseling practice creates as much stress and anxiety as crisis situations. For purposes of this chapter, crisis is defined as situations in which a client poses a danger to self or others. This includes clients who may be potentially suicidal, those who threaten to harm a third party (e.g., homicidal ideation or to commit serious physical injury), and cases of child abuse and neglect. Due to the nature of client crisis, there are ethical and legal ramifications for counselors to consider and to follow. Essentially, the guideline is "What decisions would a reasonable professional make in crisis situations?" (Wheeler & Bertram, 2015). Reasonable decisions are typically not defined, although following ethical guidelines and applicable laws would be the beginning. Consult with your supervisor and if necessary notify pertinent outside officials (e.g., the police, hospital, parent or guardian). The final responsible act is to accurately document your actions in the case record.

Most practicum and internship settings, whether in schools, agencies, residential treatment centers, hospitals, and so forth, likely will try to screen potential crisis clients away from practicum and internship students due to the complexity and potentially litigious nature of a crisis regarding harm to self or others. Because no screening system is perfect, however, counseling programs must prepare students for the possibility that they will encounter crisis clients on practicum. In fact, many supposed "noncrisis" clients assigned to the practicum or internship student may, because of stressful circumstances, escalate into a crisis. This chapter provides an overview of crisis situations and ways interns can begin to address it. The most important information to addressing crisis is to remain calm (easier said than done, of course!) and to consult with your supervisor or a senior counselor if the supervisor is unavailable.

## THE DUTY TO WARN

Before we discuss crisis situations, it is necessary to review confidentiality and its exceptions, which are discussed in detail in Chapter 3. Confidentiality is not absolute, and federal and state laws mandate several exceptions where confidentiality must be broken (state laws vary, so you must know the laws of your jurisdiction). These situations include the following:

- Potential suicide
- Credible threats made against third parties
- Abuse (children, the elderly, or vulnerable persons)
- Court-mandated disclosure
- When the client signs a release of information

As discussed in Chapter 3, the landmark court case involving confidentiality is *Tarasoff v. The Regents of the University of California* (1976). In the *Tarasoff* case an ex-boyfriend named Prosenjit Podder informed a psychologist at the University of California Berkeley that he intended to kill his ex-girlfriend Tatiana Tarasoff when she returned from overseas. Neither the campus police nor the counseling center notified Ms. Tarasoff, and Podder murdered Ms. Tarasoff when she returned to the United States. The Tarasoff family sued the University of California citing negligence; upon appeal to the California State Supreme Court the decision was reversed and the plaintiff awarded damages. The California State Supreme Court specifically stated:

> Once a therapist does in fact determine, or under applicable professional standards reasonably should have determined, that a patient poses a serious danger of violence to others, he bears a duty to exercise reasonable care to protect the foreseeable victim of that danger. (p. 345)

Thus, the *Tarasoff* decision established a therapist's duty to warn and protect. This decision has radically changed the nature of the counseling relationship in a manner that has created more responsibility for the counselor. The duty to warn exception is sometimes referred to as the mental health profession's "Miranda" rule (Remley & Herlihy, 2014). When clients disclose a viable threat to themselves or another party, the counselor must breach confidentiality and notify appropriate parties (e.g., the police and potential victims) of serious and foreseeable risk to the individual or others. Failure to adequately address a crisis or to warn appropriate parties could result in legal and ethical sanctions, and suspension of a counselor's license or certification (Remley & Herlihy, 2014; Wheeler & Bertram, 2015).

Now, having read the preceding paragraph, students should be aware of two notable exceptions to the *Tarasoff* decision. Texas is one of two states where a judge has explicitly ruled *Tarasoff* does not apply. In 1999, the Texas Supreme Court declared that mental health professionals have no common law or duty to warn readily identified third parties of a patient's threats against them (*Thapar v. Zezulka*, 1999). By Texas State statute, however, counselors are permitted to make certain disclosures to law enforcement or medical personnel in situations where there is an imminent risk of physical injury to a third party (Wheeler & Bertram, 2015). Of more concern, however, there is no specific grant of immunity built into the statute, which could create a difficult decision-making challenge for the therapist (Tex. Health & Safety Code 611.004, 2013). The larger concern for counselors practicing in Texas is adherence to a state law that runs counter to the lessons of *Tarasoff*, professional ethics, and moral concerns. It will be interesting to see if the *Thapar* decision is reversed in coming years.

In 1991 a Florida appeals court declined to apply the *Tarasoff* decision ruling that imposing a duty upon therapists to warn third parties would undermine client–patient confidentiality and trust. The Florida court also opined imposing a duty to warn would be the equivalent of a therapist using a crystal ball to foresee potential violence (*Boynton v. Burglass,* 1991). Unlike Texas, however, Florida has a statute permitting therapists to warn third parties without risk of litigation, but reporting is not mandatory according to case law (*Boynton v. Burglass*, 1991; Fla. Stat. 491.0147, 2013). Thus, counselors working in Florida may breach confidentiality in the case of clear and foreseeable danger to a person and do so with less anxiety than in Texas, but no *Tarasoff* duty exists as of this publication.

In the aftermath of numerous high-profile shooting tragedies in recent years (e.g., Sandy Hook Elementary, Virginia Tech University, Northern Illinois University, Columbine High School), mandated disclosure (i.e., *Tarasoff* type) likely would be more, not less, emphasized. Nevertheless, Texas and Florida remain outliers regarding the *Tarasoff* duty to warn and protect third parties.

## SUICIDAL CLIENTS

Suicide usually is the most common concern with regard to crisis (though crisis certainly is broader than suicide). Suicide is the second leading cause of death among college students and is a serious risk among high school students and the elderly (Granello & Granello, 2007). There are several commonly held myths regarding suicide. Sadly, you may even hear mental health professionals repeating them. Common suicide myths include the following:

- Discussing suicide will cause the client to attempt it.
- Clients who talk of suicide will not attempt suicide.
- Suicides increase around Christmas and New Year's Eve.
- Only insane people attempt suicide.
- When a suicidal patient improves, it is a sign the danger is over.
- Suicide is more prevalent among poorer classes of people.
- Suicide generally happens without warning.
                              (Sommers-Flanagan & Sommers-Flanagan, 1999)

Many counselors fear they might say the wrong thing and precipitate a suicidal attempt. Fortunately, there is virtually nothing you could say to induce suicide (Captain, 2006; Granello & Granello, 2007; Sommers-Flanagan & Sommers-Flanagan, 1999). In my experience with crisis clients, all seemed visibly relieved when I inquired about the possibility of suicide. This likely is because the weighty secret the client has been carrying is no longer secret. Most clients who are contemplating suicide are actually relieved to discuss the topic and generally are appreciative that someone has asked (assuming of course that the topic is discussed in a caring, nonjudgmental way). It is also important to ask the client whether he or she has a plan (ask for details) and the likelihood to carry out that plan. The client's responses will give you a sense of his or her intent (Capuzzi & Gross, 2008).

Students occasionally disclose a fear the client will get mad if queried about suicide. In my opinion and clinical experience of more than 20 years, if the client does become angry at the question, it's likely a positive sign, as it may indicate that the client has not given up hope. I am far more anxious counseling potentially suicidal clients who appear calm. Such rationality and composure may indicate that the client has made a decision to commit suicide and is at peace with the idea of their own self-inflicted death (Capuzzi & Gross, 2008; Granello & Granello, 2007). So, counselors must of necessity ask clients if they are suicidal (or homicidal) both to assuage legal and ethical concerns and to reassure the client. An essential question in the mind of the client in crisis likely is, "Can this counselor help me through my crisis?"

## Ethical and Legal Mandates Regarding Suicide

The *ACA Code of Ethics* (2014) clearly addresses the issues of suicide and client welfare:

> The general requirement that counselors keep information confidential does not apply when disclosure is required to protect clients or identified clients from serious and foreseeable harm or when legal mandates demand that confidential information be revealed. Counselors consult with other professionals when in doubt as to the validity of an exception. (Section B.2.)

State laws also mandate that counselors and other professionals (e.g., psychologists, nurses, physicians) also breach confidentiality when the issue of self-harm arises (Remley & Herlihy, 2014). As a counselor, you must also be prepared to take appropriate measures to prevent suicide. Appropriate measures would generally include a thorough risk assessment, consulting with your supervisor, notifying the appropriate parties, documenting the actions you took in the case record, and scheduling the client for an immediate follow-up session. In many cases the client may be temporarily hospitalized depending on a variety of factors such as a suicide plan, insurance, and hospital availability.

## Talking With a Suicidal Client

Here are some suggestions for discussing the issue of suicide with a client:

- Do not panic or show any signs of discomfort. You want the client to believe you are composed in the face of his or her crisis.

- If you are concerned that a client might be suicidal, specifically ask, "I'm wondering if you might be considering suicide."
- Do not try to argue with the client about his or her plan or give him or her minimizing advice. ("It'll get better," "It's really not that big a deal," "What will your family think?" etc.)
- It is critical that the suicidal client feel "heard" and not judged. Listen empathically and let the client know you accept him or her and his or her struggles. It is also worth remembering that suicidal clients feel very isolated. You are very possibly the first person to whom the client has disclosed his or her intent for self-harm and your empathic presence may go a long way in helping to resolve the immediate crisis.
- Most crisis clients have thought of suicide but have not made a plan. If this is the case with your client, get the client rescheduled at the soonest possible time (the next day if possible). Provide the client with a 24-hour crisis number so he or she knows help is readily available.
- Remember, when the client discloses thoughts or even a suicide plan, that client is saying "Help me" to the counselor. If you can get the client to admit to suicidal thoughts or intent, you have a very good chance to stop a suicide attempt.

## How to Assess Suicidal Risk

Because suicide assessment is not an exact science, counselors would be wise to apply a broad approach to treating suicidal clients. McGlothen, Rainey, and Kindsvatter (2005) suggest that professionals consider five aspects for all potentially suicidal clients:

- Plan. The verbalization of a plan of how the client would attempt suicide suggests lethality. The more detailed and specific the plan, the greater potential lethality.
- Intent. The stated intent to follow through on a suicide plan also suggests higher lethality.
- Means. The means by which the client plans to use in a suicide attempt. The more deadly the means (e.g., gun), the greater the lethality. Women make three times the attempts but men "succeed" at suicide at approximately four times the rate of women (American Foundation for Suicide Prevention, 2013). The difference is men use more lethal means.
- Prior attempts. Previous suicide attempts also suggest the client has previously seen suicide as a viable option. This suggests higher lethality. Typically, clients must work up to making a suicidal attempt and previous attempts indicate the client is beginning to see suicide as a viable option.
- Substance abuse. A history of substance abuse—especially alcohol—increases lethality, because substance abusers often display less management of crisis situations. It's a good idea therefore to use a standard alcohol and drug assessment such as the AUDIT, SASSI-3, MAST, and so on.

McGlothen et al. (2005) also suggest the following general guidelines in gauging lethality:

- Low lethality. Suicidal ideation (thoughts of suicide) is present but intent is denied, and the client does not have a concrete plan and has never attempted suicide in the past.
- Moderate lethality. More than one general risk factor for suicide is present, suicidal ideation and intent are present but a clear plan is denied, and the client is motivated to improve his or her psychological state.
- High lethality. Several general risk factors for suicide are present, the client has verbalized suicidal ideation and intent, and he or she has communicated a well thought-out plan with immediate access to resources needed to complete the plan.
- Very high lethality. The client verbalizes suicidal ideation and intent, and he or she has communicated a well thought-out plan with immediate access to resources needed to complete the plan, demonstrates cognitive rigidity and hopelessness for the future, denies any available suicide support, and has attempted suicide in the past.

## Essential Factors of Suicide Risk Assessment

- Assessment of each person is unique.
- Assessment is complex and challenging.
- Assessment is an ongoing process.
- Assessment uses multiple perspectives.
- Assessment tries to uncover foreseeable risk.
- Assessment relies on clinical judgment.
- Assessment is treatment.
- Assessment errs on the side of caution.
- Assessment takes all threats, warning signs, and risk factors seriously.
- Assessment asks the tough questions.
- Assessment tries to uncover the underlying message.
- Assessment is done in a cultural context.
- Assessment is collaborative.
- Assessment is documented.

(Granello & Granello, 2007, p. 184)

Assessing suicide in adolescents may be particularly difficult because of the fact that this population is still developing coping mechanisms, understanding that crisis is a temporary situation, and tend to be more impulsive. In 1996, Juhnke adapted the SAD PERSONS checklist for use with adolescents and called it the Adapted SAD PERSONS checklist. The adapted scale can be used to assess suicidal risk factors and provide general intervention recommendations for school counselors and counselors working youth.

The adapted version does not assign specific points for most of the items; rather, the counselor assigns 0 to 10 points for each item based on the severity of risk.

*Adapted SAD PERSONS Scale (A-SAD)*

S—Sex (males = 10 points; females = 0 points)

A—Age (older adolescents are at higher risk and receive more points)

D—Depression or affective disorder (the more serious the disorder, the more points)

P—Previous attempts (score recent attempts and more lethal attempts higher)

E—Ethanol/drug abuse (score drug or alcohol use or abuse higher)

R—Rational thinking loss (score evidence of rational thinking loss higher)

S—Social supports lacking (score lack of close friendships or social supports higher)

O—Organized plan (score specificity and lethality higher)

N—Negligent parenting (score neglect, abuse, family stress, and suicidal modeling higher)

S—School performance (score aggressive behaviors, vandalism, or deterioration of academic performance higher)

## Scoring Guideline

Assign points (0–10) to match severity for each risk factor. Total scores can range from 0 to 100.

Scores of 0–29: Students should be encouraged to participate in counseling services and be given information about crisis services.

Scores of 30–49: Students should be strongly encouraged to receive counseling and close follow-up services. School counselors should contact parents or guardians and make a thorough suicide assessment.

Scores of 50–69: Students in this range should be strongly considered for an evaluation for hospitalization.

Scores of 70+: Scores in this range suggest both environmental turmoil and severe emotional distress. Scores at this extreme end of the continuum warrant immediate hospitalization. Child protective services should be contacted in cases where family turmoil does not allow adequate assurance of care.

Caution: Suicide risk assessment is a complex process and cannot identify all persons who will attempt suicide. The Adapted SAD PERSONS Scale should not be used as the sole or primary assessment to determine, measure, consider, or estimate suicide risk or suggest interventions. The scale and its generally suggested actions should be used as merely one component of a structured, multi-component, and thorough suicide assessment process facilitated by a suicide assessment, threat, or safety committee minimally composed of multiple clinicians, clinical supervisors, legal counselor, and a client or student ombudsman or advocate.

Reprinted by permission from Juhnke (1996).

There are other assessments for suicidality and depression (which is a significant risk factor for suicide). Perhaps the most widely used instrument for assessing depression is the Beck Depression Inventory, second edition (BDI-II; Beck, Steer, & Brown, 1996). The BDI-II is often considered as the preferred instrument because of the large amount of research validating its effectiveness

(Beck et al., 1996). It is a 21-item self-report that assesses levels of depression and predicts the likelihood of suicide in adolescents and adults. It is completed by the client and usually takes less than 10 minutes. According to Beck et al. (1996), BDI-II scores ranging from 0 to 13 represent *minimal depression*; total scores from 14 to 19 suggest *mild depression*; total scores from 20 to 28 represent *moderate depression*; and total scores from 29 to 63 suggest *severe depression*. More significantly, the BDI-II has two key items strongly correlated with suicide. One item asks about suicide potential and another hopelessness. Interestingly, it seems the latter item on hopelessness is a better predictor of suicide than the question on suicide itself (Beck et al., 1996). Given the power of the construct hope, and that of hopelessness, Frankl seems to have succinctly made the hope-life and meaning-life affirming connection decades previously (logotherapy essentially is a therapy of meaning; Frankl, 1969). Assessing hope in potentially suicidal clients is a "must" for all counselors. This may involve encouraging the client to cultivate friendships, seek ongoing counseling, consider medication (at least temporarily), join a support group, incorporate a fitness routine and healthy diet, seek appropriate opportunities through work or schooling, reduce use of alcohol and drugs, and many other things.

For more information about this instrument, go to psychcorp.pearsonas sessments.com and search on Beck Depression Inventory-II.

## Additional Risk Factors

Most people who attempt suicide have a diagnosable mental disorder (Granello & Granello, 2007), such as major depression or bipolar disorder. Here are some additional risk factors that may increase the risk for suicidality:

- Substance abuse
- Posttraumatic stress disorder (PTSD)
- An eating disorder
- A particular diagnosis (borderline personality disorder, histrionic personality disorder, etc.)
- Mental illness such as schizophrenia
- A history of previous suicide attempts
- Gender: Males are three to five times more likely to commit suicide than females (Granello & Granello, 2007)
- Age: Elderly Caucasian males have the highest suicide rate. In addition, suicide is the second leading cause of death among college students and is rising among high school–age adolescents (Sommers-Flanagan & Sommers-Flanagan, 1999)
- A recent and major precipitating event (death of a loved one, divorce or breakup, loss of job, major disappointment, academic difficulty, loss of home, etc.)
- For children and adolescents, peer taunting and shunning have been associated with several high-profile suicide cases in recent years (Moore, 2010).
- Access to firearms or other lethal means

## Steps to Take When a Client Is Contemplating Suicide

The most effective means of preventing suicide is to recognize the warning signs and respond to them. As mental health professionals, counselors are expected to read and interpret the signs of suicide and to intervene appropriately. Counselors should heed the following suggestions:

1. Take all suicide threats seriously. This is the first and most significant guideline of suicide prevention.
2. Of all suicidal individuals, 75% give some type of warning sign (American Foundation for Suicide Prevention, 2013). Examples of warning signs might be vague threats ("I might not be around much longer"), giving away treasured possessions, risky behavior (driving very fast, illicit drug or alcohol abuse, risky sexual behavior, etc.), nonlethal self-injurious behaviors (cutting, burning, numerous injuries, etc.), withdrawal from social activities, pessimism, sleep problems, increased alcohol use, a plan for suicide, and so on.
3. When you do encounter a potentially suicidal client, do not simply advise him or her not to commit suicide, because that is unlikely to work. Instead, ask them to postpone an attempt of suicide. When you get an agreement to delay suicide, this provides an opening for additional possibilities other than self-harm.
4. Remember: When a client discloses an intention of suicide, what he or she is saying to you is, "Help me!"
5. Fortunately, most clients who bring up suicidal thoughts or intent never make a plan for suicide. Of those who make a plan, few follow through on the plan. (But again, treat each gesture seriously.)
6. Get the suicidal client to commit to ongoing counseling. In addition, get the client a referral for a medication screening as he or she may need antidepressant medication at least temporarily. If the client refuses, be sure to document your suggestions for legal and ethical reasons.
7. Never leave the suicidal client alone. If you need to consult with a colleague or supervisor regarding a suicide-prevention plan, get a colleague or secretary to stay with the client while you consult. Furthermore, never leave sharp instruments (e.g., scissors, sharp letter opener, dinner knife) available for clients to use.
8. Always consult with your immediate supervisor about the situation. Moreover, document the situation, how you assessed the client, consultation, and the plan you made. Does the client need to be hospitalized? If the client needs hospitalization, the police or other authorized personnel should provide transportation. Suicidal clients will probably need to be screened for medication by a psychiatrist or other health care professional. Does the client live alone? Does the client have the means to attempt suicide? If so, get the means away from him or her.
9. Have the client sign a safety contract. Some research suggests that safety contracts may not be a good idea. Experts seem to be divided on this issue. Many include safety contracts because no current research indicates

contracts increase liability (Wheeler & Bertram, 2015). My own belief is signing one's name is a concrete act of commitment to health and safety.

10. Remember, it is not your role to prevent suicide, but rather to provide the best treatment plan to interrupt any suicide plan (Remley & Herlihy, 2014; Wheeler & Bertram, 2015). Basically, your job as a counselor is to provide the client with the best chance for recovery.

11. After the crisis has passed, review the case with your colleagues and supervisor to learn from the experience.

---

*The Case of Juan*

Jai-Lin is a newly graduated counselor who has just been hired as an addictions counselor at a large agency serving voluntary and mandated clients. Many of her clients have histories of violence and have been incarcerated. Lately she has been counselor to Juan, a 35-year-old ex-con who she is counseling for addictions. During the fifth session, Juan discloses he has been depressed of late. Jai-Lin inquires for more specifics. Juan states his partner has moved out and he has just lost his job. He fears his probation officer may recommend his probation be revoked, which would send him back to prison. Jai-Lin asks whether he is considering suicide. Juan says yes and that while he legally cannot possess a handgun he knows where he can get one. Jai-Lin inquires whether he has a plan for suicide and Juan answers, "Not right now." Jai-Lin is unsure whether Juan is at risk and whether she must inform Juan's probation officer.

Jai-Lin takes Juan into the waiting room while she confers with her supervisor. The supervisor suggests Juan be recommended for overnight hospitalization. The supervisor makes the decision not to inform Juan's probation officer at this point as he has not violated conditions of his parole. Jai-Lin takes Juan back into her office and informs him she will proceed with hospitalization at least on an overnight basis.

1. Did Jai-Lin make sound clinical decisions regarding Juan's treatment?
2. Did Jai-Lin's supervisor make the correct call in not informing Juan's probation officer? Explain.
3. What would you have done in this situation if you had been Jai-Lin?

---

## Assessing Suicidal Risk in Schools

Although it could be argued that assessing suicide risk is the same regardless of the setting, middle and high schools pose unique challenges because of the educational and social nature of children and adolescents. Capuzzi (2009) has proposed 15 steps in assessing suicide risk in schools.

1. Remember the meaning of the term crisis management. This initial step refers to the need to assess a crisis and manage the situation until the

risk has passed. Rapid decisions must be made by counselors and other school officials to prevent suicide.

2. Be calm and supportive. Remember that a suicidal adolescent likely feels hopeless. The demeanor and attitude of the counselor or intervener is crucial.

3. Be nonjudgmental. Statements such as "This is no big deal, it'll pass" are minimizing statements that ignore the seriousness of the student's issue and may precipitate the adolescent to slip further into depression.

4. Encourage self-disclosure. The act of talking about painful issues is the first step in getting needed help. If the adolescent feels she or he can be honest, the assessment will be more accurate.

5. Acknowledge the reality of suicide as a choice, but do not "normalize" suicide as a choice. For example, you might say, "It is not unusual for adolescents to feel upset with relationships or other disappointments. Suicidal thoughts may sometimes come up in such situations, but there are other choices, such as what you are doing now—talking about the issues."

6. Actively listen and positively reinforce. Make appropriate eye contact, encourage the student to continue talking, be soft in your tone of voice, and so on. Allowing the adolescent to be heard conveys respect.

7. Do not attempt in-depth counseling. You want to establish the relationship and get the student assessed as quickly as possible. When the crisis has passed and the student is more stable, in-depth exploration and goal setting can begin.

8. Contact another professional. A second school counselor, psychologist, or social worker may be able to catch issues you might miss. No matter what plan you establish, document all that was done.

9. Ask questions to explore lethality. The following questions may help determine the risk:
   - What has happened to make life so difficult?
   - Are you thinking of suicide?
   - How long have you been thinking of suicide?
   - Do you have a suicide plan?
   - Do you know someone who has committed suicide?
   - How much do you want to live?
   - How much do you want to die?
   - What do you think death is like?
   - Have you attempted suicide in the past?
   - How long ago was the previous attempt (or most recent attempt)?
   - Have you been feeling depressed?
   - Is there anyone to stop you (significant relationships can make a difference)?
   - On a scale of 1 to 10, with 10 being high and 1 being low, what is the number that best predicts the possibility you will attempt suicide?
   - Do you use alcohol or drugs?
   - Have you experienced significant losses during the past year or earlier losses you have never discussed?

- Have you been concerned, in any way, with your sexuality?
- When you think about yourself and the future, what do you visualize?

10. **Make crisis-management decisions.** Develop a crisis intervention plan for the suicidal adolescent to be followed until the crisis is over and long-term counseling is initiated.

11. **Notify parents or legal guardians.** Parents or legal guardians must be notified in crisis situations. Naturally, students may be very nervous about bringing their parents into the situation, but this must be done both for legal and clinical reasons. When the crisis has passed, the parents or guardians should be part of treatment planning. Family counseling may be in order.

12. **Consider hospitalization.** All suicidal adolescents should be screened for hospitalization, though many will not be hospitalized. In some cases, short-term hospitalization may be required.

13. **Write contracts.** Though suicide contracts are not foolproof, professionals may use contracts as a concrete method of getting the adolescent to commit to long-term safety. Contracts should include the following:
    - Agreement for safety
    - The adolescent's agreement to obtain enough food and sleep
    - The adolescent's agreement to discard items that could be used in a suicide attempt (e.g., guns, weapons, medications)
    - A specified time span for which the contract is in force
    - The number of an after-hours crisis line so the adolescent has 24-hour access to help
    - Phone numbers of people to contact if the feeling of crisis escalates
    - Healthy ways the adolescent will structure his or her time (e.g., walks, talks, movies)

14. **Organize suicide watches.** If hospitalization is not readily available due to insurance issues or remote location, family and friends may take shifts staying with the adolescent until the crisis passes.

15. **Refuse to allow the youth to return to school without an assessment by a mental health counselor, psychologist, psychiatrist, social worker, or other qualified mental health professional.** Some fear that the assessment may alienate an adolescent, but it establishes that treatment is ongoing and that the school took the crisis seriously. (pp. 40–47)

All middle and high schools (and colleges also) should have a written crisis management plan to deal with crisis situations such as suicide. The plan should identify key personnel (counselors, psychologists, social workers, the principal, etc.). The treatment team at the school should regularly review the plan so that everyone knows their role. The plan should identify who is responsible for ensuring that crisis management is carried out. Just as schools have conducted drills for natural disasters such as tornados and hurricanes, they should practice their crisis management plan in simulated crisis situations. This provides school personnel the opportunity to refine and improve their potential response in the face of an actual crisis. With so many high-profile school suicides and school shooter tragedies (e.g., Sandy Hook, Columbine High School, Jonesboro

High School, Paducah High School, and also higher education, with tragedies at Northern Illinois University, University of Alabama Huntsville, Virginia Tech) in the past 15 years, school personnel must have a disaster management plan. Counselors and other trained school personnel must be facile in recognizing and checking out the warning signs for suicide and homicide and intervening before such plans are actualized. Because counselors will not be able to cover all possible eventualities, some suicides, and tragically some homicides as well, will occur, so colleges, schools, and community leaders must have a plan for managing crises.

---

*The Case of Jewel*

Rachel is a school counselor at Riverdale High School, a school in a run-down section of the inner city. She is in her third year and has the respect of her colleagues and the students. One day, Jewel, a 17-year-old senior who has beaten many odds to become an honors student, comes into her office crying. Jewel tells Rachel her boyfriend has just broken up with her. She is very distraught and states, "I see my life crumbling!" She had planned to join her boyfriend, currently a freshman at a university 3 hours away, next fall. "He promised he'd never leave me," she says through tears. Complicating matters, Jewel was taken from her mother, a single parent due to her mother's addiction and is living in foster care. She has never met her father and is not close to any other family. "Life isn't worth living!" Jewel sobs.

Rachel asks Jewel if she has thought of suicide and Jewel admits she has. Rachel inquires how Jewel might harm herself and Jewel opines she will swallow a bottle of aspirin and that she is considering doing this after school. Rachel explains to Jewel she must confer with her supervisor and has Jewel wait with the secretary. Her supervisor explains the school policy of notifying the parent or guardian. The supervisor calls the foster mother while Rachel confers with Jewel back in the office. The foster mother comes to the campus and meets with Rachel and Jewel and Jewel discloses she will not attempt suicide and mainly is angry at her boyfriend and wants to "strike back at that asshole!" Jewel's foster mother is insistent on taking Jewel to their pastor for spiritual guidance. Rachel is concerned and expresses to the foster mother that Jewel could benefit from extended mental health counseling and a psychiatric evaluation. Jewel's foster mother becomes angry and exclaims, "We don't go to godless counselors, we pray!" Then, she leaves the school taking Jewel with her.

1. How well did Rachel and her supervisor handle the situation?
2. If you were Rachel, what would you do?
3. What would be the next step for Rachel or Rachel's supervisor?

---

## After-Crisis Counseling

Fortunately, few clients will attempt suicide (Granello & Granello, 2007; Sommers-Flanagan & Sommers-Flanagan, 1999). Because clients who have previously contemplated or attempted suicide are vulnerable to further attempts (Sommers-Flanagan, 2007), you will need to lay therapeutic groundwork to help them work through difficult times without becoming suicidal again. A significant part of after-crisis counseling involves assisting clients in developing resilience (Beck et al., 1996; Parr, Montgomery, & DeBell, 1998). Purpose in life, strongly correlated with hopefulness and resilience, also appears to be an important construct for counselors to nurture in their clients and students (Hodges, Denig, & Crowe, 2014; Steger, Frazier, Oishi, & Kaler, 2006).

Developing and cultivating hope are not easy or simple matters, particularly for a client who feels beaten down by life experiences. Marketing hope to a client is scarcely as simple as getting a physician to prescribe antidepressant or antianxiety medication (Glasser, 2004). Nevertheless, I have outlined some questions to help you challenge clients' negative beliefs. Regardless, while medication may reduce depression and anxiety, it does nothing to promote skill development. Developing skills to combat depression and anxiety are important tools for clients to develop. The following self-reflection exercises are structured to assist clients (or counselors) to see beyond their present difficulty and to entertain the belief that the difficult period is temporary and will pass. Suicidal clients tend to believe crisis periods are ongoing and will not improve, thus reinforcing a sense of hopelessness (Beck, Brown, Steer, Dahlsgaard, & Grisham, 1999).

- What have you learned during this difficult period that will help you deal with stress, disappointment, or future trauma?
- In your opinion, what do you believe you most need to work through a difficult time?
- If a good friend of yours were to have attempted suicide or have contemplated suicide, what belief(s) would you want to see this friend change?
- What are your strengths? Cite three core strengths you possess. If you cannot come up with three, then ask close friends, trusted family members, coaches, ministers, teachers, or coworkers you respect.
- On a scale of 1 to 10, with 1 meaning *you have no hope in your life* and 10 meaning *you have a great sense of hope and meaning*, what score would you give yourself? If your score is, say, 1, what do you need to do to raise it to a 2? If a 2, to raise it to a 3, and so forth.
- Examine the various people in your life: family, friends, fellow students, coworkers, and members of a club or organization you are involved in. Now, find three people you admire in your various contacts. When you are ready, ask how they developed a sense of life's meaning and hope.
- How could you begin to develop self-confidence and hope in your own life? What steps could you begin to take? (*Note:* If you cannot think of specific steps, then ask close family, friends, or your counselor what steps he or she would like to see you take.)
- Having recently been through a crisis period in your life, what advice do you have for counselors, psychologists, the clergy, teachers, parents, and anyone else regarding how to be helpful to people in crisis? What could or should have been done that would have helped you?
- Consider the following questions for self-exploration: Who am I? Who do I want to be? How can I begin to become the person I desire to be? What strengths can you use to help you get there?

- Where does your sense of life's meaning or purpose come from? How could you strengthen your sense of life's meaning or purpose?
- On a scale of 1 to 10, how committed are you to making the changes that will promote your personal resilience and become the person you desire?
- Draw a picture of your present mood and circumstances. How does your picture look? Are the colors bright with hope or dark with despair. Now, draw a picture of how you would like your life to look. Compare the two pictures and ask yourself, "How can I begin to create my life to look more like the second drawing?
- Imagine when you wake up tomorrow the issues and concerns that have burdened you have disappeared. What would be different about your life?

Clients in crisis or even in postcrisis recovery will need more than the aforementioned self-reflections. Counselors will need to teach clients to set limits with others, hold themselves accountable for their destructive behavior, and encourage and challenge them to change their self-talk, behavior, and so forth. Some clients will need medication, a healthier diet, friendships, meaningful work, and so forth. In short, it takes many things to prevent and develop resilience against suicide. Counseling students also would be wise to work with their supervisor to brainstorm additional suicide prevention strategies.

## ASSESSING DANGER TO OTHERS

Like assessing suicide, predicting potential risk to third parties is not an exact science (Granello & Granello, 2007; Sommers-Flanagan & Sommers-Flanagan, 1999). There are numerous methods of prediction, which involve a multimodal approach. This section of the chapter gives an overview of practical tips for assessing difficult client situations you may encounter while on practicum and internship. As always, using the instincts you have honed through your counseling program, following the *ACA Code of Ethics*, consulting with your practicum or internship supervisor, and reading pertinent articles in relevant professional journals all are standard practices to follow.

The particular issues and challenges of your client and the circumstances with which he or she is struggling often dictate the types of interventions you will utilize. The guiding mantra in difficult cases, however, involves crafting a strong therapeutic alliance as this is one of the most critical aspects of treatment (Duncan, Miller, Wampold, & Hubble, 2010). The therapeutic alliance provides a sound relationship with the client that can make a positive difference during times of crisis. Although there have been many research studies on counseling over the past century, the following are some general guidelines that likely apply to all counseling situations:

1. Establishing a safe, secure space for counseling
2. Establishing the therapeutic alliance with the client
3. Helping the client to construct meaning in his or her life
4. Working with the client to instill hope in his or her life

5. Identifying the client's support systems: personal (optimistic attitude), familial, cultural, spiritual (if appropriate), and vocational
6. Assisting the client in developing a more balanced lifestyle (e.g., Myers, Sweeney, & Witmer's [2000] Wheel of Wellness)
7. Teaching more realistic, positive self-talk
8. Role-playing important issues in the session
9. Giving homework on the pertinent issues covered in counseling (e.g., assigning the client to make three new social contacts each week)
10. Promoting behavioral change

## Assessing the Potential for Violence

Assessing a client's potential for violence should come in the intake portion of the interview. The intake interview should consist of assessment, client history, review of case records (medical records, psychiatric records, previous counseling records, incarceration, etc.), and the client interview. A few structured assessments are available for counselors to use in determining the risk level for violence. One of the more popular threat assessment instruments is the Structured Assessment of Violence Risk in Youth (SAVRY) that has 24 at-risk factors (e.g., history, social or contextual, and individual) as well as an additional six protective factor items (Borum, Bartel, & Forth, 2002). Also, the Suicide Assessment Checklist (SAC; Rogers, Lewis, & Subich, 2002) and the SAD PERSONS Scale (Patterson, Dohn, Bird, & Patterson, 1983) target adult clients. Acts of violence occur with more frequency than many in the profession appear to think. Some research suggests around 20% of emergency department patients are violent and that 40% of psychiatrists are assaulted at least once in their careers (Tardiff, cited in Shea, 1988). It is also fair to say that certain client populations pose more risk than others. Residential psychiatric care, correctional facilities, and mandated counseling with domestic batterers all are examples.

The following is a sample of questions counselors can use to determine the potential for violence:

- First and most importantly, does the client have a history of violence (bullying, cruelty to animals, domestic violence, workplace violence)?
- Does the client make references to violence and see violence as a means to meet his or her needs?
- Does the client tend to get physically or verbally aggressive when abusing substances such as alcohol or other drugs?
- Does the client have a prevalence of violent ideation? Such clients may idealize violence and are likely more prone to commit acts of violence.
- Does the client have a history of mental illness? Although mental illness alone is not a predictor of violence, mental illness plus substance abuse can be a significant factor (Sudders, 2010).
- Does the client have a history of being the victim of violence? Clients who have been the victims are more likely to be perpetrators of violence.
- Does the client have a history of using physical and verbal violence to control people?

- Does the client have a documented history of cruelty to animals or bullying?
- Has the client made threats of violence to third parties?
- Does the client have access to weapons?
- Does the client belong to a social group that advocates and encourages violence?

The highest level of threat appears to be the following:

- Direct, plausible, and specific
- Poses imminent and serious danger to self and others
- Client implies specific steps have been taken toward violence (e.g., stalking, acquisition of a weapon; National Association of School Psychologists, n.d.)
- Client has a documented history of violent acts
- Client is male (Federal Bureau of Investigation, n.d.)

While this research concerns school violence, the indicators are generalizable to community mental health situations.

## Appropriate Interventions

The following guidelines can assist you in developing a plan of intervention:

- If the danger does not seem imminent (e.g., no specific plan for violence, no access to weapons), then continue with counseling.
- Ask the client to participate in disclosing the information to third parties (provided the client agrees to do so). Be very honest with the client that you may need to notify the police. You want to ensure the client is not surprised by disclosure to the authorities.
- Get the client screened for medication or medication change, if necessary, and arrange to get lethal weapons taken away from the client.
- Keep up-to-date and accurate records. Record the name of the threatened party, date of threat, and nature of the threat (be specific, e.g., the client threatened he would "get his ex by slashing her car"). In addition, explain why you took the course of action you took. Naturally, you will have included your supervisor in the plan of action and note that you made the plan in conjunction with your supervisor.
- Disclose only the minimal amount of information needed to the intended victim.
- Keep your supervisor informed of any and all issues related to the case. You do not want your supervisor to be surprised by any action you have taken. (Appelbaum, 1985)

## Managing Risky Clients and Situations

You need to carefully monitor the case until the danger has passed. Monitoring activities should include follow-up with the police, the intended victim, the client, and other pertinent agencies such as parole, probation, child protection, and so forth.

The following are risk management suggestions for your agency or school:

1. Risk Management Tool Kit: Create a file or binder in which you keep all copies of relevant risk management materials, which include the following:
   a. Ethical codes
      - Relevant code(s) of ethics: ACA, American School Counselor Association (ASCA), American Mental Health Counselors Association (AMHCA), and so forth
      - Ethical decision-making model (Corey, Corey, & Callanan, 2007)
   b. Laws or statutes
      - Counselor licensure statute and rules: know whether your state has a duty to warn based on a communicable threat. Does the law provide immunity for good faith acts?
      - Abuse reporting laws
      - Civil commitment (mental health and/or substance abuse)
      - Health Insurance Portability and Accountability Act (HIPAA)
   c. Subpoena checklist
      - Consult an experienced health care attorney. State law and HIPAA may apply, depending upon the circumstances. Remember that state law may outweigh HIPAA if it is more protective of the client's privacy rights. If your attorney agrees, go on to Steps 2, 3, and 4.
      - Ascertain whether the client, after consulting his or her attorney, will provide you with written authorization to release information or to testify. If you maintain psychotherapy notes as defined by HIPAA, you must have a specific authorization form in order to release these notes. (If your state has specific protection for personal notes, you might not be required to release them, even with client authorization.)
      - If the client's attorney declines to provide you with signed authorization from the client, request that the client's attorney file a motion to quash the subpoena or a motion for a protective order.
      - If the preceding steps do not produce either your client's informed authorization or a court order, send a written notice to the attorney who issued the subpoena or had the court clerk issue it. This notice should be customized to the particular facts.
      - If you are subpoenaed to court or a deposition and the time is inconvenient or you will not be available, call the attorney who had it issued. Assuming you've appropriately handled the privilege issue, it's often possible for the attorney to schedule you at a set date and time or put you "on call" in case you're not needed. Under instructions from your attorney, send a letter to the attorney who initiated the subpoena with language stating that in order to testify or release records or other protected health information, you must receive one of the following: (a) written, informed authorization

from the client to release the information requested; (b) a court order to release the information or testify, as commanded by the subpoena. Remember, you are a HIPAA-covered entity, and must follow HIPAA guidelines.

   **d.** Attorney: List of local attorneys who have expertise in mental health and health law. Also, annually review these documents to ensure current familiarity and update when/as appropriate. (Your school or agency likely has an attorney who represents them.)

2. Colleague consultation: Two heads are better than one. Obtain colleague consultation when confronted with difficult counseling situations. To that end, identify colleagues for whom you have professional regard and establish in advance the need of a reciprocal consultation relationship.

3. Informed consent: Develop an informed consent process (written document, verbal explanation, and commitment to reviewing consent as circumstances change); be sure the process clearly defines confidentiality, privilege, and privacy guidelines as well as limits and exceptions to confidentiality, privilege, and privacy and make sure these are consistent with state laws and professional ethics.

4. Institutional policies: Know the internal policies that regulate the practice of counseling in your school or agency. Adhere to these policies. If there are policies that are at odds with legal or ethical requirements, bring these to the attention of appropriate officers within the institution.

5. Termination and abandonment: Avoid terminating a client who is in crisis. Otherwise, termination should be accomplished, when appropriate, after giving adequate notice and referrals. As "adequate" is not specifically defined, make sure you have documented the client's progress (or lack thereof), timeline for preparing the client for termination, and a clear rationale for why the client is being terminated or referred. The rationale should include consulting with your supervisor or a senior colleague.

6. Document all clinical decision making and the rationale behind each decision. In the school setting, policies on documentation and record-keeping may differ from rules for private practice counselors.

7. Obtain prior medical and behavioral history. Has the client acted out violently in the past? What were the circumstances? Was it premeditated? Does the client frequently make impulsive decisions? Is substance abuse an issue? Is the client delusional? Is there reason to believe the client is only discussing a fantasy, not a real threat?

8. Manage co-occurring relationships: Co-occurring relationships (dual roles) must be effectively managed to prevent harm to clients. This is true regardless of whether the co-occurring relationship is a regular part of your job responsibilities (school counselors who counsel students and also have other relationships) or evolve from unforeseeable circumstances, or are an intentional or conscious choice. Be mindful of your state licensure board's position on boundary issues, as well as updated

guidance in the *2014 ACA Code of Ethics* on roles and relationships with clients, supervisees, and others.

9. Practice within your scope of competence: Recognize and respect the limitations of your competence; expand competence by securing the appropriate education, training, or supervision.
10. Supervision: Supervisors and supervisees are at risk if supervision is not properly administered. Supervisors and supervisees should be mindful in the selection process to ensure a good fit (theoretical approach, supervision style, availability of supervisor, etc.), clearly define the mutual expectations of both supervisor and supervisee, and monitor to ensure fulfillment of the expectations. If required, engage in regular supervision as defined by statute or policy.
11. Professional liability insurance: Obtain and maintain professional liability insurance, preferably coverage that will provide attorney representation if a complaint is brought against you by the state licensure board as well as attorney fees and settlement/damages resulting from a civil lawsuit.
12. Inquire about the client's access to weapons, homicidal ideation, and current plans.
13. Consider all appropriate responses and the consequences of each (warning the potential victim(s), calling the police, involving a psychiatrist, hospitalizing the client). If clinically appropriate, involve the client in your decision making. Do not reveal confidential information that is not necessary to protect potential victim(s).

(Adapted from Wheeler & Bertram, 2015, pp. 145–147)

Following such guidelines cannot guarantee a client will refrain from harming himself or herself or others or totally absolve a counselor from all liability should harm occur to the client or others. Regardless, following such a list certainly can help establish that the counselor is acting within the standard of care expected of professional counselors.

## A Few Additions to the Preceding Lists

As a longtime counselor and former director of counseling programs, I would also make a few additions to the preceding lists:

1. Maintain professional memberships for the duration of your professional life (ACA, ASCA, AMHCA, etc.).
2. Read professional articles that address suicide screening, risk factors, and prevention (e.g., in publications such as *Journal of Counseling and Development, Professional School Counselor, Journal of Mental Health Counseling*).
3. Attend regular relevant professional trainings on managing clients in crisis, either at a national, state, or local conference or through health providers.

## CHILD ABUSE AND NEGLECT

As discussed in Chapter 3, counselors are mandated reporters of suspected child abuse and neglect. The ASCA (2003) defines abuse and neglect as follows:

*Abuse:* The infliction of physical harm upon the body of a child by other than accidental means, continual psychological damage or denial of emotional needs (e.g., extensive bruises/patterns; burns/patterns; lacerations, welts or abrasions; injuries inconsistent with information offered; sexual abuse involving molestation or exploitation, including but not limited to rape, carnal knowledge, sodomy or unnatural sexual practices; emotional disturbance caused by continuous friction in the home, marital discord or mentally ill parents; cruel treatment).

*Neglect:* The failure to provide necessary food, care, clothing, shelter, supervision or medical attention for a child (e.g., malnourished, poorly groomed, dirty, without proper shelter or sleeping arrangements, lacking appropriate health care; unattended, lacking adequate supervision; ill and lacking essential medical attention; irregular/illegal absences from school; exploited, overworked; lacking essential psychological/emotional nurturing; abandonment). (p. 1)

Signs of potential physical abuse include the following:

- Sudden changes in behavior or school performance
- Appears very wary, as if anticipating danger or disruption
- Overly compliant or overly responsible
- Has unexplained bruises, burns, black eyes, and so forth
- Seems frightened of his or her parents and uncomfortable when time to go home
- Appears initially frightened at the approach of an adult
- Reports injury by a parent or another caregiver

Signs of potential sexual abuse include the following:

- Reports sexual abuse by parent or caregiver
- Suddenly begins sexually acting out
- Runs away or discloses he or she is considering running away
- Displays unusual sexual knowledge or behavior
- Complains of pains in the vaginal or anal area
- Becomes pregnant or contracts a venereal disease

Signs of potential emotional abuse include the following:

- Seems overly fearful at speaking up in class or in peer groups
- Appears to isolate himself or herself when on the playground or during recess

- Appears depressed and seems unattached to parents or family
- May display either overly compliant or acting-out behavior regarding disagreements with peers or authority figures

Some common signs of potential neglect may include:

- Frequent absence from school
- Often has no money for lunch or no lunch packed from home
- Frequently has medical concerns such as ear infections, dental problems that go untreated, or is underweight
- The child or the adolescent often looks poorly groomed, disheveled, or dirty
- Abuses alcohol or drugs
- Discloses he or she is responsible for own care, despite being a minor

## Reporting Child Abuse or Neglect

Counselors, like physicians, nurses, teachers, and other health and mental health professionals, are mandated reporters and must report cases where they believe child abuse or neglect is occurring (Remley & Herlihy, 2014). Counselors and other professionals must be trained in recognizing child abuse and neglect before being licensed to practice or prior to accepting educational and treatment jobs (Remley & Herlihy, 2014). Confidentiality must be breached in cases where the counselor believes there is reasonable cause to suspect abuse or neglect. All states and U.S. territories have "hold harmless" provisions that prevent mandated reporters from litigation when they report in good faith. Good faith means a professional (e.g., counselor, nurse, physician) reports child abuse or neglect based on reasonable cause (e.g., the child has marks, unusual bruising, reports being excessively disciplined [whipped with a stick], parent has abandoned the child, excessive absences with no parental support). Reporting from a lack of good faith standpoint would involve a professional filing a false report against a parent or guardian simply out of anger. A false report could result in suspension of a certification and licensure to potential incarceration.

Cases of abuse and neglect must be reported even when the minor does not want them reported (Remley & Herlihy, 2014). There may be numerous reasons why a child or adolescent would not want abuse or neglect reported, including the potential breakup of the family, fear of retribution by an abusive adult, fear of being removed from the home to the unknown (i.e., foster care), stigmatization by peers, and judgment that they snitched on family members. Counselors need to inform and prepare the child for all eventualities when they prepare to report suspected abuse or neglect. Extended counseling services are clearly in order, especially regarding victimization and displacement.

Beginning counselors should be aware of the "double-edged sword" regarding reporting child abuse and neglect. In some communities, child protection agencies may be perceived more as the villain than the alleged perpetrator because of a history of removing children from the home for perceived unfair reasons. Counselors may even find themselves under pressure from some authorities not to report some instances of abuse.

## RECOMMENDED RESOURCES FOR SUICIDE PREVENTION

Capuzzi, D. (2006). *Suicide across the lifespan: Implications for counselors.* Alexandria, VA: American Counseling Association.

Granello, D. H., & Granello, P. F. (2007). *Suicide: An essential guide for helping professionals and educators.* Boston, MA: Pearson.

Granello, D. H., & Juhnke, G. A. (2010). *Case studies in suicide: Experiences of mental health professionals.* Upper Saddle River, NJ: Merrill.

McGlothin, J. M. (2009). *Developing clinical skills in suicide assessment.* Alexandria, VA: American Counseling Association.

Westefeld, J. S. (2009). *Suicide assessment and prevention* [DVD]. Hanover, MA: Microtraining Associates.

## ORGANIZATIONS FOR THE PREVENTION OF SUICIDE

Because suicide prevention tends to be the most common type of crisis situations counselors encounter, here is a short list of organizations that provide education for counselors and others.

American Association of Suicidology (AAS; www.suicidology.org). AAS provides information to counselors, schools, colleges, and so forth.

American Foundation for Suicide Prevention (www.afsp.org). American Foundation for Suicide Prevention provides research and information to professionals and nonprofessionals.

International Association for Suicide Prevention (IASP; www.med.uio.no/iasp). IASP provides information for a broad forum of academics, practitioners, and suicide survivors.

Jed Foundation (www.jedfoundation.org). The Jed Foundation supports mental health and suicide prevention of college and university students.

National Organization for People of Color Against Suicide (NOPCAS; www.nopcas.com)

Suicide and Mental Health Association International (SMHAI; www.suicidandmentalhealthassociationinternational.org). SMHAI is dedicated to preventing suicide and related mental health issues.

Youth Suicide Prevention (www.yspp.org). An educational program providing education and training for parents and teenagers

Youth Suicide School-Based Prevention Guide (www.theguide.fmhi.usf.edu). Youth Suicide School-Based Prevention Guide provides accurate and user-friendly information.

## SUICIDE HOTLINES

*Note:* Always know the local suicide prevention/crisis hotlines and make that available to clients. Remember crisis calls are 911 in all U.S. states and territories. Most communities also have a regular crisis line and all counselors should know this number and make it available to clients. In addition, here are other resources:

**Eldercare Locator**, a public service of the U.S. Administration on Aging. Call for potential elder abuse situations, dangerous, threatening or serious. (**1-800-677-1116**). (Monday to Friday, 9:00 a.m. to 8:00 p.m. ET)

**GLBT National Help Center: 1-888-843-4564.** (Monday through Friday 1:00 p.m. to 9:00 p.m. Pacific Time, Monday through Friday 4:00 p.m. to midnight, Eastern Time; Saturday 9:00 a.m. to 2:00 p.m. Pacific Time, noon to 5:00 p.m. Eastern Time)

**National Sexual Assault Online Hotline: 1-800-656-HOPE (4673)** (24 hours a day, 7 days a week)

**National Suicide Prevention Lifeline: 1-800-273-8255** (24 hours, 7 days a week, in English and Spanish)

**TEEN LINE: 1-800-852-8336.** (The line is open nightly from 6:00 p.m. to 10:00 p.m.)

**Veterans Crisis Line: 1-800-273-8255** (press 1) (24 hours a day, 7 days a week, 365 days a year)

## CONCLUSION

Assessing and managing crisis situations are likely to be the most challenging part of your practicum and internship experience. Probably the most important thing to remember is that you do not have to go through the experience of crisis intervention alone. It is crucial that you involve your supervisor as soon as possible. Regardless of whether these issues are suicide prevention, counseling victims of trauma, or dealing with a child endangerment case, chances are very good that you will be helpful in providing resolution that will bring a reduction in stress level for the client.

## REFERENCES

American Counseling Association. (2014). *ACA code of ethics.* Alexandria, VA: Author.

American Foundation for Suicide Prevention. (2013). *Preventing suicide.* New York, NY: Author. Retrieved from http://www.afsp.org/preventing-suicide

American School Counselor Association. (2003). *Position statement: Child abuse/neglect prevention: The professional school counselor and child abuse and neglect prevention.* Retrieved May 16, 2010, from http://asca2.timberlakepublishing.com//files/PS_ChildAbuse.pdf

Appelbaum, P. S. (1985). Tarasoff and the clinician: Problems in fulfilling the duty to protect. *American Journal of Psychiatry, 142*(4), 425–429.

Beck, A. T., Brown, G. K., Steer, R. A., Dahksgaard, K., & Grisham, J. P. (1999). Suicide ideation at its worst point: A predictor of eventual suicide in psychiatric outpatients. *Suicide & Life-Threatening Behavior, 29,* 1–9.

Beck, A. T., Steer, R. A., & Brown, G. K. (1996). *Manual for Beck Depression Inventory-II.* San Antonio, TX: The Psychological Corporation.

Borum, R., Bartel, P. A., & Forth, A. (2002). *SAVRY: Structured assessment of violence risk in youth.* Lutz, FL: Psychological Assessment Resources.

Boynton v. Burglass, 590 So. 2d 446 (Fla. Dist. Ct. App. 1991).

Captain, C. (2006). Is your patient a suicide risk? *Nursing, 36*(8), 43–47.

Capuzzi, D. (2009). *Suicide prevention in the schools: Guidelines for middle and high school settings* (2nd ed.). Alexandria, VA: American Counseling Association.

Capuzzi, D., & Gross, D. R. (2008). *Youth at risk: A prevention resource for counselors, teachers, and parents* (5th ed.). Alexandria, VA: American Counseling Association.

Corey, G., Corey, M. S., & Callanan, P. (2007). *Issues and ethics in the helping professions* (7th ed.). Belmont, CA: Thomson Brooks/Cole.

Duncan, B., Miller, S. D., Wamplod, B., & Hubble, M. (2010). *The heart and soul of change: Delivering what works in therapy* (2nd ed.). Washington, DC: American Psychological Association.

Federal Bureau of Investigation. (n.d.). *The school shooter: A threat assessment perspective.* Critical Incident Response Group. National Center for the Analysis of Violent Crime. Quantico, VA: Author.

Fla. Stat. 491.0147 (2013).

Frankl, V. (1969). *Psychotherapy and existentialism: Selected papers on logotherapy.* New York, NY: Simon & Schuster.

Glasser, W. H. (2004). *Warning: Psychiatry can be hazardous to your health.* Alexandria, VA: American Counseling Association.

Granello, D. H., & Granello, P. F. (2007). *Suicide: An essential guide for helping professionals and educators.* New York, NY: Pearson/Allyn & Bacon.

Hodges, S., Denig, S., & Crowe, A. (2014). College students' attitudes on purpose in life and self-esteem. *International Journal for Existential Psychology & Psychotherapy, 5,* 124–131.

Juhnke, G. (1996). The Adapted SAD PERSONS: A suicide assessment scale designed for use with children. *Elementary School Guidance & Counseling, 30,* 252–258.

McGlothen, J. M., Rainey, S., & Kindsvatter, A. (2005). Suicidal clients and supervisees: A model for considering supervisor roles. *Counselor Education and Supervision, 45,* 135–146.

Moore, K. (2010, February 3). Residents demand answers after S. Hadley bullying death. *The Boston Globe,* p. B3.

Myers, J. E., Sweeney, T. J., & Witmer, J. M. (2000). The Wheel of Wellness counseling for wellness: A holistic model for treatment planning. *Journal of Counseling & Development, 78*(3), 251–266.

National Association of School Psychologists. (n.d.). *Threat assessment: Predicting and preventing school violence.* Washington, DC: Author. Retrieved from www.nasponline.org/resources/factsheets/threatassess_fs.aspx

Parr, G. D., Montgomery, M., & DeBell, C. (1998). Flow theory as a model for enhancing student resilience. *Professional School Counseling, 1*(5), 26–31.

Patterson, W. M., Dohn, H. H., Bird, J., & Patterson, G. A. (1983). Evaluation of suicidal patients: The SAD PERSONS scale. *Psychosomatics, 24*(4), 343–349.

Remley, T. P., & Herlihy, B. (2014). *Ethical, legal and professional issues in counseling* (4th ed.). Upper Saddle River, NJ: Pearson.

Rogers, J. R., Lewis, M. M., & Subich, L. M. (2002). Validity of the Suicide Assessment Checklist in an emergency crisis center. *Journal of Counseling and Development, 80,* 493–502.

Shea, S. C. (1998). *Psychiatric interviewing: The art of understanding: A practical guide for psychiatrists, psychologists, counselors, social workers, nurses, and other mental health professionals* (2nd ed.). New York, NY: Saunders.

Sommers-Flanagan, J. (2007). The development and evolution of person-centered expressive art therapy: A conversation with Natalie Rogers. *Journal of Counseling and Development, 85,* 120–125.

Sommers-Flanagan, R. S., & Sommers-Flanagan, J. S. (1999). *Clinical interviewing* (2nd ed.). New York, NY: Wiley.

Steger, M. F., Frazier, P., Oishi, S., & Kaler, M. (2006). The Meaning in Life Questionnaire: Assessing the presence of and search for meaning in life. *Journal of Counseling Psychology, 53*(1), 80–93.

Sudders, M. (2010, January 27). Kerrigan family faced dilemma with their adult son. *The Boston Globe*, p. B6.

Tarasoff v. The Regents of the University of California, 13 Cal. 3d 177, 529 P.2d. 533 (1976).

Tex. Health & Safety Code 611.004 (2013).

Thapar v. Zezulka, 994 S. W. 2nd 635 (Tex. 1999).

Wheeler, A. M., & Bertram, B. (2015). *The counselor and the law: A guide to legal and ethical practice* (7th ed.). Alexandria, VA: American Counseling Association.

# TEN

# PROTECTING YOURSELF DURING THE PRACTICUM/INTERNSHIP EXPERIENCE

Amid all the excitement of beginning practicum and internship, where many counseling students encounter their first actual clients, one must of necessity consider the nature of the counseling relationship. Many students likely are attracted to the profession due to the helping nature of the field. Thus, it would be no stretch to say counseling students and professional counselors are idealistic with regard to philosophical orientation. While idealism clearly holds an important place in the counseling profession, it must of necessity be grounded in realism. Many clients, particularly those in mandated situations involving domestic violence, those who are incarcerated, students in overcrowded inner-city schools, and some mentally ill populations, may be higher risks for violence. Therefore, counseling programs must be prepared to discuss the safety of practicum and intern students on placement. Many schools and agencies do a very good job of creating safety plans for students, clients, and staff though it is accurate to state some do not. This brief chapter covers some of the basics regarding safety on the practicum and internship. Naturally, no given placement, no matter how conscientious or well-staffed, can absolutely guarantee an intern's safety. (Absolute safety in life is of course a myth.)

The risks of encountering violence during your practicum/internship vary considerably depending on the nature of your setting and the population you counsel. A practicum in an elementary school, for example, is likely to be considerably less risky than interning in a maximum security prison or inpatient psychiatric facility. But all practicum and internship settings carry with them the inherent risk of violence. Therefore, all students should be prepared to deal with violence and the aftermath of potential physical and psychological symptoms of violence. In illustrating this important issue, I'll step back a few decades in time.

My first job after graduating was in a large residential psychiatric center that provided long-term treatment for children and adolescents between the ages of 8 and 19. As the unit I worked in was composed of children roughly ages 10 to 13, I felt secure regarding my physical safety. In the first 5 months of employment, however, I was assaulted twice (though not seriously). A short time later, however, I was threatened by a large male with a broken bottle. This patient had a history of violence and this encounter definitely was traumatic. Thankfully, I had a good relationship with this patient and was able to assist him to de-escalate. Nothing in my graduate counseling program had prepared me to deal with client violence directed against me. After all, I was a counselor and counselors are "nice" people, so naturally no one would want to hurt us, right? Being threatened and physically attacked served as a "slap" of reality. Fortunately, most counselors will complete their practicum and internship experience without any danger to their physical safety. Still, the potential for violence toward the clinician must be accounted for in counselor education programs as well as when out on the job as a professional counselor.

Studies of violence against mental health professionals have yielded varying estimates on the potential that a counselor or other therapist will be assaulted (Baird, 2005). Work conducted by Tully, Kropf, and Price (1993) and Reeser and Wertkin (2001) are among the few in the field to have studied violence against mental health professionals. Thackery and Bobbit (1990) reported that, among the participants in a regional conference, 59% of clinical staff and 28% of nonclinical staff indicated they had been attacked at least once. Similar percentages were reported by Perkins (1990, as cited in Baird, 2005) in a British study where 116 psychologists were surveyed. Of this group, 52% said they had been assaulted at least once by a client, and 18% reported being assaulted in the year prior to the study. Other potentially dangerous and intimidating behaviors have also been reported in the mental health profession. Romans, Hays, and White (1996) reported that out of a sample of 178 counseling staff, roughly 6% reported being stalked, and 10% had a supervisee who had been stalked. Others suggest that violence may be underreported in the field and that therapists are likely to face assault at some point in their careers (Tully et al., 1993; Whitman, Armao, & Dent, 1976). Clearly, violence against counselors and other therapists would appear as an important area of research. Likewise, more suggestions on how counselors can remain safe during internship and during their professional years would seem of paramount importance.

These studies should not be taken to mean that most clients are dangerous. In fact, most clients do not pose a significant risk to assault, stalk, harass, or threaten counselors. The studies do suggest there is some inherent risk over a long career. It would also be worth mentioning that driving an automobile over the course of a lifetime is also somewhat risky, yet few people cease driving because of the risks involved. Still, the potential of assault is real and counseling programs must prepare students to deal with it. In this chapter, we explore various ways you might identify, defuse, or deal with violence during your practicum/internship.

## PREDICTORS OF CLIENT VIOLENCE

Kinney (1995) cites several risk factors as rough predictors to use in assessing the potential for a person to commit workplace violence. These, I think, are useful to keep in mind when dealing with clients in your practicum/internship setting.

- Emotionally disturbed status
- Extreme stress in personal life circumstances and/or job
- Substance use or abuse
- Frequent disputes with supervisors or authority figures
- Routine violation of company/agency/school policy or rules
- Sexual and other harassment/bullying of coworkers or peers
- Threats of violence, either verbal or written (including electronic communication)
- Preoccupation with weapons and violence
- An isolated person with a minimal support system (p. 25)

There are other factors you should keep in mind that may help you identify a potentially violent client:

*A history of violent behavior:* A fundamental tenet in the therapeutic world is that the best predictor of future behavior is previous behavior. If a client has a history of violence, it is wise to understand the circumstances that facilitated the client's violence (e.g., a history of violence toward women, bullying others). Other factors to recognize are the triggers of violence, such as stress, alcohol, drugs, confrontation, and so forth.

*A history of victimization:* Many perpetrators of violence are themselves victims of violence. Most victims of violence will not become violent themselves (Granello & Granello, 2007). However, some victims learn that violence is a viable method of controlling others and resolving conflicts. Does the client have a history of sexual, verbal, or physical abuse? Some traumatized clients may be more prone to perceiving potential threats and striking out against those they consider a viable threat (Granello & Granello, 2007).

*Substance use and abuse:* The use of alcohol and drugs plays a major role in precipitating violence (Beck, Wright, Newman, & Liese, 1992). Granted, in most therapeutic settings, clients will not be under the influence of alcohol or drugs. However, counselors will frequently work with clients who, when under the influence of a chemical substance, become impaired in judgment, their internal controls break down, and they become aggressive.

*Going off of psychopharmacologic medications against medical advice:* The use of medications in mental health therapy has a long and controversial history. There is a little doubt, however, that medication, if properly used, can aid in counseling. One of the issues to be aware of is clients who suddenly cease taking their medications. This is particularly problematic for clients taking antipsychotic drugs to help manage their violent behavior. If you are counseling clients who have been prescribed antipsychotics, you need to monitor their behavior carefully. Have aggressive incidents suddenly increased? If so, a critical question to ask such a client is, "Have you gone off your medications?"

Although psychoactive medications usually reduce the risk of violence, there is some evidence that certain medications may actually increase the propensity for violence (Baird, 2005). Haller and Deluty (1990) reported a significant relationship between antipsychotic medication and violent attacks on psychiatric staff. An important footnote here is that it seems the patients reacting with violence appear to be a minority.

*Access to weapons*: A big factor in assessing violence potential involves the client's access to weapons. In inpatient settings, the risk of handguns is minimized, although makeshift weapons (scissors, broken glass, and other sharp instruments) are a concern. Even when staff has carefully screened a patient or client for weapons, fists, legs, and the like can become a risk.

One colleague of mine was counseling an estranged husband, who was upset with his wife's decision to file for divorce. The client admitted to the counselor he had a plan to shoot his ex. After being informed by the counselor that the police would need to be notified to detain him and take charge of the weapon, the client seemed calm. He replied, "That's why I brought this in," and reached into his coat, took out a loaded handgun, and handed it over to the astonished counselor! Although this situation ended peacefully, it illustrates the potential risk inherent in counseling work. The potential for violence, though usually small, is always present.

*Stress*: Stress is frequently the catalyst for behavioral regression (Beck et al., 1992) and clients under a good deal of pressure should be viewed with caution, particularly if they do have a history of violence.

*Ability to regulate emotions and manage behavior*: Clearly, some clients are able to regulate their emotions and manage their behavior and make healthier choices than others (Goldstein, 1999). Several factors impact a client's ability to regulate emotions and manage behavior. Mental disorders or neurological conditions, for example, may impair a client's judgment, especially under stress. Substance use or abuse will also impair a client's ability to manage his or her behavior. Clients with violent ideation who see violence as a means of justification (i.e., "might makes right") are less likely to regulate their emotions and more likely to use violence (Goldstein, 1999). Anecdotally, I have noticed school bullies and men who batter particularly likely to fall into the category of those unlikely to regulate emotions and thus have difficulty managing behavior without violent means.

*Medication noncompliance*: Clients who have gone off medication, or who have been inconsistently medicated, may not be able to respond to reason from staff. Some mental illnesses (such as some types of schizophrenia) can manifest in intense paranoia, and any attempt to dialogue with clients in this state is likely to be counterproductive. Sadly, clients who cannot manage their behavior may need to be restrained by the staff. Needless to say, graduate students should not be involved with physically restraining clients unless the health and safety of themselves, staff, or other patients dictate such a response.

## Identifying Children or Adolescents at Risk for Violent Behavior

The following checklist of early warning signs can serve as a practical technique for counselors in schools and other settings to use when assessing the potential for violence among children or adolescents. Although this is not a comprehensive list, it provides basic information for violence prevention toward self and others:

1. Expresses self-destructive or homicidal ideation
2. Expresses feelings of hopelessness
3. Has a history of self-destructive behavior
4. Begins giving away formerly valued possessions
5. Appears withdrawn from peers
6. Engages in bullying peers or cruelty to animals
7. Has significant changes in mood
8. Has difficulty with impulse control or regulating emotions
9. Experiences difficulty sleeping and has significant changes in appetite
10. Evidence of significant behavioral change
11. Has a history of trauma and tragedy
12. Engages in substance abuse
13. Has been a victim of child abuse
14. Has become involved in a gang
15. Has experienced a significant loss
16. Has been tormented or teased by others
17. Preoccupied with fighting or violence
18. Preoccupied with violent TV shows, movies, DVD games, and so forth
19. Has a history of antisocial behavior
20. Has a history of being violent

(American Academy of Experts in Traumatic Stress, 2010)

## DEALING WITH AGGRESSIVE BEHAVIORS

Workplace violence has become increasingly prevalent in American society. The National Institute for Occupational Safety and Health (NIOSH) estimated that over 2 million acts of violence occur in the workplace each year (NIOSH, 1996). Dealing with the possibility of client assault involves recognizing risks and learning how to deescalate potentially dangerous situations before they become violent. Prevention is the best measure: When you accept a practicum or internship placement, it is wise to inquire about the safety plan. If the school or agency does not have one, you should be concerned and speak with your site supervisor and advisor in the counseling program. Given gratuitous acts of violence over the past two decades (Columbine High School, Sandy Hook Elementary, Virginia Tech University, various U.S. Postal Service shootings, etc.), all workplaces need a safety plan. If you have reason to believe a client is likely to harm you, a coworker, or anyone else, you must discuss the potential threat with your supervisor immediately. Do not try to deal with a potentially dangerous situation alone. Keep in mind a few basic factors:

1. Unusual behavior (speaking to oneself, hallucinations, etc.) may be unsettling, but usually does not necessarily indicate violent or dangerous behavior. (Keep in mind non–mental health professionals will likely feel more threatened by "unusual" behavior and may want counselors and other mental health professionals to have such people committed. Remember: Unusual behavior is not necessarily a predictor of violent behavior.)

2. Developing good relationships with clients may be a good way to lessen the risk of violence. In fact, the stronger your relationship with a client/student/inmate, the more likely it is you will be able to deescalate a potentially violent situation.

3. Be aware of a client's issues so that you may notice signs of aggression and intervene before violence occurs.

4. In residential placements, be aware of bullying and how it may precipitate violence among peers. When you witness bullying, immediate intervention is necessary.

5. Be aware that developmental issues may determine the seriousness of potential violence. A 6-year-old who makes a vague threat to "get you!" obviously does not carry the same level of seriousness as a 35-year-old male prison inmate making a specific threat. Regardless, take all threats seriously and follow-up on the threat through the established channels (e.g., agency, legal).

6. However, notwithstanding the previous point, take all verbal threats seriously. Report them immediately to a supervisor or a colleague.

7. Know the violence prevention plan and the response to violence plan at your practicum/internship.

8. Get safety training if it is offered at your placement. Many residential treatment centers, for example, will have active and ongoing training on dealing with violent patients.

9. Do not attempt to intervene alone. Although numerous strategies go into preventing and dealing appropriately with violence, a common first response is for staff to make a show of numbers; in some places that I have worked, the first response to any potentially violent situation was for all available staff to converge on the scene. Even very agitated patients may become compliant in the face of a large number of staff. Certainly, never approach a potentially violent client or patient on your own.

10. Conduct yourself in a calm, confident manner with clients even when you don't feel that. This statement is not anything against Rogers (1980) core condition of genuineness, nor is it about arrogance. Rather, if you

look more confident others will have more confidence in you and you are less likely to be a victim.

## DEFUSING VIOLENCE

People use violence for various reasons. For most, violence occurs when an individual perceives a threat and responds out of fear. Fortunately, most people are not violent when they are afraid. *The Gift of Fear: Survival Signals That Protect Us From Violence* (DeBecker, 1997) says people who use violence can be understood by considering their justifications, alternatives, consequences, and abilities. Someone using violence feels justified doing so, sees few alternatives, is willing to accept the consequences, and has the ability (physical, mental, etc.) to do so (DeBecker, 1997).

However, most people who get angry do not become violent (thankfully!). People who successfully manage their anger will see other options instead of violence. For example, options other than violence might be:

- Attempting to use reason to defuse a tense encounter
- Calling for a mediator
- Walking away from the encounter

When someone is angry and potentially violent, it is helpful to try to determine why he or she is angry. Using a calm tone, you might ask, "I can see you are upset. What has led to your being so upset?" You want to send the message that you acknowledge their anger and wish to understand it. Approaching the client from the standpoint of understanding is likely the best chance of defusing a potentially violent situation. If the client's hostility level decreases, you may be able to reason with him or her and create the beginning of his or her self-understanding.

Unfortunately, it should be acknowledged that remaining calm and centered is very difficult in the face of an overt threat when adrenaline is coursing through the autonomic nervous system. Remaining calm in the face of hostility and imminent violence takes a lot of practice. Law enforcement officials and first responders who regularly face threats undergo training to practice remaining calm under duress (Tunnecliffe, 2007).

If the client continues to be agitated, you might calmly state, "I see you are very upset. I want to understand why and be helpful." This is far more likely to be effective than raising your voice tone, invading the client's physical space, or loudly demanding that the client calm down. In fact, telling an upset person to calm down will likely sound insulting and could well have the opposite effect. Your body language and voice tone may do far more to defuse the situation than anything else.

Another factor in calming angry people is to establish a dialogue. Some people may be angry because they feel misunderstood and marginalized. My counseling experience working with the unemployed, underemployed, incarcerated, and people on probation has shown me how many people feel unimportant and disempowered. When people feel such marginalization, it is no surprise they respond by lashing out in anger.

Your most effective response with angry people is to acknowledge them and then to establish a dialogue. By engaging the frustrated, angry, and potentially violent client in a conversation, you build a stronger relationship and increase the chances of being able to defuse a potentially violent situation. The following is an example of a dialogue with an upset client.

| | |
|---|---|
| **Client:** | I've had it with these fucking rules! This is bullshit! (Client is becoming more and more agitated, red in the face, and looking physically aggressive.) |
| **Counselor:** | Steve, I can see you are upset. What is going on? (The counselor speaks softly, but firmly, and asks a reflective question to get Steve to think. The counselor's question also demonstrates respect, as opposed to simply being concerned about the rules.) |
| **Client:** | I'm tired of the counselors always picking on me ... always assuming I'm using again! I'm not fucking using! (Steve is still very upset. Remember, success may not come quickly, but keep the upset person talking and see if his or her anger deescalates.) |
| **Counselor:** | Ok, well, I'm happy to hear that you feel so strongly about working your program and staying sober. |
| **Client:** | I do! But just like prison, no one believes me! |
| **Counselor:** | Well, I know Sonya had given you some real positive feedback in our last group. You seemed pretty happy about that, right? |
| **Client:** | Yeah ... (Calms down when he recalls the praise.) Yeah, she did ... I guess I forgot. |
| **Counselor:** | Steve, I'd like you to feel I was trying to be helpful to you as well. What needs to happen so that you feel we are working together? |
| **Client:** | (He pauses, considering what the counselor has just said.) I don't exactly know for sure ... maybe just what you are doing now ... taking time with me. |
| **Counselor:** | Alright, maybe this is a start. |

In this example, Steve begins feeling very angry and implying everyone is against him. The counselor, mainly by listening and soliciting information, is able to deescalate the situation before it erupts into violence. The counselor's question, "What needs to happen so that you feel we are working together?" is an example of turning the tables on an angry client in a therapeutic manner. Steve, who has complained that no one understands him, is confronted with someone who wants to understand him. Steve then puts serious thought into the question and at this point, therapy can begin to take place. A potentially dangerous situation has just been transformed into a therapeutic encounter. This is what therapy is all about. It goes without mentioning that not all such encounters would turn out as successfully. In some cases the counselor would need to be able to calmly end the session and request the client return the following day (or as soon as possible). Should the client make a clear and serious threat against the counselor or a third party, then a duty exists as in *Tarasoff v. The Regents of the University of California* (1974).

## Calming Angry Clients

Shea (1998) has outlined a number of basic warning signs to which clinicians should be attuned regarding the potential for client violence. While this is not a comprehensive list, he recommends the following:

1. Be aware if the client's verbal disclosures become increasingly hostile or threatening.
2. The client becomes agitated and paces in a threatening manner.
3. The client makes angry, threatening, violent gestures, such as pounding the table, shaking his or her fist at you, or infers assaulting someone else.
4. The client grasps his or her chair or the table very tightly, causing white knuckles.
5. The client snarls or bares his or her teeth.
6. The client has a history of violence.

(Adapted from Shea, 1998)

To calm aggravated clients and to reduce the possibility of violence, you may wish to consider the following guidelines. Naturally, many of the following are much easier said than done:

1. Position yourself in front of the client but do not block the exit. Likewise, do not let the client block the exit as this may be your escape.
2. Speak slowly and in a reassuring, conversational tone of voice.
3. Explain your actions beforehand to avoid arousing the client's suspicions. Example: "I'm going to pick up the phone and call for someone to help us."
4. Make appropriate eye contact, but do not glare or give off angry looks. Try and look as though you are concerned about a friend.
5. Provide extra space between you and the client. Slowly scoot your chair back to indicate respect for space.
6. Do not touch the client unless in the extreme situation where the client assaults you. Then, defend yourself as best you can and exit the room as soon as possible.
7. Reassure the client there is a peaceful resolution to the situation. Encourage the client to verbalize his or her anger as opposed to acting on it.
8. Do not argue with the belligerent or threatening client. Such is likely to exacerbate the situation. Be silent and display a calm body posture.
9. Be aware of your school's/agency's/hospital's safety plan. Is there a "red" button or code word to alert colleagues and security? Do you know the best escape route from the building?
10. Trust your intuition. If you believe you are in danger, explain to the client you need to leave. Notify another staff member as soon as possible. If the client has a knife or gun, ask calmly for the client to set it on your

desk. If the client threatens you, try to calm him or her with soft language then call for help or leave the office. (Do not leave a weapon with the client if you can avoid it.)

This list clearly provides no blanket of protection in the face of violent clients. All counseling practicum and intern students should address safety concerns with their field site supervisor and a member of the counseling faculty.

## SELF-DEFENSE TRAINING

To my knowledge, few, if any, graduate counseling programs provide students any training or information on how to protect themselves if assaulted. In fact, my experience is that counselor educators typically do not think of this aspect. In this era of major acts of violence in school and business settings, graduate counseling programs must consider preparing students in personal safety. Schools and agencies must also of necessity set up safety plans to protect employees, clients, and graduate interns. Naturally, no agency, hospital, prison, or addictions treatment center can *guarantee* to protect you, and most schools and agencies are not set up to be high security settings and likely should not be. Therefore, it is important that you receive training in ways to protect yourself.

There are many different types of self-defense training that may be worth looking into. The reality, of course, is that a diminutive female counselor may have limited ability to protect herself against a large male client. Still, some degree of training is better than none at all. My recommendation would be to find a reputable self-defense class that offers training, with an emphasis on defensive techniques. This should also include physical training, which has many health and stress-relieving benefits beyond the safety aspect. Better physical conditioning and some knowledge of self-defense will likely increase your confidence and that may be an asset if you are confronted by a hostile client.

Regardless of your physical size or level of training, your best asset is good common sense. Your first option is always to try to calm a potential assailant. In fact, a counselor's ability to reason with a hostile client or patient is likely far more important than physical conditioning. Many angry clients are actually frightened and thus the reason for their aggressive behavior. If you can help dispel their fear, you may avoid a potential assault and be in a better therapeutic position. Basically, you want to reason with the client and point out how avoiding a fight is to his or her benefit. Another possibility, at least in some situations, is to flee from the situation. If you cannot calm the client and you are backed into a corner and forced to defend yourself, then use whatever defense you can muster. Certainly, protect vital areas and call for help as loud as you can. Use your legs for kicking as they generate more force than arms and leave you less exposed. If you can just momentarily slow down your attacker, you may be able to reach help. Remember, safety is often about improving the odds.

It goes without mentioning, of course, that preventing an assault is the best protection of all. Prevention also involves agency policies and procedures regarding staffing, training, a viable safety plan, and making sure clients understand that the repercussions for violent behavior will be serious. Some agencies even put in their informed consent that should the client make a specific threat, the police will be called. In the event of an assault, regardless of how serious, the agency will press legal charges. Interns would be wise to ask their field site supervisors about such policies.

## WORKPLACE VIOLENCE PREVENTION PLAN

All schools, agencies, and so forth, need plans to assess for violence, prevent violence, and deal with the aftermath of violence. A few basic steps for violence prevention are the following:

1. Identify vulnerabilities in the school, agency, or treatment facility. Does the facility have a means of assessing violence? Is there an emergency plan to deal with violence after it occurs?
2. Naturally, violence prevention is the most important goal. Develop early intervention systems to identify and intervene before violence occurs (e.g., mediation programs, peer helping programs, bullying prevention programs).
3. Develop a threat protocol to assess for violence and a plan to deal with the aftermath of violence. Then, practice the plan routinely through emergency drills to ensure everyone knows their role in trauma management. In addition, when threats occur (verbal, written, text messages, etc.) always take them seriously and follow up with an investigation.
4. Establish who in the school, college, or agency will be responsible for communication to the staff, families, media, and so forth. This reduces rumors and assists with timely information and sends the message that the facility has a plan.
5. Develop feedback measures to assess how the violence prevention program is working. Use focus groups for detailed insight and survey the staff.
6. Review past incidents of violence to see how successfully they were managed.

(Kinney, 1995, pp. 46–47)

## WHAT TO DO AFTER AN ASSAULT

If the worst has come to pass and you have been assaulted, you need immediate assistance. Notify staff, medical personnel, your supervisors, and law enforcement officials (if necessary). Get a medical checkup to ensure you are not injured. If you have been injured, be aware of who is responsible to pay the cost of treatment (the practicum/internship placement? you? your insurance? your counseling program?). This is often a gray area. It goes without saying you should have your own personal insurance. In my own experience as a former clinical director and current professor of counselor education, this is an over-looked area of practicum and internship. Fortunately, in all my years as a counselor educator, no students have been assaulted. But not all programs can make the same statement and the potential for violence is always present, particularly with certain populations (e.g., domestic batterers, clients with a history of violence, psychotic clients) and placements (e.g., correctional facilities, inpatient psychiatric centers, counseling in homes).

Should an assault occur, you need to document what happened and why you responded the way you did. You also need to speak with your immediate supervisor as soon as possible, because that person will likely need to file an incident report for the agency or for insurance purposes. Your supervisor likely will request that you file a written report of what happened, including what led up to the violence, your response, and how the matter ended. Given the emotion-laden nature of violence, you may need a few days to write the report, then a little time to ensure you have been accurate. This is not to imply you are fabricating. Hastily written traumatic experiences may lead to factual errors and as the incident is likely to become a legal matter you need to be as factual as possible.

After you have received medical care, made the report, and spoken with your supervisor, it is important to debrief the traumatic experience with a supportive colleague (Tunnecliffe, 2007). Debriefing, followed by longer-term counseling, can assist you in making the transition back to feeling healthy. It should be stated, however, that in the aftermath of an assault, you are likely to experience a transition period before regaining your emotional equilibrium (Van der Kolk, 1994). Feeling tense, frightened, having higher blood pressure, and experiencing flashbacks are all normal symptoms of recovery and are nothing to hide or be ashamed about. These are all symptoms of a normal and healthy response to trauma. Most victims of trauma have symptoms that will significantly remit in 30 days. So, give yourself time to let your body and your psyche heal. As a counselor who has been the victim of an assault, I can tell you that healing does take time and will involve at least some of the symptoms mentioned earlier. Fortunately, most survivors do not develop posttraumatic stress disorder (PTSD; Tunnecliffe, 2007; Van der Kolk, 1994).

Another factor regarding healing involves the perpetrator who assaulted you. Residential treatment programs will have sanctions for assault and, depending on the severity of the assault, there may be legal charges. My recommendation is that students as well as professional counselors, psychologists, and other staff should press charges when assaulted. Pursuing legal action sends a clear message that assault is taken seriously and that sanctions will follow. Most treatment facilities will likely back you up if you decide to pursue legal action, although it is realistic to note that some may not (often because of concerns about negative publicity). Victims of violence who feel unsupported by their employers are likely to feel revictimized and may experience more significant trauma (Kinney, 1995).

Some type of restitution should be made between the perpetrator and the victim. Many schools and agencies have a written policy on this. Some communities have programs such as Victim–Offender Reconciliation Programs (VORP) that bring the victim and offender together (with the victim's approval) so that the offender can apologize and the victim can discuss how the violence has impacted him or her on a personal, medical, familial, and occupational level. Such programs can provide important closure for the victim provided the offender is truly remorseful and the victim is ready to face the assailant.

## CONCLUSION

Predicting violent behavior is at best difficult. Perhaps the best type of defense for counselors to employ is to understand the population they counsel and take appropriate precautions. Appropriate precautions would mean building appropriate relationships with clients/students/inmates, and so on so that they view you as helpful and not an authority figure. Be informed regarding the specific mental health and behavioral issues of the clients assigned to your care. Do your best to develop a caring relationship that incorporates techniques to calm angry clients. As previously mentioned, speaking calmly, and somewhat quietly, is a prudent behavior in the face of hostility. Body language is of critical importance as well. Despite the intensity of the moment, you must find a way to keep your posture as relaxed and nonaggressive as possible (again, easier said). Do not corner a client in an office. Always give them an escape route (and give yourself one as well). It is important to ask the aggrieved person, "How can I be helpful?" This may force the angry client to self-reflect, which might calm him or her somewhat. Never adopt a challenging attitude in the face of anger as that is likely to be received as a challenge at best and disrespect at worst. An angry client who feels disrespected is more likely to lash out physically.

As previously mentioned in this chapter, self-defense training is a very good idea for everyone, especially for counselors working in correctional facilities. It must be re-emphasized, naturally, that physical defense should be the refuge of last resort. No matter the size or self-defense expertise of the counselor, physical self-defense is dangerous both to the aggressor and the defender. So, use force only as a last resort. If you can, exit from the situation and seek assistance. Or, call for assistance using a "red button" or code word. Know your agency's/school's/prison's safety plan. To repeat, you will likely be safe throughout your practicum and internship and the odds certainly are with you. But be prepared as there are no guarantees.

The Occupational Safety and Health Administration (OSHA) recently published guidelines for preventing workplace violence for health care and social service workers (2015). OSHA's report offers numerous suggestions for assessing the potential for violence and addressing the aftermath of violence. Their global checklist includes:

1. Assessing risk factors for workplace violence
2. Inspecting work areas (for building security, potential hazards, locked doors, etc.)
3. Inspecting exterior building areas
4. Inspecting parking areas
5. Security measures (physical barriers, CCTV monitors, alarm systems, panic buttons, etc.)

OSHA makes the report available free of charge and counselors may download the full report at www.osha.gov/Publications/osha3148.pdf

So, good luck in your practicum and internship and stay safe.

## REFERENCES

American Academy of Experts in Traumatic Stress. (2010). *Identifying students "at-risk" for violent behavior: A checklist of "early warning signs."* Retrieved May 12, 2010, from www.aaets.org/article108.htm

Baird, B. N. (2005). *The internship, practicum, and field placement handbook: A guide for the helping professions* (4th ed.). Upper Saddle River, NJ: Pearson/Prentice Hall.

Beck, A. T., Wright, F. D., Newman, C. F., & Liese, B. S. (1992). *Cognitive therapy of substance abuse.* New York, NY: Guilford Press.

DeBecker, G. (1997). *The gift of fear: Survival signs that protect us from violence.* Boston, MA: Little Brown.

Goldstein, A. P. (1999). *The prepare curriculum: Teaching prosocial competencies.* Champaign, IL: Research Press.

Granello, D. H., & Granello, P. F. (2007). *Suicide: An essential guide for helping professionals and educators.* New York, NY: Pearson/Allyn & Bacon.

Haller, R. M., & Deluty, R. H. (1990). Characteristics of psychiatric inpatients who assault staff severely. *Journal of Nervous and Mental Disease, 178*(8), 536–537.

Kinney, J. A. (1995). *Violence at work: How to make your company safer for employees and customers.* Englewood Cliffs, NJ: Prentice Hall.

National Institute for Occupational Safety and Health. (1996). *Violence in the workplace: Risk factors and prevention strategies.* Cincinnati, OH: Author.

Reeser, L. C., & Wertkin, P. A. (2001). Safety training in a social work education: A national survey. *Journal of Teaching in Social Work, 21,* 95–114.

Romans, J. S. C., Hays, J. R., & White, T. K. (1996). Stalking and related behaviors experienced by counseling center staff members from current or former clients. *Professional Psychology: Research and Practice, 27,* 595–599.

Shea, S. C. (1998). *Psychiatric interviewing: The art of understanding: A practical guide for psychiatrists, psychologists, counselors, social workers, nurses, and other mental health professionals* (2nd ed.). New York, NY: Saunders.

Thackery, M., & Bobbit, R. G. (1990). Patient aggression against clinical and nonclinical staff in a VA medical center. *Hospital and Community Psychiatry, 41,* 195–197.

Tully, C. T., Kropf, N. P., & Price, J. L. (1993). Is the field a hard hat area? A study of violence in field placements. *Journal of Social Work Education, 29,* 191–199.

Tunnecliffe, M. (2007). *A life in crisis: 27 lessons from acute trauma counseling work.* Palmyra, Western Australia: Bayside.

Van der Kolk, B. (1994). The body keeps score. *Harvard Review of Psychiatry, 1*(5), 253–265.

Whitman, R. M., Armao, B. B., & Dent, O. B. (1976). Assault on the therapist. *American Journal of Psychiatry, 133,* 424–429.

# ELEVEN

# TERMINATION IN COUNSELING: HOW TO SAY GOODBYE

Up until recently, the process of termination in counseling has largely been avoided in the literature (Gladding, 2009; Maholick & Turner, 1979). Research by Ward (1984) concluded that the reason for this deficit is twofold. First, termination is associated with loss, which is often an avoided topic in our society. Second, termination, unlike establishing the counseling relationship, is not directly related to the skills that promote counseling. This chapter focuses on methods of termination and also illustrates some issues that impede termination both for the counselor and the client. It is worth mentioning that for some clients, the counseling relationship may represent the best relationship they have ever had. For clients whose primary positive human connection is during counseling, it is natural they would seek to remain in counseling indefinitely.

Gladding (2009) postulates that more emphasis has recently been placed on termination because of a greater societal acceptance of loss. Although much of Western society has traditionally been one of death-denying societies (Kübler-Ross, 1969), loss and grief are now popular topics in the counseling field, as numerous books, journal articles, and workshops target grief counseling. Terminations and endings are now associated with new beginnings and new adventures regarding the counseling relationship and it is this latter point that is critical for successful client termination. It should also be acknowledged that a lack of termination training in counselor education programs results in incomplete education and could be a potential liability for counselors unskilled in ending counseling relationships. After all, endings are a significant part of the life process (Maholick & Turner, 1979) and to begin a new phase in life, a former experience must be completed (Perls, 1969). Termination can also serve as a springboard for clients to move on to healthier, more growth-oriented behavior (Yalom & Leszcz, 2005). Basically, termination is an important part of the counseling process for both client and counselor. Generally counselors make the termination decisions (Gibson & Mitchell, 2008), typically based on successful completion of the treatment plan, but it is best if termination is mutually agreed upon by counselor and client.

Endings in counseling also serve as important reminders of the life process. Relationships with family begin at birth, grow and develop throughout the life span, and terminate in death. Along the way, friendships end with relocation, marriages end in divorce, and collegial relations change as people accept new jobs and leave previous ones. Healthy adjustment to change depends on acknowledgment and mourning the end of relationships and transitioning to new ones (Humphrey, 2009; Perls, 1969). Proper termination of the counseling relationship conveys respect and may help prevent harm, both of which are important ethical considerations (Vasquez, Bingham, & Barnett, 2008). Termination may of course be painful for the client but it also presents the opportunity to create new and, often, more fulfilling relationships. It likely is worth mentioning that counseling is also a relationship that by its very nature should grow toward separation.

Termination has become a more common topic in recent years, especially with the emergence of time-limited approaches, such as narrative and solution-focused counseling (Gladding, 2009). These approaches begin with the assumption that each session may be the last and that consequently, the counselor should be preparing the client for termination (O'Hanlon, 1994). Acknowledging that time in counseling is limited could also help the client in becoming more proactive and doing less procrastinating. Understanding the limits of counseling may also spur the client to make more use of his or her time and change jobs, go back to finish college, end unhealthy relationships, and set new goals.

Successful counseling will result in attitudinal and behavioral changes in clients' lives. Such growth should naturally be a clear focus of counseling. Counselors also should encourage their clients to practice their new skills each week in their personal lives. Part of the therapeutic process also involves the counselor preparing the client for the ending of the counseling relationship. This also can involve a role play. By role playing termination, clients and counselors acknowledge and honor the relationship. As Gladding (1990) says, termination puts "insights into action" (p. 130).

Naturally, not all counseling relationships end as the counselor or client would like. Circumstances and issues may arise that facilitate the counselor terminating the counseling relationship against a client's wishes (Welfel, 2010). According to Standard A.11.c of the *ACA Code of Ethics* counselors may terminate a counseling relationship in the following circumstances:

- When the client is no longer benefiting from or may be harmed through continued counseling
- When in jeopardy of harm by the client or by another person with whom the client has a relationship
- When clients do not pay the fees as agreed upon

When counselors are unable to be of assistance to clients, counselors must provide adequate notice and pretermination counseling and recommend other service providers when necessary. Also, counselors should do everything possible to ensure a smooth transition to a new counseling professional. If client insolvency is an issue, the counselor must provide a referral to a counselor or agency that offers a sliding fee scale (where allowed) or provides pro bono services. A referral to another provider will, of course, require the client to sign a release of information in order to share information and records with the new mental health professional.

It should be mentioned that clients often terminate the counseling relationship. Some research suggests that 30% to 60% of all counseling clients drop out of counseling before completing the treatment plan (Garfield, 1994). All professional counselors have experienced client's discontinuation of services even when treatment was going well. Clients often drop out without notifying their counselor. The counselor's ethical obligation in such situations is to attempt to contact the client suggesting a return to counseling to complete treatment or for a referral to another provider. Professional counselors will even experience court-mandated clients dropping from treatment even when noncompliance means a return to prison or jail! So, counselors must be prepared for clients to withdraw from counseling without notice regardless of the circumstances or consequences. In such situations, counselors must attempt to contact the client and encourage completing treatment or taking a referral. Realistically, clients who drop out of counseling are often reluctant to return.

Finally, termination serves to reinforce that the client is ready to graduate from counseling as a healthier, more well-adjusted person (Rogers, 1961). Personally, as both a counselor and a former client, I much prefer the term *graduation* over termination because it implies goals have been met. Through the crucible of the counseling relationship, the client has grown and mastered many of the obstacles that originally brought him or her into counseling. The client's increased ability to manage the demands of life results in increased self-confidence and a healthier and more meaningful life (Yalom & Leszcz, 2005). The lack of appropriate termination would actually rob the client of a lot of potential growth! So, counselors and counseling students can utilize termination as an important growth step.

In this chapter, I discuss some issues regarding when and how to terminate counseling.

## WHEN TO TERMINATE A COUNSELING RELATIONSHIP

Knowing when to terminate a counseling relationship is an inexact proposition. In the managed care system, typically insurance companies determine the session parameters of counseling. Other factors that will influence termination are legally set limits (by a judge, probation officer, etc.) and whether the client is in a residential treatment setting. In my experience, clients often make the decision to end the relationship before the counselor. Still, it is important to dialogue with the client to ensure that he or she has thought through the process. If counseling ends too soon, clients may not be able to maintain the healthy behaviors they learned in therapy. Conversely, if termination is not addressed in a timely manner, counseling may drag on with no real focus, wasting time that could be used for needy clients (to say nothing of the cost). There are several issues to address when considering termination (Gladding, 2009):

- Have clients achieved behavioral, cognitive, or affective goals? When both clients and counselors have a clear idea about whether particular goals have been reached, the timing of termination is easier to figure out. The key is to establish a mutually agreed-on contract before counseling begins.
- Can clients concretely show they have made progress in what they wanted to accomplish? Specific progress may be the basis for making a decision about termination.
- Is the counseling relationship helpful? If either the client or the counselor senses that what is occurring in the counseling sessions is not helpful, termination may be appropriate.
- Has the context of the original counseling arrangement changed? In cases where there is a move or a prolonged illness, termination (as well as a referral) should be considered. Examine whether the client's initial problem or symptoms have been eliminated or significantly reduced.
- Does the client appear capable of coping with demands in his or her life?
- Is the client better able to relate to others and to give and receive love?
- Has the client progressed in his or her ability to be productive in career and life tasks?
- Can the client "play" and enjoy life? (pp. 177–180)

I have also found it helpful to consider another factor: Is the counselor confident the client is ready for termination? This is nothing scientific, but experienced counselors often develop a sixth sense regarding a client's likelihood for success. Wise counselors will attend to this "sense" and explore the client's own readiness for termination.

It is up to the counselor to explain termination clearly to the client at the earliest possible time. The initial intake is the ideal time to cover the topic, especially as essentials such as confidentially, fees, and related topics are covered during that session. This way, the client understands that at some point in the future, the counseling relationship will end. Termination should also be framed in terms of success. For example:

Counselor:   Now, at some point in the future, when you have met your goals for counseling, you will graduate from counseling. So, we want to keep that end point in mind.

As mentioned earlier, if the client has been mandated by a judge, probation officer, or another party, then termination will likely have more fixed parameters.

Counselor:   Steve, the terms of your probation specify 12 sessions of anger management. Provided you have attended all sessions and have made progress, termination will occur at that point and I will write a report for your probation officer. Do you have any questions?

As another example:

**Counselor:**  Jade, your health plan provides eight individual counseling sessions. Now, in the event we both feel you could use more, I can ask the HMO to authorize two additional sessions. Another option after eight sessions is to get you into a local support group.

These are all examples of the counselor explaining at the onset that the counseling relationship will end. This reduces the likelihood that the client will be surprised by termination.

## DISCUSSING TERMINATION WITH THE CLIENT

In many cases, termination may be a shared decision between the counselor and the client. For example, a client may say, "I believe I have made a lot of progress the past 3 months. I'm thinking one more session would be enough. What do you think?" Or, the counselor may initiate the conversation by saying, "You appear to be in a very solid place. I'm thinking we could wrap up our relationship in two more sessions. What do you think about that?" In these examples, both the client's and the counselor's termination statements imply client growth and resolution of whatever issues brought the client into counseling. Both statements also involve verifying the message with the other party. I encourage counselors to include the client in any discussion of termination; including the client in significant discussions demonstrates your respect and trust in the client (Miller & Rollnick, 2002). The following is an example of a discussion of termination to a client:

**Counselor:**  Shoshanna, I have seen you make a lot of progress over the past 9 weeks. Your depression, as evidenced by the Beck Depression Inventory-II, seems to have dropped significantly. You have also mentioned that you are managing your grief much better and that recently you have been able to reach out and initiate social events with friends. These were the issues that brought you into counseling. So, I'm wondering how you feel about terminating from counseling in the next 2 weeks.

**Client:**  You know I'm kind of thinking the same thing. I do feel a lot better … still sad about my mother's death, but she did have a full life and she was old. I would like to have at least a couple of sessions to wrap up. Okay?

**Counselor:**  Absolutely. We can also revisit the option of the grief support group.

In the example, the counselor raises the topic of termination and frames it in such a fashion that client progress is noted in a concrete manner. The counselor also solicits the input of the client and thereby demonstrates trust and respect for the client's judgment. They agree on at least one more session and the counselor mentions a support group in the event the client would like more emotional support.

Cormier and Hackney (2008) believe that when counseling relationships last more than 3 months, the final 3 to 4 weeks should be spent discussing the impact of termination. They suggest counselors inquire how their clients will cope without the counselor's support. Counselors may also address topics such as what has changed since the client has entered therapy, what the client has learned, and how the client's life will be different in the postcounseling phase. In my experience, it has been helpful to acknowledge the growth and hard work of the client, as most clients will appreciate having their personal work acknowledged by the counselor.

De Shazer and Berg (1988), proponents of solution-focused therapy, advocate using scaling questions to assess client growth. The following dialogue is an example of using scaling questions to discuss termination:

Counselor:    Well, we are now at the end of counseling. On a scale of 1 to 10, with 10 being *high* and 1 being *low*, how helpful has counseling been?

Scaling questions provide some concrete idea of progress and allow the client to provide explicit feedback regarding what has and has not been helpful. Scaling questions focused on therapeutic effectiveness provide a forum for client and counselor discussion. Now, suppose the client answers in the following manner:

Client:       On a scale of 1 to 10, today's session has been a 2.
Counselor:    Okay, what can we do next time to move it to a 3?

In this case, the counselor does not become defensive and argue with the client, but rather accepts the client's verdict and reframes it to elicit what could be more helpful in the next session. Scaling questions could also be used at termination to help the counselor understand how he or she can be more helpful in the future.

Counselor:    Okay, I ask this question to all clients about to graduate from counseling. On a scale of 1 to 10, with 1 being counseling was *not helpful* to 10 being counseling was *very helpful*, how would you rate your experience in counseling?
Client:       I would rate it a 6.
Counselor:    Well, it sounds like our time together was worthwhile. Now, what could we have done to make our rating a 7?

When using scaling questions, it is best to keep improvements small so as to make them appear more attainable (De Shazer & Berg, 1988). As much as possible, the counselor should make the termination session as positive as possible, and discussing outcomes and soliciting feedback from the client is the most direct way to achieve this.

## THE TERMINATION PLAN

If you think a client may be ready for termination, there are several logistical issues to consider:

1. Does the client have adequate resources outside the counseling relationship to sustain whatever gains were made in counseling? Resources might include supportive family, friends, colleagues, support groups, and so forth.
2. Have you spent adequate time preparing the client for termination? Ideally, the counselor begins to prepare the client for eventual termination at the onset of therapy. Some professionals recommend an approach called *fading* (Dixon & Glover, 1984) involving a gradual decrease in counseling. For example, going to 30-minute sessions, or spacing sessions 2 weeks or more apart instead of meeting weekly. Another technique involves reminding the client about the remaining number of sessions: "Now, remember, we have three more sessions remaining." You do not want an abrupt termination or else you can undo successful therapeutic gains and potentially be liable for abandonment.
3. Have you and the client agreed on an aftercare plan (if needed)? Has the client agreed to join a support group, if necessary?
4. Have you documented in the case notes why you terminated the client?
5. In cases of mandated counseling, has the client met the conditions set down by the court, probation officer, place of employment, disciplinary board, or other concerned institutions? Does the client need a letter stating he or she has met the conditions? If subpoenaed for a court hearing, could you defend termination?

These issues will not apply equally to all clients, but they should be considered and discussed with the client before making a decision regarding termination. Counselors should also discuss termination issues with their supervisor.

## CLIENT'S RESISTANCE TO TERMINATION

Counselors should be aware that some clients will resist termination. There are several reasons why a client might desire to remain in counseling even after the reasons that brought the client to counseling have been resolved. A client's resistance to termination is most common when the counseling relationship has been long term, involves a strong connection between the counselor and the client, or involves factors such as grief, fear of rejection, and previous abandonment (Cormier & Cormier, 1998; Welfel & Patterson, 2005).

Some clients have few close relationships and find counseling hard to give up. It is worth mentioning that healthy friendships involve both parties engaging in a two-way relationship. Counseling relationships, although friendly, are not true friendships, because counseling is all about the client. Counseling is also a professional relationship, involving an ethical code, fees, time limits, and boundaries regarding time and social distance. It may be helpful for counselors to discuss the various differences between counseling relationships and friendships, should the client be reluctant to terminate.

Witness the following exchange of dialogue between the counselor and a client reluctant to terminate:

| | |
|---|---|
| **Counselor:** | Ellen, we have spent the last 6 months together. I have seen you make a lot of progress on your stated goal of managing your depression, establishing personal contacts, and recently you were able to go back to work part time. I think it's time to talk about termination. |
| **Client:** | I'm just not ready. Yeah, I am back at work, but I just went back a month ago and it's hard to get back in the swing of things. Also, I have made some progress making contacts, but have yet to make a real friend. It's true that I do feel better—maybe a combination of new medication and such, but coming to see you weekly is something I can't let go of. |
| **Counselor:** | I appreciate that you have found our time together valuable. But, as I mentioned two sessions ago, we are running up to the end of your insurance benefits in 2 weeks. I can work with you two more sessions then we refer you to a support group run by a colleague. |
| **Client:** | I think a support group is okay … and I'm willing to begin, but I want to continue counseling with you. |
| **Counselor:** | Well, we are up against a couple of issues. One, as your benefits expire, our agency requires we have a minimum charge of $60 per session. The more pressing issue is that you appear ready to graduate from counseling. You have met all your goals and seem to be well on your way. |
| **Client:** | I might be able to get the money through out-of-pocket pay. So, I can continue, right? |

There is no simple way to terminate with a client who is not ready to hear about termination. The counselor in this dialogue might have inquired of the client for some idea of how she would know when she would be ready for termination. Another possibility is, if the counselor believes he or she has taken the client as far as he or she can, perhaps a referral to another counselor. In such cases, the counselor should discuss the situation with his or her supervisor, get support, and make a plan to address client resistance to termination.

A client's fear of termination is an issue to address directly. For example:

| | |
|---|---|
| **Counselor:** | Erica, I want to follow up on the topic of termination. As I mentioned previously, we have two more sessions left. I know you have some concerns regarding termination. |
| **Client:** | Yes. I'm not ready to let go of the support I'm getting here. I agree that I've made a lot of progress the past 4 months, but I |

|  |  |
|---|---|
|  | want to keep our relationship. I don't think I can make it without you. |
| Counselor: | I appreciate the hard work you have put into counseling and both of us have noted the gains you have made, especially the past 2 months. Given how you felt when counseling began, I believe you are selling yourself short regarding your own progress and resilience. |
| Client: | But I'm not ready to end our relationship. Finally someone understands me. |
| Counselor: | The reality is that our time is coming to a close. My belief is that you are ready for the next step. I think it would be wise to explore your feelings and beliefs regarding termination today and the next couple of weeks. There are also some options regarding support groups for continued growth. |

The client in this scenario is very reluctant to end counseling. This hesitancy is best addressed delicately, but firmly. Clients reluctant to end counseling may be overly reliant on counseling. The counselor in this scenario could use some creativity. For example, the sessions could be staggered to bimonthly instead of every week, thus providing a little more transition time. However, extending the counseling relationship in such a manner might reinforce the client's neediness and be counter-therapeutic. The counselor would be wise to have the client explore her feelings regarding termination, including a list of her fears about termination as well as what she may gain by ending the counseling relationship. As previously mentioned, support groups are always an option, provided they exist.

It must be admitted, however, that some clients will be highly resistant to ending counseling. Several years ago, I encountered a woman who had been a client at an agency for more than 20 years. The agency, wisely, had recently decided that long-term clients (2 or more years, those whose insurance coverage had run out, and those who seemed more appropriate for case management) would be moved to the case management area, where they would participate in support groups, peer groups, and social activities, and meet weekly with a caseworker, not a counselor. In most cases, this policy was working well. This particular client, however, demanded to speak to the clinical director (me). When I went to retrieve her file from the office, it was as thick as the *DSM-5* (*Diagnostic and Statistical Manual of Mental Disorders*, fifth edition; American Psychiatric Association, 2013)! For this client, counseling was more about avoidance than growth. Over her strenuous objections, she was referred to the case management program.

As a new counselor, you will notice that clients have many ways to resist termination, whether at the end of the session or the end of the counseling relationship. They may request additional counseling after their goals have clearly been met, or sabotage what appears to be successful therapeutic progress because they want the counseling relationship to continue. Some clients may insist that their current counselor is the "only one" who has ever been helpful, thus using manipulation in an attempt to entice counselor guilt. With apologies to DeShazer who once held a mock funeral for client resistance (Corey, 2009), client resistance is alive and kicking!

## COUNSELOR RESISTANCE TO TERMINATION

Although the ultimate goal in counseling is to help the client move toward independence from the counseling relationship, some counselors occasionally resist termination (Corey, Corey, & Callanan, 2007). Sometimes counselors will encounter clients they feel a special bond with, or, unfortunately, clients they become infatuated with. Counselors, especially beginning counselors, must take special care to ensure they are working in the best interest of the client whenever the issue of termination arises. Counselors who find themselves reluctant to terminate a client are encouraged to consult with a supervisor or trusted colleague to critique their motivations. Goodyear (1981) has cited reasons why counselors may have difficulty with termination:

1. When termination signals the end of a significant relationship
2. When termination arouses the counselor's anxieties about the client's ability to function independently
3. When termination arouses guilt in the counselor about having not been more effective with the client
4. When the counselor's professional self-concept is threatened by the client abruptly and angrily leaving
5. When termination signals the end of a learning experience for the counselor (e.g., the counselor may have been relying on the client to learn more about the dynamics of a disorder or of a particular culture)
6. When termination signals the end of a particularly exciting experience of living vicariously through the adventures of the client
7. When termination becomes a symbolic recapitulation of other (especially unresolved) farewells in the counselor's life
8. When termination arouses conflicts regarding the counselor's own individuation (e.g., the counselor's own sense of self versus others)

In my observation, some counselors also form an unhealthy attachment based on an attraction to the client and are reluctant to see the relationship end. The ethical issues involved in dual relationships are covered in Chapter 3. Beyond ethical parameters, it must be mentioned that counseling is entirely about the client. Clients, particularly those with a history of unhealthy relationships, may mistake the counselor's professional concern with that of actual friendship. Counselors then must take special care to set and respect the boundary separating the professional from the personal. Termination for clients who believe they have a special relationship with the counselor may be particularly difficult. Such clients are likely to resist ending the relationship.

*Self-Reflections for Counselors Reluctant to Terminate With a Client*

■ List the reasons why you are reluctant to terminate with the client. Whose issues are the most significant, yours or the client's?

■ Now, in examining these reasons, whose needs are being served by keeping the counseling relationship going?

■ What would be in the best interests of the client? Also, what would be in your own best interests (ethically, legally, professionally, personally, etc.)?

■ If a friend or colleague were in the position you are in, how would you advise that friend or colleague?

■ What do you need to do to be ready to "let go" of this client and facilitate termination?

■ What have you learned from this termination? How will that knowledge help you in future situations?

When counselors find they are having difficulty in ending a counseling relationship, it would be prudent for them to carefully assess the reasons for their reluctance. It is well worth mentioning that counselors certainly will have their own personal issues, inadequacies, and struggles. The problem develops when counselors have not adequately addressed these issues or struggles. Counselors with a history of abandonment may be particularly vulnerable to fears of termination (Guy, 1987).

In cases where termination has been difficult for whatever reason, Welfel and Patterson (2005, pp. 124–125) offer four suggestions for counselors:

1. "Be aware of the client's needs and desires and allow the client to express them." The client may wish to express gratitude. Counselors should accept such expressions of gratitude with a simple "Thank you." Do not minimize the value of the client's expression.

2. "Review the major events of the counseling experience and bring the review into the present." This suggestion provides the client the opportunity to review the progress he or she has made during counseling.

3. "Supportively acknowledge the changes the client has made." The counselor should let the client know she or he recognizes the progress the client has achieved.

4. "Request follow-up contact." Counseling relationships eventually end, but the client needs to know the counselor is invested in the client's continued well-being. But, use discretion here as more "needy" clients may see this as an opening to extending the relationship. Put parameters on future contact such as "Give me a brief call ..." (Gladding, 2009, p. 187).

---

*The Case of Jordan and Yvonne*

Jordan has been counseling Yvonne for six sessions. Yvonne originally presented for counseling after a particularly painful ending to a romantic relationship. From the beginning, Jordan noticed he and Yvonne seemed to have a stronger than typical counselor–client attachment. Although he feels Yvonne is ready for termination, he is reluctant for their relationship to end because he enjoys spending time with her. Yvonne has also mentioned that she would like to be in a relationship with someone who "listens to me like you do and understands me like you." Jordan knows that ethically he should refer her or terminate with her, given both their feelings. Yet, he enjoys their sessions and looks forward to seeing her.

1. If Jordan were to consult with you, how would you advise him?
2. What ethical issues and concerns would you want Jordan to consider?

---

## REFERRALS AND FOLLOW-UP

Unfortunately, it goes without saying that most counselors will not be able to help 100% of the clients who pass through their door. My experience is that beginning counselors frequently struggle when they encounter clients who make marginal progress. Counselors need to be realistic regarding making referrals when productivity ends. A referral involves arranging continued therapeutic assistance for clients when the current counseling relationship is not making a satisfactory progress (Pietrofesa, Hoffman, & Splete, 1984). There are numerous reasons referrals are made:

- The client has an issue the counselor does not know how to handle.
- The counselor is inexperienced in a particular area (e.g., substance abuse, couples therapy, etc.).
- The counselor knows of a nearby expert who would be more helpful to the client.
- The counselor and client have incompatible personalities.
- The relationship between the counselor and the client is stuck in an initial phase of counseling. (Goldstein, 1971)

The client may resist a referral, perhaps feeling that such action implies a sense of failure on his or her part. Likewise, a client may feel rejected by the counselor. Thus, the counselor needs to make it clear that the reason for the referral to another professional is neither failure nor fault of either client or counselor. Counselors should also mention the professional to whom they are referring the client, and then volunteer to make the referral for the client, or at the very least, encourage the client to make the call before the sessions end. Ideally, the counselor would bring up the possibility of a referral during the informed-consent phase of the intake, so that the client understands from the outset that a referral is a possibility.

When the counselor begins to believe that another counselor (or other professional) would be more beneficial for the client, he or she should raise the issue for discussion with the client. Discussing the possibility of a referral provides the client a voice in the matter and also establishes a forum for the counselor and client to discuss the issue. Dialoguing on the pros and cons of referral may also take some pressure off both parties because addressing the topic of referral establishes that, perhaps, another counselor is more appropriate for the client's issue. Welfel and Patterson (2005) recommend a counselor spend at least one session with the client in preparation for the referral. Some clients may need several sessions before a referral can be made.

Following up with a client after counseling has ended has become more common in recent years (Okun & Kantrowitz, 2008). Following up with former clients also provides the counselor valuable client feedback regarding the effectiveness of counseling. It can also serve to reinforce that the counselor is still concerned about the client's progress even after counseling has ended.

Follow-up can be conducted on either a short-term (3 to 6 months after counseling has ended) or long-term (more than 6 months after counseling has ended) basis. One of the difficulties, especially for more mobile clients, is that counselors may no longer have an accurate address for agency clients (it is easier to track school students). Many clients also are less invested in participating in follow-up activities when they are no longer seeking counseling services. In fact, the percentage of clients who respond to counselors' follow-up efforts is, in my experience, quite small. Naturally, for practicum and intern students, follow-up can be challenging depending on whether the intern is leaving in 3 months or will be at the site another year. Regardless, postcounseling follow-up is challenging for counselors and the schools and agencies where they work for a variety of reasons (e.g., client relocation, other priorities, working with another professional).

Follow-up with former clients can take many forms. In the counseling centers where I have worked, follow-up consisted of a simple evaluation form accompanied by a self-addressed stamped envelope. This provides the client the opportunity to evaluate the services provided. Having had some time and distance from counseling might also be beneficial for the evaluation process as the client may have a clearer idea of how counseling has benefited him or her. In the immediate aftermath, gains that seemed so promising may look less so a few months later when the supportive structure of counseling has been removed. Conversely, clients may have a clearer understanding of the gains they have made through the counseling process. This method of sending the client an evaluation is a safe method of follow-up, although some may see it as impersonal.

A second method of follow-up is to invite the former client in for a session to discuss the progress he or she has made after counseling has concluded (Cormier & Cormier, 1998). This method is more personal and provides the counselor the most direct feedback. For counselors working in schools, bringing in former clients may not present a problem. However, the time and expense of scheduling former clients for a check-in session in many clinical settings can be prohibitive. Does the client need to pay? Is the follow-up session free? If the counselor works in an agency, college center, or another high-volume center with a waiting list, bringing in former clients for follow-up sessions is not feasible. It is also likely that the only clients who would show for a follow-up session are ones who felt counseling was a real success.

Another common way for counselors to check on clients is to call them on the phone, or to request the former client to call in after 3 to 6 months after counseling has concluded. This method provides easy access and is both time- and cost-efficient. This approach does involve some preparatory work, as the counselor should ask the client for permission to call before doing so. E-mail could also be used, although there are concerns about the privacy and security of such a method. Secure systems exist, though no system is totally secure. Agencies and schools must take reasonable precautions in follow-up with clients and students.

Although follow-up can be time-consuming, it can be very important to the counseling process. Follow-up provides the counselor a concrete method of evaluating the success of counseling. In my experience, most clients appreciate the opportunity to have a voice in the evaluative process. Counselors can also receive some helpful feedback regarding their own sense of effectiveness and what techniques worked best for the particular client. Counselors may also discover the client had a different idea of what was and was not helpful. Counselors must also be ready to receive critical feedback regarding themselves, their approach, and their effectiveness. The important thing for counselors (particularly beginning counselors) to remember is that the feedback and evaluation process provides valuable feedback into the effectiveness of their work. This piece of the counseling process may well be the most important of all.

## ABANDONMENT

Counselors must be careful to avoid abandonment when terminating a client. Abandonment is a form of inappropriate termination and occurs when the client's treatment needs are not adequately addressed by the counselor when treatment ends or when the counselor simply drops the client from treatment (Vasquez et al., 2008). The *ACA Code of Ethics* (2014, Standard A.11.a) and court decisions related to the medical profession (*Allison v. Patel*, 1993; *Manno v. McIntosh*, 1994) prohibit counselors from client abandonment. When the counseling relationship has been established, the counselor cannot arbitrarily discontinue services if said action puts the client at risk.

To prevent abandonment, counselors should provide reasonable notice prior to termination. In planned termination, that is when a client has, say, a total of 12 sessions as per insurance coverage, the counselor could simply remind the client of the number of remaining sessions around session eight:

**Counselor:**  So, Consuelo, we have three more sessions left after today.
**Client:**  Alright. It's good to be reminded.

Counselor:  Absolutely. Now, during our last session in 3 weeks, we'll review treatment progress so you'll be ready to graduate from therapy.

**The following week:**

Counselor:  Consuelo, we have two more sessions left after today.

In addition to termination, counselors must also provide clients reasonable notice or a substitute counselor when a planned absence such as a pregnancy, vacation, or other prolonged absence. Counselors must document their planning in the case record in the event the counselor's absence becomes an issue.

Hilliard (1998, in Remley & Herlihy, 2014), an attorney who represents mental health professionals sued by their clients, offers practical recommendations. Hilliard has recommended counselors never terminate a professional relationship over a client's objection when the client is angry or in a serious crisis situation. Providing additional time to address the client's anxiety or distress likely would help the client address unresolved issues and help make the transition from one counseling professional to another. As important, a judge or jury likely would not look favorably on a mental health professional's decision to abruptly end a relationship in the middle of a crisis (*Allison v. Patel,* 1993; *Manno v. McIntosh*, 1994). If the client is in crisis, even if the client's insurance benefits have expired, the counselor should continue treatment until the crisis phase is over (Packman & Harris, 1998).

To protect mental health professionals from litigation for abandonment, Hilliard (1998) and Macbeth, Wheeler, and Onek (1994) have developed the following guidelines for mental health professionals to use when they are terminating clients who are resisting termination:

- Honestly discuss with the client your intention to terminate and the specific reason for your decision.
- Give the client an opportunity to make changes that would be necessary to continue the relationship.
- Give written notice to the client that the relationship will be terminated.
- Offer the client one to three termination sessions.
- Give your client up to three referrals.
- Give your client places to contact in the event of emergencies.
- Place a summary of your interactions with the client around the termination issue in the client's file. Do not transfer that document to another individual or entity without an expressed written request from the client.
- Give the client plenty of time to find another mental health professional. If more time is requested, allow it.
- Transfer records to the new mental health professional.

(Remley & Herlihy, 2014, p. 94)

## CONCLUSION

Terminating with clients can be difficult for both the counselor and the client. It is natural for clients to want to "hang onto" a relationship that has been positive and growth-oriented for them. After all, for some clients, the counseling relationship may have been their closest relationship. Nevertheless, termination is necessary for continued growth and development of the client. Counselors would do well to frame termination as "continued growth" and portray it as a type of "commencement."

For counselors, especially graduate student counselors-in-training, learning to "let go" of clients they have worked with for extended periods can be very difficult, especially if the client has made significant progress. It is important for counselors to remember that the welfare of the client is of utmost importance. An important aspect of client welfare is acknowledging the completion of major treatment goals and the subsequent "graduation" from counseling. Counselors having difficulty with termination should seek out their supervisor for advice on the matter. It is also recommended that counselors engage in self-reflection and ask themselves, "What makes termination with this client so difficult?" The difficulty may arise from issues within the counselor that need addressing. If a counselor continues experiencing difficulty with termination, individual counseling is recommended in order for the counselor to examine personal issues regarding relationship endings.

Though many people would prefer not to think about it, endings are a natural part of the life process as people move away, divorce, take new jobs, marry, launch adult children to college, work, join the military, and so on, and of course everyone eventually dies. That endings are as common as beginnings, however, scarcely makes them easy and in fact terminations often present hardships for everyone. As covered in this chapter, some clients will resist and perhaps even sabotage termination as they may see they are losing a "friend" or a major support system. Thus, dialoguing with the client on termination is an important part of counseling treatment and presents a valuable opportunity. Work with your field site supervisor and university supervisor to manage such challenging situations as termination may present difficulties for you, the counseling student. The good news is that the more experience you gain with termination, the more competent you will become with such endings. It is also accurate to say that many clients will see termination as a positive sign of growth and will be looking forward to "graduating" from counseling. Some counselors and counseling sites will even hold "graduation" for clients. This practice is more common in 12-step programs (1 year of sobriety), residential programs, group treatment, and even some schools. At one residential psychiatric agency where I worked, the person completing treatment was honored with a cake, testimony from counselors, parents, guardians, and peers regarding the client's growth and progress. Whatever the counselor does, acknowledging completion by honoring the client's accomplishment is a good idea.

# REFERENCES

Allison v. Patel, 211 Ga. App. 376 (1993).

American Counseling Association. (2014). *ACA code of ethics.* Alexandria, VA: Author.

American Psychiatric Association. (2013). *Diagnostic and statistical manual of mental disorders* (5th ed.). Arlington, VA: Author.

Corey, G. (2009). *Theory and practice of counseling and psychotherapy* (8th ed.). Belmont, CA: Thomson Brooks/Cole.

Corey, G., Corey, M. S., & Callanan, P. (2007). *Issues and ethics in the helping professions* (7th ed.). Belmont, CA: Thomson Brooks/Cole.

Cormier, L. S., & Cormier, W. H. (1998). *Fundamental skills and cognitive behavioral interventions* (4th ed.). Pacific Grove, CA: Brooks/Cole.

Cormier, L. S., & Hackney, H. (2008). *Counseling strategies and interventions* (7th ed.). Boston, MA: Pearson/Allyn & Bacon.

De Shazer, S., & Berg, I. (1988). Doing therapy: A post-structural revision. *Journal of Marital and Family Therapy, 18,* 71–81.

Dixon, D. N., & Glover, J. A. (1984). *Counseling: A problem-solving approach.* New York, NY: Wiley.

Garfield, S. L. (1994). Research on client variables in psychotherapy. In A. E. Bergin & S. L. Garfield (Eds.), *Handbook of psychotherapy and behavior change* (4th ed., pp. 190–228). New York, NY: Wiley.

Gibson, R. L., & Mitchell, M. H. (2008). *Introduction to counseling and guidance* (7th ed.). Upper Saddle River, NJ: Merrill/Prentice Hall.

Gladding, S. T. (1990). Coming full cycle: Reentry after the group. *Journal for Specialists in Group Work, 15,* 130–131.

Gladding, S. T. (2009). *Counseling: A comprehensive profession* (6th ed.). Upper Saddle River, NJ: Merrill/Prentice Hall.

Goldstein, A. P. (1971). *Psychotherapeutic attraction.* New York, NY: Pergamon Press.

Goodyear, R. K. (1981). Termination as a loss experience for the counselor. *Personnel and Guidance Journal, 59,* 347–350.

Guy, J. D. (1987). *The personal life of the psychotherapist.* New York, NY: Wiley.

Hilliard, J. (1998). Termination of treatment with troublesome patients. In L. E. Lifson & R. I. Simon (Eds.), *The mental health practitioner and the law* (pp. 216–221). Cambridge, MA: Harvard University Press.

Humphrey, K. M. (2009). *Counseling strategies for loss and grief.* Alexandria, VA: American Counseling Association.

Kübler-Ross, E. (1969). *On death and dying.* New York, NY: Macmillan.

Macbeth, J. E., Wheeler, A. M., Sither, J. W., & Onek, J. N. (1994). *Legal and risk management issues in the practice of psychiatry.* Washington, DC: Psychiatrists Purchasing Group.

Maholick, L. T., & Turner, D. W. (1979). Termination: The difficult farewell. *American Journal of Psychotherapy, 33,* 583–591.

Manno v. McIntosh, 519 N.W.2nd 815 (Iowa App. 1994).

Miller, W. R., & Rollnick, S. (2002). *Motivational interviewing: Preparing people for change* (2nd ed.). New York, NY: Guilford Press.

O'Hanlon, W. H. (1994). The third wave: The promise of narrative. *Family Therapy Networker, 18*(6), 19–26, 28–29.

Okun, B. F., & Kantrowitz, R. E. (2008). *Effective helping: Interviewing and counseling techniques* (7th ed.). Belmont, CA: Thomson Brooks/Cole.

Packman, W. L., & Harris, E. A. (1998). Legal issues and risk management in suicidal patients. In B. Bongar, A. I. Berman, R. W. Maris, M. M. Silverman, E. A. Harris, & W. L. Packman (Eds.), *Risk management with suicidal patients* (pp. 150–186). New York, NY: Guilford Press.

Perls, F. S. (1969). *Gestalt therapy verbatim.* Lafayette, CA: Real People Press.

Pietrofesa, J. J., Hoffman, A., & Splete, H. H. (1984). *Counseling: An introduction* (2nd ed.). Boston, MA: Houghton Mifflin.

Remley, T. P., & Herlihy, B. (2014). *Ethical, legal and professional issues in counseling* (4th ed.). Upper Saddle River, NJ: Pearson.

Rogers, C. R. (1961). *On becoming a person.* Boston, MA: Houghton Mifflin.

Vasquez, M. J. T., Bingham, R. P., & Barnett, J. E. (2008). Psychotherapy termination: Clinical and ethical responsibilities. *Journal of Clinical Psychology: In Sessions, 64,* 653–665.

Welfel, E. R. (2010). *Ethics in counseling and psychotherapy: Standards, research, and emerging issues* (4th ed.). Pacific Grove, CA: Brooks/Cole.

Welfel, E. R., & Patterson, L. E. (2005). *The counseling process: A multitheoretical integrated approach* (6th ed.). Belmont, CA: Thomson Brooks/Cole.

Yalom, I., & Leszcz, M. (2005). *The theory and practice of group psychotherapy* (5th ed.). New York, NY: Basic Books.

# TWELVE

# COMPLETING THE PRACTICUM/ INTERNSHIP AND PREPARING FOR THE FUTURE AS A PROFESSIONAL COUNSELOR

This chapter is devoted to completing the practicum/internship sequence and preparing for your job search. The first part of the chapter addresses termination of the field supervisor–intern relationship. The latter section will be devoted to preparing for the job search, including preparing a résumé or curriculum vitae (CV), letters of reference, cover letters, interviewing, and issues of licensure and credentialing.

As you complete your final semester of field placement, it is important to keep in mind that you carry the reputation of your counseling program with you during internship. Counseling students who perform well on internships showcase their counseling program in a favorable light. Conversely, counseling students whose performance is subpar, or who have ethical issues, potentially harm their program's reputation. Because future practicum and internship placements depend on the willingness of the field placement site, it is important that you always be mindful of how you complete your final internship placement. Ideally, besides completing all internship requirements, you will express your gratitude to your field site supervisor and colleagues in the school, agency, hospital, and so forth, in addition to saying goodbyes to your clients.

## TERMINATING THE FIELD SUPERVISOR–INTERN RELATIONSHIP

In the previous chapter, we reviewed termination with clients. A key question during that process clearly is, "Has this client (or student) made adequate progress in counseling?" A similar question could be asked of graduate counseling interns prior to termination: "Has this intern made the type of progress we would expect a beginning counselor to have made?" Because interns are usually in the final stage of their graduate program, field supervisors are preparing them to be future counseling professionals (Remley & Herlihy, 2014). As completion of the final internship is a critical step in the education of future counselors, field supervisors and interns should ensure ample time is set aside for evaluation and discussion of the intern's development prior to the intern's completion of the final internship.

Most interns will experience some formal type of evaluation process (Remley & Herlihy, 2014; Williams, 1995). A sample evaluation form is shown in Exhibit 12.1. Such evaluation forms should be filled out and then forwarded to the graduate counseling program. Before the form is sent on to the appropriate faculty member, the field supervisor and intern should meet to discuss the evaluation.

The most difficult part of the evaluation process lies in the giving and receiving of critical feedback (Herlihy & Corey, 2015). As a longtime counselor educator and supervisor, I have witnessed interns who receive 95% positive feedback and perhaps 5% critical feedback. Frequently it's the 5% that the intern focuses on! Although it may be human nature to focus on the deficit, interns must learn to address both, keeping strengths and deficits in the proper perspective. Praise can help the intern develop confidence, and constructive criticism assists the intern in shoring up the areas of concern. Constructive criticism ideally provides the type of information interns can use for improvement.

One method of soliciting constructive criticism is for the field supervisor to require the intern to write a self-evaluation, identifying his or her strengths as well as areas of concern (Baird, 2005; Capacchione, 2000; Hodges & Connelly, 2010). This exercise requires the intern to engage in intense self-reflection, which is required for future success as a counselor (Covey, 1996). Then, when the supervisor and intern meet, they can compare and contrast the two evaluations. My recommendation is for the field supervisor to go over the intern's self-evaluation first; this not only provides a window into the intern's thinking, but also sets the stage to compare and contrast the intern's evaluation to the supervisor's evaluation.

Many field site supervisors may simply ask the intern to write up a narrative of their strengths and areas of concern. Others may simply ask the intern to do this verbally. For posterity's sake, my recommendation is for the intern to write the self-evaluation because this provides more structure and organization to the reflection process. A sample of a written self-evaluation is shown in Exhibit 12.2.

Interns who have had a good working relationship with their supervisor will likely experience only mild anxiety heading into the formal evaluation meeting. In such cases where the intern has already completed a self-evaluation and has had the benefit of several months (or in some cases years) of feedback from the supervisor, the fear factor regarding the final evaluation is likely quite low. Regardless of the field supervisor–intern relationship, I would encourage the student to prepare for the formal evaluation by considering the following suggestions:

- Remain composed and do not become defensive. Even if you disagree with the supervisor's evaluation, do not react with anger. It is sometimes very difficult to receive critical feedback, but doing so with respect and a cool head is good preparation for the future. After all, the final internship evaluation will not be the last time you receive critical evaluation. Remember, you do not have to agree with the feedback; you do need to remain present and respectful during the evaluation meeting.

---

**EXHIBIT 12.1   Internship Evaluation**

---

**Site Supervisor's Evaluation of Student Counselor's Performance**
**(Return to: Counseling Program, Niagara University, College of Education)**

*Note:* This form should be completed at the conclusion of each practicum and internship. Clinical supervisors are encouraged to go over the results with their students.

**Name of Student Counselor:** _____

**Name of Clinical Supervisor:** _____

**Directions:** The supervisor will circle the number most closely approximating the student counselor's skill rating in each of the following areas.

| GENERAL SUPERVISION RATING: | POOR | | SATISFACTORY | | EXCELLENT | |
|---|---|---|---|---|---|---|
| 1. Demonstrates a personal commitment to developing professional competencies. | 1 | 2 | 3 | 4 | 5 | 6 |
| 2. The student possesses a good working attitude. | 1 | 2 | 3 | 4 | 5 | 6 |
| 3. Accepts and uses constructive criticism. | 1 | 2 | 3 | 4 | 5 | 6 |
| 4. Communicates well with peers and supervisors. | 1 | 2 | 3 | 4 | 5 | 6 |
| 5. Recognizes both strengths and limitations and works to improve clinical skills. | 1 | 2 | 3 | 4 | 5 | 6 |
| 6. Punctual with case notes and other documentation. | 1 | 2 | 3 | 4 | 5 | 6 |
| 7. Keeps appointments on time. | 1 | 2 | 3 | 4 | 5 | 6 |
| 8. Researches client information prior to session. | 1 | 2 | 3 | 4 | 5 | 6 |
| 9. Appears relaxed and confident in dealing with counseling and clinical issues. | 1 | 2 | 3 | 4 | 5 | 6 |
| 10. Presents a nonjudgmental attitude regarding clients and their issues. | 1 | 2 | 3 | 4 | 5 | 6 |
| 11. Able to gain client trust. | 1 | 2 | 3 | 4 | 5 | 6 |
| 12. Facilitates client's exploration of personal issues. | 1 | 2 | 3 | 4 | 5 | 6 |
| 13. Student is professional and ethical. | 1 | 2 | 3 | 4 | 5 | 6 |
| 14. Student is able to deal with mandated or hostile clients. | 1 | 2 | 3 | 4 | 5 | 6 |

*(continued)*

---

**EXHIBIT 12.1    Internship Evaluation (*continued*)**

| | | | | | | | |
|---|---|---|---|---|---|---|---|
| **15.** Recognizes and deals with client manipulation. | 1 | 2 | | 3 | 4 | 5 | 6 |
| **16.** Uses silence effectively in counseling. | 1 | 2 | | 3 | 4 | 5 | 6 |
| **17.** Uses self-disclosure appropriately. | 1 | 2 | | 3 | 4 | 5 | 6 |
| **18.** Student is aware of own biases and how they impact the therapeutic relationship. | 1 | 2 | | 3 | 4 | 5 | 6 |
| **19.** Student is skilled in using confrontation in session. | 1 | 2 | | 3 | 4 | 5 | 6 |
| **20.** Facilitates realistic goal setting with the client. | 1 | 2 | | 3 | 4 | 5 | 6 |
| **21.** Writes clear, appropriate treatment plans. | 1 | 2 | | 3 | 4 | 5 | 6 |
| **22.** Explains, administers, and interprets tests correctly. | 1 | 2 | | 3 | 4 | 5 | 6 |
| **23.** Terminates/refers clients at appropriate times. | 1 | 2 | | 3 | 4 | 5 | 6 |
| **24.** Able to use appropriate techniques and interventions properly. | 1 | 2 | | 3 | 4 | 5 | 6 |
| **25.** Makes sound clinical decisions in counseling. | 1 | 2 | | 3 | 4 | 5 | 6 |

Additional Comments (Use back if necessary): _____

_____

_____

_____

Clinical Supervisor _____     Date: _____

Student Counselor _____     Date: _____

---

- If you find yourself feeling overly anxious about the formal evaluation, find ways to combat the stress—a workout routine, talking with friends, family, a support group, through counseling, and so forth.
- Make a "worst case/best case" list of what you may hear in the evaluation meeting. After each item on the list, write out a respectful response (which may include saying nothing and listening). On the other hand, if a compliment is given, a simple "thank you" may be appropriate.
- If you feel the need, have a classmate, friend, family member, or counselor role-play being the supervisor giving you a formal evaluation. During

---

**EXHIBIT 12.2   Intern's Self-Evaluation of the Practicum/Internship Performance**

On the following issues, rate yourself based on the scale as follows:
**1** = *Needs Improvement*;   **2** = *Below Average*;   **3** = *Average*;   **4** = *Above Average*;
**5** = *Excellent*;   **N/A** = *Not Applicable*

1. Counseling skills:
     1    2    3    4    5

2. Writing clear, concise case notes:
     1    2    3    4    5

3. Competence and confidence in leading a group session:
     1    2    3    4    5    **N/A**

4. Competence and confidence in leading a psychoeducational presentation:
     1    2    3    4    5    **N/A**

5. Understanding and applying the ethical code (ACA, AMHCA, ASCA, etc.):
     1    2    3    4    5

6. My professional dispositions on the placement (e.g., being on time, completing case notes in timely manner, showing respect to the staff, dressing appropriately, managing critical feedback):
     1    2    3    4    5

7. Taking initiative by reading relevant books, journal articles, viewing DVDs, and attending offered trainings and workshops (if offered):
     1    2    3    4    5    **N/A**

8. My own work ethic while on the practicum/internship:
     1    2    3    4    5

9. Readiness for the job market through my growth on the practicum/internship and having an updated résumé/CV, cover letter, and practiced interviewing skills:
     1    2    3    4    5

10. Because of my experience on the practicum/internship, I have clear and measurable professional goals:
     1    2    3    4    5

11. Overall, I would rate my progress during this placement as (note longer scale: **1** = Poor, **5** = Average; **10** = Excellent):
     1    2    3    4    5    6    7    8    9    10

*(continued)*

---

**EXHIBIT 12.2   Intern's Self-Evaluation of the Practicum/Internship Performance (*continued*)**

**Narrative Section**

In the space provided, please comment on additional areas of interest related to your development while on the practicum/internship. Use an additional sheet of paper if you need more space.

**12.** As a counselor, my greatest strength appears to be _____

_____

**13.** The area I most need to improve in is

_____

**14.** Additional comments regarding my experience in practicum/internship:

_____

_____

_____

_____

_____

_____

_____

_____

_____

_____

_____

_____

_____       ____/____/____

Practicum/Internship Student's Signature                          Date

---

this "mock evaluation," write down both strengths and weaknesses you believe the supervisor will point out. Then, have the mock supervisor mention these. Practice provides a greater likelihood you will manage the evaluation session with more professionalism and less distress.

- Let the supervisor control the meeting. This conveys respect and illustrates maturity on your part. Supervisors will likely resent an intern trying to take over the evaluation meeting.
- The supervisor may ask if you have questions or comments regarding the evaluation. This is your opportunity to clarify anything that seems unclear to you. Again, work to manage your emotions even if the evaluation is disappointing in some areas. If you have made it to the end of the placement with this particular school, agency, or university counseling center, the strengths likely outweigh the weaknesses.
- At the conclusion, regardless of how the meeting has gone, thank the supervisor for the opportunity to work at the setting. Remember, your counseling program needs practicum and internship placements and a respectful departure will help maintain good relations between your program and the field organization.

In addition to the field supervisor's evaluation of the intern, some counseling programs have the interns complete a field supervisor evaluation form, even though such evaluations are not always shared with the field supervisor. A sample student evaluation of field supervisor form is available in Exhibit 12.3.

If you are asked to evaluate your field supervisor, you need to be prepared to offer honest and constructive insights, yet use discretion when delivering critical feedback, as of course you may need that supervisor's support for your job search. First, it would be prudent to ask for a form, such as the one shown in Exhibit 12.3. A form provides you with a format to convey your opinions in a reasonable way. Reflect on the following considerations prior to evaluating your field supervisor:

- How strong is your relationship with the supervisor? If the relationship is strong, you will likely feel more confident in evaluating him or her.
- What is your level of trust in your supervisor?
- What do you know about this supervisor's ability to receive criticism? Have you seen the supervisor take constructive criticism? Does the supervisor occasionally solicit critique from coworkers?
- How important is this supervisor's recommendation for you? If this supervisor has been the only one you have had, the reference is critical. If this supervisor is one of two or three, then perhaps his or her reference is less weighty for you.
- You may wish to practice providing feedback. Have a friend, classmate, family member, counselor, and so on, do a role-play with you.
- If you are still concerned, consider speaking with your faculty advisor, another professor, or someone you trust for advice.
- An alternative to providing face-to-face feedback would be to write the supervisor a letter after you have completed all work at the site and grades have been turned in. (It may be wise to consider whether such a letter might jeopardize a future reference from the supervisor.)

**EXHIBIT 12.3  Student Counselor's Evaluation of On-Site Supervisor**

**Directions:** Circle the number that best represents how you, the Practicum/Internship Student, feel about the supervision received from your on-site (agency) supervisor. This information will not be shared with your on-site supervisor without your consent.

| My Supervisor: | Poor | | Fair | | Good | |
|---|---|---|---|---|---|---|
| 1. Gives appropriate time for individual and/or group supervision. | 1 | 2 | 3 | 4 | 5 | 6 |
| 2. Provides constructive feedback in supervision sessions. | 1 | 2 | 3 | 4 | 5 | 6 |
| 3. Recognizes and encourages further development of my clinical strengths and capabilities. | 1 | 2 | 3 | 4 | 5 | 6 |
| 4. Encourages and listens to my ideas and suggestions. | 1 | 2 | 3 | 4 | 5 | 6 |
| 5. Helps to define specific, concrete goals for me during the practicum or internship experience. | 1 | 2 | 3 | 4 | 5 | 6 |
| 6. Is available when I need consultation. | 1 | 2 | 3 | 4 | 5 | 6 |
| 7. Through his or her professional behavior, my supervisor models ethical practice. | 1 | 2 | 3 | 4 | 5 | 6 |
| 8. My supervisor makes the effort to remain current in the counseling field. | 1 | 2 | 3 | 4 | 5 | 6 |
| 9. Maintains confidentiality within the clinical setting. | 1 | 2 | 3 | 4 | 5 | 6 |
| 10. Helps me formulate my own theoretical approach to counseling. | 1 | 2 | 3 | 4 | 5 | 6 |
| 11. Explains his or her criteria for evaluating student interns in clear terms. | 1 | 2 | 3 | 4 | 5 | 6 |
| 12. Applies these criteria fairly in evaluating my counseling performance. | 1 | 2 | 3 | 4 | 5 | 6 |
| 13. Demonstrates respect to clients, staff, and student interns. | 1 | 2 | 3 | 4 | 5 | 6 |
| 14. Encourages me to discuss concerns encountered in the practicum or internship setting. | 1 | 2 | 3 | 4 | 5 | 6 |
| 15. Through my work with this supervisor, I have learned new counseling techniques, interventions, or assessments. | 1 | 2 | 3 | 4 | 5 | 6 |
| 16. The supervisor has helped to make this practicum/internship a valuable experience. | 1 | 2 | 3 | 4 | 5 | 6 |
| 17. Because of my experience with the supervisor and this agency, I would recommend this site to other students. | 1 | 2 | 3 | 4 | 5 | 6 |

**Additional Comments and/or Suggestions:**

_____

_____

_____

Date: _____/ _____/_____        Student: _____

Good supervisors will desire feedback on ways to enhance their supervision skills. Regardless of the outcome, a two-way evaluation in which both the supervisor and the intern provide feedback is the healthiest process when termination arrives.

---

*Self-Reflection Exercise for the Conclusion of the Internship*

Through your practicum and internship experience, you have gained a broader understanding of how to identify and address the educational, career, emotional, and mental health needs of the students and clients you have counseled. Another aspect of your field placement is how what you have learned fits into the needs of your chosen career. Examine and respond to the following questions.

1. What specific skills and interests have you gained through your practicum and internship experience?
2. The practicum and internship experience is a challenging one. During this process of counseling others, what have you learned about yourself?
3. What lessons have you learned from working with different types of people (clients, supervisors, colleagues, fellow students)?
4. In what ways have you benefited from your practicum and internship experience?
5. What specific skills, talents, and interests are you likely to use in your new counseling position?
6. What type (or types) of counseling setting are you considering for your first job after graduate school?
7. Regarding item number 6, what specifically interests you about working with the settings you have listed?
8. What advice would you give to a fellow graduate counseling student regarding choosing a practicum or internship?
9. Considering your experiences on practicum/internship and in your graduate counseling program in general, what changes would you like to see (e.g., course or curricular changes, changes to the practicum/internship, changes in the counseling profession, or anything that seems relevant)?

---

## PREPARING FOR THE JOB SEARCH

Because the practicum/internship is all about preparing to become a professional counselor, this book would not be complete without some basic orientation to prepare for the job search. Although this section of the text is a brief overview (there are many more comprehensive job search books and websites available), it will provide some basic information and point the way for further information that may be helpful in assisting you in landing that initial job.

A job search involves many facets: planning, résumé writing, mock interviewing, applying, interviewing, following up, dealing with rejection, entertaining an offer, accepting a job, negotiating salary, and relocating to name a few. The remainder of the chapter focuses on the basics of this process.

## THE VISIONING PROCESS: CREATING YOUR DREAM CAREER

Career professionals will tell you the first step to success is the ability to visualize a desired goal. Surprisingly, many clients I have counseled and students I have taught do not have a clear vision for their careers. The lack of a clear vision may set up a graduating counseling student for some degree of struggle. Richard Nelson Bolles, author of *The New York Times* bestseller and iconic *What Color Is Your Parachute?*, has a popular saying, "If you don't know where you're going, you'll likely end up somewhere else." Thus, the need for vision works regarding a career (and personal life as well). The second, and more important task, is to strategize on how to achieve the goal. One of the most popular methods for strategizing is creative visualization, or *visioning* for short (Capacchione, 2000). Successful people in every occupation tend to use some type of visioning process. Some notable visionaries are Nelson Mandela, Mohandas Gandhi, Martin Luther King, Jr., and Mother Teresa. Vision includes optimistic thinking, which is strongly correlated with success (Seligman, 1998). Visioning is a simple process requiring just a few basic pieces of information:

- **Personal history**. How did you arrive at your current station in life? What experiences led you to becoming a professional counselor or counselor educator? What valuable lessons have you learned along the way? What advice might you give to someone considering counseling as a career?
- **Values**. What values are important to you? Psychologist Milton Rokeach (1979) conducted extensive research in the study of values. His findings suggest that the most successful people find work that is congruent with their personal values. For example, if your spirituality is important to you, then perhaps you should find a spiritually affiliated school or agency. If working with inner-city youth is where your passion lies, a job in a wealthy suburban school may not be a good fit for you. So, what are your top five values? How might these values guide your job search and counseling career?
- **Professional identity**. Sure, you know you want to be a professional school/rehabilitation/career/mental health/addictions counselor. However, professional labels such as "counselor" do not tell the entire story. For example, some mental health counselors may decide to retrain to become school counselors or vice versa. In addition, many experienced counselors may move into administrative roles, such as clinical director, and do more administrative work and less actual counseling. A few readers may even wish to earn a doctorate in Counselor Education and become a counselor educator! Would your long-term goals include moving into administration? Would those changes be healthy for you? Why or why not?

- **Goals.** What are your immediate, short-term, and long-term career goals? Are you interested in running a school counseling center? Being director of a college counseling center? Becoming dean of students at a large university? Moving overseas? Becoming president of the American Counseling Association (ACA), American School Counselor Association (ASCA), American Rehabilitation Counseling Association (ARCA), American College Counseling Association (ACCA), and the like? Goals are fluid and subject to personal changes over time, but it is still a good idea to set goals and to revise them periodically as your interests and values change over time and through experience.
- **Action Plan.** Everyone with a vision needs an action plan to achieve it. An action plan is a rough road map to success and should consist of concrete steps leading up to the vision. The visioning process should also involve estimated time frames to provide a sense of how you are proceeding toward your goal. Action plans also are flexible as circumstances will intervene. As John Lennon wrote in one of his last songs, "Life is what happens when we're busy making other plans." Life will happen, but plan anyway.

---

*Sample Action Plan*

If your ultimate goal is to become president of the ACA, your action plan might look something like this:

1. Become active in the state affiliate of ACA (1–3 years).
2. Transition into a state leadership role through the following steps (1–2 years):
   a. Serving on the planning board for the state conference
   b. Serving on the editorial board of the state journal
   c. Running for president, vice president, or another office of the state organization
   d. Submitting manuscripts to the state journal and national ACA-affiliated journals
3. Attend the annual ACA conference for networking opportunities.
4. Volunteer, make presentations, and host receptions at ACA conferences to boost your profile with the organization (3–6 years).
5. Get published in academic journals, national newsletters, and in venues such as *Counseling Today*. Sit on ACA subcommittees to further boost your profile and understand the organization (3–4 years).
6. Run for secretary or vice president of ACA (2 years).
7. Finally, you run for president, using everything you have learned previously regarding visibility, a coherent platform, networking, and so forth. You win!

---

Even if you are not presently interested in becoming ACA president, this example illustrates that setting a clear goal helps you strategize how to work to reach that goal. You should also be flexible with timelines and remember that you will have some failures along the way. Do not let failures get you too down as they offer the opportunity for self-reflection and reassessment. In fact, failures can provide the incentive and the wisdom for future success. Perhaps inventor Thomas Edison is the best example of this ethic. Edison's experiment failures far outnumbered his successes. Yet, he needed the failures to help pave the road to his success. So, be of the mindset of allowing your failures to teach you healthy lessons.

Thus, when creating a visioning plan:

1. **Be conscious of the present.** Think long term as in the previous example. However, do not let long-term planning trip you up in the present. Doing well in your present is the first step to achieving your long-term goals.
2. **Set a time frame.** Remember, long-term goals will take time and you will need to revise them when setbacks and life circumstances change (e.g., marriage, divorce, children, moves, promotions, job loss). Disappointments will happen. I can recall numerous job rejections and feeling very discouraged. Then, I received some prudent counsel. I was encouraged to reframe each rejection as "One rejection closer to landing that first job." This simple act of reframing provided a greater sense of purpose and lessened my sense of failure. So, when you are not having the success you desire, reframe your thoughts accordingly.
3. **Be flexible.** Your goals will change over time and that may be good. For example, you may start out with the long-term goal of running a university counseling center but decide over time you are more interested in being a training director at a college counseling center. This would be an example of clarification, or simply learning that the original goal was not as congruent with your values and interests as previously thought. Remember, life is dynamic and all about change.
4. **Review your action plan periodically.** You need to check on your progress regularly. If you are not being successful, why not? In addition, what does success actually mean to you? Have your interests and values changed?
5. **Be mindful.** Be grounded in the center of your own being while connected to others. Make sure the goals you have set actually fit with your values. This may be the most difficult process you encounter in your career journey. You may need years of struggle, professional counseling, and some type of meaningful self-reflecting practice to a mindful career.

Some techniques for career visioning are as follows:

- **Open-ended questions.** "What do I want in my career?" and "Now that I know what I want career-wise, how can I create it?"
- **Meditation.** Many people have a meditation practice that calms and centers them. Some people use meditation as part of the creative process.
- **Visualization.** When you picture yourself 5, 7, or 10 years down the line, what does that picture look like? What does your career involve? Where are you living? Who else is in the picture?

- **Focusing**. This assists in clarifying how to plan and prioritize the preceding visualization process. For example, what needs to happen before you can open your own private practice?
- **Career journaling**. For many people, journaling allows them the opportunity to document how their career is proceeding, what challenges, satisfactions, struggles, changes, failures, successes, and so on, they face. Not everyone finds journaling helpful, but for those who enjoy it, journaling can be a type of self-discovery regarding career and personal insights.
- **Collage making**. Do not denigrate this potentially creative exercise. Collage making can be fun as well as helping you create a picture of your career dreams. Use a collage to explore your future dreams and goals.
- **Informational interviewing**. Choose two or three people whom you respect and who know you well. Ask them to address the following questions about you:
  1. What qualities do you possess that will help make you successful in your career?
  2. What steps do you need to take to realize your career goal(s)?
  3. What is your strongest quality?
  4. What is your chief weakness?

(Hodges & Connelly, 2010, p. 14)

## THE CAREER CENTER

The career center on your campus can offer numerous services for the soon-to-be-graduated intern. One of the most valuable services is the letters of reference bank. With this, your field supervisor(s) and advisor can write letters of reference that can be stored at the center. Reference letters can be open or closed. Open references mean that the student has the right to inspect the letter. Closed letters cannot be read by students.

Students frequently ask me, "Should I have an open or closed file?" I always feel somewhat torn, because I believe when we agree to serve as a reference it should be an open process. However, I also know that some hiring committees view closed files as more authentic. So, make the best decision you can. You may feel more confident in closed files if you are confident about the people who are writing the letters. I have written reference letters both for open and for closed files and my letter would be the same for both. Once again, it also comes down to how much trust you have in the person writing the reference letter. Ideally, people would not write reference letters for students unless they honestly had faith in the students' counseling ability.

The career center counselors can also critique your résumé and cover letter (you might show them to your supervisor as well). It never hurts to have fresh eyes examine your materials for errors, accuracy, and to make sure you present yourself in the strongest possible light to a potential employer. Remember, initial screenings of résumés and cover letters often are to screen out applicants. You want to be "screened in," so spelling errors, wrong dates, or simply misleading information will get your application relegated to the recycle bin.

## PROFESSIONAL NETWORKING SITES

You should also consider using appropriate social networking sites such as LinkedIn. LinkedIn provides a method of building vocational connections. Refrain from using social sites such as Facebook as a professional networking vehicle. Facebook works fine for transmitting social and familial information but many people post compromising photographs and information on such sites. Professional sites such as LinkedIn are typically understood to be more appropriate sites for networking with other counseling professionals. LinkedIn offers an easy, quick method of linking with fellow counselors and even soliciting recommendations. It is likely that in this rapidly accelerating electronic world, sites such as LinkedIn represent future "career centers" or at least as an ancillary career center (though certainly not as good as an actual career counselor). Naturally, the American Counseling Association (ACA), American Mental Health Counselors Association (AMHCA), American School Counselor Association (ASCA), and organizations such as the National Board for Certified Counselors (NBCC) have their own networking capabilities (another reason to have membership).

## REQUESTING REFERENCES

As you complete your final internship and prepare for the job search, you should be soliciting letters of recommendation from professors and field supervisors. Your letters of reference ideally should be written by counseling professionals—professors in your counselor education program, your faculty advisor, major professor, field site supervisors, and possibly supervisors or professionals in related fields who may be able to address pertinent areas related to counseling work. These references may be required to either write a formal letter on your behalf, or merely be accessible for a verbal discussion about you with a potential employer. Although most counseling applications typically require three references, some may ask for five. So be prepared for the possibility of needing additional references. Again, you are wise to seek references from those with whom you have a good relationship as they likely will write you the strongest reference.

Prior to sending off your résumé or cover letter, you must *ask* each person on your list if he or she would be willing to serve as a reference. This may seem elementary, but you might be surprised how many times I have received a phone call from an employer asking about an applicant who never asked if I would serve as a reference. Such unexpected calls are always embarrassing and usually sink the counselor's candidacy. Failure to ask if a former supervisor or professor will serve as a reference sends the message you potentially don't respect your references well or that you were sloppy in your approach. Ask!

Consider the strength of the referral before asking anyone to serve as a reference. As one who has written scores of reference letters for the past two decades, my guideline is I must be able to write a strong letter of reference or I will refuse to serve as a reference. Be aware that weak or nebulous references are worse than none at all. So, as soon as possible during your final semester, line up your references. As you do so, consider the following:

1. Provide your referral sources with a résumé or CV. This helps them fill in the gaps about your vocational life. No matter how well I know a student, I always learn something additional from his or her résumé or CV.

2. Do not ask your references to write a letter at the last moment. This shows poor planning on your part and your reference may not be able to write the letter with short notice, or might be annoyed at such a last-minute request. Ideally, give your references 2 weeks to write letters of reference.

3. Make sure you keep your references informed as to how your job search is proceeding. I personally appreciate hearing how my students are progressing on the job search. When you land a job, let your references know—they will be happy to know their supervision and hard work has paid off.

4. Although many applications now suggest e-mailing letters of reference and may not require a mailed letter of reference, it is a good idea to provide your references with self-addressed stamped envelopes just in case.

## DEVELOPING A RÉSUMÉ OR CURRICULUM VITAE

A résumé or CV provides a description of your educational and occupational life. The résumé or CV provides a sketch of you for a potential employer's perusal. This is no time to be overly modest; your résumé is your calling card and summary of your professional life. Be your best self. But be honest in whatever you write on your CV or résumé! Overly embellishing on a résumé or CV can cost you a job and maybe even a career.

The recommended reading list at the end of the chapter offers many comprehensive references to help you craft a résumé and conduct other aspects of your job search. I highly recommend you consult one or more of them. Here are some basic tips to get you started (Hodges & Connelly, 2010, p. 34):

- Your education and transferrable skills are of critical importance. Your experience, training, education, and skills serve as a bridge to desired employment. Make sure you design your résumé or CV in a manner that clearly highlights your training and skills areas. List all degrees, degrees in progress, certifications, work history, awards, and so forth.
- Make sure your résumé makes chronological sense. Begin with the most recent position and work your way back. In addition, I recommend that you list your graduate assistantship just as you would list a job—because in essence, it is *job-like*.
- Claim the highest skills ethically possible. For example, if you have co-facilitated counseling groups for 2 years, certainly list that. Do not, however, list that you developed and oversaw the group treatment model at your school or agency if this is untrue.

- Be able to elaborate on anything you list. For example, if you list that you are proficient in dialectical behavioral therapy (DBT), you must be prepared to demonstrate you have mastered the basic concepts of this theoretical approach.
- Include membership in relevant professional organizations. Membership demonstrates a stronger commitment to the profession. It also suggests you are more likely to keep informed of research and emerging trends in the counseling field. My personal opinion: All counseling graduates and professional counselors should hold membership in the ACA, their particular counseling specialty area (e.g., ASCA, AMHCA, American Rehabilitation Counseling Association [ARCA]), and their state counseling organization.
- Make your résumé or CV reader friendly. When a search committee member first looks at your résumé or CV, he or she will give it a 30- to 45-second speed read (Bolles, 2015). Make sure it is clearly organized. Use a common 12-point font (such as Times New Roman).
- Do a spelling and grammar check. Have a career counselor or someone else you trust read it for content and mechanics. Misspellings and poor grammar are likely to get your application eliminated from consideration.
- There is no one "right" résumé or CV format. Make sure your résumé makes sense, flows logically, is factually accurate, and fits with the counseling position for which you have applied. For example, if you are applying for an inner-city high school counselor position, make sure your application letter reflects the particular demographics of that school, as opposed to an elite private school.
- Cover your most recent years of work experience in the greatest detail, depending on your age and years in the field. Do not be discouraged if you are a recent graduate of a counseling program. At your age and experience level, you are not expected to have many years of professional experience. After all, everyone starts somewhere.
- Having held multiple jobs is no longer the problem as it was in previous generations. In this era, people are expected to have held three, four, or even more jobs (Bolles, 2015). In higher education, the general understanding is that you must "move out to move up," and that is likely to be reflected in your résumé or CV. However, when you enter into a professional counseling position, you will be expected to stay at that job for 4 to 5 years. Job hopping—leaving or trying to leave a job every 1 to 2 years— will hurt you in future job searches.
- Be factually correct. You are responsible for anything you list in your résumé or CV. If you are caught lying or embellishing, the least you will lose is a job. In some cases, you may forfeit your career. Be warned: Potential employers have little tolerance for the ethically challenged!
- Provide all contact information. List landline and cell phone numbers, e-mail, and so forth.

In developing your résumé and cover letter, I encourage you to use language that describes your experience, skills, and interest in a concise, descriptive, and eloquent voice. The best way to illustrate your work in the cover letter and résumé is with action words that present your case in a lively manner. Here is a sampling of action words:

| | | |
|---|---|---|
| Accomplished | Directed | Negotiated |
| Achieved | Drafted | Organized |
| Advised | Edited | Planned |
| Assisted | Established | Presented |
| Chaired | Facilitated | Presided |
| Collaborated | Implemented | Reorganized |
| Consulted | Integrated | Researched |
| Counseled* | Lectured | Revised |
| Developed | Monitored | Supervised |

*Use of this word should occur only after completing a counseling practicum and internship!

Exhibit 12.4 displays a sample résumé. Remember, there is no one right résumé format. The books listed at the end of this chapter give plenty of additional styles to choose from.

---

**EXHIBIT 12.4   Sample Résumé**

Reggie Martinez, Master's Candidate, BA, AA
327 Springdale Ave.
Palouse Hills, WA 96332
(817) 555-0234 (c)
rmartinez@hotmail.com

**Profile**

Master's degree candidate seeking a challenging counseling position at a community mental health clinic.

**Summary of Qualifications**

- Five years experience supervising college students in collegiate living groups, providing peer advising, crisis intervention, and educational programming.
- Nearing completion of 700-hour practicum/internship in community counseling agency.
- Trained in grief counseling during practicum/internship.
- Developed an outreach program for Latino youth.
- Selected as the Graduate Student of the Year at Washington State University.

**Education**

Master's Degree Candidate (will graduate in June 2015) in Clinical Mental Health Counseling, Washington State University, Pullman, WA (CACREP-accredited program)
Bachelor's of Arts (2012) in Cultural Anthropology at Western Washington University, Bellingham, WA (Minor: Psychology)
Associate's of Arts (2010) in Psychology at Seattle Area Community College

---

(continued)

**EXHIBIT 12.4   Sample Résumé (*continued*)**

### Related Work Experience

Mental Health Counseling Practicum and Internship (2013–2015), The Rainbow Center, Moscow, ID.

- Provided individual and group counseling to clients in Spanish and English.
- Co-facilitated support groups for parents of gay and lesbian children.
- Developed a grief support group for parents who have had children die.
- Presented psychoeducational workshops to schools, service organizations, and law enforcement officers.
- Served as crisis counselor for evening crisis call center.
- Assisted in rewriting the *Rainbow Staff Employee's Manual.*

Resident Director, Department of Housing and Residence Life, Washington State University, Pullman, WA (2012–2015)

- Director of International Student residence hall, with students from 33 countries.
- Oversight of 150 undergraduate and graduate students and scholars-in-residence.
- Supervisor for five residence advisors.
- Responsible for coordinating educational programming in residence hall.
- Mediated conflicts between residents in the residence hall.
- Provided crisis intervention and referred students to the university counseling center.
- Participated in Safe Haven training for gay, lesbian, and transgender students.

Resident Advisor, Department of Residential Life, Western Washington University, Bellingham, WA (2010–2012)

- Floor supervisor in coeducational collegiate residence hall (30 students).
- Responsible for educational programming.
- Served as peer counselor for students.
- Referred students to the counseling center, health services, and the career center.
- Mediated disputes between students on the floor.

President, Student Government Association, Seattle Area Community College, Seattle, WA (2005–2006)

- President of student organization representing 25,000 community college students.
- Responsible for oversight of student fee budgeting, programming approval, and selecting committee chairs.
- Voting member of Seattle Community College's Board of Trustees.
- Charged with lobbying for student needs, such as a new student union, recreation center, and campus residence halls.

### Awards

2014–2015, Graduate Student of the Year. Presented by the Association for Gay, Lesbian, and Transgender Student Association, Washington State University, Pullman, WA

2006, 2007, Seattle Area Community College's Presidential scholarship

(*continued*)

---

**EXHIBIT 12.4   Sample Résumé (*continued*)**

**Publications**

Martinez, R. (2013). Barriers to providing counseling services to Latino clients: Some reflections from the trenches. *Journal of the Washington Counseling Association, 12*, 22–34.

Martinez, R. (2013). Experiences as a first generation Latino graduate student. *The Advocate, 10*, 3–5.

Martinez, R. (2014, October 15). Racism and homophobia: One Latino's struggle for acceptance. *Seattle Post, 57*, pp. A.1, 22.

**Additional Training**

Trained in Dialectical Behavioral Therapy (Rainbow Center, 2014–2015)

Washington State Certified Mediator

Solution-Focused Counseling, Pullman, WA, June 22–25, 2014

**Professional Memberships**

Chi Sigma Iota (Counseling Honorary)
American Counseling Association (ACA)
American Mental Health Counselors Association (AMHCA)
Washington State Mental Health Counselors Association (WSMHCA)

**Hobbies**

Running, cycling, traveling, and writing poetry

**References**

Sam Cogan, PhD, Associate Professor of Counseling, Counselor Education program, College of Education, Washington State University, Pullman, WA, (509) 633-0134, e-mail: scogan@wsu.edu.

Angela Hermes, MS, LMHC, The Rainbow Center, Moscow, ID, (509) 714-1027, e-mail: hermesa@yahoo.com.

Harriet Wilson, EdD, Assistant Dean of Students/Coordinator of International Students, Washington State University, Pullman, WA, (509) 618-9090, e-mail: hwilson@wsu.edu.

---

## WRITING A COVER LETTER

In writing the cover letter, you want to keep several elements in mind:

1. Open the letter with a respectful businesslike address such as "Dear Director," "Dear Search Committee," or another title that conveys respect. Do not use informal titles even if you know the persons to whom you are writing. Remember, the cover letter indicates you understand professional protocol.
2. As with your résumé, type using a standard 12-point font (such as Times New Roman or another more traditional style). If you are delivering

hard copies—less common in this electronic era—have your résumé and cover letter printed on quality, heavy stock paper.

3. In the opening paragraph, explain why you are interested in the job and show that you understand the population the organization serves. For example, if you are applying for a position as a school counselor in an inner-city school or alternative school, briefly illustrate your knowledge of the student population.

4. Keep it brief: one to one and one-half pages.

5. Hit the highlights of your qualifications for the position: cite your counseling experience (practicum/internship) and theoretical approach. (If the school or agency uses a particular approach, indicate your knowledge and experience with it if appropriate.) In addition, if you have special training in a particular approach, indicate that as well.

6. If you have experience related to the counseling field, you certainly want to mention that. Related experience (such as working as a case manager, teaching assistant, resident advisor, bachelor's-level addiction counselor, etc.) should also be mentioned.

7. In the final paragraph, wrap up by stating that you look forward to meeting to discuss your interest and fit for the job. Provide a phone number and e-mail.

Exhibit 12.5 shows a sample cover letter.

---

**EXHIBIT 12.5  Sample Cover Letter**

March 13, 2015
1339 Easy Street
Vista View, AR 72301

Personnel Department
Hickory Ridge School District
5555 Cardinal Lane
Hickory Ridge, AR 72709

Dear Personnel Officer:

Please consider me an applicant for the school counseling position at Hickory Ridge High School. I noticed the advertisement in a recent online edition of the *Northwest Arkansas Times*. Currently, I am a graduate student completing my studies and will graduate with my master's degree in school counseling this May at the University of Arkansas. In addition to coursework, I have completed 700 hours of practicum and internship at a local high school. I have also served as a teacher's aide in a public school for 5 years and have a good understanding of both academic and personal issues that impact a student's learning environment.

My practicum and internship were spent at Fayetteville Technical High School, where I assisted the school counseling staff with academic, career, and personal counseling. This past semester, I co-facilitated two counseling groups for students at risk for dropping out of school. I also led an after-school group targeted at gang prevention.

During my counselor education studies at the University of Arkansas, I was selected for the counseling honorary Chi Sigma Iota, and have even served as president. During this

---

*(continued)*

---

| **EXHIBIT 12.5**   **Sample Cover Letter (*continued*)** |
| --- |
| past year, I also worked part time at the Beacon Light Center, where I provided personal, career, and academic counseling to at-risk adolescents.<br><br>My résumé and three letters of reference requested in the advertisement are being forwarded from the Career Center at the University of Arkansas. I would welcome the opportunity to discuss my interest in the school counseling position with you in the near future. If you have additional questions, please feel free to contact me at (123) 456-7890 or through e-mail at noone@hotmail.com.<br><br>Respectfully yours,<br><br>*Althea Jefferson*<br><br>Althea Jefferson |

## THE JOB INTERVIEW

Some questions you will face in an interview will be generic, whereas others will be specific to a school, agency, or college counseling center. The sample questions in this section are not comprehensive, but will hopefully give you a sense of the types of questions you should be prepared to answer. It may also be helpful to have a career counselor, classmate, spouse, or friend play the role of interviewer. As previously stated, practice is *highly* recommended.

There are a couple of important points to consider before interviewing. If you do not know the answer to a question, say, "I don't know." This displays both honesty and a lack of pretension. After all, you have just completed a master's program and are not expected to know everything.

Second, you do not want to be too lengthy with your answers, as those interviewing you will lose interest. Bolles (2015) suggests the 50/50, 2-minute rule. The 2-minute maximum suggests that you keep your answers thorough, but brief. The longer you talk, the less interest the interviewer (or search committee) will have in your answers. After all, if you are too wordy at the interview, you may be too talkative as a counselor. In addition, the longer you speak during an interview, the greater the likelihood you will disclose something you would rather not disclose (Hodges & Connelly, 2010). Be brief, thorough, and discrete.

Here are some sample interview questions:

1. **Why do you want this job?** This is a critical question. You want the search committee to believe this school, agency, or college counseling center is your primary interest and focus. Be able to tie your answer to the mission of the organization. Something like, "I enjoy the challenge of working in an addictions treatment agency and wish to make my career in this counseling field. Your agency treats addicts in recovery utilizing CBT and DBT for trauma and offers an extensive training program and continuing education for employees." Don't say, "I think your school is a good stepping stone for my career." This latter response says, "You're just a short step on my career path and I'm not committed to you."

2. **Tell me about yourself.** This is your opportunity to take initiative in the interview. What interviewers want to hear is how you can tie your brief biography into why you are a good fit for the job. I would suggest that you weave your personal experience and strengths into a 60-second answer that sums up your "fit" for the position. For example, "I grew up in a family of teachers, with my mother a principal and my father a school counselor and have maintained a high value on education. I volunteer with disadvantaged children every year in the Big Sister/Big Brother program. I believe my personal background and training as a school counselor have provided me valuable experience for working alongside teachers, counselors, and administrators such as those at the Levett Middle School."

3. **What special training or skills do you offer?** This is where additional training or related skills and experience come in handy. For example, if you are a trained or certified mediator, mention that. Perhaps you have several years supervising collegiate residential living communities, or advanced training in art therapy or adventure-based therapy; mention this and tie the experience into how much it has enhanced your counseling ability. Remember, administrators are always interested in getting multitalented employees.

4. **What is your experience with this particular clinical population?** This is where your practicum/internship comes in handy, as does any related experience. Again, use your professional and related experiences to address the question. Weave in your practicum and internship experience, training, related experience volunteering with special populations, and so forth.

5. **Could you describe your strengths and weaknesses?** Everyone has weaknesses, and you are no exception. An overused line I have heard *way* too many times in job interviews goes something like: "I'm a perfectionist and very hard on myself." To me, this sounds contrived and scarcely original. So try to relate a weakness that can be turned around into a strength. For example, "Well, I am young and have just completed my graduate degree. But, I'm a quick learner and in a couple of years I will be older and more experienced. I'm also very willing to take coaching and feedback." The strength aspect of this question is much easier. Cite your experience on practicum and internship, related work, and so forth.

6. **If offered this position, how long could you see yourself working here?** In most cases, it is best not to give a specific time. Instead, you might answer something like, "I would like to work here as long as I have fresh challenges and opportunities. And, I hope to be challenged and have opportunities here for several years to come."

7. **What theoretical counseling approach do you work from?** This is often a tough question for recent graduates of master's degree counseling programs, as the program may not have provided one single approach. So, cite the approaches you have primarily used and under what situations you used them. Also, let the committee know you are open to learning new skills, techniques, and approaches.

8. **What are your professional goals?** Wise interviewees will tie their answer to the job at hand. For example, if you are interviewing for a school counseling position, you might express that you would like to direct a high school counseling office. You might also mention a few marking points along the way (such as attaining licensure, national certification, additional training, etc.). The dreaded "I have no goals" or "I don't believe in setting goals" is guaranteed to end your candidacy for the job. You might be surprised at the number of interviewees who have answers similar to the ones here! Set goals and measure your progress regularly.

9. **How do you handle conflict?** Be judicious with your answer, but be authentic. Inability to get along with coworkers is a huge reason people are fired or quit their jobs. A possible answer to this question might be something like this: "I work to calm myself, reviewing the main points of the disagreement. Then, I try to seek out the other party from the standpoint of trying to understand his or her point of view. If we then cannot come to agreement, perhaps asking a colleague or supervisor to mediate might be a good idea."

10. **What if a parent, teacher, coach, and so forth, demand to know what you and a student or client is working on in counseling?** For school counseling applicants, this is a question to see how well you remember your professional ethics (and legal issues as well!). You might want to briefly allude to the relevant legal issues in your answer. Remember, laws vary from state to state. So, know the relevant laws for the state you plan to work in.

11. **Regarding research, what is your specialty area?** If you are completing a doctorate in Counselor Education and Supervision and applying for an academic position or a research position, you need to be able to articulate your research interests, experience, and publications. In addition, check out the department's website to see how your research interests match those of the faculty. It's also worthwhile to scope out whether the opening is a replacement position ("Why did the last person leave?") or a newly created position.

12. **Have you ever been fired from a job?** If you were terminated for a cause, explain what that was. Emphasize how you have learned and grown from this experience. Remember, the world is full of successful people who were fired from previous jobs.

13. **What did you like about our agency/school/treatment center that interested you enough to apply for the job?** This is a critical question. The interviewer wants to hear your in-depth knowledge of the agency or school and its programs, missions, goals, client population, talented staff or faculty, and so forth. Be brief but thorough. Illustrate that you are knowledgeable about what they do. For sure, check out the website to learn as much as you can. If you know someone who works at the school/agency, ask him or her relevant questions.

14. **What do you see as the pressing issues in the field for the next decade?** This question is designed to see how well you understand the profession and potential changes. Good answers also illustrate that you have kept up on professional reading of journals. The "pressing issues" are subjective, so be prepared to support any answers you give. For example, a potential answer might be, "I believe multiculturalism is the most

important issue because of the large influx of immigrant and multicultural populations and the fact we live in a globally interconnected era."

15. **How have you or how would you support multiculturalism?** Be prepared to address how you support multiculturalism and include specific examples. Concrete examples might include having served on the school district's diversity task force, having counseled multicultural populations, having studied and/or worked abroad, and so forth. Remember, everyone has some part in multiculturalism as multiculturalism includes race, culture, socioeconomics, gender, sexual orientation, geography, and so on.

16. **What professional counseling organizations do you hold membership in?** If you are preparing for a job search and are not a member of a professional counseling organization, I'd strongly suggest you join the pertinent one: e.g., ACA, ASCA, ARCA, etc. The lack of a professional membership, especially in ACA, suggests you may not be committed to your profession and that you may not stay current in your profession.

17. **What salary would you expect to receive?** Never quote a specific figure. Answer with something like, "Somewhere in the advertised range," or "Something reflecting my training or experience." Never state a dollar amount until you receive a job offer! This is a mistake too many inexperienced job seekers—and even some experienced ones—make.

18. **What do you know about the mission of this university, school, or agency?** This is a question that is becoming more commonly asked in interviews. Make sure you have read and understood the mission, which should be posted on the university/school/agency's website. In addition, be prepared to explain why your experience and background fits the mission of the organization. If you do not know the mission, search committees will interpret that to mean you were not prepared for the interview, and do not understand the school or agency.

19. **Why should we hire you?** All interviews are an attempt to address this overarching question. This question usually comes at the end of the interview and is the candidate's opportunity to state his or her special qualifications and fit for the job. You need to be brief and sound confident, but not cocky. Here is one possible answer, "I believe myself to be the best candidate for the addiction counseling position because I have spent the past 2 years counseling in a residential addiction treatment center. I also have experience counseling trauma survivors and have completed DBT training. My plan is to make a career as an addictions counselor and one day to run a clinic such as this one. Hire me as a counselor and I'll make you very happy you did."

20. **Do you have any questions for us?** Of course you do! This is your opportunity to take control of the interview and it comes at the tipping point. I cringe when I hear job candidate's state, "No, I have no questions." Such an answer implies the candidate did not do his or her homework. You must always have questions to ask, even if you already know the answers to them. Chapter 2 offered suggested questions when choosing a practicum/internship placement; many of these questions would also be appropriate for a formal job interview. (Hodges & Connelly, 2010, pp. 68–70)

## Inappropriate Questions

Unfortunately, some interviewers will ask inappropriate questions during interviews. This may be unintentional (although ignorance is no excuse) or deliberate. Most public and private institutions sign an Equal Opportunity Employment Commission (EEOC) statement that pledges they will not discriminate based on race, creed, national origin, disability status, veteran status, gender, and so on. Many schools, agencies, and colleges also include sexual orientation as a status they will not discriminate against. Thus, questions concerning any of these issues should generally not be raised in an interview.

Examples of inappropriate questions might include:

- "Are you married?" or "Do you have children?"
- "What church do you attend?"
- "Mind if I ask you some personal questions?" (Of course you would mind—everyone minds!)
- "What political party do you belong to?"
- "Do you have a *normal* sexual orientation?"
- "How many times a day do you pray?"
- "I don't see a ring on your finger. Are you dating anyone?"
- "Are you related to anyone who could help us politically?"

The professional way to respond to illegal or inappropriate questions is to be tactful and ask clarification-type questions. While it might be very understandable if you were to get angry and respond in a likewise manner, you are a professional and professionals conduct themselves professionally even when the interview team or an administrator does not.

Example of illegal/inappropriate question: "Are you married?"

**Potential Answer:** "How does that question relate to the job?" or "Why is this important information to know?" You might use humor to defuse the situation: "Hmmm . . . I don't think the interview police allow that question." A more low-key and humorous approach does not suggest that illegal or inappropriate questions are any laughing matter, but rather they provide the interviewee an opportunity to set a message in a manner that does inflame the situation.

Inappropriate or illegal questions should rightfully lead you to wonder about the day-to-day ethics of the workplace. Should you be asked illegal or inappropriate questions on an interview, you may wish to consider whether you want to work at a school or agency with such lax ethics. Once the interview is over, you may consider contacting the appropriate person (usually in human resources) and informing him or her of your experience. You also have the right to contact your state's department of labor and file a complaint. Naturally, as a vulnerable person on a job search, it is wise to consider the ramifications of reporting versus not reporting. Consider the potential risks versus the rewards. Just as important for you, ask yourself what type of school, agency, or academic department you want to work in. If the potential job site does not seem a good fit for your personal values, you will likely be unhappy working there. As a counselor who spent more than 20 years providing career counseling and career advising, I have heard many sad stories from employees whose values are not a good fit for their place of work. Accepting a job is a bit like a marriage; you can get out of it (thankfully!) but the getting out is emotionally draining and very expensive.

## DEALING WITH REJECTION

On the path to career success, you will experience some rejection. This section of the chapter offers concrete suggestions to manage your disappointment if you do not get a position that you wanted. Fortunately, such rejection is not personal (except in rare cases), will pass, and does not have to keep you from landing another viable job. Rejection is also universally experienced as everyone has been rejected for something he or she desired.

So, you have just suffered a setback in your job search. That dream job—the one you seemed perfect for—was given to someone else. Perhaps you had a great interview where the search committee seemed to hang on your every word (or so you thought). You left the interview convinced you would soon be getting a call with a job offer. Then, with a brief and stilted phone call, your dreams burst into flames of disappointment. You hang up the phone stunned and numb from the shock of rejection. You try to make sense of it, but your mind cannot seem to accommodate the unexpected setback. "How could they have selected someone else?"

This scenario has been experienced by just about every job seeker in history. The critical factor is to acknowledge that you will have failures. For each job advertised, typically only one person will be selected. This means, of course, that if 30 applicants apply for a mental health counseling opening, 29 will be disappointed.

There are several reasonable reasons for job rejection:

1. A more qualified candidate was selected. Or, the committee *thought* the successful candidate was more qualified.
2. The successful candidate seemed a better fit for the position. A candidate with less experience might be hired because he or she has a counseling specialty area other candidates lack (e.g., trauma counseling, play therapy experience, mediation training) or simply seemed to connect better with the search committee.
3. Fit has cultural and gender implications. For example, if all the current counseling staff at a school are female, a male candidate may have a better chance at the job. No interviewing committee will admit to making such considerations, but believe me, they do consider such.
4. The successful candidate was simply better prepared than the other finalists. Bolles (2015) makes the point that the most prepared applicant will likely be hired over a more qualified one. Preparation includes a well-crafted résumé or CV, succinct and error-free cover letters, and good interviews. A more qualified candidate could torpedo his or her candidacy by lack of preparation in these areas.
5. A candidate's behavior was inappropriate during the interview. Inappropriate behavior could be having more than one drink at dinner

with search committee members, making racist or sexist jokes, rudeness to committee members, or raising inappropriate topics during the interview.

6. A candidate displayed a lack of confidence at the interview. You might be the most qualified candidate, but if you do not present as such, someone else will get the job offer. Self-critical comments such as "It's nothing," or "Anyone could have done it," or, "My colleagues actually did most of the work," send the wrong message. Be confident, not cocky or self-absorbed but confident.

7. A candidate was dishonest. Were you caught in a lie on your résumé or CV? Did you overly embellish your credentials during the interview phase?

8. A candidate's appearance was unprofessional. Granted, the counseling profession is not as formal as that of, say, banking or finance. Nevertheless, play it conservative; women should wear dress slacks, skirt, or dress. Men should wear a tie or sport coat. Do not go overboard with cologne or perfume or jewelry.

9. The search was a failed one. Sometimes a committee will not hire because of a shallow applicant pool or a general dissatisfaction with the finalists.

10. There was behind-the-scenes politicking. You can never really know what goes on behind closed doors. Politics certainly comes into play at times and a surprise candidate emerges as the top choice. Or the interview committee ranks the candidates 1 to 5 and the pertinent administrator selects the fourth- or fifth-ranked candidate.

11. A candidate posted inappropriate content on the Internet. Social networking sites have created a medium for sharing information and meeting new people. They also contain and chronicle much outlandish behavior. Make sure your online persona matches what you wish to convey in your job search.

(Hodges & Connelly, 2010, pp. 88–91)

## Transforming Your Disappointment

Fortunately, most applicants are resilient and understand there will be other job opportunities. The important point is to learn from disappointment and adapt that knowledge to new opportunities. When you get the disappointing phone call, e-mail, or thin envelope, here are some suggestions for dealing with job rejection:

1. Allow yourself some time to adjust to the situation. Do not push yourself to feel "okay." Talk the situation over with a trusted friend or colleague. Be honest with yourself about the disappointment and pain.

2. Stay physically active. Activity routines are a staple of health, especially during a job search. Physical activity works off anxiety and depression and promotes relaxation.

3. When you have a little distance from the disappointment, reflect back on the experience. What went wrong? What seemed to go well? How could you improve for the next application or interview? This aspect of self-reflection is a critical task in the job search process.

4. Get feedback from someone in the professional field. If you are seeking a school counseling position, ask a professional school counselor to look

over your résumé or CV and for tips. Practice interviewing with a career counselor or a professional counselor and have him or her grade you.

5. Identify two or three close friends/colleagues you can get support and a reality check from.

6. If needed, go in for personal counseling to address your frustration and the stress generated by the lack of getting hired.

7. Monitor and reframe your self-talk. Notice if you are telling yourself negative messages, such as "I'll never get hired" and "Nobody wants me." Reframe to more positive and realistic self-talk, such as "I'm having difficulty but I'll keep applying and improving and someone will hire me," or "Someone will eventually give me an opportunity and I'll be ready."

---

*Professional Self-Reflection*

1. How would you describe your current job search?
2. Ideally, where would you like to be in your professional life? Describe the job, geographic location, salary, and anything else that seems pertinent.
3. How can you begin to create the professional life you described in the previous question? Cite anything that could help you accomplish your professional goals.
4. If you were recently rejected for a job (or jobs) you wanted, what did you learn that could help you in future job searches?
5. What supports do you have for this transitional time? Examples of support can be family members, friends, a spiritual community, fellow graduate students, support groups, and the like.
6. What personal strengths do you have that will assist you in coping with this transition time? Examples of personal strengths are a positive outlook, good work ethic, fitness routine, and the like.
7. Think of when you were faced with previous challenges. How have you coped with previous disappointments? How can previous experience assist you now?
8. Think of someone who has been successfully transitioned through job rejection and then found success. Ask them for tips on how you can do the same.
9. Ask yourself, "What else can I do to become the strongest candidate possible?"
10. When you do land a professional counseling position, how will your life be different?
11. What would potential employers find attractive about you? What criticisms might they have? What is your ratio of strength to criticisms?
12. Networking is an essential component of a successful job search. What can you do to create an effective supportive network?
13. When writing cover letters, résumés or CVs, interviewing, and so forth, what message would you like to convey? How can you create that desired message?
14. If you were looking to hire a counselor or counselor educator, what qualities would you be looking for? Now, how well do you match up to those qualities? If you do not match up to the desired qualities, what do you need to do to meet them?
15. If a potential employer were to say, "Tell me five reasons why I should hire you," how would you answer? (Hodges & Connelly, 2010, pp. 94–96)

## EVALUATING A JOB OFFER

Congratulations, you have a job offer! This is a big deal even if you are not interested in the job. When you receive an offer, it may be tempting to accept on the spot, especially during tough economic times. Be aware that if you accept the job unconditionally, you may be losing any leverage you might have in the negotiation process. Certainly, you want to express excitement and gratitude on receiving the offer and you may even feel the salary and benefits are very good. Still, as this is a big step, ask for a few days to think it over. Most employers, reasonable ones anyway, will respect this request.

Be thorough in your decision-making process, because you do not want to hastily accept a job only to find there is something you missed in the process (e.g., moving expense reimbursement, annual raises). There are many issues to consider:

- What life changes would accepting this job entail?
- What expenses would I incur by accepting the job (e.g., moving expenses, selling or buying a home, uprooting children from school and friends, moving away from family)?
- What would I be gaining by accepting this offer (other than a paycheck)?
- What would I be giving up by accepting this job?
- Does the salary range seem equitable compared to other jobs of this type? Will it be enough to live on? In addition, what will my counter offer be?
- How excited am I about this offer? Would I want to work with the staff? Does this position offer good potential for professional growth?

If you are still unsure about accepting the job, a simple and common technique to try is a pro–con exercise. Using a pen, split a sheet of paper down the center. Label the left side "pro" and the right side "con." Then, list all the pros and cons you can think of. Naturally, you want the pro list to be longer than the con list. If the con list is longer or the lists are of about equal length, this should give you pause before accepting the offer. Let us examine such a list:

| Pro | Con |
|---|---|
| 1. It is a job. | 1. It is an expensive area. |
| 2. It includes good salary and benefits. | 2. It requires an expensive move. |
| 3. It is in a desirable area of the country. | 3. It is far from friends and family. |
| 4. It has good potential for promotion. | 4. I might get other offers. |
| 5. I would have likable colleagues. | |
| 6. The area has job potential for my partner. | |
| 7. I am excited about the job! | |

In this case, the pros outnumber the cons, although there are significant cons in the list. Thus, this candidate has a difficult decision to make. There are some significant pros as well, and the most significant one may be item number 7— excitement about the job. Some readers may be in the enviable position of entertaining several offers at once, and the pro–con lists would be longer than a list for one offer. Regardless, the ultimate decision to accept or reject the offer can be a difficult one. Talking the matter over with friends, family, spouse, or partner and if need be, a counselor all can be helpful.

Here is another example of a counselor weighing an offer:

| Pro | Con |
|---|---|
| 1. It is a very good job. | 1. It is a 500-mile move. |
| 2. We love the location! | 2. I will be leaving friends. |
| 3. They will help my partner search for a job. | 3. My partner will need to find a new job. |
| 4. Excellent potential for promotion. | |
| 5. I like the staff/faculty. | |
| 6. The salary and benefits are very good. | |
| 7. They will pay $3,000 for the move. | |
| 8. We are close to family. | |
| 9. I am very excited about the job! | |

In this example, the pros seem to far outnumber the cons. It is likely that this counselor would have an easier time making a decision of whether to accept the position than the previous scenario. Another method of assessing whether or not to accept a job involves a decision tree. In the following example, continue down the list until you arrive at a "no" answer. A "no" answer would suggest that you seriously consider whether accepting this job is a wise decision.

Step 1: Do I want really this job? Yes or no?

Step 2: Does this job fit my needs or my family's needs regarding professional challenge, financial security, benefits, stability, and lifestyle? Yes or no?

Step 3: If taking this job necessitates a move, would I or my family be willing to relocate? Yes or no?

Step 4: Would the relocation be worth the disruption in our lives (distance from family, friends, school change, spouse's or partner's job change, etc.)? Yes or no?

Step 5: Are the administration and staff (or faculty) at this position actually supportive of diversity? Yes or no?

Step 6: Do I feel committed to this job for 3 to 5 years? Yes or no?

Step 7: Does the job environment seem healthy (e.g., healthy collegial relations, small annual turnover rate, supportive supervisor)? Yes or no?

Step 8: Can I say, "This is the type of job I'm excited about?" Yes or no?

Step 9: Do the pros of accepting this job outweigh the cons? Yes or no?

If you answered "yes" to the question, "Do the pros significantly outweigh the cons? Yes or no?" this should provide you some insight. If you answered "no," that answer has the same guiding principle as "yes." Another critical question to consider is: "Am I excited about the prospect of this job?" Well, *are you*? (Hodges & Connelly, 2010, p. 81)

## If You Reject the Offer

Be professional. Thank whoever has offered you the position. If the person asks why you are turning down the offer, be as honest as you feel comfortable. For example, if the staff seemed rude, you might want to consider whether you would actually disclose that. If you are rejecting the offer because of salary, because you found a job that offers a better fit with your goals, or because you have found one in a preferred geographic location, that likely will not be as difficult to mention. Remember, the counseling profession can be very small, so do not burn any bridges.

## If You Accept the Offer

This is the place all job seekers want to be; they have an offer and have decided to accept it. Now, your work is still not done. Anyone extending a job offer understands that a savvy candidate will attempt to negotiate the best possible terms. Many people, and this may especially be true of counselors fresh out of graduate school, may be uncomfortable with negotiation, especially during tough economic times. Determine what salary you and your family need, then practice negotiating with a career counselor or friend. Here are some things to keep in mind regarding negotiation:

- You may have been given a specific salary figure (likely). Your ability to move that figure upward will depend on what you have to offer (e.g., special training, related experience, publications), your apparent skill level, and how much the employer wants you.
- Beyond salary, what are the other negotiables? Is a costly move involved? Are you a dual-income family and losing one income with the move? Can the employer assist your spouse or partner in finding a job?
- How good are the benefits? What and *who* does the health plan include (e.g., domestic partners, stepchildren)? What about the retirement package? If you are young do not discount this issue because it will become increasingly important over time. In fact, many Americans have inadequate pensions (Olen, 2014).
- How many vacation days do you receive per year? How many sick days?
- What type of annual salary increase or merit increase is offered? Will you have a probationary period? Does the job involve tenure, and, if so, what is the length of time before you can apply for tenure?
- What opportunity is there for advancement in this clinic/school/agency?
- Will the employer pay for you to receive additional training (e.g., attending conferences, workshops)?
- Regardless of what transpires, be courteous during the negotiation phase. Do not become rigid and make statements such as "This is my final offer!"

Be flexible when necessary without giving in on everything. For example, you might be more flexible on salary, but hold the line on moving expenses.
- When you agree to a package, get the agreement in writing.

Your new employer will expect you to be enthusiastic when you begin. Be realistic and give yourself time to adjust to a new place, new colleagues, and new challenges. Remember that most people struggle in their jobs not because they lack the skill, but because of conflicts with coworkers (Bolles, 2015). Therefore, extend yourself to your new colleagues by asking for their input, ideas, and critique. Be respectful when you disagree in staff meetings, and learn to listen to people you find difficult.

## FINAL THOUGHTS ON CONCLUDING YOUR PRACTICUM/INTERNSHIP AND BEGINNING YOUR CAREER

- Remember, your career as a professional counselor is just beginning. The work setting you begin with is unlikely to be the one you finish your career with.
- Because you are new in the profession (e.g., recent graduate) and lack licensure (or certification for many school counselors), your initial job out of graduate school may not be one you stay with for the long term. However, remember that, although the initial job after graduation may not be ideal, it provides you the opportunity for professional growth and to receive supervision for licensure. State licensure and 3 to 5 years' experience give you professional mobility.
- Although graduate school experiences vary, many graduate students experience their counseling programs as nurturing environments. Do not expect your first professional job to be like your graduate program.
- Make sure to keep your résumé or CV current so that when more desirable positions become available, you are ready to apply.
- Take advantage of all trainings your school, agency, college, and so forth, has to offer. As a professional counselor, you should be a lifelong learner. Certificate trainings in specific clinical, legal, or professional issues are great ways to upgrade and expand your skills. Take advantage of these.
- If the agency, school, or college counseling center has a preferred treatment approach (e.g., DBT, cognitive behavioral therapy [CBT], solution-focused therapy [SFT]) keep an open mind about it, even if you prefer a different theoretical approach. Working from a new theoretical modality also broadens your experience and enhances your clinical skills.
- Keep in mind that this is simply your first professional (post-master's) experience. It is likely, in fact almost a certainty, that you will change jobs in the future. However, remember that you will be more marketable when you are licensed and have a few years of post-master's experience under your belt.
- Set some professional goals for yourself, such as to develop expertise in the treatment model you are learning (e.g., CBT, DBT), to develop

harmonious relationships with the staff, to stay in the job for 2 years, to receive training in a new skill area, and so forth.

- Keep a folder of the applications you make for employment. Many students, especially doctoral students looking for an academic job, may make 20 to 30 applications. You want to keep the positions you apply for from merging together in your mind and a file of all applications filed can assist with organization. In addition, some search committees work slower than others do. I once applied for a job and did not hear from the search committee until 6 months later.
- Anytime you apply for a counseling position, be sure to examine the website of the organization.
- Use appropriate social medial sites for career networking. LinkedIn is one of the preferred networking sites career professionals use. LinkedIn is relatively easy and simple to use and provides an efficient way to link with colleagues in your area, state, country, and abroad.

## RECOMMENDED READING

Here are a number of texts I have used and found helpful in counseling students regarding résumé and cover letter writing, self-exploration, visioning career goals, and the job search process in general:

Bolles, R. N. (2015). *What color is your parachute? A practical manual for job-hunters and career-changers.* Berkeley, CA: Ten Speed Press (updated annually).

Capacchione, L. (2000). *Visioning: Ten steps to designing the life of your dreams.* New York, NY: Tarcher/Putnam.

Enelow, W. S., & Kursmark, L. M. (2007). *Cover letters: Trade secrets of professional resume writers.* Indianapolis, IN: JIST Works.

Hodges, S., & Connelly, A. R. (2010). *A job search manual for counselors and counselor educators: How to navigate and promote your counseling career.* Alexandria, VA: American Counseling Association.

Parker, Y. (2002). *The damn good resume guide: A crash course in resume writing.* Berkeley, CA: Ten Speed Press.

Yate, M. (2007). *Knock' em dead 2007: The ultimate job seekers guide.* Avon, MA: Adams Media.

## REFERENCES

Baird, B. N. (2005). *The internship, practicum, and field placement handbook: A guide for the helping professions* (4th ed.). Upper Saddle River, NJ: Pearson/Prentice Hall.

Bolles, R. N. (2015). *What color is your parachute? A practical manual for job-hunters and career-changers.* Berkeley, CA: Ten Speed Press.

Capacchione, L. (2000). *Visioning: Ten steps to designing the life of your dreams.* New York, NY: Tarcher/Putnam.

Covey, S. R. (1996). *The seven habits of highly effective people.* New York, NY: Simon & Schuster.

Herlihy, B., & Corey, G. (2015). *ACA ethical standards casebook* (7th ed.). Alexandria, VA: American Counseling Association.

Hodges, S., & Connelly, A. R. (2010). *A job search manual for counselors and counselor educators: How to navigate and promote your counseling career.* Alexandria, VA: American Counseling Association.

Olen, H. (2014, February/March). You call this retirement? Boomers still have work to do. *AARP The Magazine*. Retrieved from http://www.aarp.org/work/retirement-planning-little-savings-means-working.html

Remley, T. P., & Herlihy, B. (2014). *Ethical, legal and professional issues in counseling* (4th ed.). Upper Saddle River, NJ: Pearson.

Rokeach, M. (1979). *Understanding human values: Individual and societal*. New York, NY: Simon & Schuster.

Seligman, M. E. P. (1998). *Learned optimism* (2nd ed.). New York, NY: Pocket Books.

Williams, A. (1995). *Visual and active supervision: Roles, focus, technique*. New York, NY: W. W. Norton.

# LIST OF PROFESSIONAL COUNSELING ORGANIZATIONS

(*Note:* Be aware licensing and credentialing requirements are subject to periodic change.)

## AMERICAN COUNSELING ASSOCIATION (ACA)

ACA is the flagship organization for counselors and the world's largest organization representing the counseling profession. All counselors should hold a membership in the ACA. Membership in the ACA also includes a subscription to the *Journal of Counseling and Development*, the monthly magazine *Counseling Today*, and numerous other tools for professional development.

The ACA (www.counseling.org) also includes 20 affiliate divisions representing various counseling specialties and many different counseling interest groups:

- **American College Counseling Association (ACCA)**
  ACCA is the primary professional organization for college, university, and community college counseling professionals. ACCA membership is also open to psychologists, social workers, and so forth.
  www.collegecounseling.org

- **American Mental Health Counselors Association (AMHCA)**
  AMHCA is the professional division representing clinical mental health counseling.
  www.amhca.org

- **American Rehabilitation Counseling Association (ARCA)**
  ARCA represents the profession of rehabilitation, rehabilitation counseling faculty, and graduate students in rehabilitation counseling.
  www.arcaweb.org

- **American School Counselor Association (ASCA)**
  ASCA promotes the profession of school counseling.
  www.schoolcounselor.org

- **Association for Adult Development and Aging (AADA)**
  AADA serves as the professional organization devoted to supporting counselors serving senior populations.
  www.aadaweb.org

- **Association for Assessment and Research in Counseling (AARC)**
  AARC promotes the ethical and effective use of assessment (testing) in the counseling profession.
  www.theaaceonline.com

- **Association for Child and Adolescent Counseling (ACAC)**
  Association for Child and Adolescent Counseling aims to focus on the training needs of counselors who work with children and adolescents while also providing professional support to those counselors, whether they are school counselors, play therapists, counselor educators, and so on.
  www.acachild.com

- **Association for Counselor Education and Supervision (ACES)**
  ACES is an umbrella organization for counselor educators in all counseling affiliates (clinical mental health counseling, school counseling, marriage and family counseling, etc.), as well as counseling supervisors out in the field. ACES membership is also open to counseling psychologists and members in related mental health professions.
  www.acesonline.net

- **Association for Creativity in Counseling (ACC)**
  ACC is a professional affiliate organization for creative arts counseling (e.g., art, music, dance, drama therapy) as well as novel counseling approaches. ACC also encourages creative expression in the manner of poetry, prose, musical performance, and so forth by individual counselors.
  www.creativecounselor.org

- **Association for Humanistic Counseling (AHC)**
  AHC, formerly C-AHEAD, a founding association of ACA in 1952, provides a forum for exchange of information about humanistic-oriented counseling practices and promotes changes that reflect the growing body of knowledge about humanistic principles applied to human development and potential.
  www.afhc.camp9.org

- **Association for Lesbian, Gay, Bisexual, and Transgender Issues in Counseling (ALGBTIC)**
  ALGBTIC educates counselors on concerns regarding the needs of lesbian, gay, bisexual, and transgender clients. ALGBTIC also serves as an advocacy organization both within and beyond the counseling profession.
  www.algbtic.org

- **Association for Multicultural Counseling and Development (AMCD)**
  AMCD strives to improve the understanding of multicultural issues in counseling. Multicultural issues could be related to race, sexual

orientation, class, disability, culture, religion or spirituality, and many other issues.
www.amcdaca.org/amcd/default.cfm

- **Association for Specialists in Group Work (ASGW)**
ASGW provides professional leadership and promotes research in the field of group counseling in schools, colleges/universities, correctional facilities, hospitals, and so forth.
www.asgw.org

- **Association for Spiritual, Ethical, and Religious Values in Counseling (ASERVIC)**
ASERVIC is devoted to exploring and addressing spiritual, religious, and ethical issues in counseling.
www.aservic.org

- **Counselors for Social Justice (CSJ)**
CSJ is one of the newest ACA divisions and is committed to plurality on a broad array of social justice issues including an end to oppression and injustice impacting clients, students, families, communities, schools, workplaces, governments, and other social and institutional systems.
www.counselorsforsocialjustice.com

- **International Association of Addictions and Offender Counselors (IAAOC)**
IAAOC advocates for the development of effective practice in substance abuse treatment, counseling juvenile offenders, and counselors working in correctional facilities.
www.iaaoc.org

- **International Association of Marriage and Family Counselors (IAMFC)**
IAMFC is the ACA division devoted to studying and promoting the field of couples and family counseling.
www.iamfc.com

- **Military and Government Counseling Association (MGCA); formerly Association for Counselors and Educators in Government (ACEG)**
MGCA is dedicated to exploring counseling issues and concerns in municipal, state, federal, and military settings.
www.acegonline.org

- **National Career Development Association (NCDA)**
NCDA's mission is to promote career and vocational counseling and development.
www.associationdatabase.com/aws/NCDA/pt/sp/Home_Page

- **National Employment Counseling Association (NECA)**
NECA's charge is professional leadership and development for counselors working in employment settings.
www.employmentcounseling.org

## ADDITIONAL PROFESSIONAL ASSOCIATIONS (INDEPENDENT OF THE AMERICAN COUNSELING ASSOCIATION)

- **American Art Therapy Association (AATA)**
  The American Art Therapy Association is an organization of professionals dedicated to using art in a therapeutic, healing manner. AATA provides standards of professional competence and promotes knowledge in the field of art therapy.
  www.arttherapy.org

- **American Association of State Boards of Counseling (AACSB)**
  AACSB promotes unification and reciprocity among U.S. state counseling licensure requirements.
  www.aacsb.org

- **American Dance Therapy Association (ADTA)**
  The American Dance Therapy Association, founded in 1986, is a professional organization dedicated to the profession of dance/movement therapy.
  www.adta.our

- **Association for Play Therapy (APT)**
  The Association for Play Therapy (APT) is a national professional society established in 1982 to foster contact among mental health professionals interested in exploring the therapeutic power of play to treat clients, particularly children.
  www.a4pt.org

- **International Association of Counseling Services (IACS)**
  IACS serves as the professional accrediting organization for college and university counseling centers and community clinics.
  www.iacsinc.org

- **International Association of Counselors and Therapists (IACT)**
  IACT is the professional counseling organization promoting the international counseling profession.
  www.iact.org

## PROFESSIONAL ACCREDITING ORGANIZATIONS FOR THE COUNSELING PROFESSION

- **Center for Credentialing and Education (CCE)**
  CCE, an affiliate of the National Board for Certified Counselors, Inc., provides credentialing to counselors and related professionals. CCE offers several certifications including Approved Clinical Supervisor (ACS), Distance Certified Counselor (DCC), Board Certified Coach (BCC), and several more.
  cce-global.org

■ **Commission on Rehabilitation Counselor Certification (CRCC)**
CRCC, like NBCC, provides certification for individual rehabilitation counselors. Certification, unlike licensure, is usually a voluntary credential for counselors. Licensure, often a mandatory credential, is overseen by state licensure boards (see State Licensure Boards).
www.crccertification.com

■ **Commission on Rehabilitation Education (CORE)**
CORE accredits graduate programs in rehabilitation counseling. Though separate from CACREP, CORE and CACREP are affiliates. CCE also offers the Counselor Preparation Comprehensive Examination (CPCE) utilized by some 400 counselor education programs.
www.core-rehab.org
e-mail: core@core.org

■ **Council for Accreditation of Counseling and Related Educational Programs (CACREP)**
CACREP, an ACA organizational affiliate, is the international accrediting organization for counseling programs. CACREP accredits graduate programs in colleges and universities. The types of graduate counseling programs accredited by CACREP are doctoral programs in counselor education, and master's degree programs in clinical mental health counseling, marriage and family counseling, school counseling, student affairs and counseling, and college counseling. (*Note:* CACREP does not accredit rehabilitation counseling [see the Commission on Rehabilitation Education].)
www.cacrep.org
e-mail: cacrep@cacrep.org

■ **National Board for Certified Counselors (NBCC)**
NBCC serves as an independent credentialing organization for the counseling profession. Although U.S. states and territories are responsible for licensing counselors, NBCC provides certification for specialty areas. Examples of NBCC specialty area certification are National Certified Counselor (NCC), National Certified Clinical Mental Health Counselor (NCCMHC), National Certified Career Counselor (NCCC), and Approved Clinical Supervisor (ACS). NBCC also offers certification examinations that most U.S. states and territories use for licensure examinations, such as the National Counselor Examination (NCE), Certified Clinical Mental Health Counselor Examination (CCMHCE), and more.
www.nbcc.org
e-mail: nbcc@nbcc.org

# STATE LICENSURE BOARDS AND REQUIREMENTS

Here is some basic information regarding licensure requirements by state as of 2010. For complete information, please visit the state licensing board website.

**ALABAMA**
Alabama Board of Examiners in Counseling
950 22nd St. North, Suite 765
Birmingham, AL 35203
(800) 822-3307
(205) 458-8716
(205) 458-8718 (fax)
Walter H. Cox, Ex. Officer: Walter.Cox@abec.alabama.gov
www.abec.state.al.us

**Title of License**: Licensed Professional Counselor (LPC)
                     Associate Licensed Counselor (ALC)

*Note:* ALCs work under LPCs to attain hours for licensure.

**Educational Requirements**: Master's degree in counseling from a CACREP- or CORE-accredited program (or its equivalent) defined as 48 semester hours or 72 quarter hours.

**Experiential Requirements**: ALC is given when master's is verified. No experiential requirements. LPC: 3,000 hours of supervised experience in professional counseling with board approved supervision. An applicant may subtract 1,000 hours of the required professional experience for every 15 graduate semester hours (or 22.5 quarter hours) obtained beyond the master's degree from a regionally accredited college or university, provided that such hours are clearly related to the field of professional counseling. This formula can be used for up to 2,000 hours.

(*Note:* In the ACA book on state licensure, numbers are written as 2,000, not two thousand.)

**Exam Required**: NCE

## ALASKA
AK Division of Occupational Licensing
Board of Professional Counselors
P.O. Box 110806
Juneau, AK 99811-0806
(907) 465-2551
(907) 465-2974 (fax)
Eleanor.vinson@alaska.gov
www.dced.state.ak.us/occ/ppco.htm

**Title of License**: LPC

**Educational Requirements**: Master's degree in counseling from a regionally or nationally accredited institution approved by the board and consisting of at least 60 graduate semester hours. The degree must include coursework in eight core areas. Related professional field includes psychology, marital and family therapy, social work, and applied behavioral science.

**Experiential Requirements**: 3,000 post-master's supervised hours including 1,000 hours of direct client contact and 100 hours of face-to-face supervision over a 2-year period. The supervisor must be a licensed mental health professional.

The face-to-face supervision can be by telephone or electronic means due to remote distances. Supervision must be under an LPC or other licensed mental health professional approved by the board.

**Exam Required**: NCE

## ARIZONA
AZ Board of Behavioral Health Examiners
3443 N. Central Avenue, Suite 1700
Phoenix, AZ 85012
(602) 542-1882
(602) 364-0890 (fax)
Counseling Contact:
Pamela Osborn
Pamela.Osborn@azbbhe.us
www.azbbhe.us

**Title of License**: LPC

> Licensed Associate Counselor (LAC) must practice only under direct supervision as prescribed by the board and shall not engage in independent practice.

**Educational Requirements**: Master's degree in counseling or a related field from a CACREP or CORE-accredited program or a program that includes a minimum of 60 semester hours and completion in 14 content areas. As of October 31, 2015: If a program is not accredited by CACREP or CORE, it must require 700 clinical supervision hours and a minimum of 24 semester hours in 8 content areas.

**Experiential Requirements**: 2 years/3,200 hours of full-time post-master's supervised work experience in psychotherapy, including assessment, diagnosis, and treatment. 100 hours of clinical supervision and 1,600 hours of direct client contact are required. No more than 400 of the additional hours can be psychoeducational.

Applicant must receive a minimum of 10 hours of clinical supervision obtained during direct observation or a review of audiotapes/videotapes by the clinical supervisor while the applicant is providing treatment and evaluation services to a client.

**Exam Required**: NCE, NCMHCE, or CRCE

## ARKANSAS
AR Board of Examiners in Counseling
P. O. Box 989
Little Rock, AR 72201
(501) 683-5800
(501) 683-6349 (fax)
arboec@sbglobal.net
www.state.ar.us/abec

**Title of License**: LPC

> Licensed Associate Counselor (LAC): An applicant with less than 3 years of post–master's-level supervision experience, if all other requirements have been met.

**Educational Requirements**: Master's degree or higher in counseling from a program that reflects the CACREP or CORE curriculum and consists of 60 semester hours from a regionally accredited institution.

**Experiential Requirements**: 3 years/3,000 hours of post-master's supervised counseling experience (1 year = 1,000 hours). 50% of the hours have to be Client Contact Hours.

One year of experience may be gained for each 30 semester hours earned beyond master's degree (up to 2 years) provided the hours are clearly counseling in nature and acceptable to the board.

Supervision must be under an LPC approved by the board. Telephone supervision is allowed for less than 25% of the total amount.

**Exam Required**: NCE and an oral exam.

**CALIFORNIA**
CA Board of Behavioral Sciences
1625 N. Market Boulevard
Suite S-200
Sacramento, CA 95834
(916) 574-7830
(916) 574-8625 (fax)
www.bbs.ca.gov

California Association for Licensed Professional Clinical Counselors
P.O. Box 280640
Northridge, CA 91328
www.calpcc.org

**Title of License**: Licensed Professional Clinical Counselor (LPCC)[1]
Professional Clinical Counselor Intern (PCCI): An unlicensed person who has completed the education requirements and is registered with the board to complete the supervision requirements to be licensed as an LPCC. (Has to renew annually for up to 5 years.)

**Educational Requirements**: Master's degree or higher that is counseling or psychotherapy in content:
Enrolled before 8/1/12 and graduate before 12/31/18: Minimum of 48 graduate semester hours.
Enrolled after 8/1/12 or graduate after 12/31/18: Minimum of 60 graduate semester hours.
**Additional Educational Requirements:**

1. 15 contact hours in alcoholism and other chemical substance abuse, dependency
2. 10 contact hours in human sexuality
3. A two-semester unit or three-quarter unit survey course in psychopharmacology
4. 15 contact hours in spousal or partner abuse assessment, detection, and intervention strategies[1]
5. 7 contact hours in child abuse assessment and reporting
6. 18 contact hours in California law and professional ethics for professional clinical counselors[1] (possible that graduate coursework will suffice)
7. 10 contact hours in aging and long-term care[1]
8. 15 contact hours in crisis or trauma counseling[1]

---

[1]There are stipulations regarding the types of hours that will be accepted. Please consult your state regulations.

**Experiential Requirements:** 3,000 hours of post-master's supervised counseling experience; 1,750 have to be Direct Client Contact hours.
Areas with guidance on:

- 500 hours maximum for group counseling
- 250 hours maximum for phone crisis counseling
- 150 hours minimum of clinical experience in a hospital or community mental health setting
- Combined total of 1,250 hours combined total maximum:
  (A) Direct supervisor contact
  (B) Client centered advocacy
  (C) 250 hours maximum in administering tests
  (D) 250 hours maximum in attending conferences

**Exam Required:** NCMHCE (as of January 1, 2014)—taken after experiential requirements have been fulfilled. AND: California jurisprudence exam—taken while acquiring supervision.

**COLORADO**
CO Division of Professions and Occupations
1560 Broadway, Suite 1350
Denver, CO 80202
(303) 894-7768
(303) 894-7764 (fax)
Karin.gleichauf@state.co.us
mentalhealth@dora.state.co.us
www.dora.state.co.us/mental-health

**Title of License:** LPC
Licensed Professional Counselor Candidate (LPCC)[2]: An applicant who has completed the education requirements and is under a licensed supervisor; valid for 4 years (if not registered as an LPCC, must register as a Registered Psychotherapist in the Registered Psychotherapist Board Database).

**Educational Requirements:** Master's degree or higher in professional counseling from a CACREP-accredited program, or equivalent program from a regionally accredited college/university consisting of 48 semester hours, completion of coursework in core areas and a practicum and/or internship. *Note:* If enrolled after August 31, 2014, the program must consist of 60 graduate semester hours.

**Experiential Requirements:** 2 years/2,000 hours of post-master's practice in applied psychotherapy under board-approved supervision. (Doctoral degree

---

[2]There are stipulations regarding the types of hours that will be accepted. Please consult your state regulations.

can be 1,000 in 12 months). 100 hours of supervision is required, 70 of which must be face-to-face individual supervision.

The teaching of psychotherapy can count up to 600 hours and 30 hours of required supervision.

*Note:* Electronic supervision is allowed—initial 2-hour meeting must be in person and every 6 months an in-person meeting must be held and the electronic supervision must be audio and visual (as of July 20, 2012).

**Exam Required:** NCE and CO jurisprudence exam.

**CONNECTICUT**
CT Department of Public Health
Professional Counselor Licensure
410 Capitol Ave., MS# 12APP
P. O. Box 340308
Hartford, CT 06134-0308
(860) 509-7603
(860) 509-8457 (fax)
oplc.dph@ct.gov
www.ct.gov/dph

**Title of License:** LPC

**Educational Requirements:** Master's degree or higher in counseling or a related mental health field from a regionally accredited institution of higher education consisting of at least 60 semester hours and completion of required coursework.

**Experiential Requirements:** 3,000 hours of post-master's supervised experience in professional counseling.

A minimum of 100 hours of direct supervision by an appropriately licensed individual is required.

**Exam Required:** NCE or NCMHCE

**DELAWARE**
DE Board of Mental Health and Chemical Dependency Professionals
Cannon Building
861 Silverlake Blvd.
Suite 203
Dover, DE 19904-2467
(302) 744-4500
(302) 739-2711 (fax)
www.dpr.delaware.gov

**Title of License**: Licensed Professional Counselor of Mental Health (LPCMH)
Licensed Associate Counselor of Mental Health (LACMH):
An individual licensed for the purpose of gaining experience required for licensure as an LPCMH; must work under direct supervision of an LPCMH or other health professional approved by the board.

**Educational Requirements**: Master's degree or higher in clinical mental health, including a minimum of 48 semester hours.

Must also be certified by NBCC as a National Certified Counselor (NCC), or certified by another national mental health specialty certifying organization approved by the board.

**Experiential Requirements**: 2 years/3,200 hours full-time clinical professional counseling experience to be completed within a 4-year period.

1,600 hours must be under professional direct supervision acceptable to the board (100 hours must be face-to-face supervision; live video-conferencing is considered face to face but cannot exceed 50% of the supervision). 1,500 hours must be direct client contact hours (750 hours have to be individual).

30 graduate semester hours or more beyond master's degree may be substituted for 1 year/1,600 hours of required experience, provided that hours are clearly related to the field of counseling and acceptable to the board.

*Note:* If your degree was conferred after June 30, 2012, you will receive credit only for experience that you gained as a Delaware-licensed Associate Counselor of Mental Health.

**Exam Required**: NCE or NCMHCE

**DISTRICT OF COLUMBIA**
DC Board of Professional Counseling
Board of Professional Counseling
717 14th St. NW, Suite 600
Washington, DC 20005
(202) 724-4900
(877) 672-2174
(202) 727-8471 (fax)
hpla.doh.dc.gov/hpla

**Title of License**: LPC

**Educational Requirements**: 60 graduate semester hours including a master's degree in counseling or a related field from an accredited institution.

Master's degree to include coursework in 10 core areas, including a counseling practicum or internship.

**Experiential Requirements**: 2 years/3,500 hours of post-master's supervised professional counseling experience.

200 hours of supervision (100 hours must be immediate supervision under an LPC).

**Exam Required**: NCE

*Note:* Will accept NCMHCE or CRCE if already taken in another jurisdiction.

## FLORIDA

FL Board of Clinical Social Work, Marriage and Family Therapy, and Mental Health Counseling
4052 Bald Cypress Way, BIN C-08
Tallahassee, FL 32399-3258
(850) 245-4474
(850) 921-5389 (fax)
mqa_491@doh.state.fl.us
www.doh.state.fl.us/mqa/491

**Title of License**: Licensed Mental Health Counselor (LMHC)
Provisional Mental Health Counselor: A person provisionally licensed to provide mental health counseling under supervision; valid for 24 months. Issued to licensure applicants who have completed their clinical experience requirement intending to provide services in Florida while satisfying coursework and/or exam requirements.

**Educational Requirements**: Master's degree or higher from a CACREP-accredited mental health counseling program that includes 60 semester hours, a course in human sexuality, and a course in substance abuse.
OR
Master's degree or higher from a program related to the practice of mental health counseling from an accredited institution that includes 60 semester hours, 12 specific course content areas, and 1,000 hours of supervised practicum, internship, or field experience.
AND for both options:
Completion of an 8-hour Laws and Rules course and a 2-hour Prevention of Medical Errors course from a board-approved provider
and within 6 months of licensure have to complete from a board-approved provider:
3-hour course on HIV and AIDS
2-hour domestic violence course from a board approved provider.

**Experiential Requirements**: 2 years of supervised post-master's clinical experience in mental health counseling that consists of at least 1,500 hours providing psychotherapy face-to-face with clients and at least 100 face-to-face hours of supervision (50 of which can be group supervision).

Supervision must be under an LMHC or equivalent.

**Exam Required**: NCMHCE

**GEORGIA**
GA Composite Board of Professional Counselors, Social Workers, and Marriage and Family Therapists
237 Coliseum Dr.
Macon, GA 31217-3858
(478) 207-2440
(866) 888-7127 (fax)
www.sos.state.ga.us/plb/counselors

**Title of License**: LPC
Associate Licensed Professional Counselor (ALPC): Applicant who has met the educational requirements and has registered with the board an acceptable contract for obtaining post-master's experience under direct supervision; valid for 5 years.

**Educational Requirements**: Master's degree or higher in a program that is primarily counseling in content, or in applied psychology, from an institution accredited by a regional body recognized by the Council on Higher Education Accreditation (CHEA).

Completion of specific coursework and a supervised practicum or internship consisting of at least 300 hours is required.

**Experiential Requirements**: 4 years/2,400 hours of supervised, post-master's directed experience in professional counseling in a work setting acceptable to the board, with a minimum of 120 clock hours of supervision (can count up to 1 year of experience from practicum/internship).

*Note:* On December 6, 2013, there was a proposal to increase the number of required hours to 3,000.

A minimum of 2 years of supervision must be provided by an LPC. Please consult your state regulations for requirements regarding clinical supervision for licensure.

**Exam Required**: NCE

**HAWAII**

HI Department of Commerce and Consumer Affairs—Professional and Vocational Licensing (PVL)
Mental Health Counselor Program
P. O. Box 3469
Honolulu, HI 96801
(808) 586-2697
counselor@dcca.hawaii.gov
www.hawaii.gov/dcca/areas/pvl/programs/mental

**Title of License**: LMHC

**Educational Requirements**: Master's degree or higher in counseling or an allied field related to the practice of mental health counseling, with a minimum of 48 semester hours (or 72 quarter hours) of coursework in core areas, from an accredited institution. Also, two academic terms of a supervised mental health practicum intern experience for graduate credit of at least 3 semester hours (or 5 quarter hours) per academic term in a mental health counseling setting, with at least 300 hours of supervised client contact under a licensed supervisor.

July 5, 2007: Changes in Hawaii Revised Statutes Chapter 453D-7(c)(1) and (2) allow individuals who obtained a graduate degree before July 1, 2007 an alternate method to verify the practicum and postgraduate experience.

**Experiential Requirements**: 2 years/3,000 hours of post-master's supervised experience in the practice of mental health counseling, with 100 hours of face-to-face clinical supervision under a licensed supervisor.

Experience shall be completed in no less than 2 years and in no more than 4 years.

**Exam Required**: NCE

*Note:* Will accept the NCMHCE or the CRCC (if taken after 1/1/2000 and before 7/1/2005).

**IDAHO**

ID State Licensing Board of Professional Counselors and Marriage and Family Therapists
700 W. State St.
Boise, ID 83702
(208) 334-3233
(208) 334-3945 (fax)
Deborah.Sexton@ibd.idaho.gov
cou@ibol.idaho.gov
www.ibol.idaho.gov

**Title of License:** LCPC
LPC
Registered Counselor Intern (RCI): A counselor performing under supervision as part of the supervised experience requirement.

**Educational Requirements:** Master's degree or higher in a counseling field from an accredited college or university with 60 semester hours and completion of a 6-semester hour advanced counseling practicum.

**Experiential Requirements:** LPCC: Hold a valid LPC, 2 years/2,000 hours of supervised direct client contact experience accumulated after licensure in any state, 1,000 hours must be under supervision of an LCPC. Minimum of 1-hour face-to-face, one-on-one supervision for every 30 hours of direct client contact. Successful completion of a diagnostic evaluation graduate course or equivalent training/experience acceptable to the board.

LPC: 1,000 hours is defined as one thousand clock hours of experience working in a counseling setting, 400 hours of which shall be direct client contact. Supervised experience in practica and/or internships taken at the graduate level may be utilized. The supervised experience shall include a minimum of 1-hour face-to-face or one-to-one or one-to-two consultation with the supervisor for every 20 hours of job/internship experience. Face-to-face may include a face-to-face setting provided by a live video connection between the supervisor and supervisee. As stated under Subsection 150.01.a.iv, counseling practicum experience as opposed to job or internship experience shall be supervised at a ratio of 1 hour of supervision for every 10 hours in the settings. **Supervised practicum and/or internship taken at a graduate level may be utilized.**

**Exam Required:** LPCC: NCMHCE
LPC: NCE

**ILLINOIS**
IL Professional Counselor Licensing and Disciplinary Board
320 W. Washington St., 3rd Floor
Springfield, IL 62786
(217) 785-0800
(217) 524-6735 TDD
(217) 782-7645 (fax)
www.idfpr.com/DPRdefault.asp
or
www.idfpr.com/PROFS/Info/ProfCounselor.asp

**Title of License:** Licensed Clinical Professional Counselor (LCPC): Holds license authorizing independent practice of clinical professional counseling in private practice.
LPC: Holds license authorizing the practice of professional counseling.

**Educational Requirements**: LCPC: A master's or higher in professional counseling or a related field from a regionally accredited college/university OR hold a current CCMHC credential issued by NBCC (meets all requirements for licensure as an LCPC).

*Note:* Certain other certifications meet all or part of the LPC or LCPC licensure requirements; please contact the board for more information.

LPC: Master's degree or higher in professional counseling or related field of at least 48 semester hours from a regionally accredited college/university in a program approved by the IL Dept. of Professional Regulation.

CACREP- and CORE-accredited programs in professional counseling are approved programs for both LPC and LCPC licensure.

**Experiential Requirements**: LCPC: 2 years/3,360 hours of full-time, satisfactory, supervised employment experience working as a clinical professional counselor in a professional capacity under the direction of a qualified supervisor, subsequent to degree.

Of these, 1,920 hours must be direct face-to-face service to clients.

One year = maximum of 1,680 hours, including 960 hours of direct face-to-face service to clients.

If applicant holds a doctoral degree, 1 year must be subsequent to the degree and internships may count toward professional experience.

**Exam Required**: LCPC: NCE and NCMHCE or ECCP or CRCE
LPC: NCE or CRCE

**INDIANA**
IN Behavioral Health and Human Services Licensing Board
402 W. Washington St., Rm. W072
Indianapolis, IN 46204
(317) 234-2064
(317) 233-4236 (fax)
pla5@pla.in.gov
www.in.gov/pla/social.htm

**Title of License**: LMHC
Licensed Mental Health Counselor Associate (LMHCA): A counselor performing under supervision as a part of the supervised experience requirement (required after July 1, 2014)—cannot apply for until AFTER degree is conferred.

**Educational Requirements**: Master's degree or higher in an area related to mental health counseling from a CACREP- or CORE-accredited program, or equivalent program, from a regionally accredited institution, which includes 60 semester hours of graduate coursework in counseling in 12 specified content areas.

Completion of a practicum (100 hours), internship (600 hours), and advanced internship (300 hours) with at least 100 hours of face-to-face supervision are required.

An area related to mental health counseling includes counseling, clinical social work, psychology, human services, human development, family relations, or programs accredited by CACREP or CORE.

**Experiential Requirements**: 3,000 hours of postgraduate supervised clinical experience over a 21- to 48-month period. Does not start to count until approved as an LMHCA.

100 hours of face-to-face supervision under an LMHC or equivalent supervisor is required.

**Exam Required**: LMHC: NCMHCE
LMHCA: NCE

*Note:* If a passing score is achieved on the initial try, the applicant can apply up to 1,500 hours accrued. If a passing score is not achieved, the applicant can no longer accrue hours until a passing score is achieved.


**IOWA**
IA Board of Behavioral Science Examiners
Lucas State Office Building, 5th Floor
321 E. 12th St.
Des Moines, IA 50319-0075
(515) 281-4422
(515) 281-3121 (fax)
Judith.Manning@idph.iowa.gov
www.idph.state.ia.us/licensure

**Title of License**: LMHC

*Note:* Can get a temporary license while meeting supervision requirement—expires in 3 years.

**Educational Requirements**: Master's degree or higher in mental health counseling from a CACREP-accredited program, or the content equivalent, with at least 60 semester hours (or equivalent quarter hours). For applicants who entered the program of study prior to July 1, 2010: 45 semester hours (or 60 quarter hours) are required. Degree must be from a nationally accredited college/university; or hold a current CCMHC credential issued by NBCC (meets educational and experience requirements). Applicants who did not graduate from CACREP-accredited mental health counseling program as of July 1, 2012 will need to submit to an education review.

**Experiential Requirements**: 2 years/3,000 hours of full-time, supervised postgraduate work experience in mental health counseling including 1,500 hou direct client contact and 200 hours of clinical supervision concurrent with the work experience.

At least 100 of the 200 hours of clinical supervision must be individual supervision.

For applicants who entered a program of study prior to July 1, 2010: 2 years of full-time supervised postgraduate work experience in mental health counseling, including 200 hours of clinical supervision concurrent with 1,000 hours of mental health counseling conducted in person with individuals, couples, and families.

At least 100 of the 200 hours of clinical supervision must be individual supervision or hold a current CCMHC credential issued by NBCC (meets experience requirements).

**Exam Required**: NCE, NCMHCE, or CRCE

**KANSAS**
KS Behavioral Sciences Regulatory Board
712 S. Kansas Ave.
Topeka, KS 66603
(785) 296-3240
(785) 296-3112 (fax)
www.ksbsrb.org

**Title of License**: LCPC: May diagnose and treat mental disorders independently. LPC: May practice under the direction of an LCPC, licensed psychologist, a person licensed to provide mental health services as an independent practitioner and whose license allows for diagnoses and treatment of mental disorders, or a person licensed to practice medicine and surgery.

**Educational Requirements**: LCPC: In addition to or as part of the graduate degree completion of 15 credit hours of supporting diagnosis and treatment of mental disorders with use of the American Psychiatric Association's *Diagnostic and Statistical Manual of Mental Disorders (DSM)*, and a graduate-level supervised clinical practicum of professional experience.

LPC: 60 graduate semester hours, including a master's degree in counseling from a university approved by the board that consists of 45 graduate semester hours distributed among 10 core categories (this includes a supervised practicum).

**Experiential Requirements**: LCPC: Licensed as an LPC or meets all requirements to be licensed as an LPC, and 4,000 hours of supervised clinical professional counseling experience under an approved clinical training plan, which 1,500 hours of direct client contact and 100 hours of clinical supervision must be individual supervision).

**Exam Required**: LCPC: NCMHCE
LPC: NCE

## KENTUCKY

KY Board of Licensed Professional Counselors
P.O. Box 1360
Frankfort, KY 40602
Diana Jarboe, Board Administrator: Diana.Jarboe@ky.gov
(502) 564-3296
(502) 564-4818 (fax)
lpc.ky.gov

**Title of License**: LPCC
Licensed Professional Counselor Associate (LPCA): Credential holder who has met all qualifications to engage in the practice of professional counseling under an approved clinical supervisor authorized by the board.

**Educational Requirements**: Master's degree or higher in professional counseling or a related field from a regionally accredited institution, with a minimum of 60 semester hours in nine specified areas and a 400-hour practicum/internship.

**Experiential Requirements**: No experiential requirements for LPCA.

LPCC: 4,000 hours of post-master's experience in the practice of counseling under approved supervision, which includes 1,600 hours of direct counseling and 100 hours of individual, face-to-face clinical supervision. Applicants are encouraged to include 10 hours of direct counseling with individuals in a jail or correctional setting as part of the 4,000 hours.

**Exam Required**: NCE or NCMHCE

## LOUISIANA

LA Department of Licensed Professional Counselors Board of Examiners
8361 Summa Ave.
Baton Rouge, LA 70809
(225) 765-2515
(225) 765-2514
lpcboard@eatel.net
www.lpcboard.org

**Title of License**: LPC
Counselor Intern: Those with a master's degree in counseling while practicing counseling under the board-approved supervision of an LPC. (There are three parts to registration and hours cannot begin to be accrued until all three are complete.)
Counselor interns have up to 7 years to complete their internship from the date of registration.

**Educational Requirements**: Master's degree or higher, the substance of which is professional mental health counseling in content, from a regionally accredited institution, with 48 semester hours and coursework in eight content areas. Completion of a supervised practicum (100 hours) and a supervised internship (300 hours) in mental health counseling.

Beginning September 1, 2015, all applicants whose academic background has not been previously approved by the board must have accumulated at least 60 graduate semester hours as part of the graduate degree plan containing the eight required areas, the supervised mental health practicum, and supervised internship in mental health counseling (as defined in Chapter 5 in this textbook). Applicants may apply post-master's counseling courses toward licensure if their degree program consisted of less than 60 hours. *Note:* Rule change July 20, 2013.

**Experiential Credentials**: 2 years/3,000 hours of post-master's supervised experience in professional mental health counseling under the clinical supervision of a board-approved supervisor, to be completed in no more than 7 years. Hours to include: 1,900 to 2,900 hours of direct client contact in individual or group counseling; a maximum of 1,000 hours additional client contact, counseling-related activities, or education at the graduate level in the field of mental health; and a minimum of 100 hours of face-to-face supervision. Only 50 hours may be group supervision. Up to 25 of the hours can be synchronous videoconferencing. 500 hours of supervised experience may be gained for each 30 graduate semester hours beyond master's degree, but must have no less than 2,000 hours of supervised post-master's experience.

**Exam Required**: NCE or NCMHCE

**MAINE**
ME Board of Counseling Professionals Licensure
35 State House Station
Augusta, ME 04333
(207) 624-8674
(888) 577-6690
(207) 624-8637 (fax)
www.maine.gov/pfr/olr

**Title of License**: LCPC
LPC
Conditional LCPC: A license granted to an applicant for licensure as an LCPC who has met all the requirements except for the supervised clinical experience; valid for 2 years.
Conditional LPC: A license granted to an applicant for licensure as an LPC who has met all the requirements except for the supervised clinical experience; valid for 2 years.

**Educational Requirements**: LCPC/Conditional LCPC: Master's degree or higher from a regionally accredited institution that consists of 60 semester hours and is CACREP accredited, or consists of coursework in 10 core areas, 3 additional areas, and a practicum and internship of 900 clock hours.

LPC/Conditional LPC: Master's degree or higher from a regionally accredited institution that consists of 48 semester hours and is CACREP or CORE accredited, or consists of coursework in 10 core areas and a practicum and internship of 600 clock hours.

**Experiential Requirements**: LCPC: 2 years/3,000 hours of post-master's supervised clinical counseling experience (4,000 hours if qualifying degree did not have practicum/internship). To include 1,500 hours of direct client contact and 1 hour of clinical supervision per 30 hours of client contact with an approved supervisor.

LPC: 2 years/2,000 hours of post-master's supervised counseling experience. To include 1,000 hours of direct counseling and 67 hours of supervision with an approved supervisor.

**Exam Required**: LCPC: NCMHCE, LPC/Conditional LCPC/Conditional LPC: NCE

**MARYLAND**
MD Board of Examiners of Professional Counselors and Therapists
4201 Patterson Ave.
Baltimore, MD 21215
Anna.sullivan@maryland.gov
(410) 764-4732
(410) 358-1610 (fax)
www.dhmh.state.md.us/bopc

**Title of License**: LCPC
Licensed Graduate Professional Counselor (LGPC): Title used while fulfilling the supervised clinical experience requirement.

**Educational Requirements**: (Same for both license tiers.)
Master's degree or higher in professional counseling or related field from an accredited educational institution, with a minimum of 60 graduate semester hours in specific coursework, including completion of an alcohol and drug counseling course, and supervised field experience.
    OR
Doctoral degree with a minimum of 90 graduate semester hours in counseling training approved by the board.

**Experiential Requirements**: 3 years/3,000 hours of supervised clinical experience in professional counseling (2 years/2,000 hours must be post-master's). 1,500 hours must be direct face-to-face client contact and 100 hours minimum of face-to-face clinical supervision. Supervision must be under a board-approved supervisor. At least half of hours need to be accumulated under the supervision of an LCPC approved by the board. If obtained a doctoral degree: 2 years/2,000 hours of supervised clinical experience in professional counseling (1 year/1,000 hours must be postdoctorate). 1,000 hours must be face-to-face client contact and 50 hours minimum of face-to-face clinical supervision. Supervision must be under a board-approved supervisor.

**Exam Required**: NCE and MD Professional Counselors and Therapists Act Exam

## MASSACHUSETTS
MA Board of Registration of Allied Mental Health and Human Services Professionals
100 Washington St. Suite 710
Boston, MA 02118-6100
Board Administrator: leija.t.meadows@state.ma.us
(617) 727-3080
(617) 727-1627 (fax)
www.mass.gov/dpl/boards/mh

**Title of License**: LMHC
**Educational Requirements**: Minimum of 60 graduate semester hours in counseling or a related field from a regionally accredited institution of high education. This includes a minimum of 48 semester credit hour master's degree in mental health counseling or a related field, including a practicum (100 hours), an internship (600 hours), and coursework in each of the 10 content areas as defined by the board; or hold a current Certified Clinical Mental Health Counselor (CCMHC) credential issues by NBCC.

**Experiential Requirements**: 2 years/3,360 hours of full-time post-master's supervised clinical experience in mental health counseling after obtaining 60 graduate semester hours. To include 960 hours of direct client contact (250 hours may be group client contact), 130 hours of supervision (75 hours must be individual supervision and 25 hours must be under a LMHC). These hours do not include the pre-master's practicum and internship supervision requirements.

**Exam Required**: NCMHCE

## MICHIGAN
MI Board of Counseling
P.O. Box 30670
Lansing, MI 48909
(517) 335-0918
(517) 373-2179 (fax)
bhphelp@michigan.gov
www.michigan.gov/healthlicense

**Title of License**: LPC

>Limited Licensed Professional Counselor (LLPC): A limited license is issued to those who have not yet completed the 3,000-hour supervised counseling experience; valid for 1 year and may be renewed.

**Educational Requirements**: (Same for both licenses.)
Master's degree or higher in professional counseling from a program that reflects the CACREP curriculum, including a minimum of 48 semester hours and 600 clock hour internship.

**Experiential Requirements**: 2 years/3,000 hours of postdegree supervised counseling experience. To include a minimum 100 hours under immediate physical presence of the supervisor. Supervision must be under an LPC. For persons with 30 semester hours or 45 quarter hours beyond the master's degree: 1 year/1,500 hours of postdegree supervised experience. To include a minimum of 50 hours under immediate physical presence of the supervisor. Supervision must be under an LPC. *Note:* Supervisors of LLPCs are required to have training in supervision.

**Exam Required**: NCE or CRCE

**MINNESOTA**
MN Board of Behavioral Health and Therapy
2829 University Ave. SE, Suite 120
Minneapolis, MN 55414
(612) 617-2178
(800) 627-3529 TTY
(612) 617-2187 (fax)
Bbht.board@state.mn.us
www.bbht.state.mn.us

**Title of License**: Licensed Professional Clinical Counselor (LPCC)[3]

>Licensed Professional Counselor—Independent designation.
>
>Licensed Professional Counselor—Supervision designation (LPC), working on supervision hours toward LPC.

**Educational Requirements**: LPCC: Meet all LPC educational requirements, and in addition to or as part of the graduate degree in counseling or a related field—completion of 24 graduate-level semester credits in six clinical content areas.
LPC: Master's degree or higher in counseling or a related field from a CACREP-accredited program or regionally accredited institution recognized by the Council for Higher Education Accreditation (CHEA), which includes a minimum of 48 semester hours and supervised field experience not fewer than 700 hours that is counseling in nature.
    The degree must include specific coursework in 10 core content areas.

---

[3]Has completed supervision experience for LPC licensure.

**Experiential Requirements**: LPCC: Already has LPC credential; 4,000 hours of post-master's supervised professional practice in the delivery of clinical services in the diagnosis and treatment of mental illnesses and disorders in both children and adults. Supervision must comply with the board's Supervision Contract for LPCC applicants. Practice must include 1,800 hours of clinical client contact. At least 50% of supervision must be individual supervision. Supervisor must have independent CLINICAL license.

LPC: 2,000 hours of post-master's supervised professional practice that is acceptable to the board OR submission of Supervision Plan for the first 2,000 hours of professional practice. Supervision must be completed in not less than 1 year and not more than 3 years. Practice must include 100 hours of supervision under a board-approved supervisor.

**Exam Required**: LPCC: NCMHCE. *Note:* ECCP is no longer offered by NBCC. LPC: NCE or other national exam that is determined by the board to be substantially similar to the NCE.

### MISSISSIPPI

MS State Board of Examiners for Licensed Professional Counselors
239 North Lamar St., Suite 402
Jackson, MS 39201
LeAnn Mordecai, Executive Director: LPMordecai@lpc.ms.gov
(601) 359-1010
(888) 860-7001
(662) 716-3021 (fax)
infor@lpc.ms.gov

**Title of License**: LPC

> Licensed Professional Counselor: An applicant who has satisfied experience and educational requirements but still needs to pass the exam.

**Educational Requirements**: Master's degree or educational specialists degree in counselor education or a related program from a regionally or nationally accredited college/university program, subject to board approval, with 60 semester hours (or 90 quarter hours) and completion of coursework in 10 content areas, or doctoral degree primarily in counseling, guidance, or related counseling field from a regionally or nationally accredited college/university program, subject to board approval, with 60 semester hours (or 90 quarter hours) and completion of coursework in 10 content areas.

**Experiential Requirements**: 2 years/3,500 hours of supervised counseling experience in a clinical setting (1,750 hours must be post-master's experience). 1,167 hours must be direct counseling service to clients to include counseling-related activities. Minimum of 100 hours of supervision required

(50 hours may be group supervision). Supervision must be under an LPC that has met the requirements to be a MS Board Qualified Supervisor.

**Exam Required**: NCE; will accept the NCMHCE but not required.

## MISSOURI
MO Committee for Professional Counselors
3605 Missouri Blvd.
P.O. Box 1335
Jefferson City, MO 65102
profcounselor@pr.mo.gov
Loree.Kessler@pr.mo.gov
pr.mo.gov/counselors.asp

**Title of License**: LPC
> Counselor-in-Training: Issued automatically when supervision is registered and approved and all other requirements are met.

**Educational Requirements**: Master's degree or higher in counseling, counseling psychology, or school psychology from a regionally accredited college or university, with at least 48 semester hours reflecting the CACREP or CORE curriculum, and a practicum, internship, or field experience consisting of 6 semester hours in the practice of counseling.

**Experiential Requirements**: 2 years/3,000 hours of post-master's continuous experience (full or part time), to be completed within 60 months. 1,200 hours must be direct client contact. 30 hours of post-master's study may be substituted for 1,500 of the 3,000 hours.

If a doctorate or specialist's degree: 1 year/1,500 hours of counseling experience (full or parttime), to be completed within 36 months; 600 hours must be direct client contact.

For both degree paths: 15 hours of supervised counseling experience per week are required, with 1 hour a week of face-to-face supervision. If electronic supervision is continuously interactive, it can count toward required hours. Supervision must be under an LPC or licensed psychologist or psychiatrist approved and registered with the board.

**Exam Required**: NCE

## MONTANA
MT Board of Social Work Examiners and Professional Counselors
301 S. Park 4th Fl.
P.O. Box 200513
Helena, MT 59620
dlibsdswp@state.mt.us
www.swpc.mt.gov

**Title of License**: LCPC

**Educational Requirements**: A 60-semester hour (or 90-quarter hour) counseling-in-nature graduate degree from an accredited institution that includes specific coursework and a 6-semester hour advanced counseling practicum, or applicants may apply for licensure with a minimum of 45 semester hours (67.5 quarter hours) master's degree in counseling that includes specific coursework and a 6-semester hour advanced counseling practicum. Applicants must complete the remaining hours within 5 years of the original application approval date. Applicants are not eligible for full licensure, nor are they eligible to test until the hours are completed.

**Experiential Requirements**: 3,000 hours of supervised counseling experience, 1,500 hours of which must be postdegree. 1,000 of the 1,500 hours must be direct client contact (250 can be group). Must have 1 hour of supervision for every 20 hours. Supervision must be under a licensed professional counselor or licensed allied mental health professional who has had 20 clock hours of supervision training and the agreement has been approved by the board.

**Exam Required**: NCE

**NEBRASKA**
NE Board of Mental Health Practice
P.O. Box 94986
Lincoln, NE 68509
(402) 471-0185
(402) 472-3577 (fax)
Program Manager: kris.chiles@nebraska.gov
www.dhhs.state.ne.gov/crl/mhcs/mental/mentalindex.htm

**Title of License**: Licensed Mental Health Practitioner-Certified Professional Counselor (LMHP-CPC) or Licensed Professional Counselor (LPC): This additional appellation is available for LMHPs who have a graduate degree from a CACREP-accredited program or a program with equivalent coursework.
    Licensed Mental Health Practitioner (LMHP): An individual who is qualified to engage in mental health practice or offers or renders mental health practice services.
    Provisional Licensed Mental Health Practitioner (PLMHP): An individual beginning the 3,000-hour experience requirement; valid for 5 years.

**Educational Requirements**: Master's degree or higher from an approved educational program that is primarily therapeutic mental health in content, in a CACREP-accredited program (or complete equivalent coursework), from a regionally accredited institution. Completion of a practicum or internship with a minimum of 300 clock hours of direct client contact under the supervision of a qualified supervisor.

**Experience Requirements**: LMHP-CPC/LPC, LMHP: 3,000 hours of post-master's supervised experience in mental health practice accumulated during the 5 years immediately preceding application for licensure. To include a 1,500 hours of direct client contact (not more than 1,500 hours of nondirect service). Supervision must be under an LMHP, LIMPH, licensed psychologist or licensed physician with mental health treatment training.

**Exam Required**: LIMHP and LMHP with CPC credential: NCE of NCMHCE

**NEVADA**
The Board of Examiners for Marriage and Family Therapists and Clinical Professional Counselors
P.O. Box 370130
Las Vegas, NV 89134-0130
(702) 486-7388
(702) 486-7258
nvmftbd@mftbd.nv.gov
www.marriage.state.nv.us

**Title of License**: Licensed Clinical Professional Counselor (LCPC)
Licensed Clinical Professional Counselor Intern

**Educational Requirements**: (Same for both licenses.)
Master's degree or higher in mental health counseling or community counseling from a program approved by CACREP or equivalent program of at least 48 semester hours and completion of the minimum required coursework, including 3-semester hour courses or 4-quarter hour courses in Supervised Clinical Practice by way of either practicum or internship in mental health counseling, accomplished over a period of 1 academic year.

**Experiential Requirements**: 2 years/3,000 hours of post-master's supervised counseling experience. To include 1,500 hours of direct client contact, 1,200 hours in the practice of clinical professional counseling, and 100 hours of direct supervision under an approved supervisor of which at least 1 hour per week was completed for each work setting at which the applicant provided counseling.

**Exam Required**: NCMHCE

**NEW HAMPSHIRE**
NH Board of Mental Health Practice
121 S. Fruit St.
Concord, NH 03301
mlynch@dhhs.state.nh.us
(603) 271-6762
(800) 735-2954 TDD
(603) 271-3950
www.nh.gov/mhpb

**Title of License**: LCMHC

**Educational Requirements**: All applicants shall have a master's degree or doctoral degree in clinical mental health counseling from a CACREP-accredited institution or have a 60 credit degree in clinical mental health counseling or its equivalent from an institution which has received regional accreditation from the Association Secondary Schools and Colleges. A minimum of 1 academic year of full-time graduate study in mental health counseling should be completed in residence at the institution granting the college degree. There are 11 content areas.

**Experiential Requirements**: 2 years/3,000 hours of paid post-master's supervised clinical work experience in a mental health setting, to be completed in no more than 5 years. Each year shall not be less than 1,500 clock hours. 100 hours of face-to-face supervision provided by a state-licensed, board approved, mental health professional is required.

**Exam Required**: NCMHCE and an essay exam provided by the board.

**NEW JERSEY**
NJ Board of Marriage and Family Therapy Examiners, Professional Counselor Examiners Committee
P.O. Box 45007
Newark, NJ 07101
(973) 504-6415
(973) 648-3536 (fax)
www.state.nj.us/lps/ca/medical/procounsel.htm

**Title of Credential**: LCMHC, LPC
> Licensed Associate Counselor (LAC): After acceptable documentation of the satisfaction of the LPC education and examination requirements, an individual may be granted licensure as an Associate Counselor to practice counseling under the direct supervision of an LPC or a supervisor acceptable to the committee.

**Educational Requirements**: Minimum of 60 graduate semester hours, which include a master's degree in counseling from a regionally accredited institution of higher education (45 of 60 hours must be distributed in eight of the nine defined course content areas).

As of April 20, 2006, an acceptable graduate degree means that the word "counseling" or the word "counselor" appears in the title of the graduate degree awarded and that the institution offering the degree states in the catalog or in another format acceptable to the committee that the purpose of the graduate degree is to prepare students for the professional practice of counseling.

**Experiential Requirements**: LCMHC: Already holds an LPC. Certification by the Academy of Certified Clinical Mental Health Counselors, or any successor thereto; passage of a comprehensive qualifying examination prepared by the Academy; evidence satisfactory to the committee that the clinical mental health counselor has satisfied the continuing education requirements of the committee; and evidence satisfactory to the committee that certification of the clinical mental health counselor has been renewed by the Academy. 2 years/3,000 hours of post-master's degree supervised field experience, 100 hours of face-to-face supervision.

LPC: 3 years of full-time supervised counseling experience in a professional counseling setting, 1 year of which may be obtained prior to the granting of the master's degree. 1 year/1,500 hours of the experience may be eliminated by substituting 30 graduate semester hours beyond the master's degree. In no case may an applicant have less than 1 year of post-master's supervised work experience.

LAC: No experiential requirements.

**Exam Required**: NCE

**NEW MEXICO**
NM Counseling and Therapy Practice Board
2550 Cerrillos Rd.
Santa Fe, NM 87505
(505) 476-4610
(505) 476-4633 (fax)
counselingboard@state.nm.us
www.rld.state.nm.us/counseling

**Title of License**: LPCC
      LMHC: An individual who is pursuing the LPCC license but still
          needs to complete the supervised experience requirement.

**Educational Requirements**: Master's degree or higher in counseling or a counseling-related field with no less than 48 graduate hours from an accredited institution. Related field degree must meet the clinical core curriculum. Counseling-related field is mental health, community counseling, agency counseling, psychology, clinical psychology, family studies, art therapy, or education.

**Experiential Requirements**: 2 years of postgraduate professional clinical counseling experience, with 3,000 hours of clinical client contact and a minimum of 100 hours of face-to-face supervision. 1,000 hours of clinical client contact may come from the applicant's internship/practicum. Supervision must come from an LPCC or licensed MFT, professional art therapist, psychiatrist, clinical psychologist, or independent social worker.

**Exam Required**: LPCC: NCE, and NCMHCE
      LMHC: NCE

**NEW YORK**
NY State Education Department
State Board for Mental Health Practitioners
Office of the Professionals
89 Washington Ave., 2nd Floor
Albany, NY 12234-1000
(518) 474-3817 x450
(518) 486-2981 (fax)
mhpbd@mail.nysed.gov
www.op.nysed.gov/mhclic.htm

**Title of License**: LMHC
> Limited Permit: Applicants who have met all requirements except experience and/or exam may apply for a 2-year permit to practice under supervision; may be renewed for one year, upon new application and permit fee.

**Educational Requirements**: Master's degree or higher in counseling that includes 60 semester hours and completion of specific coursework. *Note:* If counseling degree was completed prior to January 1, 2010, 48 credit hours were required. Completion of a 1-year/600 clock hours supervised internship or practicum in mental health counseling. Completion of coursework or training approved by the education department in the identification and reporting of child abuse.

**Experiential Requirements**: Completion of a minimum of 3,000 hours of post-master's supervised experience providing mental health counseling in a setting acceptable to the department. 1,500 of the hours must be direct client contact.

**Exam Required**: NCMHCE

**NORTH CAROLINA**
NC Board of Licensed Professional Counselors
P.O. Box 1369
Garner, NC 27529
(919) 661-0820
(919) 779-5642 (fax)
ncblpc@mgmt4u.com
www.ncblpc.org

**Title of License**: LPC
> Licensed Professional Counselor Associate (LPCA): Individuals who are pursuing the LPC license but still need to complete the supervised experience requirements.

**Educational Requirements**: Master's degree or higher in counseling from a regionally accredited institution of higher education that includes coursework in nine areas of study and meets the following additional requirements:

- If enrolled prior to July 1, 2009, 48 semester hours (or 72 quarter hours) are required.
- If enrolled prior to July 1, 2013, but after June 30, 2009, 54 semester hours (or 81 quarter hours) are required.
- If enrolled after June 30, 2013, 60 semester hours (or 90 quarter hours) are required.

A practicum and internship must be completed as part of the graduate course of study:

- Must cover at least a combined total of 17 hours of graduate counseling supervision.
- Must consist of a combined minimum of 300 hours of supervised graduate counseling experience at a rate of not less than 1 hour of clinical supervision per 40 hours of graduate counseling experience.
- At least 60% of this counseling experience shall be direct graduate counseling experience.

**Experimental Requirements**: 3,000 hours of supervised professional practice; 2,000 hours must be direct counseling. No hours can be applied from the practicum/internship. Not less than 8 hours per week but no more than 40 hours per week. 100 hours of clinical supervision required. 75 hours must be individual supervision. Must have a minimum of 1 hour of clinical supervision for every 40 hours of professional practice. Supervision shall be based on direct (live) observation, co-therapy, audio and video recordings, and live supervision. Supervisor must be approved by the board.

**Exam Required**: LPC/LPCA: NCE, NCMHCE, or CRCE and NC jurisprudence exam
LPCA: NCE, NCMHCE, or CRCE

**NORTH DAKOTA**
ND Board of Counselor Examiners
2112 10th Ave. SE
Mandan, ND 58554
(701) 667-5969
(701) 667-5969 (fax)
ndbce@btinet.net
www.ndbce.org

**Title of License**: LPCC
LPC: Full professional license after LAPC criteria are met and supervised experience has been completed.
Licensed Associate Professional Counselor (LAPC): A 2-year license, which allows for completion of the supervised experience. A 2-year plan of supervision and passage of the NCE required.

**Educational Requirements**: LPCC: Master's degree in counseling from an accredited college or university, including 60 semester hours, core clinical coursework (a minimum of 15 contact hours in each of three categories determined by the board), and 800 hours of clinical training in a supervised practicum and internship.

LPC/LAPC: Master's degree in counseling or closely related field from an accredited college or university including 48 semester hours and specific core counseling coursework within the master's degree.

**Experiential Requirements**: LPCC: Must already possess the first-level LPC credential, and 2 years/3,000 hours of post-master's supervised clinical counseling experience in a clinical setting. Experience to include 100 hours of direct supervision (60 hours must be individual, face-to-face supervision) by a board-approved supervisor.

LPC: 400 hours of direct client counseling contact during the 2-year LAPC supervisory period. Experience to include 100 hours of direct supervision (60 hours must be individual, face-to-face supervision) by a board-approved supervisor.

**Exam Required**: LPCC: NCMHCE and a videotaped clinical counseling session of at least 30 minutes.
LPC/LAPC: NCE

## OHIO

OH Counselor, Social Worker, and Marriage and Family Therapist Board
50 W. Broad St., Suite 1075
Columbus, OH 43215
(614) 466-0912
(614) 728-7790 (fax)
Cswmft.info@cswb.state.oh.us
www.cswmft.ohio.gov

**Title of License**: Licensed Professional Clinical Counselor (LPCC)
Professional Counselor/Clinical Resident (CR): Title used while completing the 3,000 hours of supervised experience required for the LPCC license.
LPC: Title used after completing coursework including practicum and internship.
Registered Counselor Trainee (RCT): Title used while enrolled in a practicum or internship in a counselor education program.

**Educational Requirements**: Master's degree or higher in counseling from an accredited program, with 60 semester (or 90 quarter) hours, from an accredited institution. 20 hours (or 30 quarter hours) must be in clinical content areas. 100 hours practicum and 600 hours internship required.

**Experiential Requirements**: LPCC: Must already possess the first-level LPC credential and 2 years/3,000 hours of post-master's clinical counseling under the supervision of an LPCC holding the supervision credential. 50% must be clinical experience. The supervision must include the diagnosis and treatment of mental and emotional disorders; 50% of the time must be face-to-face contact delivering clinical counseling services. Supervisor will fill out an evaluation to evaluate competence to diagnose and treat mental and emotional disorders. No experiential requirements for LPC, CR/RCT.

**Exam Required**: LPCC: NCMHCE
                 LPC: NCE
                 OH jurisprudence exam

**OKLAHOMA**
OK State Board of Licensed Professional Counselors
1000 N.E. 10th St.
Oklahoma City, OK 73117
(405) 271-6030
(405) 271-1918 (fax)
nenaw@health.ok.us
pcl.health.ok.gov

**Title of License**: LPC
                 Licensed Professional Counselor Candidate: An individual may be granted licensure as Licensed Professional Counselor Candidate to practice counseling under the direct supervision of an approved LPC supervisor.

**Educational Requirements**: Master's degree or higher in counseling or a related mental health field with 60 graduate semester hours (or 90 quarter hours) from a regionally accredited college or university. Completion of coursework in 10 areas and a counseling practicum/internship of 300 clock hours. The board will define what qualifies as counseling related.

**Experiential Requirements**: 3 years/3,000 hours full-time postapplication professional counseling experience supervised by an approved LPC supervisor. For each 1,000 hours, 350 hours must be direct face-to-face contact. Face-to-face supervision must be 45 minutes for every 20 hours of experience. Up to 2 years of required experience may be gained at a rate of 1 year for each 30 graduate semester hours beyond the master's degree, provided that such hours are clearly related to the field of counseling and acceptable to the board. The applicant shall have no less than 1 year of supervised-time experience in counseling.

**Exam Required**: NCE and Oklahoma Legal and Ethical Responsibilities Exam (as pertains to LPCs)

**OREGON**
OR Board of Licensed Professional Counselors and Therapists
3218 Pringle Rd., SE, Suite 250
Salem, OR 97301-6312
(503) 378-5499
(503) 373-1427 (fax)
Lpc.lmft@state.or.us
www.oregon.gov/pblpct

**Title of License**: LPC
Registered Intern: An applicant registered to obtain postdegree supervised work experience toward licensure.

**Educational Requirements**: Master's degree or higher in counseling, with 48 semester hours in a CACREP- or CORE-accredited program, or the content equivalent, from a regionally accredited institution. Completion of an internship/practicum consisting of 600 clock hours. If graduating after October 1, 2014: Master's degree or higher in counseling, with 60 semester hours (or 90 quarter hours) in a CACREP- or CORE-accredited program, or the content equivalent, from a regionally accredited institution.

**Experiential Requirements**: 3 years of full-time supervised experience in counseling, to include 2,400 hours of direct client contact. The supervision must take place concurrently with the direct client contact hours and must total no less than 2 hours of supervision for months where 45 or fewer direct client contact hours are completed, or total no less than 3 hours of supervision for months where 46 or more direct client contact hours are completed. Up to 75% of the individual supervision can be electronic and 50% of total supervision can be group. An approved supervisor must provide supervision. 600 (from 48 credit hours) or 700 (from 60 credit hours) client contact hours may be obtained during the clinical portion of the qualifying degree program.

**Exam**: NCE, CRCE, NCMHCE, or other exam as approved by the board and Oregon Law and Rules (open book).

**PENNSYLVANIA**
PA State Board of Social Workers, Marriage and Family Therapists, and Professional Counselors
One Penn Center
2601 N. 3rd St.
Harrisburg, PA 17110
(717) 783-1389
(717) 787-7769 (fax)
ra-socialwork@pa.gov
stsocialwork@state.pa.us
www.dos.state.pa.us/social

**Title of License**: LPC

**Educational Requirements**: Successful completion of a planned program of 60 semester hours (or 90 quarter hours) of graduate coursework in counseling or a field closely related to the practice of professional counseling, including a 48 semester hours (or 72 quarter hours) master's degree in professional counseling or in a field closely related to the practice of professional counseling.

OR a doctoral degree in counseling or in a field closely related to the practice of professional counseling.

AND for both: Completion of coursework in nine core areas including a supervised practicum (100 hours) and internship (600 hours). The supervised internship experience shall begin after completion of the supervised practicum experience.

**Experiential Requirements**: 3 years/3,600 hours of supervised clinical experience after completing 48 graduate-level credits (or 72 quarter hours). (Have to complete at least 600 hours a year and no more than 1,800 a year.) If obtained a doctoral degree in counseling: 2 years/2,400 hours of supervised clinical experience. 1 year/1,200 hours must be obtained postdegree.

Supervision must be provided by a qualified supervisor. At least 1,800 hours must be completed under an LPC that has 5 years of experience within the last 10 years as a professional counselor. There should be 2 hours of supervision for every 40 hours of client hours. The remaining hours may be completed under an individual that holds a license and has at least a master's degree in a related field and 5 years of experience within the last 10 years in that field.

**Exam Required**: Any one of the following: NCE, CRCE, ATCB, CBMT, PEPK, AAODA, EMAC

**PUERTO RICO**
PR Office of Regulation and Certification of Health Professions
Board of Examiners of Professional Counselors
P.O. Box 10200
San Juan, PR 00908
(787) 723-0102
www.salud.gov.pr

**Title of License**: Licensed Professional Counselor (LPC)
Professional Counselor with Provisional License (PCPL): Person who is granted a temporary/provisional authorization by the board to offer counseling services under supervision to meet the experience requirement; valid for 3 years.
Certified Mentor (CM): A licensed PC who has been certified by the board to supervise those who wish to obtain licensure.

**Educational Requirements**: Master's degree or higher in counseling from an institution accredited by the Council of Higher Education of Puerto Rico. Specific coursework required in 8 out of 10 areas.

**Experiential Requirements**: Completion of a minimum of 500 hours of practice supervised by a CM. Upon approval of the exam required, the board shall issue a provisional license.

**Exam Required**: NCE

**RHODE ISLAND**
RI Board of Mental Health Counselors and Marriage and Family Therapists
3 Capitol Hill, Rm. 104
Providence, RI 02908
(401) 222-2828
(401) 222-1272
www.health.ri.gov/hsr/professions/mfcounsel.php

**Title of License**: Licensed Clinical Mental Health Counselor (LCMHC)

**Educational Requirements**: Master's degree or higher specializing in counseling/therapy from a college/university accredited by the New England Association of Schools and Colleges or an equivalent regional accrediting agency. OR master's degree, certificate in advanced graduate studies, or a doctoral degree in mental health counseling or allied field from a recognized educational institution.

For all options: Completion of 60 semester hours (90 quarter hours) (master's must be 48 semester hours or 72 quarter hours) within the graduate counseling/therapy program, coursework in eight core areas, a supervised practicum (12 semester hours), and 1 calendar year of a supervised internship consisting of 20 hours per week in counseling.

**Experiential Requirements**: 2 years/2,000 hours of direct client contact offering clinical or counseling or therapy services with emphasis in mental health counseling. To include 100 hours of post-master's supervised casework spread over a 2-year period. Supervision must be under a board-approved supervisor.

**Exam Required**: NCMHCE

**SOUTH CAROLINA**
SC Board of Examiners for the Licensure of Professional Counselors, Marriage and Family Therapists, and Psychoeducational Specialists
P.O. Box 11329
Columbia, SC 29211-1329
(803) 896-4658
(803) 896-4719 (fax)
www.llr.state.sc.us/pol/counselors

**Title of License**: LPC

> Professional Counselor Intern (LPC/I): An applicant who has met the education and exam requirements, but not the 2-year supervised experience requirements.

**Educational Requirements**: Master's degree or higher in professional counseling or a related discipline from a regionally accredited institution that includes at least 48 graduate hours, coursework in 10 content areas, and a 150 hours supervised counseling practicum.

**Experiential Requirements**: Must already possess the first-level LPC/I credential, and 2 years/1,500 hours of full-time, post-master's supervised clinical experience in the practice of professional counseling. The 1,500 hours must be direct counseling with individuals, couples, families, or groups. A minimum of 150 hours of the 1,500 hours must be clinical supervision provided by a board-approved LPC supervisor (100 hours must be individual supervision).

**Exam Required**: NCE or NCMHCE

**SOUTH DAKOTA**
SD Board of Examiners for Counselors and Marriage and Family Therapists
P.O. Box 2164
Sioux Falls, SD 57101
(605) 331-2927
(605) 331-2043 (fax)
sdbce.msp@midconetwork.com
www.counselor.sd.us

**Title of License**: Licensed Professional Counselor-Mental Health (LPC-MH)
LPC

**Educational Requirements**: Master's degree or higher with an emphasis in mental health counseling from a CACREP-accredited program, or equivalent program from an accredited institution that includes specific coursework and a supervised practicum (100 hours) and internship (600 hours). 48 semester hours required for LPC licensure; 60 semester hours or completion of all required coursework for LPC-MH licensure.

**Experiential Requirements**: LPC-MH: Must already possess the first-level LPC credential. 2 years/2,000 hours of post-master's direct client contact in a clinical setting and 100 hours of direct supervision, at least 50 hours of which shall be face-to-face. 1,000 hours of post-master's direct client contact hours and 50 hours of face-to-face supervision earned under the LPC credential may be counted toward these requirements if LPC-MH supervision condition were met.

LPC: 2,000 hours of post-master's counseling experience, with 800 hours of direct client contact and 100 hours of direct supervision, at least 50 hours of which shall be face-to-face.

**Exam Required**: LPC-MH: NCMHCE
LPC: NCE

**TENNESSEE**
TN Board for Professional Counselors, Marital and Family Therapists, and Clinical Pastoral Therapists
227 French Landing, Suite 300
Nashville, TN 37243
(615) 532-3202, ×25138
(800) 778-4123, ×25138
(615) 532-5369 (fax)
health.state.tn.us/boards/pc mft&cpt

**Title of License**: Licensed Professional Counselor-Mental Health Service Provider (LPC/MHSP)
LPC

**Educational Requirements**: LPC/MHSP: In addition to or as part of the graduate-degree completion of 9 graduate semester hours of coursework related to diagnosis, treatment, appraisal, and assessment of mental disorders.

LPC: 60 graduate semester hours in professional counseling or a related field from an institution accredited by the Southern Association of Colleges and Schools, CACREP, or a comparable accrediting body, which includes a master's degree in professional counseling and a supervised 500-hour practicum or internship (300 hours of which must be completed in a clinical setting).

**Experiential Requirements**: LPC/MHSP: 2 years of post-master's professional experience consisting of 3,000 hours of direct clinical experience (not less than 10 hours per week); 1,500 hours have to be direct client contact and 1,500 hours need to be clinically based. Must have 150 hours of supervision.

LPC: 2 years of post-master's professional experience consisting of 3,000 hours of direct clinical experience (not less than 10 hours per week). *Note:* As of January 31, 2013, supervisors had to be licensed for 5 years, conform to section F of the *ACA Code of Ethics*, and have at least 12 clock hours of supervision training.

**Exam Required**: LPC/MHSP: NCMHCE, NCE, and TN jurisprudence exam all required.
LPC: NCE and TN jurisprudence exam

**TEXAS**
TX State Board of Examiners of Professional Counselors
P.O. Box 149347, MC 1982
Austin, TX 78714
(512) 834-6658
(512) 834-6677 (fax)
lpc@dshs.state.tx.us
www.dshs.state.tx.us/plc

**Title of License:** LPC

Licensed Professional Counselor Intern (LPC-I): An applicant practicing under supervision; valid for 5 years.

**Educational Requirements:** Master's degree or higher in professional counseling or related field from and accredited college/university consisting of 48 graduate semester hours. Completion of specific coursework and a 300 clock hour supervised practicum with at least 100 hours of direct client contact. Counseling-related field: A mental health discipline utilizing human development, psychotherapeutic, and mental health principles including, but not limited to, psychology, psychiatry, social work, marriage and family therapy, and guidance and counseling. Non–counseling-related fields include, but are not limited to, sociology, education, administration, dance therapy, and theology.

**Experiential Requirements:** 3,000 hours of post-master's supervised experience, including 1,500 hours of direct client contact. Supervision must be provided by under a board-approved LPC.

**Exam Required:** NCE and Texas jurisprudence exam

**UTAH**
UT Professional Counseling Licensing Board
P.O. Box 146741
Salt Lake City, UT 84114
(801) 530-6628
(866) 275-3675 (Utah toll-free number)
(801) 530-6511 (fax)
dopl.utah.gov/licensing/professional counseling.html

**Title of License:** LCMHC

Licensed Associate Clinical Mental Health Counselor: LACMHC credential required before starting the supervised experience requirement; valid for 3 years.

**Educational Requirements:** Master's degree or higher in mental health counseling from a CACREP-accredited program, including a minimum of 60 graduate semester hours (or 90 quarter hours) in specific coursework. A minimum of

3 semester hours or 4½ quarter hours of a practicum. A minimum of 6 semester hours or 9 quarter hours of an internship.

**Experiential Requirements**: Must already possess the LACMHC. 4,000 hours of post-master's supervised professional counseling experience. 1,000 hours must be supervised experience in mental health therapy. 100 hours of face-to-face supervision required. Supervision must be under a licensed mental health therapist on site with a contract.

**Exam Required**: NCE, NCMHCE, and the Utah Professional Counselor Law, Rules, and Ethics Exam.

## VERMONT
VT Board of Allied Mental Health Practitioners
89 Main St., 3rd Floor
Montpellier, VT 05620
(802) 828-2390
(802) 828-2465 (fax)
dlafaill@sec.state.vt.us
vtprofessionals.org

**Title of License**: LCMHC

**Educational Requirements**: Master's degree or higher in counseling from an accredited institution, with a minimum of 60 semester hours and 1,000 hours of a supervised practicum, internship, or field experience in a clinical mental health setting. (Master's degree must be 48 semester hours.)

**Experiential Requirements**: 2 years/3,000 hours of post-master's experience in clinical mental health counseling, including 2,000 hours of direct client contact. 100 hours of face-to-face supervision required. Supervision should be 1 hour per 30 client hours and 50 must be individual supervision. Supervision must be under a board-approved Licensed Mental Health Professional.

**Exam Required**: NCE and NCMHCE and VT jurisprudence exam

## VIRGINIA
VA Board of Counseling Perimeter Center
9960 Mayland Drive, Suite 300
Richmond, VA 23233
(804) 367-4610
(804) 527-4435 (fax)
coun@dhp.virginia.gov
www.dhp.virginia.gov/counseling

**Title of License:** LPC

> Licensed Professional Counselor Resident: An applicant practicing under supervision.

**Educational Requirements:** Master's degree or higher in counseling that includes 60 semester hours (or 90 quarter hours) of graduate study in counseling. Completion of a supervised internship consisting of at least 600 hours. Programs that are approved by CACREP or CORE are recognized as meeting the definition of graduate degree programs that prepare individuals to practice counseling and counseling treatment intervention.

**Experiential Requirements:** 4,000 hours of postgraduate supervised counseling experience, including 2,000 hours of direct client contact. 200 hours of supervision required (100 hours must be under the supervision of an LPC approved by the board). Graduate-level internship hours may count toward the 4,000 hours.

**Exam Required:** NCMHCE

## WASHINGTON

WA Licensed Mental Health Counselors, Marriage and Family Therapists, and Social Workers Advisory Committee
P.O. Box 47877
Olympia, WA 98504-7877
(360) 236-4700
(360) 236-4818 (fax)
hpqa.csc@doh.wa.gov
www.doh.wa.gov/licensing

**Title of License:** LMHC

> Licensed Mental Health Counselor Associate (LMHCA): A prelicensure candidate who has a graduate degree in mental health counseling or related field and is working toward meeting the supervised experience requirements (may renew annually up to six times).

**Educational Requirements:** LMHC/LMHCA: Master's degree or higher in mental health counseling or related field from a regionally accredited college or university that includes a supervised counseling practicum or internship. Individuals who are certified as NCC or CCMHC are considered to meet educational requirements.

ALL professionals must complete 4 hours of HIV/AIDS education training.

**Experiential Requirements:** 3 years of full-time counseling or 3,000 hours postgraduate supervised mental health counseling in an approved setting. To include 1,200 hours of direct counseling with individuals, couples, groups, or families and 100 hours of immediate supervision by a board-approved supervisor. Graduate from CACREP-accredited programs can count up to 50 hours of supervision and 500 hours of experience from their practicum/internship.

**Exam Required:** LMHC: NCE or NCMHCE
LMHCA: None

## WEST VIRGINIA

WV Board of Examiners in Counseling
815 Quarrier St., Suite 212
Charleston, WV 25301
(800) 520-3852
(304) 558-5496 (fax)
counselingboard@msn.com
Roxanne Clay: RCLAY27@msn.com
www.wvbec.org

**Title of License:** LPC
Provisional Licensed Professional Counselor: An applicant who has met the education and exam requirements, but not the 2 years supervised experience requirement.

**Educational Requirements:** Master's degree or higher from a program accredited by CACREP or CORE, or a comparable accrediting body, that includes 60 graduate semester hours (or 90 quarter hours) and a practicum and internship. Acceptable graduate degrees include a specialization in community agency counseling, mental health counseling, pastoral counseling, rehabilitation counseling, school counseling, and substance abuse or addictions counseling. Similar degrees that include the word "counseling" and include specific coursework, and are determined by the board by a closely related field, are also acceptable.

**Experiential Requirements:** Must already possess provisional license. 2 years/3,000 hours of post-master's supervised professional counseling experience. If obtained a doctoral degree: 1 year/1,500 hours of postdegree supervised professional counseling experience. At least 50% of the supervised counseling experience must be in the direct provision of counseling services to clients. A minimum of 1 hour of direct individual supervision is required for every 20 hours of practice. Supervision must be under a board-approved professional.

**Exam Required:** NCE, CRCE, or NCMHCE

**WISCONSIN**
WI Examining Board of Marriage and Family Therapists, Professional Counselors, and Social Workers
P.O. Box 8935
Madison, WI 53708
(608) 266-2112
(608) 261-7083 (fax)
drl.wi.gov/prof/coun/def.htm

**Title of License**: LPC
> Licensed Professional Counselor Trainee: An applicant who has completed the degree requirements but not the supervised experience; valid for 48 months.

**Educational Requirements**: Master's degree or higher in professional counseling or equivalent program approved by the board, from a regionally accredited institution that includes a minimum of 42 semester hours (or 63 quarter hours). 3 semester hours of counseling theories and 3 semester hours of a supervised counseling practicum are required.

**Experiential Requirements**: 2 years/3,000 hours of post-master's supervised professional counseling practice, including 1,000 hours of face-to-face client contact. Supervision must include 1 hour per week of face-to-face supervision and must be provided by a board-approved mental health professional.

**Exam Required**: NCE, CRCE, or equivalent exam approved by the board, and Wisconsin jurisprudence exam

**WYOMING**
WY Mental Health Professions Licensing Board
2001 Capitol Ave., Room 104
Cheyenne, WY 82002
Michelle M. Lamorie, Executive Director: Michelle.lamorie@wyo.gov
(307) 777-7788
(307) 777-3508 (fax)
plboards.state.wy.us/mentalhealth/index.asp

**Title of License**: LPC
> Provisional Professional Counselor (PPC): An applicant who has received a master's degree, but has not passed the NCE exam or completed the supervised experience requirement; valid for 36 months.

**Educational Requirements**: Master's degree or higher in counseling, with a minimum of 60 semester hours (or 90 quarter hours) from a CACREP- or

CORE-accredited program, or a regionally accredited college or university which meets the CACREP criteria for coursework, instructor qualification, and supervision.

**Experiential Requirements**: 3,000 hours of supervised post-master's clinical experience (1,200 must be direct client contact and 100 hours must be face-to-face supervision). Supervision must be provided by a licensed mental health professional.

**Exam Required**: NCE, NCMHCE, or CRCE

Acronyms in the list of state licensure requirements refer to the following:

| | |
|---|---|
| AAODA | The Advanced Alcohol and Other Drug Abuse Counselor Examination (administered by the International Certification and Reciprocity Consortium/Alcohol and Other Drug Abuse, Inc.) |
| ATCB | The Art Therapy Credentials Board Certification Examination |
| CACREP | Council for Accreditation of Counseling and Related Educational Programs (an organizational affiliate of ACA that provides professional counselor-training accreditation) |
| CBMT | The Certification Board for Music Therapists Examination |
| CCMHC | Certified Clinical Mental Health Counselor (an NBCC professional counseling specialty title; not a required credential) |
| CORE | Council on Rehabilitation Education (an independent rehabilitation counselor-training accreditation board) |
| CRC | Certified Rehabilitation Counselor (a CRCC professional counseling specialty title; not a required credential) |
| CRCC | Commission on Rehabilitation Counselor Certification (an independent, nongovernmental rehabilitation counselor-credentialing board) |
| CRCE | Certified Rehabilitation Counselor Examination (administered by CRCC for the certification of rehabilitation counselors; also administered by some states for their own credentialing process as an alternative to their clinically oriented exam) |
| EMAC | The Examination for Master Addictions Counselors (administered by NBCC) |

NBCC National Board for Certified Counselors (an independent, non-governmental professional counselor-credentialing board and an organizational affiliate of ACA)

NCE National Counselor Examination (administered by NBCC for national certification of professional counselors, also used by most states for their own credentialing process)

NCMHCE National Clinical Mental Health Counselor Examination (administered by NBCC for national certification of mental health counselors, also administered by some states for their own licensure process)

PEPK The Practice Examination of Psychological Knowledge (administered by the North American Association of Masters in Psychology)

Exam acronyms listed because of a number of different examinations:

AAODA Advanced Alcohol and Other Drug Abuse Counselor Examination (administered by the International Certification and Reciprocity Consortium/Alcohol and Other Drug Abuse, Inc.)

ATCB Art Therapy Credentials Board Certification Examination

CRCE Certified Rehabilitation Counselor Examination (administered by CRCC for the certification of rehabilitation counselors, also administered by some states for their own credentialing process as an alternative to their clinically oriented exam)

CBMT Certification Board for Music Therapists Examination

EMAC Examination for Master Addiction Counselors (administered by NBCC)

NCE National Counselor Examination (administered by NBCC for national certification of professional counselors; also used by most states for their own credentialing process)

PEPK Practice Examination of Psychological Knowledge (administered by the North American Association of Master in Psychology)

# DOCUMENTS FOR PRACTICUM AND INTERNSHIP

**Old State University**
**Mental Health Counseling Program**
**Practicum and Internship Contract**

This agreement is made on _____ by and between _____
(Date)             (Practicum/Internship Site)

and the Old State University Mental Health Counseling Program. The agreement will be effective for a period from:

_____ to _____ for 100/300* semester clock hours for _____
(Name of Student)

### Purpose

The purpose of this agreement is to provide a qualified graduate student with a practicum/internship experience in the field of counseling.

### The University Program Agrees:

To assign a university faculty liaison to facilitate communication between university and site;

To provide weekly classroom supervision and instruction for the practicum/internship student through EDU 679, EDU 685/686/687;

---

*Practicum requires a minimum of 100 clock hours. Internship requires 300 clock hours. For practicum, 40 of the 100 hours must be direct contact hours. For internship students, 120 of the 300 hours must be in direct service. Direct service is defined as individual, group, couples or family counseling, co-counseling, clinical intakes, phone crisis counseling, team counseling and observation through a two-way mirror, running psychoeducational groups, and so forth.

To provide to the site, prior to placement of the student, the following information: profile of the student named above and an academic calendar that shall include dates for periods during which student will be excused from field supervision;

To notify the student that he or she must adhere to the administrative policies, rules, standards, schedules, and practices of the site;

That the faculty liaison shall be available for consultation with both site supervisors and students and shall be immediately contacted should any problem or change in relation to student, site, or university occur; and

That the university supervisor (or practicum/internship instructor) is responsible for the assignment of a fieldwork grade. Grades are the S/U type.

**The Practicum/Internship Site Agrees:**

To assign a practicum/internship supervisor who has appropriate credentials, time, and interest for training the practicum/internship student;

The clinical site must provide weekly supervision for 1 hour per week;

To provide opportunities for the student to engage in a variety of counseling activities under supervision and for evaluating the student's performance (suggested counseling experience included in the "Practicum/Internship Activities" section);

To provide the student with adequate work space, telephone, office supplies, and staff to conduct professional activities;

To provide supervisory contact that involves some examination of student work using audiovisual tapes, observation, and/or live supervision;

To provide written evaluation of student based on criteria established by the university program; and

To not involve students in any form of billing for professional services.

Within the specified time frame, _____ will be the primary on-site practicum/internship site supervisor. The training activities (checked below) will be provided for the student in sufficient amounts to allow an adequate evaluation of the student's level of competence in each activity.

_____ will be the faculty liaison/supervisor with whom the student and practicum/internship site supervisor will communicate regarding progress, problems, performance evaluations, and grading.

**Practicum/Internship Activities**

This list below is a list of possible clinical activities for the practicum/internship student. It is not necessary that field sites have the student counselor complete all or even most of these. Check all areas that seem to apply. Additional areas of responsibility may be added in the future.

1. **Individual Counseling/Psychotherapy** _____
   Personal/Social Nature _____
   Occupational/Educational Nature _____

2. **Group Counseling/Psychotherapy** _____
   Co-leading _____
   Leading _____

3. **Intake Interviewing** _____

4. **Couples or Family Counseling** _____
   Leading _____
   Co-leading _____

5. **Testing and Assessment** _____
   Administration and Interpretation _____

6. **Report Writing** _____
   Record Keeping _____
   Treatment Plans _____

7. **Consultation** _____
   Referrals _____
   Team Consultation and Case Staffing _____

8. **Community/Psychoeducational Activities** _____
   Family Conferences _____
   Community/Campus Outreach _____
   In-Service Presentations

9. **Career Counseling** _____

10. **Other (please specify):**
    _____
    _____
    _____

**Type of supervision student will receive:**   Individual _____   Group _____
(_Needs 1 hour of formal supervision per week_)

**Clinical Site Supervisor:** _____   Date _____

**Student:** _____   Date _____

**Faculty Liaison:** _____   Date _____

**Field Supervision**

As per the Council for Accreditation of Counseling and Related Educational Programs' (CACREP) guidelines, on-site supervisors must hold a minimum of a master's degree earned in counseling or a closely related field. Closely related fields include Clinical Social Work, Counseling or Clinical Psychology, Marriage and Family Therapy, Psychiatric Nursing, and Psychiatry. On-site supervisors must have a minimum of 2-year post-master's degree experience and must be licensed in their field (LMHC, LCSW, LP, etc.)

On-site supervisors also provide individual or group supervision for 1 hour each week the practicum/internship student accrues hours. The on-site supervisor submits a written evaluation of the student's performance at the end of each semester. On-site supervisors also sign off on student's time logs.

### Evaluation of Practicum Student/Intern's Performance

At the conclusion of each semester, the field supervisor will complete an evaluation of the student practicum/internship student. The evaluation form can be copied from the NU MHC manual. The site supervisor should return the evaluation to:

**Coordinator, Mental Health Counseling Program**
**College of Education**
**Old State University, NY 14190**
**712-285-8327**
**ssegdoh@oldstate.edu**

### Concerns Regarding the Student Intern

*The Field Site Supervisor:*

If the field supervisor has concerns regarding the student's abilities to meet the goals and objectives of the agency, the supervisor has the following options:

The field supervisor apprises the university supervisor of the concern.

The field supervisor discusses the concern with the student.

If resolution does not occur, the field supervisor should notify the university supervisor.

The university supervisor will schedule an appointment with the field supervisor and the student to facilitate the resolution.

If no resolution occurs, the field supervisor may terminate the placement.

For the student, in the event the placement is terminated, the student must find another placement and repeat the practicum or internship.

*The University Supervisor:*

If the university supervisor has a concern regarding the student's performance:

The university supervisor will inform the student that the field supervisor will be notified.

The university supervisor will seek feedback regarding the student's performance at the site.

If the concern cannot be resolved, the university supervisor will decide if the student will be placed in another setting.

If the student will receive an unsatisfactory grade, he or she will inform the student and the field supervisor that the student will need to repeat the class.

If the student does not pass the classroom or the on-site portion of the practicum/internship, the student will need to repeat the class.

Because of the nature of student practicum/internships, either the clinical site or the counseling program reserves the right to dissolve this contract should concerns arise.

*Note: The agency hosting the placement, the graduate program representative, and the practicum/internship student should all keep a copy of this agreement.*

## Sample Consent to Audiotape or Videotape Permission Form

Sample University and the agency provide counseling opportunities for individuals, couples, families, and groups. Signing this form provides the counselor-in-training the opportunity to record your counseling session and to play the recording for the counselor's supervisor and graduate students in the Practicum/Internship class, all of whom are held to confidentiality. The recording will not be made available to anyone outside the agency or the Practicum/Internship cohort. Feel free to ask your counselor any questions about the purpose of recording and use of the recording.

Your signature below indicates that you give _____ _____ (name of your counselor-in-training) permission to be recorded (audiotaped or videotaped; circle one or both) and that you understand the following:

1. I can request the recorder be turned off at any time and may request the recording be erased.
2. The purpose of recording is for use in training and supervision. This will allow the counselor-in-training to consult with her or his supervisor(s) in an individual or group format.
3. The contents of these recorded session(s) are confidential and will not be shared outside the context of individual and group supervision.
4. The recording will be stored in a secure location and will be used only for training and supervision purposes as stated above.
5. The recordings will be erased after they have served their purpose.

_____

Name of Client (Please Print)


_____

Signature

## Weekly Practicum/Internship I Hours Log
## 300 Hours (120 Direct/180 Indirect Needed)

| Dates | Direct Hours* | Clock Hours** | Supervisor Signature |
|-------|---------------|---------------|----------------------|
|       |               |               |                      |
|       |               |               |                      |
|       |               |               |                      |
|       |               |               |                      |
|       |               |               |                      |
|       |               |               |                      |
|       |               |               |                      |

| Dates | Direct Hours* | Clock Hours** | Supervisor Signature |
|---|---|---|---|
|  |  |  |  |
|  |  |  |  |
|  |  |  |  |
|  |  |  |  |
|  |  |  |  |
|  |  |  |  |
|  |  |  |  |

| Dates | Direct Hours* | Clock Hours** | Supervisor Signature |
|-------|---------------|---------------|----------------------|
|       |               |               |                      |
|       |               |               |                      |
|       |               |               |                      |
|       |               |               |                      |
|       |               |               |                      |
|       |               |               |                      |
|       |               |               |                      |

Total Direct Hours _____     Total Clock Hours Completed _____

_____     _____

Student Signature                    Date


_____     _____

On-Site Supervisor Signature         Date


_____     _____

University Supervisor Signature      Date

_____

*Direct Hours = Individual, group, couples, family counseling, co-counseling, intakes, assessment, phone crisis counseling, psychoeducational or support groups, and any direct contact with clients.

**Total Clock Hours = Any work activity that does not involve direct contact with clients. Practicum requires a minimum of 100 clock hours, which include 40 hours of direct contact. Internship requires 300 clock hours, which include 120 hours as direct contact.

## Sample School Counseling Referral Form

Student name: _____

Date of birth: _____

Teacher referring: _____

Parent/guardian: _____

Home address: _____

Home phone: _____ Cell phone: _____

Please check the behaviors indicated below that serve as a reason for the referral:

___ Unable to sit still                    ___ Fails to complete homework

___ Impatient                              ___ Wastes time

___ Easily distracted                      ___ Appears inattentive in class

___ Peer conflicts                         ___ Withdrawn during class

___ Noncompliant with rules                ___ Appears worried/preoccupied

Estimated level of classroom functioning: Scale of 1 to 100. Higher scores indicate greater functioning.

___ Math            ___ Reading          ___ Language Arts

___ Science         ___ Social Studies   ___ Physical Education

Please cite any remedial services presently being rendered:

_____

_____

_____

Briefly describe the issue(s) placing the student at risk. Be as specific as possible:

_____

_____

_____

Briefly specify the desired behaviors you would like to see from this student in your classroom:

_____

_____

_____

Teacher making this referral:

_____

Signature

_____

Title

_____

Date

## Mental Status Checklist

|   |   | Check | Circle | Counselor's Note |
|---|---|---|---|---|
| **1.** | Posture | Normal ____ | Rigid, slouches | _____ |
| **2.** | Grooming | Normal ____ | Well-groomed<br>Disheveled, dirty | _____ |
| **3.** | Dress | Appropriate ____ | Ragged<br>Too revealing | _____ |
| **4.** | Facial<br>expression | Appropriate ____ | Poor eye contact,<br>stares, downcast | _____ |
| **5.** | Speech |   |   |   |
|   | **a.** Pace | Normal ____ | Pressured,<br>slow | _____ |
|   | **b.** Volume | Normal ____ | Loud, low | _____ |
|   | **c.** Tone | Normal ____ | Monotone,<br>angry, low | _____ |
|   | **d.** Content | Normal ____ | Profane,<br>hostile, illogical | _____ |
|   | **e.** Clarity | Normal ____ | Scattered, stutters<br>Loose associations | _____ |

Affect and Mood

|    |           | Check       | Circle                                    | Counselor's Note |
|----|-----------|-------------|-------------------------------------------|------------------|
| 1. | Attention | Normal ___  | Brief, unable to sustain attention        | _____  |
| 2. | Affect    | Normal ___  | Inappropriate, flat                       | _____  |
| 3. | Mood      | Normal ___  | Irritable, labile, depressed, euphoric    | _____  |

Perception and Thought Content

Check if applies   Description

1.  Hallucination

    **a.** Auditory ___          _____

    **b.** Visual ___            _____

    **c.** Tactile ___           _____

    **d.** Taste ___             _____

    **e.** Smell ___             _____

2.  Delusion

    Paranoid ___  Grandeur ___       Persecutory ___  Thoughts ___

    Control ___  Broadcasting ___     Other (name) _____

3.  Phobias (name): _____

4.  Obsessions (name): _____

**5.**  Compulsions (name): _____

**6.**  Suicide/homicide

Ideation: _____ Plan: _____

Timetable to carry out suicide plan: immediate, future, etc.:

_____

Orientation: This client/student is oriented to (check all that apply):

**a.** Time ____      **b.** Place ____      **c.** Person ____

Judgment     Good ____                    Impaired ____

Memory/Ability to Concentrate

**1.** Immediate recall          Good ____        Poor ____

**2.** Reversals                      Good ____        Poor ____

**3.** Serial sevens                 Good ____        Poor ____

Abstract Reasoning

**1.** Similarities     Good ____        Poor ____        Bizarre ____

**2.** Absurdities     Understands ____        Does not understand ____

**3.** Proverbs    Normal ____     Literal ____     Concrete ____     Bizarre ____

Insight

Good ____  Fair ____        Poor ____

## Mental Status Exam (Brief Version)

Now, I'm going to ask you a series of questions to test your concentration and memory. Answer to the best of your ability. Ok, any questions before we begin?

1. **Orientation to time:**

   **a.** What year is this? (1 point)

   **b.** What season is this? (1 point)

   **c.** What is the month and date? (1 point)

   **d.** What day of the week is it? (1 point)

   (Maximum of 4 points)

2. **Orientation to place:**

   **a.** What is the name of this institution/school/agency? (1 point)

   **b.** What floor are we on? (1 point)

   **c.** What city and state are we in? (1 point)

   **d.** What county is this? (1 point)

   (Maximum of 4 points)

3. **Immediate Recall:**
   I am going to say three objects. After I say them I want you to repeat them. They are *"ball," "flag,"* and *"tree."* Now say them. Remember them because I will ask you to repeat them later. (Interviewer: **1 point** for each; maximum of **3 points**)

4. **Attention: (Serial 7s or Spelling. Choose from either item below but not both)**

   **a.** Subtract 7 from 100 and continue until I tell you to stop. (Interviewer, continue until subject makes an error. **1 point** for each correct answer up to a maximum score of **5 points**)

   **b.** Spell the word "world" backwards. (**1 point** for each correct letter; maximum of **5 points**)

5. **Delayed Recall:**
   What are the three words I asked you to remember? (**1 point** for each; maximum of **3 points**)

6. **Naming:**
   Show subject a pen and wristwatch and ask to name them. (**1 point** for each; maximum of **2 points**)

**7. Repetition:**
Repeat the following sentence exactly as I say it. "No ifs, ands, or buts."
(**1 point** for each word; maximum of **3 points**)

**8. Stage Command:**
"Now I want to see how well you can follow instructions. I'm going to give you a piece of paper. Take it in your right hand, use both hands to fold it in half, and then put it on the floor." (**1 point** for each command; maximum of **3 points**)

**9. Reading:**
Show the subject the headline on the following page and ask her or him to read what it says silently and then to do what it says. (**1 point**)

**10. Copying:**
Give subject a clean sheet of paper and ask her or him to draw two interlocking geometric figures (e.g., triangles, squares). If necessary draw an example for client. (**1 point**)

**11. Writing:**
On the same sheet of paper, ask the subject to write a complete sentence. (**1 point**)

**Scoring Procedures:**
**Total (Maximum Score) = 30**

*Note:* Scores of 23 to 30 indicate expected or "normal" functioning. Scores under 23 suggest the presence of cognitive impairment.

**23–30 = no cognitive impairment**

**18–23 = mild cognitive impairment**

**0–17 = significant cognitive impairment**

*MSE scores may be invalid if the subject has less than a ninth-grade education, is intoxicated, or is under the influence of drugs.*

**Adapted from** Folstein, M. F., Folstein, S. E., & McHugh, P. R. (1975). "Mini-mental state." A practical method for grading the cognitive state of patients for the clinician. *Journal of Psychiatric Research, 12,* 189–198.

## Intake and Psychosocial Case History Interview

Name of Client*:

Date of Interview:

Place of Interview:

Purpose of Interview:

Name of Interviewer:

### I. Introduction:
Introduce yourself, your role, explain the nature of the interview (to assist with treatment), and ask if the client has any questions.

### II. Childhood:

Where were you born and raised? (Did you move? When and why did you move?)

Were your parents married?

Did your mother have problems while she was pregnant with you?

Did you reach your developmental milestones such as walking, talking, potty training, on time?

With whom did you live while growing up?

Who did you feel closest to?

Who in the family was most affectionate to you?

How did you get along with_____? (whoever raised you)

Who made the rules and enforced discipline?

Were the family rules clearly and consistently applied?

Do you believe the rules were fair?

How often did you get punished?

How did they usually discipline you?

_____

*Pseudonym.

Were you ever spanked? (If "yes," were there ever bruises? Did you have to see a doctor?)

Did you witness violence in the family? (verbal, physical, sexual)

Did anyone sexually abuse you or a sibling? (If "yes," what happened? How much did this upset you? How upset are you now?)

How would you describe your personality as a child?

How would peers have described you?

Did you have many friends as a child? (Any close friends? Best friends?)

Were you a leader or a follower?

### III. School:

At what age did you begin school?

Did you go to special education classes or regular classes?

(If special classes, why?)

Were you a good student?

Did you ever repeat a grade? (If "yes," what was the last grade you repeated?)

Were you involved in school activities? (If "yes," what types?)

What did you do after you graduated (or dropped out) of school?

Did you attend college or get advanced technical training? (If "yes," did you graduate from college, tech school, etc.?)

Did you like school? (Explain whether "yes" or "no")

### IV. Parenthood:

Do you have any children? (If "yes," how many? Their ages and sexes? How well do you get along with them?)

### V. Friendships and Marriage:

Do you have many friends now? (Any close friends you can trust with secrets? Do your friendships tend to be long-lasting?)

Have you ever been married? (If "yes," how many times? How would you describe your marriages? If divorced, why did you divorce? If never married, why?)

Almost all couples argue or fight at times. I'd like to know a little bit about what happens when you and your partner argue or fight. Do you or your partner ever get pushed, grabbed, or hit? Ever throw things?

If "yes": Describe the most recent or most serious time this happened. How often does this happen? Have one of you ever had to go to the doctor after an assault?

If "no": Did the above ever happen in previous relationships? Are you ever afraid you will be physically hurt during an argument with your spouse/partner?

### VI. Relationships With Other Family Members:

Who is your immediate family? Extended family? Do you have in-laws? Grandparents? Grandchildren? Any other family?

### Are your parents still alive?

If "yes": Are you close?

How do you get along with them?

How often you visit them?

How often do you speak with them?

Have you had any recent arguments with them?

When you get angry with them, how long do you stay angry?

### Do you have siblings?

If "yes": Are you close?

How do you get along?

Have you spoken with them recently?

Have you argued with them recently?

When you argue, how long do you stay angry with them?

### VII. Occupation:

Are you employed?

If "yes": What type of work do you do?

How long have you worked there?

Do you like the work?

Why did you leave?

What is the longest job you have ever held?

If "no":  When was the last time you worked?

What kind of job was it?

What other jobs have you had?

What is the longest job you have had?

## VIII. Living Situation:

Where do you live? (A house? Apartment? Condominium?)

How long have you been living there?

Where did you previously live?

Why did you move? (Have you moved often?)

Have you ever been homeless or lived in a shelter?

How long were you homeless (or lived in a shelter)?

With whom do you currently live?

## IX. Health:

Do you have any serious health problems? (If "yes," describe.)

Has your illness/condition impacted your close relationships? (If "yes," how?)

Have you been more withdrawn?

Do you argue more or less due to your health concerns?

### X. Spirituality and Religious Beliefs:

Do you consider yourself a spiritual/religious person?

How important are your beliefs to you?

Would you say your spiritual/religious beliefs assist you in dealing with stress, anxiety, and health concerns? (If "yes," briefly explain how.)

### XI. Satisfaction in Life:

Are you generally satisfied with your life?

    If "no": Which areas of life are you dissatisfied with?

        How much are you dissatisfied?

    If "yes": What areas are you satisfied with?

How could you develop more satisfaction in your life?

Would you say your life has been meaningful?

    If "yes": What accounts for the meaning in your life?

    If "no":  How could you develop meaning in your life?

# School Counseling Intake Interview

Date: _____

Student: _____

Age: ___ GPA: ___ Band: ___ Sports: ___ Honor Society: ___ Other Organization: ___

Reason for interview (circle): Academic, Social, Personal, Career, Other

Briefly explain reason cited above: _____

_____

Discipline history (e.g., suspensions, fighting): _____

_____

Student's family:

Mother's name: _____

Father's name: _____

Sibling's names and ages: _____

_____

Parents married or living together: Yes___ No___

Has student had previous counseling? Yes___ No___. If "yes," reason for previous counseling: _____

Any history of physical/emotional/sexual abuse? Yes___ No___

What community resources is student involved with? (e.g., religious community, YMCA/YWCA, Youth League sports)

Has this student ever been removed from his or her home? Yes___ No___. If so, for what reason:

_____

Has student been arrested? Yes___ No___. If "yes," what was student arrested for: _____

_____

Is student currently taking medication(s): Yes____ No____. If "yes," what medications:

_____

What are the student's strengths? _____

_____

How does parent/guardian describe student's behavior at home? (If known)

_____

_____

Has student acted out in socially unacceptable ways? If so, describe: _____

_____

Does student have friends? Yes____ No____

Has student made a suicide threat? Yes____ No____. If "yes," how long ago? _____

Is student suicidal? Yes____ No____. If "yes," must activate school plan to notify parent/guardian and appropriate authorities for mental health assistance.

Does student have a history of alcohol or drug use? Yes___ No____. If "yes," what type: _____?

_____

Student: What are your future goals? _____

_____

Student: What are you happiest about? _____

Student: What are you most concerned about? _____

Student: What would you most want the counselor to know? _____

_____

Student: On a scale of 1 to 10, with 1 being *low* and 10 *high*, how optimistic do you feel regarding your life (or school performance or whatever seems appropriate depending on type of student concern). Score: ____. How could you raise that score one number in the next week? _____

_____

Student: On a scale on 1 to 10, with 1 being *low* and 10 *high*, how effective was today's time?

Score____. How could the session improve one point next time? _____

_____

# SOAP Progress Note

S.O.A.P. stands for Subjective, Objective, Assessment, and Plan. Some people prefer D.A.P. notes—D.A.P. stands for Description, Analysis, and Plan.

### S.O.A.P. Notes

Subjective: Subjective experience of the client as related/reported by the client. Often direct quotes from the client of his or her problems or complaints. Examples include: "I had an awful week," "I'm feeling really depressed," "I hate my mother," "I can't seem to stop worrying about my grade," "I haven't slept in two days." Also, there can be statements made by the client that you summarize without using quotes.

Objective: An objective account of the client's appearance and behaviors. May include client dress/clothing, posturing, eye contact, timeliness to session, affect, activity, speech, and so on. All the information in this section should be objective in the sense that it could be verified by observers and contains no analysis/judgment on your part. The objective section should provide a behavioral picture of the client.

Assessment: Your **theory-specific** analysis or interpretation of the client's issues and the session. Examples include: "The client seemed to accept his anger" or "The client's thinking was irrational in the following ways...." This is your chance to hypothesize and define your conceptualization of your client's issues.

Plan: What you plan to do in the next session. Includes homework assignments, planned exercises or techniques, and so on. When writing this section, ask yourself, "Following this theory, what is it I want to remember to do with this client?" or "What do I want to cover with the client next week?" **A plan should always be theory specific.**

# Client's Evaluation of Counseling Session

Date: _____

_____                    _____
Counselor                                       Client

Rate each statement below on a 10-point scale, where 1 = Strongly Disagree, 10 = Strongly Agree, and 5 = Neutral.

1. This session assisted you in developing a better understanding of your issue(s) and the primary problem(s).

   Strongly Disagree        Neutral           Strongly Agree

   1      2      3      4      5      6      7      8      9      10

2. This counselor seemed to have listened very well and understood my concerns.

   Strongly Disagree        Neutral           Strongly Agree

   1      2      3      4      5      6      7      8      9      10

3. Through this counseling session, I have gained a better understanding of myself.

   Strongly Disagree        Neutral           Strongly Agree

   1      2      3      4      5      6      7      8      9      10

4. This interview helped me identify new strategies to address my issues and concerns.

   Strongly Disagree        Neutral           Strongly Agree

   1      2      3      4      5      6      7      8      9      10

5. This session assisted me in identifying strengths and resources to address my concerns.

   Strongly Disagree        Neutral            Strongly Agree

   1      2      3      4      5      6      7      8      9      10

6. Because of this session, I am more inclined to change my thinking and behavior.

    Strongly Disagree          Neutral          Strongly Agree

    1    2    3    4    5    6    7    8    9    10

7. The counselor was instrumental in making today's session productive.

    Strongly Disagree          Agree          Strongly Agree

    1    2    3    4    5    6    7    8    9    10

8. I would rate today's session as: (Scale 1–10. 1 = Unhelpful, 10 = Very Helpful)

    Circle the appropriate score.

    1    2    3    4    5    6    7    8    9    10

9. What could you and the counselor do to raise your score by one point during the next session? (Write your answer on line below.)

    _____

10. What is one cognitive or behavioral change I can begin using today? (Write on line below.)

    _____

## Student Counseling Session Rating Form

Date: _____/_____/_____

Student: _____ Evaluator: _____

Audio Recording: ___        Video Recording: ___   In-Class Role Play: ___

Brief Summary of Session Content: _____

_____

_____

Specific Criteria:                          Rating (1 = Least; 5 = Best)

**1.** Opening:                             1   2   3   4   5

Was informed consent thorough and professional? Was confidentiality covered?

**2.** Rapport:                             1   2   3   4   5

Did the counselor establish a good therapeutic alliance? (e.g., voice tone, appropriate eye contact, paraphrasing, summarizing)

**3.** Attending Skill:                     1   2   3   4   5

Did the counselor use minimal encouragers and refrain from unnecessary interruptions? (Also, was counselor skilled in using therapeutic silence?)

**4.** Open-Ended Questioning:              1   2   3   4   5

Did the counselor make appropriate use of open-ended questions?

**5.** Affective Domain:                    1   2   3   4   5

Did the counselor demonstrate appropriate empathy?

**6. Challenging/Confrontation:**                    1   2   3   4   5

Did the counselor confront the client? (If necessary)

**7. Solution Skills:**                               1   2   3   4   5

Did the counselor offer appropriate solution-seeking input?

**8. Cultural Issues:**                               1   2   3   4   5

Did the counselor appear to understand and respect cultural issues?
(Culture would include race, ethnicity, gender, sexual orientation, religion/spir-
ituality, etc.)

**9. Goal Setting:**                                  1   2   3   4   5

Did the counselor set effective goals for a follow-up session?

**10. Closing:**                                      1   2   3   4   5

Was closing well-orchestrated? (Or, was it abrupt?)

On the following 1 to 10 scale, how effective was the student counselor in facilitating the counseling session? (1 = lowest score, 10 = highest score) Circle the
appropriate number below:

1      2      3      4      5      6      7      8      9      10

Constructive comments for the student counselor's further development:

_____

_____

_____

_____

_____

_____

_____

_____

_____


_____

Signature of Evaluator

## *DSM-5* and S.O.A.P. Client Case Notes Format

Page 1 of 3

Name(s) and age(s) of client(s): _____

_____

_____

Date: _____/_____/_____ Code(s): _____ Session #: _____

Presenting Problem: _____

_____

_____

_____

_____

<u>Medications</u>:

<u>*DSM-5*\*</u>:
Diagnosis: (Cite Principal *DSM-5* diagnosis and diagnostic criteria)

\*Prescriptive. Not intended as a final diagnosis.

Subjective (S): _____

_____

_____

_____

_____

_____

_____

Objective (O): _____

_____

_____

_____

_____

_____

_____

Assessment (A):_____

_____

_____

_____

_____

_____

_____

Plan (P):_____

_____

_____

_____

_____

_____

Counselor's Signature _____

## Client Initial Intake Form

Name: _____ Date: ____/____/____

Address: _____ City: _____ State: ____

Zip Code: _____ Phone: _____ (H) _____ (W/C)

**Identifying Information:**

Age: _____ Date of Birth: ____/____/____ Place: _____

Sex: Female _____ Male _____ Height: ____ Ft. _____ In. Weight: _____ Lbs.

Marital Status: M ____ S ____ D ____ Sep. ____ Other: ____

Ethnicity: Caucasian: __ Hispanic/Latino: __ Asian: __ African American: __

American Indian: __ Multiethnic: __

Spouse's/Partner's Name: _____ Age: _____

Occupation: _____ Employer: _____

Name(s)/Age(s) of Children (If applicable)

_____

_____

Referral Source: _____

Address of Referral Source: _____

**Treatment History:**

Are you currently taking medication?　　　　Yes: _____　　No: _____

If "yes," name of medication(s): _____

Provider of medication(s): _____

Have you received previous psychiatric/psychological treatment?

Yes: _____　　No: _____

If "yes," name the psychiatric treatment provider: _____

_____

Dates of counseling/psychiatric treatment: _____

_____

Has any close relative ever had psychiatric treatment or been committed to a psychiatric hospital? Yes: _____　　No: _____. If "yes," please explain:

_____

_____

What factor(s) led you to seek counseling services? _____

_____

_____

Symptoms: _____

_____

_____

**Family History:**

Father's name: _____Living: _____ Deceased: _____

Occupation: _____

Mother's name: _____ Living: _____ Deceased: _____

Occupation: _____

Brother(s)/Sister(s):

Name: _____ Age: _____ Living: ___ Deceased: ___

Name: _____ Age: _____ Living: ___ Deceased: ___

Name: _____ Age: _____ Living: ___ Deceased: ___

**Educational History:**

(Name of institution, location, dates attended, degree)

High School: _____

College/University: _____

Technical School: _____

Graduate/Professional: _____

**Military Information: (If applicable)**

Branch of Military: _____

Dates of Active Service/Reserve Commitment: _____

Were you in a combat zone? Yes:__ No:__

Did you receive any medical treatment as a result of injuries? Yes:__ No:__

If "yes," what injuries were you treated for?_____

_____

_____

# INDEX